Communicating Ethically

Communicating Ethically

Character, Duties, Consequences, and Relationships

William W. Neher
Butler University

Paul J. Sandin
Butler University

Boston ■ New York ■ San Francisco
Mexico City ■ Montreal ■ Toronto ■ London ■ Madrid ■ Munich ■ Paris
Hong Kong ■ Singapore ■ Tokyo ■ Cape Town ■ Sydney

Series Editor: Brian Wheel
Series Editorial Assistant: Jenny Lupica
Marketing Manager: Suzan Czajkowski
Editorial Production Service: Integra
Manufacturing Buyer: JoAnne Sweeney
Cover Administrator: Joel Gendron
Electronic Composition: Integra

Between the time Website information is gathered and then published, some sites
may have closed. Also, the transcription of URLs can result in typographical errors.
The publisher would appreciate notification where these occur so that they may be
corrected in subsequent editions.

Library of Congress Cataloging-in-Publication Data
Neher, William W.
    Communicating ethically : character, duties, consequences,
        and relationships / William W. Neher and Paul J. Sandin.
        p.   cm.
    Includes bibliographical references and index.
    ISBN 0–205–39363–2 (alk. paper)
    1. Communication—Moral and ethical aspects.   I. Sandin, Paul J.   II. Title.

P94.N44 2007
175—dc22

                                                           2006001686

Printed in the United States of America

C O N T E N T S

PREFACE

This book serves as a text for undergraduate courses in communication ethics, or as a companion text for courses in interpersonal, organizational, business, small group, or other communication courses. Faculty who teach general introductions to the field of communication or capstone courses for communication majors will also find the book useful. Outside the field of communication studies, the text can be used for business administration courses in leadership, management, organizational development, and similar courses. In addition, it can serve as a supplementary work for service learning, experiential courses, or internships in areas of communication. These purposes reflect our belief that more and more colleges and universities are emphasizing ethics in both their general curriculum and their disciplinary curricula. The text is organized and grounded in ethical theories, with realistic cases for study and analysis in each chapter, and is responsive to this growing concern about the ethics of communication in our contemporary world.

The text can also serve as a general reference for professionals in the fields of communication (media relations, public relations, corporate communications, and the like) or for people in helping professions, particularly those working with the disabled, in interpersonal counseling, or in employee relations.

Plan for the Book

We intend to make students aware of the major philosophical grounds for analyzing and thinking about ethical decisions in their or others' communication. In doing so, we begin in Chapter 2 with the basic questions about the ethical nature of rhetoric and communication that go back as far as the classical foundations of the field. The issues first enunciated by Plato challenging the Sophists' teaching about rhetoric and the answers advanced by Aristotle continue to be basic to the whole field of communication, especially in light of television, cable, and computerized technologies of communication.

Each of the five chapters, constituting Part One, presents an overview of major systems of ethical reasoning developed over many years to guide our thinking in making ethical decisions: *Character*, emphasizing virtue ethics; *Duties*, covering Kantian and universalistic systems of ethics; *Consequences*, including utilitarianism and egalitarian or contractualist theories of ethics; *Relationships*, which deals primarily with dialogical ethics; and, in a final chapter in Part One, postmodern and feminist responses to these traditional approaches to ethics.

In Part Two, Chapters 7 through 13 cover applications of ethics in various communicative settings. In these chapters, we consider the special ethical issues arising when dealing with interpersonal communication and communication with diverse others, such as people with disabilities or from other cultures or subcultures. We will also devote chapters to the ethical questions and situations that arise in mass communication, politics, and organizational settings. Specific topics include questions of political advertising and campaigning, the employment of political action committees, political consultants, lobbyists, whistle-blowing, ethics in corporate communication, and the like.

Each chapter includes a chapter outline at the beginning to foreshadow the topics to be covered, a chapter summary at the end, and topics and questions intended to stimulate discussion of the issues covered in the chapter. In carrying out the overall plan for the text, we include some distinctive features as aids for teaching and learning:

- Use of case studies illustrating principles for each chapter except in the capstone chapter.
- Incorporating communication with people with disabilities in the chapters on diversity.
- Including a chapter on ethics of computer-mediated and Web-based communication.
- Including a Capstone chapter to pull together the various themes and topics covered through the text.
- A Glossary of important terms following the Capstone Chapter.

Reasoning about Communication Ethics

In this text, we do not intend to *teach* communication ethics but, rather, to *teach about* communication ethics, especially to *teach reasoning about communication ethics*. Our framework for such reasoning is represented by a model borrowed from argumentation theory, in which we say there are three forms of *propositions* for arguing or reasoning about ethics. A proposition is a statement that is to be proved, in this case, to be proved by the argument being advanced. The three kinds of argumentative propositions are Fact, Value, and Policy. The distinction among these three types is essential to understanding how we go about making arguments about ethical decisions.

A *proposition of fact* upholds a statement about a factual state of affairs, which could be demonstrated by an objective or scientific process. Such a proposition is not the same as a fact, but it should be based on the facts as we can discover them. A statement about a fact to be proved is a statement that is in some way controversial, people disagree about what the facts are. The person making the argument, then, is hoping to get people to agree with her interpretation of the facts. For example, people who maintain conspiracy theories about the assassination of former President Kennedy state a proposition of fact: "President Kennedy was killed by a group of conspirators rather than the lone gunman, Lee Harvey Oswald." Before the second Gulf War against Iraq, proponents of the war argued for the proposition of fact: "Saddam Hussein possesses weapons of mass destruction." The statements may or may not describe a factual situation—that is what the argument is all about.

The second kind of argumentative proposition is a *proposition of value*. The point of the argument shifts from trying to prove what the facts of the case are to what value we should place on the state of affairs. A value proposition thus upholds that something is good or bad. Ethicists tend to point out that ethics deals with such propositions of value. In analyzing ethics, we judge an action to be good or bad to the extent that it can be so judged. A proposition of value thus takes the form of making a value judgment: "Cheating on your income tax is wrong." Note that the statement "Cheating on your income tax is illegal" is different in that the legality can be determined as a matter of fact. Rightness or wrongness, however, lies in the realm of our values rather than in the realm of facts. It is on this basis that many philosophers claim that ethics or morals ultimately are matters of preference, perhaps preferences that are widely shared by most people, but preferences nonetheless.

The third kind of argumentative proposition is a *proposition of policy*, which is concerned with action, while the first two types are concerned with belief. In a proposition of policy, someone advocates a particular course of action—we should do something. This type of argument stresses the notion of *should* or *ought*. In ethics, we use a proposition of policy when we argue for doing or not doing something. A proposition of policy hence takes the form of calling for a specific action: "We should provide full and truthful information for all stakeholders in this particular case," for example.

Because the kind of evidence that it takes to prove each kind of proposition is different, we say that each proposition has different standards of proof. The easiest type for most people to understand is the standards of proof for propositions of fact. You have to determine what the state of affairs really is. The proof of such a proposition requires a clear statement and understanding of known facts in the case and demonstrations that the facts in the argument are relevant, complete, and justified.

People are often less sure about how to approach a proposition of value—the issues here seem more *subjective* than *objective*. We shall see in this text that ethicists have suggested various ways to go about arguing for acceptable and even universal values to guide decisions in these cases. Arguing a proposition of value must go beyond proving what the facts are. It is necessary to argue why those facts should be interpreted as good or bad. Some standards or criteria must be advanced with which those involved can agree. The crux of a value proposition lies in gaining assent to the criteria to be used for making the judgment that something is good or bad. The next step then is to compare the situation in the case to the criteria to see whether they meet or do not meet the criteria of a good or bad thing.

A proposition of policy requires that the advocate show that there is a need or a cause to take the proposed action, that the action will result in achieving the objective intended, and that it is the best or most expedient action to take under the prevailing circumstances. In many cases, the advocate of a policy proposition should also show that the benefits of the action called for outweigh its costs or harmful side effects. Some of the major theories about ethics we will discuss do not agree on this last step, since some systems claim that consequences (costs or benefits) are not germane to matters of ethics.

Reasoning through ethical issues, dilemmas, or problems can follow a process of arguing propositions of facts, values, and policies. First, one ought to determine what the facts in the case are. Does the statement of the ethical problem point to all the relevant elements or facts in the situation? Second, one needs to determine what set of criteria for judgment make the most sense for analyzing the problem. What ethical principles should we bring to bear in determining what is right or wrong about the situation? Finally, we need to argue a proposition of policy. What would be the most ethical action to take? What does our ethical reasoning tell us is the right action to take?

Given this framework, we feel it is important for students to develop an understanding of the various criteria that have been formulated for making ethical judgments. Part One presents these various systems of value criteria and reasoning about them. Utilitarianism, for example, emphasizes the *consequences* of one's action, while a universalistic system such as Kant's lays most stress on one's *intentions* for carrying out an action. Part Two considers applications of ethical principles in various communication contexts. We hope that the issues presented in the chapters as well as the case studies in each will allow students to try out and discuss, even argue about, different reasoned approaches to the issues and cases.

ACKNOWLEDGMENTS

Many people have encouraged and supported us in the developing and writing of this text. The students we have worked with over the years in our classes on communication ethics have afforded us an appreciation for the importance of ethical thinking and feeling in their lives. They have often challenged us, helping us to sharpen and refine our own thinking about how people think through ethical challenges in their own communication.

We wish to express our gratitude to the professionals at Allyn & Bacon who helped us with their advice and suggestions in bringing the work to publication. Especially we wish to thank Brain Wheel, the series editor and Jenny Lupica, the series editorial assistant.

We are grateful for the very helpful suggestions and comments made by those who participated in various stages reviewing this text: Andy Denhart, Stetson University; Jon A. Hess, University of Missouri; Mike Ingram, Whitworth College; L. David Schuelke, Bethel College and June Smith, Angelo State University.

Finally, we thank our families for their patience and support as we spent long hours and days (and nights) at our keyboards and computer screens researching and writing–Bill owes special thanks to Linda, his wife, and Paul, to his wife, Laura, and to his daughter, Erin for their special encouragement and support.

Communicating Ethically

1 Introduction to Communication Ethics

CHAPTER OUTLINE

Susan, a senior student in our capstone class, presented her professors and classmates with this dilemma. She had been accepted into three graduate schools but hoped to attend the one that offered the best package of financial aid, assistantships, or stipends. Each school, she explained, required a student to commit or indicate an intention to attend that school before considering the financial aid package they could offer the student (this was her understanding of the communication she had from the grad schools).

She told us, "I feel that I have to commit myself and promise to attend all three under these circumstances, until I find out what kind of financial aid they are going to give me."

Feeling a little concerned about the ethics of her communication with the universities, she asked for advice from friends, who generally supported her in her deception, most by saying that was "how the game is played."

In the discussion, other students revealed that they had sometimes found themselves in similar situations and *reassured* Susan that they will mislead a prospective employer or grad school in the same fashion. One student, Jonathon, reported that in a job interview he had communicated complete interest and dedication to that employer, without revealing he was really looking at several different offers. His reasoning was that one has to do that in order to protect oneself, to cover all the bases so as not to be caught without any offers or prospects.

Our discussions with students and colleagues concerning these situations reveal several different responses to the ethical issues they raise. Many students expressed the feeling that the graduate or law schools put students in untenable situations by requiring commitment on the students' parts before committing financial aid on their part. Their point implies the question, "If you are not being treated fairly or ethically, is it all right to reciprocate with a deception on your part?"

Others maintained that these institutions are just institutions rather than real people with feelings—and that lying to them is not morally the same as lying to actual people. These institutions expect people will try to mislead them in these instances anyway, because, after all, "everybody does it."

In this kind of situation, students recognize that outright lying to others is a breach of communication ethics, but they maintain that circumstances, and especially the need for self-protection, change the equation. This sort of lying or deception is not really wrong, or at least not too bad, because of the circumstance, the parties involved, or the justification that these are standard practices and expectations. Again, the assumption is that this is the way *the game* is played.

Another student, Michaela, seemed more concerned about the implications, however. "What about other students also wanting to go the same grad school and also needing financial aid?", she wondered. Would they be closed out or denied a spot, because Susan was essentially taking up three places instead of one? Michaela was exploring the issue of potential harm coming to others because of Susan's communication committing to all three schools. Susan then admitted that another reason she was feeling uneasy about her actions was that the faculty adviser at one of the colleges seemed very excited about her attending that school. The adviser described the other students and the faculty she would be working with and even suggested people she could live with while settling in. It seems that this college became personal an institution as a result of this kind of interaction. Michaela as well as Susan were beginning to show how we reason about ethical issues. At first, students

Zits

© Zits Partnership. Reprinted with special permission of King Features Syndicate.

believed that Susan's deception was victimless, except for the institution, which was not really a person. But Michaela's contribution requires us to question that assumption. And, Susan was pointing out that the lifeless institution itself did include some real people who may have real feelings.

Reasoning about Communication Ethics

Susan's dilemma, as well as the issue facing the student in the job interview, raises issues of communication ethics. By an ethical issue, we mean just this sort of case, in which one can raise a question about whether a particular communication behavior is *right or wrong*. The question of whether something is *right or wrong* may seem like a loaded one. Who is to say whether what a person does is right or wrong for that person or that situation? We often feel that a person's ethics or moral judgments are a matter of personal values and beliefs: can we really judge a person in such a case or, at least, judge their action?

The arguments made and the questions raised by the students suggest we often make these judgments. At least, our feeling the need to justify or rationalize what might seem questionable actions shows a sense that we can give reasons for or against them. This book is about trying to answer this and similar questions. We feel that you can reason about and give arguments for or against behaviors that can be considered ethical or unethical. Over many years philosophers, especially in the branch called *ethics*, have tried to develop systematic ways to reason about ethical issues. Let's consider some of the approaches one could take to thinking in a systematic way about the dilemma in Susan's case.

First, one could argue that her decision about whether to mislead the graduate schools reflected her upbringing and character. Does one action, in a case such as this, indicate that a person has a certain kind of character, or does her acting this way in one case lead to behaving deceptively in later cases? One instructor tried to explore this question with the class by asking what kinds of commitments were more important than others. For example, if one student has become engaged to another, that represents a commitment. Could this commitment be taken as lightly as the one involving the grad schools or the job offers? Certainly not! At least, that was the response of nearly everyone in the room.

This first approach to reasoning about ethics assumes a person with the right kind of character, one who possesses virtues such as honesty and truthfulness, will behave in an ethical way. The first kind of ethical system is based on the notion of character used in this sense, and is usually referred to as *virtue ethics*. This system may be the oldest of the ones we shall be considering and is linked, historically, with the oldest tradition of theories about human communication. Virtue ethics assumes that by practicing the right sort of virtues, one will have a guide to making ethical decisions. In addition, the system assumes that there may be competing virtues that apply to any single case, requiring that a virtuous person be able to balance the different virtues appropriately.

Second, one could argue that the moral or ethical thing to do is based on a set of rules that are universal. This system would hold that lying is always wrong, although there may be differences in how wrong a given lie might be given certain circumstances. This system assumes that any sort of falsehood or lying is presumed wrong until proven otherwise. The great philosopher most often associated with this way of reasoning about ethics was the German thinker, Immanuel Kant. He held that any kind of lying, even for a good cause, such as to save an innocent person from a murderer, was always wrong. Ethics according to this view is based on a set of unchanging duties, which may be based on *divine command*, that is, based on religious precepts, or on human nature, or on the unalterable laws of reason and logic. Because the ancient Greek word for duty was *deon*, this type of ethical reasoning is called *deontological ethics*. The question about Susan's actions would be put in terms of whether or not her actions constituted a violation of a universal ethical rule or commandment. We should first determine whether or not in this particular case Susan had a duty to tell the exact truth to each grad school. Did her misleading them constitute lying (deliberately saying something that one knows not to be true)? If lying is always wrong, then was Susan wrong in this case?

Third, one could argue that the question should revolve around what action results in the best outcome for the most people. This kind of system considers the *outcome*, the consequences of the behavior as the sole or at least major determining factor in the rightness or wrongness of an action. The most famous of the systems based on this sort of *consequentialism* is *Utilitarianism*. This word, coined in the nineteenth century and associated with the British philosophers Jeremy Bentham and John Stuart Mill, means that the utility, the usefulness, of an action determines whether it should be considered ethical or not. We should emphasize that *usefulness* here means specifically the greatest, beneficial usefulness for the greatest number of people.

Another form of the so-called *consequentialism* is concerned with whether or not the outcomes, the consequences, affect everyone involved equally. This system is based on the principle that everyone should be treated in the same way—for that reason, it is referred to as *egalitarianism*. If we were applying utilitarianism in Susan's case, we would ask who was benefited by her communication. Obviously, she stood to gain by her action, but the question would be the total effect on other persons as well. Michaela's question about other students wanting to be admitted to the same program seems relevant in this application. Similarly, the egalitarian viewpoint would seek to know whether others were less likely to receive equal consideration for admission or financial aid because of her action.

A fourth way of looking at these issues grows from a concern for human *relationships*. How are relationships between individuals affected by one's communication behavior? It seemed that Susan may have developed an interpersonal relationship with a person at one or more of the schools. Did the relational nature of this interaction bring with it certain ethical obligations or expectations? This sort of consideration is associated with *dialogical ethics*, which derive from one's responsibilities to another human being when engaged in meaningful dialogue or communication with that other person.

In summary, the first four types of systems for reasoning about communication ethics involve issues based on the following broad concepts:

1. Character
2. Duties
3. Consequences
4. Relationships.

Our first goal, then, is to make you familiar with each of the major systems for making ethical judgments so that you can see how they would be applied in communication. The field of ethics has been studied for a very long time and from many different perspectives, so we should not be surprised to learn that these are not the only systems for debating ethical decisions that have been developed. Also, we emphasize here the word *major*, since there are many variations and permutations of these systems which will not be covered, at least not in detail.

The second chapter will take up the application of virtue ethics, because of its early association with the study of persuasive communication in public life. In the third chapter, we will turn to very influential system developed by the philosopher, Immanuel Kant, and his system of universalistic ethics. We shall also consider some contemporary systems that derived from the Kantian approach. Also, important and traditional systems of universal ethics are derived from, first, *divine command* theories, which bring in religious traditions, and, second, theories based on the concept of *human nature*. The human nature arguments for universal rules of ethics are sometimes but not always developed from biological theories of evolution— bioethics.

In the fourth chapter we discuss the system of utilitarianism, as developed by John Stuart Mill. Egalitarianism and social contract (or *contractualism*) theories of ethics are covered in this chapter as theories concerned especially with the outcomes or consequences of communicative behavior.

The fifth chapter turns our attention to the ethics of dialogue, as represented in the works of Martin Buber, Carl Rogers, Emmanuel Levinas, and Paulo Freire. These related systems of dialogic ethics are especially important when we engage in interpersonal interactions.

In the concluding chapter of Part I, we take up issues presented by the challenges of some contemporary approaches or concerns in ethics and the field of communication. First, we need to be aware of the challenge to any sort of rationalist system for ethical decision making represented by postmodern critics and theorists. We then need to make you aware of systems that emphasize differences rather than universalistic principles for ethics. In this vein, we will discuss feminist theories of ethics, cultural relativism, and situational ethics.

Thoughtful people have been able to reason and therefore to debate rationally ethical issues. The purpose of this book is to guide you through some of the various systems that you could adapt for judging whether a particular tactic or behavior could be considered to ethical or not. In order to proceed, however, we should clarify exactly what we are talking about when we use the term *ethics* and *communication ethics*.

Definitions

First, we should clarify what we mean by *ethics* and *ethics of communication*. In a technical sense, ethics is a branch of the field of philosophy, which concerns judgments about right and wrong actions. Beyond the discipline of philosophy, many fields include the study of and applications of ethics to their domain. Ethics refers to a systematic method for making judgments concerning voluntary actions of people. We need to highlight several aspects of this definition.

- First, ethics is intended to provide us with a system so that *the decisions or judgments one makes can be justified to others and to oneself in a clear and objective manner.*
- Second, ethics is concerned with judgments *about actions that can be determined to be right or wrong* according to the principles of this method.
- Third, the judgments are to be made about actions, in which the actors appear to have a *choice*; they could have done otherwise.
- And, fourth, the actions are seen as *intentional*: the persons seemed to know what they were doing and intended to do what they did.

Communication ethics is the application of ethical thinking to situations involving human communication. In this book, we are concerned with interpersonal communication, in which two people are interacting face-to-face; public communication, such as public speaking; political communication; religious communication; and mass communication. All these situations face-to-face, public, and mass or mediated communication can also involve intercultural or cross-cultural communication. We further recognize that the so-called *new media*, represented by digital telecommunications and computer-mediated communication, can also cut across these various dimensions affecting the ethics of communication.

Communication Ethics and Integrity

A word that represents what we mean by communication ethics is *integrity*. One of the main characteristics many people say they look for in a leader is integrity. Most of us hope that other people will think of us as a person of integrity. The word shares a root with *integral* and *integrate*, both of which bear the connotation of completeness or unity. An integral part of something is necessary to complete it, to make it whole. When we integrate something into something else, we make it a fitting and necessary part of the greater whole. In the same way, we think of someone with integrity as someone in whom principles or virtues are such a part of that person that they would not be complete, not be who they are, without that characteristic. The word then implies wholeness and completeness. It also implies consistency and steadfast commitment to principles.

The problem is that we often claim a need to be flexible at times, because we feel that integrity can be too demanding given the needs of everyday, modern life. Integrity in other words is an ideal but not really practical. A second problem is that people do not always agree on exactly what constitutes integrity. Of course, many believe that ethics and integrity are relative, depending on the culture or society in which one is born and brought up. Still, even in the same, homogenous culture, there is disagreement on exactly what is the moral or ethical thing to do. It is our hope that in this text, you derive some systematic and principled way to argue or reason through those situations in which there are competing views of right and wrong.

The Inconvenience of Integrity and Ethics

Will Rogers an American humorist, was supposed to have remarked that he could resist anything but temptation. We are all often of the same mind. In principle, we can resist the temptation to wiggle around some ethical principle for reasons of expediency. But, when the real life situation does come up, we find the temptation to make one exception in order to get that great job, to achieve some personal dream, to get into the best law school, to get the coveted promotion more powerful than it seemed when it was only a theoretical matter. As we begin our study of communication ethics, it may be useful to remember that ethical issues or dilemmas arise only when those principles seem to go against our personal wishes or what we would really like to do in a specific instance.

Let's return to a case similar to the one with which we began this book. A student, David, brought up a familiar dilemma. He intended to go on to graduate school but after laying out a year to work and gain some experience and money. At a job interview, it became clear that he could have a really good job if he committed to stay with the firm for at least two or more years. The question he had for the class was what he should do. The immediate response of several students, many of whom had completed one or two classes in ethics, was "You lie." They believed that getting the well-paying job took precedence over the *theoretical* principle of integrity. The general feeling was that the world is impersonal and competitive, and in this kind of world "you have to do what you have to do." The *real world* requires hard-headed acts of self-interest, according to this way of thinking. If the world presented us with only cases in which the action in our self-interest is also the action that accords with high principles and personal integrity, there would be no need for the study of ethics. We hope that in studying this text, you come to develop a method for thinking through dilemmas involving ethics and communication that you may face in the *real world*. We are not intending to give you the *right answers*, but rather a system or a process for analyzing such situations.

The *Game*

We have found that when we bring up real-life decisions that people have to make, in which it is in their interest to lie or prevaricate, they are often able to rationalize their action in doing so. Certainly the authors have found themselves in the same situation when faced with some of life's ethical dilemmas. The justification that we encounter most often as the basis for such rationalization can be summed up in these words: "That is how the game is played." So, if business is a game, politics is a game, and even courtship and marriage are games, do different or special rules of the game apply when we are playing? Our class discussions showed many people would feel it is all right for the student faced with having to commit to one graduate school without knowing which would give them the best financial package or for the student faced with the need to commit to one employer even when they did not intend to meet that commitment to lie or mislead the other party. The justification is that everyone knows or should know how to play the game. These institutions, it is felt, ought to know the game as well as anyone; and if they don't, that is their fault. One who does not play the game is simply naïve and is likely to come out worse off than another person who is a more skillful player. The metaphor of the game allows us to blame the other party when they are indignant about having been misled.

The problem with the *rules of the game*, especially when our own preferences or desires are involved, is that it becomes easy to change them or simply to make up the rules as we go along. Another problem with the game image is that it assumes that all other involved parties know about the game and how it is played. Consider the graduate school faculty or the people in the business in our two running examples. If they knew that the commitments being made to them were simply ploys or moves in a game, would they take them seriously? Are the commitments being asked for like bluffs in the game of poker?

Notice that the justifications advanced for lying or misleading others in these cases also depend on two other factors:

- First, the other party is not really a person but an organization or an institution.
- And, second, the other party is also being unfair or unreasonable.

The serious business of the games we play in life, it would appear, allows us to take into account the supposed personhood of the other party (or the lack thereof) and the issue of assumed reciprocity. The rules of the game allow us to treat institutions differently from *real* people. And, the rules allow us to do unto others what they are trying to do unto us, or at least what we think they will try to do unto us.

As we discuss the various approaches to ethics and communication in this text, we will often return to the image of the *game*, as we try to make systematic the dilemmas and decisions people face in communicating, ethically, with other people.

The Scope of Communication Ethics

The specific cases we have referred to so far involve decisions being made by individuals in regard to their own goals—graduate school, employment, and the like. Communication ethics is of concern, however, beyond our own immediate lives and relationships. It does not take much effort to discover all sorts of questionable practices in the marketplace, media, and everyday interactions. Unfair political attack ads, *spin doctors* putting the best possible face on a bad political decision, speakers playing to prejudices in courtrooms and election campaigns, the so-called *white lie*, deceptive accounting reporting, racist or sexist or ageist jokes, overly-aggressive telemarketing, misleading mailers suggesting "You may already be a winner!"—this list of familiar, questionable communication practices emphasizes that the ethics of communication is a highly salient and relevant concern in our lives.

At the beginning of the twenty-first century, ethics has become a dominant concern in political, business, and social lives. Campaigning for political office, especially at the national level, is truly big business, bigger than ever. Faced with mounting costs of media advertising and the presumed short attention span of viewers and listeners, political campaign spots have to be shorter and simpler than ever. Often the easiest and quickest point to make in these circumstances is to attack the character of the opponent. While the political smear is certainly nothing new in American political life, the range and far-reach of the mass media today have made it nearly ubiquitous. The spread of political communication through the Internet has made questionable political communication even more insidious and difficult to correct.

Ethical questions are not limited to political communication, of course. Several major business scandals in the early 2000s such as those at Enron and others centered around unreliable or misleading financial reports communicated by auditors, accountants, and top executives. Whistle-blowers brought the wrongdoing to light, raising questions about the ethical responsibilities of people to communicate misdeeds to the press, government, or the general public. Conflicts of interest raise similar concerns about ethical communication. A stock analyst, for example, ran afoul of a large telecommunication supplier when he raised questions about the reliability of the company's financial reporting. The chief financial officer of the company was soon calling the head of the investment analysis firm complaining about these reports.[1] As in the cases of questionable political communications, the businesses were trying to mislead the public and customers. Is there any wonder that a member of Board of Trustees of the State University of New York stated, "Does anyone doubt the need for heightened standards of ethics in all the professions? In recent scandals, too many accountants, lawyers, bankers, security analysts, and corporate officers allow self-interest and greed to trump long-standing principles of integrity."[2]

In a more ethnically and religiously diverse society, people worry about communications that inflame or prejudice people against specific groups. In some cases, such *hate speech* is highly public, such as the so-called *shock-jocks*, radio personalities whose shows are intended to shock listeners. Officials at colleges and universities have grown increasingly concerned about *hate speech* on their campuses. Several campuses have tried to institute speech codes, intended to prevent prejudiced or bigoted speech among students, staff, and faculty. Such attempts provoked a backlash from some groups, both conservative and liberal, concerned about perceived restrictions on freedom of speech.

All these cases focus on communication intended to persuade people by words, by the use of rhetoric, the art of persuasive communication. The communication in these examples is often labeled unethical because it is based on partial truth, misleading statements, incorrect or irrelevant evidence, and similar tactics.

Many of these cases have prototypes, ancestors that reach far back in the history of human communication. The classical Greeks, such as Plato and Socrates, over two thousand years ago, condemned practices similar to these contemporary questionable tactics. Ethics has always been at the center of the systematic study and practice of human communication. The next chapter begins by placing communication ethics within that tradition of the discipline of rhetoric and communication.

QUESTIONS AND TOPICS FOR DISCUSSION

1. Discuss your response to the dilemmas presented by the students in this chapter. When is it OK to play the game and mislead others in order to achieve your career goals? Do people often expect to be misled in these kinds of situations? What would you do if you were faced with the situation of the student forced to commit to a graduate school in order to be considered for financial aid, even if you were not sure you really wanted to attend that graduate school? Is it true that most institutions expect to be misled about these matters anyway, since they know how the game is played?

2. Is it true that everyone knows that when advertisers claim their product is the best, or the most popular, or the favorite whatever, it is just hype or permissible boasting? If that is true, why do advertisers do it anyway?

3. Do you think that most politicians (all politicians?) are likely to withhold the whole truth or mislead voters or make promises they really cannot deliver on in order to get elected? Do most voters think of politics as a *game* of the sort we have described in this chapter?

NOTES

1. Jesse Drucker and Jathon Safsford, "Analyze This: Firms Chafe at Criticism," *The Wall Street Journal*, November 22, 2002, p. C1.

2. Candace de Rossy, "Professional ethics begin on the college campus," *Chronicle of Higher Education*, September. 19, 2003, p. B20.

PART ONE

Theories and Perspectives

2 Character in Communication and Virtue Ethics

In earlier times, Americans looked to the simple maxims of someone like Benjamin Franklin as a model for virtuous behavior. While still in his twenties, Franklin set down a list of thirteen virtues:

- Temperance; don't overindulge in food or drink.
- Silence; avoid chattering.
- Order; be organized.
- Resolution; fulfill your obligations.
- Frugality; waste not.
- Industry; don't waste time in idle pursuits.
- Sincerity; speak honestly and forthrightly.
- Justice; do right by others.
- Moderation; avoid extremes, as in emotional responses.
- Cleanliness; keep body, home, and clothes clean.
- Tranquility; don't be upset by insignificant events.
- Chastity; keep a good reputation.
- Humility; imitate Jesus and Socrates, according to Franklin.

Franklin's list of virtues has a distinctly American flavor, emphasizing practical behaviors that would help one *get ahead*. These maxims and others were popularized in his famous *Poor Richard's Almanac*. In the end, Franklin himself abandoned his project to practice his thirteen virtues, because he saw it would be almost impossible, but being aware of these virtues, at least, he felt was worth the effort.[1]

The generation of American leaders we think of as the *Founders* of the republic offer several versions of the virtues associated with the American character. Thomas Jefferson was known as a moral philosopher in addition to his many other intellectual talents. Jefferson's ideas about the virtues and character are evident, first, in the Declaration of Independence. In his other writings and reflections he also extolled the virtues of justice, benevolence, the *agrarian virtues* of industry, moderation, patience, self-reliance, and independence, and of course the public virtues of patriotism and political democracy.[2] George Washington was looked to for generations as an exemplar of the American virtues in his person and conduct, especially as commander of the Continental Army during the Revolution itself. Of course, one can hardly forget famous story about George Washington and the cherry tree—"Father, I cannot tell a lie."

During the 1990s, William J. Bennett reminded Americans of this heritage of the virtues of the American character, when he compiled stories intended to teach character in *The Book of Virtues*. Bennett, who served as Director of the Office of National Drug Control Policy under the first President Bush and as Secretary of Education and Chairman of the National Endowment for the Humanities under former President Reagan, invoked the founders as well as many of the virtues associated with Franklin, Washington, and Jefferson. The chapters reveal a list of virtues similar in many ways to those of Franklin and Jefferson:

- Self-Discipline
- Compassion
- Responsibility
- Friendship
- Work
- Courage
- Perseverance
- Honesty
- Loyalty
- Faith.

Bennett's first book led to others, especially concerned with character education for children and young people. These works even became the basis for a Public Broadcasting System (PBS) educational series aimed at children.

This emphasis on character and practicing the virtues represents perhaps the oldest tradition in the study of ethics: the system known as *virtue ethics*. The earliest Greek philosophers—Socrates, Plato, and Aristotle—formulated the seminal ideas about virtue ethics. The major religious traditions have also taught systems of virtue and the development of character. The ancient Chinese sage, Confucius, for example, believed that the right character of the superior person, or the educated gentleman, was required for right conduct. In these philosophical as well as religious traditions, the ideals of the virtues are more important than fallible human conduct. After all, as noted above, Franklin, who fathered at least one illegitimate son, decided to abandon his attempt to live up to all the virtues on his list as being impossible. Jefferson held to his ideals despite being a slave-owner and his fathering of children, it is alleged, with his slave, Sally Hemmings. In the May of 2003, even William Bennett was forced to admit that he had indulged a huge gambling habit, which seems a vice at odds with the virtues he upheld in his books.[3]

Background of Virtue Ethics

A person practicing virtue ethics decides the ethical course of action in any given situation by asking, "What would the person of exemplary character do in this circumstance?" In other words, ethical action is not determined by applying a set of rules, but rather is the result of good character and sound judgment. Our students often find this definition a little circular—it seems to say that virtue ethics requires being virtuous. The complication arises because practicing virtue ethics requires a way of living rather than following a set of rules. The person who has integrity or good character relies on his or her good judgment to act ethically in each given situation.

Socrates laid down the basis for virtue ethics when he argued that a person would not do evil knowingly. Let us be clear about the claim that is being made here. Socrates is saying that a person who truly and carefully contemplates the truth and the circumstances of his or her life will believe doing good and suffering evil is preferable to any alternative. The *character* of the contemplative person, that person's virtue, results in following these principles. Virtue ethics hence does not lay down rules for dealing with various situations a person might encounter but maintains that the person who has the proper virtues will act correctly in all circumstances. In contrast to virtue ethics, many of the ethical systems encountered later in this text are *rule based.*

The classical Greeks believed that human virtue was manifested in a quality they called *arête* (which is often translated simply as *virtue*). *Arête* implied not only doing the right thing but also leading a noble life. We might say that it consists in living well, which means that one acts virtuously or ethically.

In other words, one does not do the ethical thing because it is a duty or in order to achieve some good end: *doing the ethical thing is simply part of the most fully human way of living.* One does not behave ethically in order to get the benefits of living well, but in living well one performs ethical actions. Ethical behavior is hence the consequence of character. The ethical action is performed not to achieve a desired consequence, but the action itself is the consequence of character.

Because character is more important than rules in this system of ethics, it allows for flexibility in making ethical judgments. The key attribute the ethical person requires is good judgment. The upshot is that one cannot easily predict in advance what the ethical act will be in all circumstances. It is better to leave decisions up to the person with mature and wise practical reason rather than try to provide one with rules, guidelines, or laws. Having the right kind of person at the right time is essential. But, of course, one might complain, how can we be sure of having the right person at the right time, and how do we, as fallible and inexperienced people, know what the right action might be under future circumstances?

The answer to this question is not easy, although the implication is to do what the *virtuous person* would do. We often rely on models for good behavior in trying to develop the character to behave in the most ethical way. For example, some religious people refer to the phrase *WWJD* (*What Would Jesus Do*) as a guide for thinking through ethical decisions. Even professional athletes are enjoined to behave well because they could be *role models* for young people.

Virtue ethics has had a long association with the field of communication studies. This association results from the fact that the earliest systematic study of the art of persuasion, called *rhetoric*, was developed in classical Greece, as was the early study of the ethics as a field of philosophy. The three most famous early Greek philosophers, Socrates, Plato, and Aristotle all took a hand at investigating the relationship between the art of communication and ethics. First, we will see that Socrates and Plato attacked the teaching of the art of persuasion as being basically unethical. Second, we see that Aristotle tried to rescue the teaching of persuasion (*rhetoric* as it was called in those days) from this charge by linking the fields of persuasion and ethics.

For our purposes, the interesting point is that the field of communication has had to deal with charges concerning its ethics from the earliest days of its inception. Some things hardly ever change.

The Art of Communication and Ethics

When one tries to persuade other people, he or she is trying to get them to believe or to do something they would not have otherwise believed or done. Persuasion thus puts one's own interests ahead of those of the other person, or so some would argue. Obviously, we can think of instances in which the persuasion is really for the benefit of the one being persuaded: when a doctor persuades a patient to take a particular medicine; when a parent convinces a child not to experiment with dangerous drugs, or not to drink and drive; and so on.

In one of the earliest discussions about persuasive communication, Plato attacked the way persuasion was taught in his day, over two thousand years ago. The art of persuasion then was highly practical, aimed at winning cases and votes in assemblies. The teaching was based on the observation that members of the general public, who comprised the juries and assemblies, were not always able to follow complicated arguments and proofs. The art taught, therefore, focused more on what such audiences would accept as probably true, rather than what was actually true.

Plato presented his philosophical works as dialogues, that is, fictionalized conversations written like a play. The protagonist of these dialogues is often Plato's revered teacher, Socrates. Plato (the real author of the dialogue) has Socrates lay out his most famous charge against the art of persuasion.[4] It is no art at all, he contends, but is merely a *knack* for producing gratification or pleasure among the hearers, not true knowledge or edification. To clarify this charge, Socrates compares rhetoric (the art of persuasion) to cookery. When we cook food, we present it in such a way that we don't perceive the meal as flesh of a dead animal or dead plants. Cooking makes the items more palatable, more easily digested. In the same way, the art of political persuasion consists of presenting unpalatable situations in ways that make them appear in a better light, according to Socrates. He also compares rhetoric to cosmetics, a skill aimed at making people appear more attractive than they might actually be. If there were a true art of rhetoric, of political persuasion, it would consist in communicating in a way that improved the listeners and made them better people. A true art of rhetoric would aim at speaking truth and instilling justice. The skill of persuasion, not based on *true art*, could be taught to corrupt people for their own selfish ends, since it was not grounded in ethical or moral instruction.

This charge against teaching persuasion has a very contemporary ring to it. Plato is contending persuasive communication, especially political communication, should be aimed at enhancing the well-being of the listeners, not at advancing the fortunes or purposes of the speakers themselves. But sometimes, professionals in the fields of political campaign communication, public relations, advertising, and so on, seem more concerned precisely with advancing the interests of the speakers or advocates. Success, defined as winning, is everything. (Hence, we see the need for professionals in those fields to be especially attentive to the issues of ethical communication.)

In line with Plato's thinking, a distinguished American political scientist, James MacGreor Burns, wrote a classic study on leadership in the twentieth century.[5] In this well-known work, Burns develops the concept of what he calls a *transformational leader*, as representing the best kind of political leader. The transformational leader is so called because she has the effect of *transforming* her followers, making them better people and bringing out the best in them. Most leaders, even the best, are often more what Burns calls *transactional leaders*, who lead as a result of transactions with the followers, in which both sides are looking out for their own interests. The transformational leader, on the other hand, resonates with Plato's vision of the best leader or the true speaker.

Aristotle: The Foundation for Communication Theory and Ethics

Aristotle linked the teaching of persuasion to the fields of ethics and politics directly. Virtue or character is required for the best practice in all three areas, he argued. As we shall see, Aristotle devoted major works to the practical fields of politics, ethics, and rhetoric, and his books on these three fields have become classics.

Now, we should be clear at the outset that the art of communication of most interest (perhaps of only interest) to Aristotle was communication in the public arena, literally in the open-air agora and law courts of Athens. The highest and noblest calling for an Athenian, and by extension the citizens of similar Greek city-states, was to be a political leader and statesman. His *Art of Rhetoric* was intended as a guide and instruction for such leaders, as were his works on ethics and obviously politics. Amelie Oskenberg Rorty says this concerning Aristotle's purpose in his ethical work: "He writes the *Nicomachean Ethics* for those who have the traits, constitutions, and some of the habits that would enable them to become virtuous, for those capable of responsible action, and particularly for those who might be statesmen."[6] We now turn to Aristotle's classic attempt to develop an ethical theory of communication.

The Rhetoric

In this book on the art of persuasion, Aristotle begins by defining the field. The proper domain of political communication, or *rhetoric*, as Aristotle called it, is not based on the logical exposition and proof associated with mathematics and science. Logic and science attempt to get at general truths that apply across all circumstances as do mathematical proofs and scientific laws. In the political arena, however, we do not deal with general truths themselves but with the application of principles to specific events and circumstances. In real life, those who debate public policy—say in Congress or a municipal city council—do not have the advantages of the scientist in her laboratory, where she can take as much time as she needs and control nearly all the variables affecting the outcome of an experiment. In making political decisions people do not have the luxury of knowing all the circumstances or factors that could affect the outcome. There is usually an urgent need to act without waiting for all the information to come in.

Rhetoric is therefore concerned with developing arguments that will be persuasive to an audience under real-life conditions. Similarly, Aristotle maintains ethics and politics are arts in which *practical reason* must guide decisions rather than *scientific reason*. This is the major link among the three fields of study: rhetoric, politics, and ethics are concerned with making judgments under real-life constraints, requiring mature and practical reason.

The distinction between logical reason and practical reason leads Aristotle to define *rhetoric* as the ability or faculty that allows a person to discover the best possible proof or most persuasive argument for any given case.[7] The *best possible proof* implies that what is sought is not the final or universal proof, as one hopes to find in the natural sciences, but the most effective proof under the circumstances of ongoing public life. Therefore in political communication, we rely on rhetorical proofs rather than logical or scientific proofs for our arguments.

A person who studies rhetoric is therefore trying to learn a systematic procedure for developing and presenting *good arguments* in *realistic situations* to audiences of *typical citizens*. Aristotle is most concerned in his *Rhetoric* with what we call *invention*, with the methods for devising rhetorical proofs and arguments. He does include in his book sections on organizing, wording, and delivering speeches, which we would expect to find in a modern text book on public speaking, but most of his attention stays on the process of finding good arguments.

Although Aristotle gives most attention to logical proof in his work, he also maintains that the *ethos*, the character of the speaker, can be the most powerful means of support in a speech, when he says, "character is almost, so to speak, the controlling factor in persuasion."[8] In order to be effective in using all forms of proof, the speaker must be able to develop arguments or syllogisms and "be observant about characters and virtues . . ."[9]

This emphasis on character and the virtues sets Aristotle's teaching on rhetoric apart from those of the earliest speech teachers, called *Sophists*, and other theories of persuasion concerned mainly with strategies for achieving one's own ends. An overarching concern with strategy suggests one tries to develop strategies concerned only for winning, winning an election, winning a market share, and so on. *Strategic communication* here means communication intended to achieve the speaker's personal objectives whether or not these outcomes are in the best interests of the listeners or the community at large. For example, some advertising communication is aimed at selling a product often without concern for whether there is truly a need for the product. We may not really need another high-definition TV in our family room or a larger SUV on the road, but the purpose of some advertising is to use communication strategies to make us believe we need these things. The success of the commu-nication is measured in terms of the number of units sold rather than some larger, moral goal. Aristotle makes the same point in his work on ethics when he points out that "a morally weak or a bad man will, as a result of calculation, attain the goal which he has proposed to himself as the right goal to attain. He will, therefore, have deliberated correctly, but what he will get out of it will be a very bad thing."[10]

In other words, the communicator will have been successful in the short run, as measured in a superficial way, but in the long run, he or she will not be living the flourishing, best possible life.

Aristotle intends to teach an ethical rhetoric, to be practiced by the per-son with good moral character, acting for the benefit of the political commu-nity. His own summary of his definition is translated as follows: "The result is that rhetoric is a certain kind of offshoot of dialectic [formal logic] and of ethical studies (which it is just to call politics)."[11] We can understand more about what he means by the *ethical* by turning to a discussion of his most famous work on ethics, the *Nicomachean Ethics*.[12]

The Ethics

At the beginning of his major work on ethics, Aristotle says that living an ethical life implies knowing the purposes of human life. The first line of the book lays out the issue: "Every art of applied science and every systematic investigation, and similarly every action and choice, seem to aim at some good; the good, therefore, has been well defined as that at which all things aim."[13] His system of ethics aims at some desired end (*telos* in Greek, which is why this system is called *teleological*).

This end is to live the good life, which is desired in and for its own sake. The aim of politics, as well, is to discern what is required to live well in a community. This ultimate goal, of course, is happiness. This happiness, he maintains, is understood to be the same as *living well* and *doing well*.[14] Doing well, or *flourishing* as a human being, requires fulfilling the highest functions characteristic of being human.

So the meaning of happiness as used by Aristotle may not be the same as we mean by happiness today. A good person, therefore, is someone who excels at being a complete human being, and so the highest virtue is excel-lence in being fully human.

Behaving ethically is the result of habits of living the best possible life. When we judge whether people have behaved in an ethical fashion, three factors must be present. First, they must *know* what they are doing, and not acting rightly or wrongly because of accident, chance, or misunderstanding. For that reason, truth is not the test of the act of lying, as Sissela Bok points out in her famous book titled *Lying*. If we honestly believed what we said was true, even though we were mistaken, our statement would not be a lie because we did not act from accurate knowledge. Secondly, people must *choose* to act in the way they do. Telling a lie requires a conscious choice to tell someone what we truly believe to be false. Third, according to Aristotle, the decision to act in a certain way is based on the *character* of the speaker, as he puts it, "the act must spring from a firm and unchangeable character."[15] The three elements are thus knowledge, choice, and character. The essential point about Aristotle's system of ethics is that *character* is the most important defining feature of ethical conduct.

One cultivates the character of a virtuous person by practicing the virtues, which are tendencies to act in certain ways under certain conditions. So, as there is the general concept of *virtue*, there are also various individual virtues themselves. It is essential to bear in mind that for Aristotle and other classical virtue ethicists, moral virtue was equated with *excellence*. A virtue was a predisposition to act in a way that produced the highest excellence that a person could achieve.

To illustrate what this perspective entails, we could turn to some examples of excellence in various activities. For example, for a track athlete, excellence requires speed and stamina; for that athlete these two attributes are *virtues* in that they allow her to achieve the highest level of excellence in that sport. Aristotle is concerned with excellence in general for human beings, and thus he asks what are the attributes required to allow a person to achieve the highest level of excellence as a human being, that is, in living the best possible life. As the sprinter requires speed and stamina, the human being in general requires the general excellences or virtues of character.

This understanding of the meaning of *virtue* is different from our everyday use of this term today, so we need to be sure that this concept of a *virtue as excellence* is explicit before going into the list of the virtues proposed by Aristotle. Aristotle's belief that a virtue allows a person to achieve excellence explains his notion that a virtue is a mean (average) between two extremes. For example, in athletics again, a basketball player must be aggressive and competitive to be successful, but if he is too aggressive he will not achieve excellence. Too much aggressiveness will lead the athlete to break rules, foul his opponent too much, and lose effectiveness. So, the successful player exhibits just the right amount of aggressiveness, a mean between unnecessary roughness and insufficient competitiveness. This is the idea behind Aristotle's notion that a virtue is a mean between two extremes. We can also think of the virtue as the peak between two valleys, which are the extremes on either side.

The virtues can be further explained by looking at the list proposed by Aristotle, which also gives us a picture of what would have been considered excellence among the classical Greeks of his day and can be compared to the virtues of Benjamin Franklin and others of our own day. The set of virtues may be different in different times and under different circumstances, as we shall see. These, then, are virtues that would have been seen as leading to excellence in the classical world of Athens.

- Courage, which is the mean between rashness and foolhardiness, on one extreme, and timidity or cowardice, on the other.
- Self-control, referring to mastery of self, that is, control of one's passions. The extremes on either side would be self-indulgence and extreme asceticism or self-denial. In certain religions, asceticism or self-denial are seen as virtues, so this indicates how the list of virtues may differ from time to time and place to place.
- Generosity, between the extremes of extravagance and stinginess. In some cultures, generosity in hospitality is the mark of the highest excellence. Chinua Achebe, in his great novel, *Things Fall Apart*, describes how his protagonist shows himself to be a great man by the magnificence of the feast he presents to his guests as he prepares to return to his own home after a period of exile.
- *Magnificence*, a term or concept which is hard to translate into modern English. Aristotle seemed to intend to refer to people who today we would say are very public-spirited and contribute to worthy causes. The extremes would be vulgarity (giving too ostentatiously) and being uncharitable.
- High-mindedness, which Aristotle explains as appropriate to one's greatness. Today, we might refer to this virtue as a sense of honor. The extremes on either side are pettiness, when we make too much of every slight, and vanity.
- An appropriate desire to achieve or excel. Aristotle leaves this virtue unnamed, allowing it is possible we do not have a word for every virtue. The extremes on either side of this attribute would be overly ambitious and lack of all ambition.
- *Gentleness*, again a concept for which we lack a good match in English. Aristotle seems to have in mind the sort of *gentle* used in referring to an English *gentle*man. The person remains unruffled and does not get too emotional under stress. The extremes would be short-tempered or easily angered, on the one hand, and apathetic, on the other.
- Friendliness, appropriate to the relationship one has with another person. The extremes are obsequiousness, on one side, and grouchiness, on the other. Aristotle devotes a great deal of attention to friendship in the latter part of his book on ethics, stressing that friendship is the conceptual basis for political states.
- Truthfulness, especially in regard to oneself and one's accomplishments. The idea here is clarified by thinking of the mean between being boastful and being self-deprecating. In the discussion of this virtue, however, it is clear that Aristotle also has in mind *truth-telling* in the general sense of the term.
- Wittiness or tact. The person is able to participate in a conversation without resorting to buffoonery (too much effort at being witty or funny) or to boorishness (being a boring companion).

- Ability to feel shame, which remains an unnamed virtue between too much shame and shamelessness, or brazenness. Although a person of good character is unlikely to do something that would bring shame on him or her, the person should still have the capability of feeling shame.
- Sense of justice, honesty, or righteousness in dealings with others.

In addition, a truly virtuous person also possesses the fundamental characteristic of sound practical reason, or what Aristotle called *phronesis*, which through its Latin translation gives us our word, *prudence*. Aristotle goes to great lengths to explain the necessity for and characteristics of this practical wisdom. Having the virtues allows us to see what the goals should be, but it requires practical wisdom to know how to bring about the goals and how to act virtuously in various specific circumstances.

Some of the classical virtues given by Aristotle may seem at odds with what we today might consider to be virtues. For example, we may not be sure of high-mindedness or magnificence or wittiness as virtues of the same level of importance as truthfulness or justice. In the tradition of Western civilization, the most obvious competing traditions concerning the virtues are religious ones, as found in Judaism and Christianity.

The Christian virtues as set forth in "The Sermon on the Mount" include meekness, the hunger for righteousness, mercifulness, purity of heart, and forgiveness.[16] Such virtues seem to conflict with those espoused by Aristotle, who gives no mention to such traits as meekness, mercy, or forgiveness. High-mindedness and a desire to excel also seem to contrast with Christian virtues.

Still, clearly, parts of the message in the *New Testament* are consistent with what we have been calling *virtue ethics*. Specifically, when the "Scribes and Pharisees" try to catch out Jesus in breaking some point of the Jewish Law by healing people (doing work) on the Sabbath or consorting with tax collectors or questionable women, he replies that strict enforcement of those rules is at odds with the greater virtues, requiring one to love others and to show compassion for them. One of the most famous examples of relying on wisdom and compassion in place of strict adherence to rules is the case of the woman accused of adultery brought before Jesus to be stoned (recounted in the *Gospel of John*, Chapter 8). The virtues of compassion and forgiveness trump the strict interpretation of the law calling for the stoning of the woman. As noted earlier, when people rely on the formula *WWJD*, they are applying a form of virtue ethics, asking what the virtuous person would do in their present circumstances.

The culture and education of classical Greece was passed on to Rome. The two most famous theorists of the art of rhetoric in Rome were Cicero, a contemporary of Julius Caesar in the first century B.C.E., and the lawyer turned teacher, Quintilian, in the century after. Cicero, in his work on rhetoric, upheld a highly ethical vision of the best form of rhetoric. For example, in one of his early books on rhetoric, Cicero recognized that rhetoric was sometimes used by unworthy speakers to attain gain, but the answer to that problem was for good men to study rhetoric in order to combat such misuse of communication skills.

Specifically, Cicero maintains, "Therefore, in my opinion at least, men ought none the less to devote themselves to the study of eloquence although some misuse it both in private and in public affairs. And they should study it the more earnestly in order that evil men may not obtain great power to the detriment of good citizens. . . "[17] And, Quintilian, one of the most famous early teachers of the art of rhetoric, maintained rhetoric aimed to produce "The good man, speaking well," with emphasis on the *virtue* of the speaker.

In sum, the major authorities on the teaching of classical rhetoric, the art of persuasion, emphasized the importance of ethics in communication. The issues were not all that different from the kinds of issues students of communication face today. Are the techniques of effective communication essentially tools that can be used for any cause or do students of communication have a special responsibility to consider the ethical choices they reveal in the communications and interactions with others?

If the ethical communicator is the good person communicating well, the aim of the communicator must be to assure the best outcomes for the listeners. In doing so, the communicator will exhibit the virtues of good character.

Contemporary Virtue Ethics

We have considered the classical background of virtue ethics, which had its beginnings with the philosophy of Aristotle and was grounded in the public arts of rhetoric, ethics, and politics. Virtue ethics can be compared with the other major ethical systems of utilitarianism and the universalism of Kant, which are discussed in subsequent chapters.[18] The philosopher Rosalinde Hursthouse explains the distinctions among these three systems in the following way. The universal system of ethics associated with Kant is based on the premise that ethical behavior follows a moral rule or principle that is given to us by one of the following: divine authority or natural law or the dictates of reason. Utilitarianism follows the premise that an act is ethical if it promotes the most happiness for the maximum number of people.

In virtue ethics, however, an action is ethical if it is what a virtuous person would do under the given circumstances with the understanding that a virtuous person is one who exhibits the virtues.[19] A behavior is right or ethical because of the *character* of the person performing it. A person is not virtuous or ethical because they perform certain right actions, but it is the other way around. The action is virtuous because of the nature of the person who performs it.[20]

An impetus for this new interest in virtue ethics is the growing importance of feminist ethics, especially as derived from the work of the philosopher of education and ethics, Nel Noddings in her *Caring: A Feminine Approach to Ethics and Moral Education*,[21] and Martha C. Nussbaum, eminent professor of law and ethics at the University of Chicago. Noddings, however, does try to distinguish her meaning for an ethics of care from some modern interpretations of virtue ethics as character education. The difference she sees is that an ethics of care does not concern itself with enumerating specific virtues to be cultivated but a certain kind of caring relationship.[22] She further clarifies this distinction when she points out that caring is a character trait and basically virtue, but the impetus for caring must lie in the relationship with the other person, the caring itself, not in the cultivation of the virtue itself.[23] The emphasis is on the relationship rather than the abstract virtue. In that sense, the *ethics of care* is close to the system of dialogic ethics discussed in Chapter 5.

We will take up more detailed discussion of feminist ethics at a later point, but there is a connection with virtue ethics. In a system based on caring for individuals, a person acts for the best interests of a particular person rather than following a rules-based approach to ethical decision making. If that person has a special relationship to you, as a mother or husband or lover, your ethical obligations are different toward that person than to someone who does not enjoy the same kind of relationship with you. Christian ethics, as illustrated by Jesus' view that love takes precedence over the law and rules, are similar to this kind of thinking. In other standard systems of ethics, one is supposed to be *person-neutral*, that is, one should not be swayed to act in a partial way to benefit another because of special relationships. Because of the virtues of caring, love, or friendship, it is ethical to be partial to individuals in this way. The virtues of being a parent or a friend or a lover require that we treat the loved one or the friend in a special way.

This is not say that we do not have moral obligations to humanity in general and to others who are personally distant from us. Humanitarian concerns are not ruled out, but one seeks a realistic balance between caring for known individuals and concern for all people. Practical wisdom is called for in figuring out how to achieve this kind of balancing. The difficulty of reconciling partiality for loved ones, on the one hand, with humanitarian concern for all human beings, on the other, has been a major contemporary criticism of virtue ethics.

How shall we identify the virtues that represent the best life for people in today's world? The approach of virtue ethics emphasizes that the virtues are those attributes or functions that allow one to live the fullest, most flourishing life. Regardless of differences represented by different cultural and historical contexts, Martha Nussbaum maintains that there are universal human capabilities desired by all people across all regions and cultures. For example, being able to live out a life of normal length, one worth living would be such a universal.[24] At another point, she argues, "Everyone has some attitude and behavior toward her own death; toward her bodily appetites and their management; toward her property and its use; toward the distribution of social goods; toward telling the truth; toward being kindly or not kindly to others; toward cultivating or not cultivating a sense of play and delight; and so on."[25]

Nussbaum's list implies that there are human goods or concerns that are found just about everywhere regardless of cultural differences. Disease and premature death are seen as universal negatives and therefore virtues that uphold health for all people could be seen as universal. Other virtues seen as universal based on her categories include truthfulness, kindliness toward others, and respect for others' rights to property, food, and well-being. *The Declaration of Human Rights* of 1948 adopted by the United Nations after World War II similarly suggests that there are some universal moral or ethical principles. By implication these kinds of principles should provide the foundation for the virtues of the good life. We will have more to say about universal ethical principles in the following chapter.

For purposes of public policy, Nussbaum implies, there are nearly universal ethical principles derived from the virtues that are related to each of these human needs or desired capabilities. The ethical action is the one that the person applying sound practical reason believes will best allow people to realize these capabilities. One cannot lay down laws and rules in advance that will cover all circumstances, so one must bear in mind the needs for a flourishing life and act in a way intended to realize such a life.

Implications for Communication Ethics

What does virtue ethics suggest for our communication behaviors?

First, it should be clear that Aristotle viewed the art of persuasive communication, rhetoric, as one of the branches of the practical arts that included ethics as well as politics. These three arts required the application of practical wisdom, informed by good character, to make ethical decisions about circumstances encountered in the *real world*. Rhetoric, the art of persuasion, was not divorced from ethics, as some early practitioners had implied. Persuasion does not rely simply on a set of techniques that could be applied in any situation for any end. *Ethos*, the character of the speaker, remained one of the most important means of persuasion available to a communicator. Aristotle thus advocated a philosophical rhetoric that went beyond mere technique. The emphasis on the good character of the speaker continued in the traditions of Roman rhetoric, as evidenced by Cicero and Quintilian. If a speaker or communicator in any circumstance loses his or her credibility as a person of good character, he or she will lose effectiveness in future interactions.

Second, we should be able to derive specific ethical principles for communication from the virtues and from the concept of the good person speaking well. Let's consider for illustration the virtue of *courage.*

Courage in Ethical Communication

Courage can be the relevant virtue when we need to speak up and challenge an authority, especially when such speaking out places us in some jeopardy. For example, in the aftermath of the events of 9/11 an FBI whistle-blower named Coleen Rowley became well known for a scathing letter she had written to higher-ups in the Bureau accusing them of hindering efforts to investigate one of the potential hijackers being held in Minneapolis. She was well aware that her letter could have jeopardized her career and chances for promotion in the FBI. She shared the *Time Magazine* Person of the Year Award with two other whistle-blowers in 2002: Sherron Watkins was the Enron vice president who tried to warn the company president of improper accounting practices; Cynthia Cooper similarly revealed to her company board of directors that WorldCom had covered up $3.8 billion in losses by phony accounting as well.

These women all exhibited the virtue of courage in speaking out, putting themselves at risk. The notoriety of their circumstances allowed these three women to escape some of the harsh consequences that often befall organizational whistle-blowers. Nonetheless, their actions at the time required great courage on their parts.

The French philosopher, Michel Foucault, has analyzed this concept of courageous speech in a series of lectures on *Fearless Speech*, under the classical Greek concept of *parrhesia.*[26] The notion of fearless speech sums up the idea of courageous speech, in that the person speaks frankly, telling the whole truth, which in some way criticizes a person who has some authority or power over the speaker. One who practices such fearless speech assumes this risk because she feels that she has an obligation to speak frankly and truthfully under the circumstances. This is not easy, as most people are understandably reluctant to point out their superiors' shortcomings.

In religious traditions, the characteristic of fearless speech is associated with prophetic communication. In the *Old Testament* tradition, the most striking example may be the case of Nathan, who admonished King David for wrongdoing. David caught sight of a beautiful young woman bathing while he was walking about the roof of his palace. He sent to find out the identity of the woman and to whom she was married. When he discovered that her husband was Uriah, a Hittite soldier in David's army, he arranged to have him placed in a battle and then had the other soldiers suddenly desert him so that he was caught and killed by the enemy. As soon as the period for mourning was over, David immediately sent for the widow and married her. Nathan went to the King to ask for his *advice* on a matter involving two men. One was rich, and one was poor. The rich man naturally had many flocks of sheep and goats, while the poor man had only one lamb, but he loved it very much. When a traveler visited the rich man, instead of taking one of his many lambs to feed the stranger, as required by hospitality, he seized the poor man's lamb and slaughtered it. David was angered and charged that the rich man should be punished and be made to compensate the poor man. At this point, Nathan rises and points at the King, saying, "Thou art the man!"

The fear of criticizing authority is rationalized by people who say that they must maintain their access and usefulness in order to have any effect at all. They say, in other words, that is "how the game is played." Irving Janis has written extensively about what he calls *Groupthink,* which develops out of the desire to go along with the decisions of popular leaders or groups. The rationalization is that if people become known as *boat-rockers*, they will lose any effectiveness they might have had with the leader or with the group. In the case of the famous Watergate scandal that brought down former President Nixon, John Dean exhibited the virtue of courage and broke with groupthink in coming forward to challenge the former president and his close advisers concerning the danger of covering up the White House' involvement in the Watergate break-in. Dean was White House Counsel to the president at the time and came forward to Nixon to warn him of what he called a "cancer growing on the Presidency." He was referring to the efforts by other White House aides to cover up their involvement in the break-in at the center of the Watergate scandal.

The person who displays this courage in communicating may not always succeed, as was the case with the Morton Thiokol engineer, Roger Boisjoly, who tried to convince NASA not to launch the Challenger Space Shuttle in 1986. He was not successful, with the tragic results of the explosion after launch the next day, but he did speak up and did the ethical thing in so doing. The pivotal point occurs for the speaker when something is at stake, when the speaker knowingly takes a risk but feels obligated to do so.

Courage, however, as a virtue of communication, must be balanced with other communication virtues as well. The other virtues of self-control, magnanimity, or friendship may require that one temper frankness in order to enact these virtues as well. And, other classical authors, such as Plato and Isocrates, claim too much *parrhesia*, unbridled free speech, by demagogues and others can lead to more harm than good for the state or society. Aristotle reminds us that sound, practical wisdom and sound character must always be the guide in these situations. So, an ethic of caring for persons close to one, such as family and friends, must temper one's communication.

We can further explore the implications of virtue ethics for communication by considering a case study, taken from the contemporary world of business.

CASE STUDY: COMPARING APPLES TO HAMMERS

Many organizations, profit and non-profit, have had to struggle with the issue of equal benefits for all their employees. In our university, members of the faculty or staff can send their dependent children through the university at no cost, that is, tuition is waived for these students. Because we are a private university, and therefore relatively costly, this benefit can be equivalent to a very large sum of money, especially if the faculty or staff member sends more than one child through the school tuition-free. On the other hand, those faculty members and staff members who have no children, through their own choice or otherwise, may complain that they are not able to take advantage of this rather valuable benefit nor do they receive anything comparable in value. Obviously, these people can feel that they system treats them unfairly in comparison to their counterparts who put their children through the university.

This sort of situation is recounted in a case study that appeared in the *Harvard Business Review* of March 2001 (pp. 33–42; used by permission of Harvard Business School Publishing). The following case study is excerpted from that case.

The case uses fictitious names for the company and the people involved, but it is based on a real-life scenario. The company is called *ClarityBase* and is described as a software support company located in Virginia in the vicinity of Washington, D.C. The company provides database applications to help other companies run their operations. There are eight account managers, whose job is to provide support for the company's major clients, who have purchased the software. These managers must spend a great deal of time in communication with the clients to help them maintain and troubleshoot all the software.

One account manager, named Megan, had a shortened workweek, because when hired she negotiated a four-day week (in return for a 20% less than normal salary) to take care of two young children. As a result of this arrangement, the supervisor tended to give Megan less-demanding clients, meaning that the other managers had more than their share of demanding clients. Jessica Gonon, the supervisor for the eight account managers, including Megan, was fairly new in her position, appointed after Megan was hired. She then faced two other members of the eight-person team who also wanted reduced hours for their personal needs.

First, Jana Rowe wanted a four-day workweek and was willing to take the corresponding 20% cut in pay. In addition, Davis Bennet, another account manager, requested the same workload so that he could train for the Ironman Triathlon World Championships, the premier competition in that event held annually in Hawaii. He hoped to make the U.S. Olympic team in 2004.

When Jana first met with Jessica, she declined to elaborate on what her *personal reasons* were. When Jessica did not immediately respond, since she was pondering whether she ought to ask for more specifics about the *personal reasons,* Jana added, "All I'm asking for is the same deal that Megan has. Please don't tell me that I need to have a baby to have this time off."

Jana was pointing to a potential bone of contention in ClairyBase's family friendly policies. The company provided family medical insurance, adoption assistance, and paid maternity and paternity leaves. Those employees who were not parents occasionally grumbled about what some construed as *special treatment,* and felt discriminated against in the use of flex-time, special leaves, and so on, because they were expected to work at odd hours, on weekends, and on holidays, and to take on the more demanding or needy clients. Giving more of the eight team members flex-time would add to the burden and demands on those who did not have shortened weeks.

Jessica took Jana to lunch to get a better handle on why she needed the reduced work week. "I want to understand your situation better," Jessica began, "Yesterday you cited 'personal reasons.' The last thing I want to do is pry into your personal life, but is there anything else you would feel comfortable in telling me?"

"I don't mean to be disrespectful," Jana responded, "Honestly, I don't. Nor do I mean to be mysterious. But I really don't think I should have to explain why I want the time off. Suffice it to say that it's very, very important to me."

"I see," replied Jessica. "I'm sorry to have asked. I just wanted to understand your situation better."

After a pause, Jana continued, "The thing that gets me is that somehow all the family stuff is deemed more important—the soccer games, the school plays, the graduations. Well, I have important things going on in my life, too. They just don't involve children."

Breakfast the next morning with Davis went more smoothly, partly because he did not feel discriminated against because of not being a parent. Jessica then asked, "I guess what I need to know from you is how much flexibility you might have—I'm not sure how much time you'll need to train."

"It varies. Everyone seems to have a different training regimen," Davis responded. "But here's what I think will work best for me: for the summer, I'd like to leave work at 3 p.m. on Tuesdays and Thursdays. Then, during the Fall, I'd want to leave early maybe four days a week. But on the days I left early, I could definitely come in at 6 a.m. to make up some of that time, or I could stay late on the other days."

Jessica then asked, "But with this new schedule, do you think you could keep up with the needs of your clients?"

"I've thought about that a lot and, to be honest with you, I don't know," Davis replied.

When Jessica consulted her old mentor, he pointed out that the firm had no solid policies in place regarding flex-time. When Jessica complained that she had trouble deciding among the different requests, because it was like comparing apples to hammers and vases, the mentor responded, "And let me be frank with you. The reason you were promoted to vice president is precisely because of your ability to compare apples with hammers and vases. You run a large department and, yes, it's not always easy to meet the needs of your staff while also making your quarterly numbers. So, no, you can't go out and hire two more account managers to cover for the people who want flex-time. There is no simple, tidy solution here."

What communication strategies represent the most ethical way for Jessica to deal with this problem?

QUESTIONS FOR ANALYSIS OF THE CASE

1. Identify the issues presented in this case in terms of the competing virtues that are involved. Does each person described communicate in an ethical fashion? For example, has Jana communicated all that is ethically required? Do you feel that she needs to provide more information about her *personal reasons?* Or, would it be unethical for Jessica to try to get more information from her in order to compare her situation to that of a young parent with children?

2. Discuss the communication practices of the firm itself: have they communicated ethically in regard to their policies concerning flex-time and family friendly benefits?

3. Consider the mentor, and presumably more senior executive in the case, who tells Jessica that she is in a position where she has to rely on her good judgment, in the absence of specific rules of company guidelines: what virtue or virtues does he display (or not display)?

4. Discuss what Jessica's next steps ought to be. How should she communicate with Megan, Jana, and Davis about their respective situations? What are the virtues that she must balance in this case? How can character help her in coming to a decision in this matter?

Chapter Summary

According to the principles of virtue ethics, one acts virtuously as part of living the best, most flourishing life. A person with the developed character of such a person will be able to apply practical wisdom in specific cases to make the ethical decision and act in the most ethical way. One cannot lay down guidelines or rules to be applied in each case, because real life is too complicated for rules to cover every conceivable eventuality. One must rely on the character and wisdom of the virtuous person.

Virtue ethics has a long and traditional connection with the theories about communication, especially persuasive communication. Aristotle linked the fields of ethics, persuasive communication or rhetoric, and politics in his practical arts. A true philosophical rhetoric, he taught, was ethical and relied on the persuasion derived from the character of the speaker. Aristotle taught that the virtues represented types of human excellence, and that excellence required the wisdom to avoid extremes in their application (e.g., too much courage became sheer recklessness).

Contemporary virtue ethics has been found appealing because the rule-based systems, usually represented by utilitarianism and Kantianism, seem inadequate to some ethicists on at least two counts. First, they do not seem to allow for our humane tendencies to respond to our actual relationships with people in authentic relationships. And, secondly, these other systems can seem too inflexible in dealing with realistically complex situations. Some interpretations of religious ethics based on love as well as some of the feminist theories of ethics seem close to the approach of virtue ethics.

For communication behaviors, virtue ethics emphasizes ethical rhetorical appeals and arguments, harking back to the notion of the good person speaking well, the ethic of Roman rhetoric. Virtue ethics seems to emphasize the need to act from character by showing courage in speaking out, while tempering such frankness (*parrhesia*) with virtues based on humane feelings, self-control, and magnanimity.

QUESTIONS AND TOPICS FOR DISCUSSION

1. Chapter 1 began with some conversations with students concerned that they felt they had to mislead potential employers or graduate schools about their real intentions in order to "keep their options open." Analyze their dilemmas from the perspective of virtue ethics. Is there a way to determine what the *virtuous person* would do in these cases?

2. Virtue ethics implies a flexible approach to ethical decision making rather than relying on rules or guidelines. Does this approach allow one to rationalize some decisions without holding to a strict set of principles? Does virtue ethics allow for a relativistic approach to ethical decisions?

3. How does one become a virtuous person and come to have the character and practical wisdom to know what is ethically required in our communication with others?

4. Does love for another person, such as a parent for a child, take precedence over strict ethical guidelines? Is it ethical to lie in order to protect a loved one from shame or punishment?

5. Review the list of virtues taken from Aristotle's work on ethics. Which ones seem to be especially applicable to our communication with each other?

NOTES

1. Randy Cohen, The Ethicist, *The New York Times Magazine,* at ethicist@nytimes.com. *New York Times,* 2002.

2. Jean M. Yarborough, *American Virtues: Thomas Jefferson on the Character of a Free People* (Lawrence, KS: University of Kansas Press, 2000).

3. Anita L. Allen, *The New Ethics* (New York: Miramax Books, 2004), pp. 11–12.

4. Plato, "Gorgias," in *The Collected Dialogues of Plato,* ed. Edith Hamilton and Hunington Cairs (Princeton, NJ: Princeton University Press, 1961), pp. 229–307.

5. J. M. Burns, *Leadership* (New York: Harper and Row, 1978).

6. Amelie Oskenberg Rorty, ed., *Essays on Aristotle's Ethics* (Berkeley: University of California Press, 1980), p. 2.

7. George A. Kennedy, ed. and Trans., *Aristotle on Rhetoric: A Theory of Civic Discourse* (New York: Oxford University Press, 1991), p. 36.

8. Kennedy, *Aristotle on Rhetoric,* p. 38.

9. Kennedy, *Aristotle on Rhetoric,* p. 39.

10. Aristotle, *Nicomachean Ethic's,* trans. Martin Ostwald (Indianapolis: Bobbs-Merrill, 1962), pp. 162–163.

11. Kennedy, *Aristotle on Rhetoric,* p. 39.

12. The *books* attributed to Aristotle today are not books in the modern sense. In the first place, they are not actual writings of Aristotle himself but the compilation of lecture notes, often as taken down by students at his school, the Lyceum. For that reason, the books do not all flow in a sequence of thought one might expect; there appear to be interpolations or places where editors have inserted material from different works or sets of lectures. Two works on ethics are attributed to Aristotle, the *Eudemian Ethics* and the more famous and influential *Nicomachean Ethics,* which is the basis for the discussion that follows.

13. Aristotle, *Nicomachean Ethics,* p. 3.

14. Aristotle, *Nicomachean Ethics,* p. 6.

15. Aristotle, *Nicomachean Ethics,* p. 39.

16. See Matthew 5:3–16, NRSV.

17. Cicero, *De inventione,* trans. H. M. Hubbell (Cambridge: Harvard University Press, 1949), pp. 11–13.

18. Michael Slote, "Virtue Ethics," in *The Blackwell Guide to Ethical Theory,* ed. Hugh LaFollette (Malden, MA: Blackwell Publishers, 2000), p. 325.

19. Rosalinde Hursthouse, "Virtue Theory and Abortion," *Philosophy & Public Affairs* (1991), 20:1, 224–225.

20. See Justin Oakley and Dean Cocking, *Virtue Ethics and Professional Roles* (Cambridge: Cambridge University Press, 2000), pp. 9–20.

21. Nel Noddings, *Caring: A Feminine Approach to Ethics and Moral Education* (Berkeley: University of California Press, 1984). See also, Nel Noddings, *Educating Moral People: A Caring Alternative to Character Education* (New York: Teacher College Press, 2002).

22. Noddings *Educating Moral People,* p. 2.

23. Noddings *Educating Moral People,* p. 14.

24. Martha C. Nussbaum, *Sex and Social Justice* (New York: Oxford University Press, 1999), p. 41.

25. Martha C. Nussbaum, "Non-relative Virtues: An Aristotelian Approach," in *Ethics: The Big Questions,* ed. James P. Sterba (Malden, MA: Blackwell Publishers, 1998), p. 262.

26. Michel Foucault, *Fearless Speech,* ed. Joseph Pearson (Los Angeles: Semiotext(e), 2001).

CHAPTER

3 Duties

Is Lying Always Wrong?

One of the enduring debates about ethics concerns whether there is one set of rules or principles, good for all situations and times, or whether, on the other hand, the rules vary from time and place, and from culture to culture. Given our modern sense of tolerance and acceptance of diversity, we may be comfortable with the idea that what is right or wrong can vary according to circumstances. For example, we accept that lying is wrong, but hold out the possibility that there are times or situations in which lying may be all right or even the best course of action. We all probably tell *white* lies from time to time, when giving someone a compliment or making excuses for why we can't attend a friend's dinner party. We feel it is almost obligatory to lie to enemies, in order to prevent their gaining an advantage over us. We expect and accept some shading of the truth in politics or the law courts. At times, we want our physicians to err on the side of optimism when giving us a prognosis of our own or a loved-one's illness. Occasionally, people will *puff up* their qualifications on a resume they send out to prospective employers, perhaps calling their stint as a camp counselor in high school *Youth Athletic Director.*

On the other hand, we seem to demand strict accountability for prominent political and business leaders. The major business scandals a few years
ago have highlighted public concern about shading the truth on income and
accounting reporting of corporations. Back in 2001, the University of Notre
Dame hired a football coach who had to resign after only five days on the job
when it came to light that he had lied on his resume regarding his academic
and athletic background. Years earlier, the man had claimed in an application
for a position at Syracuse University that he had a master's degree in Education and had played college varsity football for three years.[1] Former President
Clinton was nearly removed from office, not because he had had an affair
with an intern, but because he had lied to cover it up. President Nixon was
forced to resign the presidency largely because he had tried to cover up his
Administration's involvement in an illegal break-in at the Democratic Party's
headquarters in the Watergate complex.

The theme of this chapter is *Duty*, just as the theme of the first chapter
was *Character*. Ethical duties or obligations comprise a set of rules that are
universal for all people and all times. Many people feel that they have a
strong sense of right and wrong, and an ability to see what their duty is in
regard to that sense. Another way of saying this is to say that we have an
obligation; in fact we might say a moral obligation, to do the right thing
regardless of the consequences. The question becomes how can we determine what our duty is, especially in complicated situations.

One of the most influential systems of ethics developed, that of the
eighteenth-century philosopher Immanuel Kant, rejects tolerance of relativistic ethics. His system allows no room for white lies or *beneficial lies,* as
when the doctor tells you there is nothing to worry about when she just
wants to make you more confident facing a threatening illness.

Kant did not even permit lies to achieve some greater good. The most
famous case deals with the situation in which a would-be murderer bursts in
on you demanding to know where his intended victim is. Should you lie to
the criminal to protect the victim, possibly a good friend or family member?
While we feel instinctively that a lie is justified in this extreme case, Kant
does not.[2] To understand this result, surprising perhaps to most of us, we
need to explore how Kant developed his ideas about ethics.

Kant was one of the most important figures in the period of history
known as the Enlightenment (see Box). The overriding goal of this movement was to be objective and scientific in thinking about all aspects of both
the physical and the human world. *Reason* was the supreme judge for
knowledge and explaining the physical world. The Enlightenment thinkers
maintained that people could reason out for themselves how the world
really worked, without having to rely on faith or revelation that could not be
explained rationally or scientifically.

Immanuel Kant taught that it should be possible to rely solely on the
power of human reason to figure out the nature of human life and knowledge.

Kant and the Enlightenment

Kant was a major figure in the intellectual movement historians now refer to as the *Enlightenment*. This period ran through most of the 1700s, centered primarily in Western Europe. The movement developed into what we think of as the *modern* way of doing things and of thinking. In Britain, Enlightenment thinkers included John Locke, who influenced modern democratic institutions; Jeremy Betham, responsible for the idea of utilitarianism; and the founder of modern economics, Adam Smith. These British thinkers applied the methods of the *scientific revolution* to political philosophy. The scientific understanding of the physical world seemed so successful to people like Locke, Bentham, Adams, and other philosophers, such as Thomas Hobbes, that they believed it should be possible to develop scientific theories of human behavior, just as the natural scientists had unlocked the mysteries of physics and chemistry.

In France, a group of highly influential thinkers, called the *Philosophes* (which means intellectuals rather than philosophers) popularized this idea. The leaders of this group were people like Jacque Rousseau and Voltaire, who believed that it was possible to understand the realities of human life and society without resort to religious or mystical principles, just as the scientists had dispensed with spirits in explaining how gravity or combustion works. As you may know from your history, the American leaders such as Franklin, Jefferson, and Adams were very much influenced by Locke and the French intellectuals, especially Montesquieu, the writer associated with the political concept of the separation of powers manifested in the U.S. Constitution.

The natural scientists had demonstrated that the laws of physics and chemistry were universal and that the laws of science were the same everywhere. In the same way, Kant reasoned, the principles underlying human thought and behavior should be universal as well. Although Kant himself was religious and a firm believer in Christianity, he believed that people should be guided by reason rather than religion when it came to ethical or moral conduct, so that individuals were responsible for their thinking and actions.

Ethical decisions, therefore, should be the result of reasoning rather than the result of dictates or commandments given by religion. If we behave morally so as to avoid eternal punishment or to achieve salvation, we are not being moral for its own sake, he believed. Such reasoning set him apart from those of many other thinkers and philosophies of morality and ethics, many of whom maintained that religion must be the basis for morality and ethics (as we explore in the next section of this chapter). Since the laws of reason or logic are the same for all people and cultures, the ethical duties derived from reason should be the same every where.

In this chapter, we will first discuss Kant's highly influential theory of ethics, duty derived from reason. Then we will look at the other two basic methods advanced to determining universal moral duty: the theory of *divine command* and the idea of ethics based on *human nature* or *natural law.* We will then consider some ways of thinking about ethics that would run counter to such universal ethics to sharpen our understanding of the ethics of *duty.*

The Basis for Kant's Universalism: The Categorical Imperative

The most famous part of Kant's ethical theory revolves around what he called the *categorical imperative.* Let us first understand the meaning of this term. Most of our daily decisions are based on what he called *hypothetical* imperatives. These decisions concern actions aimed at achieving some particular end. If we want to be in good physical shape, we ought to exercise regularly, for example. The decision depends on the conditions laid down as the goal or objective of the activity (being in good shape). A hypothetical imperative applies only under the specified conditions. It doesn't mean that we have an obligation to exercise under all conditions, but only when we are trying to achieve some particular goal. On the other hand, a *categorical imperative* applies in every situation, regardless of the circumstances or the consequences. There are no exceptions. Because there are no exceptions, the principle means that we have a *duty* to act the same way every time we are faced with an ethical decision. This emphasis on an unchanging duty is the basis for calling Kant's ethical system a *deontological* system, from the classical Greek word for duty, *deon.*

Let us emphasize that Kant is not concerned about the outcomes or the consequences of doing one's duty in behaving ethically. "Thus the moral worth of an action does not lie in the effect expected from it and so too does not lie in any principle of action that needs to borrow its motive from this expected effect," he argues.[3] The only thing that counts is doing one's duty regardless of what happens as a result.

Kant believed that this categorical imperative provided a rational basis for making ethical decisions without relying on any other commandment or directive. It meant that human beings could determine the ethical thing to do in every situation based on their reason alone. The most basic formulation of the categorical imperative by Kant is as follows: "Act only according to that maxim by which you can at the same time will that it should become a universal law."[4] If we cannot reasonably intend that our action should be the basis (a *maxim* is like a rule) for action by *everyone every* time, then it is not an ethical action. If we lie in order to achieve some end, then we must want it to be a rule that everyone else lies to us and others when it suits their purposes as well. The result would be that no one could ever trust anyone else or believe anything another person says. If I misrepresent my credentials on my resume in order to get a job, then I must want all other people, including those competing with me for the job, to misrepresent themselves on their job applications as well. So, later on when I am interviewing someone to hire, I must assume that they also would misrepresent their experience or education. Kant concludes that human interaction and communication would become impossible if everyone made it a universal rule that one lies in order to get ahead. Since no one (who is rational) would want human communication to be impossible, no one should want to lie and thereby undermine the basis for such communication. Kant hence believed that someone who thinks through the ultimate implications of lying will discover that they have a duty to tell the truth in every circumstance, regardless of the consequences.

If we act on the maxim, or rule, that we can promise what we want in order to protect ourselves or to achieve ends that are very important to us, we are intending that *everyone* act that same way in the same conditions. In the opening chapter, we discussed some typical cases in which people felt they had some justification for promising something or committing to do something, when in fact they reserved the right (without telling the other party) not to follow through on their promise or commitment. Obviously Kant would disapprove of playing the game this way. Kant would have us ask how these individuals would feel if someone made promises or commitments to them that the other party did not intend to keep. In other words, what if it were a general rule that people made promises and commitments just for getting what they wanted without intending to meet their obligations. There would be no point for making promises or commitments— everyone would expect them to be worthless.

A second way that Kant formulated his categorical imperative stressed the humanity of each person. "Act in such a way that you always treat humanity, whether in your own person or in the person of any other, never simply as a means, but always at the same time as an end."[5] This formulation of the imperative emphasizes that you should not treat people as means to an end, because, presumably, you would not want to be treated that way yourself. Whenever you manipulate others for your own ends, you are using them as a means to get your way, not treating them as uniquely valuable individuals. If you mislead or deceive another person, you are diminishing his or her humanity—the other person becomes more of an object than a person. This second form of the imperative suggests why some people have said that Kant's categorical imperative is similar to the *golden rule*, "do unto others as you have them do unto you." Or, as it is sometimes stated, "do not do to others what you would not have them do to you." There is a further twist to Kant's point, however. Take the case of the *white lie*, when you tell someone what they want to hear (or so you think). He says you should treat yourself as an end as well, which means that if you thought out the situation clearly you would not want someone to lie to you just to give you a false sense of security or self-worth. If you are to be a fully functioning, autonomous individual, you want to hear the actual truth.

Other Universal Ethics of Communication

Kant's deontological system of ethics is thus a universal system of ethics. The duties are the same for everyone everywhere, in any culture, time, or place. When most people think of ethics and integrity they think they are dealing with a universal set of rules or commands. The whole point of integrity is that you are the same today as you were yesterday and as you will be tomorrow. People can depend on your word in any situation. Of course, most people given more time for reflection, even most philosophers, are not comfortable with the ramifications of such an inflexible stance (deceiving the murderer seeking victims being perhaps the most obvious case of wanting some wiggle-room). There are other bases for systems of ethics that are both deontological (based on unchanging duties) and universal (the same for all people in all places). First, there are ethical systems built on religious foundations, holding that our ethical duties are laid down by divine authority. Second, some people base ethics on the foundation of a universal human nature or what some call natural law.

Divine Command

While driving to lunch one afternoon, one of us saw a bumper sticker on a car ahead, reading: "God is THE true judge. Everything else is Reality TV." This message illustrates a basic theme in *divine command* theory, which holds that the ultimate rules of morality and ethics come from God. The major religions of the world provide teachings on moral conduct: the *Bible*; the *Torah* (the *Written Torah* or the *Tanakh*); the *Koran*; the Vedic (Hindu) scriptures, such as the *Baghavad Gita* (part of the *Mahabharata*); the *Analects of Confucius*; the *Dao De-jing*; the discourses of the Buddha; and so on. Sections of all these scriptures include rules or commandments concerning right conduct. Observe that one can be religious but not necessarily be a believer in divine command theory, Kant being a case in point. Recall that he believed that ethical conduct must arise from one's own reasoning and will to count as truly ethical. On the other hand, many religious people do follow some form of this theory as the foundation for their ethics: we have heard deeply religious students in our class in communication ethics claim, "The *Bible* is really the only book on ethics I need." Also, we cannot fail to notice that when panels on ethics are formed to advise agencies or even political figures (think of former President Clinton's calling on pastors to serve as advisers to him on his own ethics), they almost always include several members of the clergy.

For many, reliance on religious direction in ethics provides an objective and universal basis for making ethical decisions. Religion provides a moral clarity avoiding the ambiguities of relativism and uncertainties of modern living. The deontological component of divine command theory is, of course, that it is our *duty* to obey the rules of God. One's religious convictions thus provide the motivation to behave in an ethical fashion. We see at least two ways that divine command can operate to support an ethical system. First, such religious belief can *define* what ethical or right conduct is and is not. Secondly, as already noted, religious belief can *motivate* one to behave ethically and to avoid behaving unethically. In other words, the commands of the religion cause us to do our duty as well as defining what those duties are.

The first basis of support, then, is defining our ethical duties. The *Ten Commandments*, for example, set out a short list of things to do and things not to do. The *Koran* and ethical teachings of Islam divide right and wrong behavior into five categories instead of only two: Required actions, Recommended ones, Neutral actions that are neither right nor wrong, Acts one ought not to do, and Forbidden acts. An act is said to be ethical or not because God has commanded it to be so. Some critics of the divine command theory at this point raise a familiar objection based on the age-old dilemma posed by Socrates in the Platonic dialogue, *The Euthryphro*: Is something pious or right because God has said that it is, or has God said it is pious and right because it is? If the answer is that the first statement is correct, then morality is based on arbitrary rules: presumably, God could have commanded something we think of as evil to be good. If we respond that God would not do such a thing—that he would not designate something to be good which we know to be wrong, such as murder—then we acknowledge there is some standard external to God for knowing what is right or wrong.

Followers of the divine command point of view would respond that the purpose of religious directives is to clarify and provide guidance on these matters. They would argue that because God is all-knowing and thus infallible, He provides the ideal guidance on ethical issues. The dilemma in the paragraph above oversimplifies the nature of divine command, they would say, by assuming that God is not essentially good in the first place.

Many adherents of the divine command theory are more comfortable with the motivating force of the system than with the defining aspect. A person wants to do the ethical thing as a fundamental part of being a good Christian or Jew or Muslim (in this case, divine command theory may appear closer to virtue ethics than to deontological ethics). One can point to conflicts among the different rules of conduct associated with different religions. Rules setting forth what is ethical or moral to eat or not to eat, for example, vary greatly among the major religions. Of course, for an adherent of a particular faith, it is assumed that the rules of his or her religion are in fact universal.

What does divine command theory suggest regarding ethical communication? Nearly all systems of belief emphasize the duty of truth-telling and forbid most forms of lying. Interestingly, the *Ten Commandments* do not contain a straightforward condemnation of lying in general, only the command that one should not bear *false witness* (although clearly other parts of the *Bible* strongly condemn deceit and lying). In addition, there are often injunctions concerning the use of references to the Deity and religious concepts. For example, a Muslim is required to state aloud the Confession of Faith (the *Shahada*) in order to be accepted as a true believer. Most major religions have restrictions on blasphemy, denying God or "taking the name of the Lord in vain." Religious systems also usually prize courage in speaking, as noted in the last chapter in regard to fearless speech. Many of the major religions are *proselytizing* religions, which means they actively seek to win converts to their belief, through the spoken word.

These examples point up a very important fact about most religious systems concerning communication and ethics: the *spoken word* is judged to be a critical form of human behavior. Speech defines who we are and what we are, especially our identities as moral creatures. In most religions, acts are performed by speaking. Speech is seen as potentially powerful in and of itself.

Human Nature

After reason (the Kantian method) and divine command, a third way to derive universal rules of ethics is to base such rules on the fundamental nature of human beings and the world. This method can also be conceptualized as based on *natural law*. The term *natural law*, has different definitions: it can mean a type of moral or ethical theory, as we mean to use it here, or it can mean a certain kind of theory about law. *The Internet Encyclopedia of Philosophy* explains the first meaning of the term this way: "According to natural law ethical theory, the moral standards that govern human behavior are, in some sense, objectively derived from the nature of human beings."[6] Such systems are also referred to as *naturalistic ethics*, or *naturalism*.

There is not necessarily a divorce between divine command theory and ethics based on human nature. Major theologians, such as St. Thomas Aquinas, base their theories about ethics partly on their understanding of human nature. Aquinas taught that natural law is a subset or an aspect of the eternal, divine law and is the basis for people's moral sense. Often, religious leaders will say that some act is immoral or unethical because it is *unnatural*. For example, they may say that cloning of human beings is unethical because it is unnatural, in that it intends to produce a human offspring by some way other than the *natural* way.

But, our ideas about human nature can also come from the nonreligious contemplation of scientific theories about biological human nature and evolution. Sociobiologists, like Edward O. Wilson, or, to use a more current term, *evolutionary psychologists* try to deduce ethical principles from the biological nature of people as developed during human evolution. They would claim that the natural process of evolution has led to social creatures, especially those like human beings, who possess some sort of moral sense. For example, they note that such beings display altruistic behavior, such as risking oneself in order to save others, as a result of natural selection because species that do so are more likely to perpetuate themselves.

Whether our principles are derived from theological natural law or from the human nature as described by evolutionary psychology, the question remains just what is human nature and just what is *natural*. What is natural and what is unnatural may not always be objectively clear. If it is my nature to be *near-sighted*, or myopic, is it unnatural and therefore wrong for me to take advantage of glasses? If someone has a pace-maker or similar device implanted in their body to regulate their heart or other organs, is that unnatural interference in the course of events, and therefore wrong? At what point does interference with nature cross the line to become immorally unnatural?

So, what do theories from natural law or human nature tell us about what our duties are when communicating ethically? The first sort of natural law philosophers, such as Aquinas, maintain the natural purpose of human communication is to convey knowledge from one person to another. It is human nature to assume that speech and language are being used for this natural purpose. Messages that intentionally convey false information are therefore against nature, in that they subvert the natural function of human language and speech. Lying, for instance, misrepresents what is actually in the mind of the person sending the false message. Recall that lying requires intentionally communicating what the speaker believes is not true. We say, as communication theorists, that there are many functions of language and speech beyond conveying information from one person to another. In fact, strictly information sharing may not be the most important function of speech. The natural functions of spoken greetings are to signal awareness of the other person and readiness to interact. So, when we say "Fine," when someone greets us by asking how we are, we are not naturally expected to go into clinical detail, even if the truth be that we are not *fine* in every sense.

The evolutionary approach to human nature is not quite so clear-cut on the rightness or wrongness of truth-telling. A professor at the University of New Hampshire, David Livingtone Smith, has pointed out that deceit can give certain creatures an edge in the struggle for survival. Successful liars may have an advantage. Of course, one can dissent from the direction this line of reasoning may be taking us by pointing out that such scientific theories describe what has happened or does happen but tells us nothing about whether the facts are to be judged as right or wrong. For example, killing the offspring of rivals, as female pack leaders among African wild dogs are said to do, also provides one with an evolutionary advantage, but it hardly would be accepted as right for us to do so to the children of other human beings. Lying may give some people an advantage in the way Professor Smith describes, but that does not necessarily tell us that lying is therefore ethical or unethical. Also, it is possible that liars may not be picked as suitable marriage partners, since they may be seen as unreliable providers.[7] In short, we sometimes are left with speculation about what is natural and hence ethical and what is not.

But, there appears to be other research looking at ethics in terms of natural selection that may be enlightening in a different way. A long-range project at Harvard University, in which over 60,000 people have taken a short, online survey concerning responses to ethical dilemmas, has suggested that people make fairly quick and consistent ethical judgments.[8] The researchers reason from this that people have some kind of built-in moral intuition which leads them to react emotionally rather than intellectually to moral dilemmas. Instead of thinking through ethical dilemmas, and applying arguments based on a rational system, people seem guided by some sort of emotional response to the issues. The researchers suggest responses that would have helped people survive in prehistoric times have been integrated into our makeup, our human nature. Still, such results may help explain *why* we behave the way we do, but not necessarily prove that is how we *ought* to behave. The fact that most people do respond this way does not demonstrate it is the *best* way to deal with ethical matters.

In short, theories about ethics based on human nature display the weakness of the arbitrariness of deciding what is *human nature* or what is *natural*, and what isn't. The assumption behind such theories often is that the way we do things, for example in the dominant North American culture, defines what *human nature* is. We accept some deviations from nature, such as the use of antibiotics or eye glasses, but not others, also seemingly on a somewhat arbitrary basis.

The scientific hypotheses derived from evolutionary psychology and related fields may tell us what people do or why they have done certain things, but they do not really tell us whether those actions are morally right or wrong. There is an evolutionary advantage for a species in which members display altruistic behavior, let us grant, but whether altruism is a good or bad thing is up to us to decide. Eating is also necessary for survival, but we don't think of the decision to eat food as a moral decision (apart from the separate issue about *what* we choose eat—meat-eating as seen by vegetarians and so on).

So far, we have considered three grounds for justifying universal rules of ethics; those based on reason and the categorical imperative, divine command theories, and theories derived from human nature and natural law. It has been difficult to demonstrate definitively that any of these grounds ultimately succeed in providing a solid foundation for universal rules for all people in all circumstances. So the obvious next question is what ethics would look like if there were no universal standards. Can ethical systems be different for different people in differing situations and cultures? In the next section we turn to ethical theories at odds with the attempt to build a universal set of ethical rules in the hope of further clarifying the deontological approach.

Alternatives to Universal Rules Systems

Let us return to the question we began this chapter with: Is lying always wrong? Most people can think of many situations in which they feel that is all right to lie and even situations in which it may be the right thing to do. While we generally agree that we have a duty to tell others the full truth, there are situations in which we feel it is OK to remain silent. Deception is often considered to be acceptable when dealing with enemies or a dangerous criminal or in playing a game. The game of poker, for example, would not be fun if all the players were strict Kantians. The police are praised for setting up successful *sting* operations to catch crooks. Good manners often require a certain amount of shading the truth. We tell the earnest host, "Everything was delicious, but we couldn't possibly eat another bite," when we actually find the main entrée nearly inedible. These examples also reveal why so many people find Kant's unbending stance on lying to be impractical as well as extreme.

American business people and government officials have found that there are cultures in which saying *no* directly to another person is considered unethical. To avoid the direct denial, which Americans may think is the truthful response, various circumlocutions may be used. They are told "matters are complex at the moment," or "this sounds reasonable but we must check with our superiors first," and the like. The American stews about how difficult it is to get a *straight answer* from these people, while the Japanese or other Asian business person frets about how aggressive or rude the American is (Chapter 8 of this text further discusses the ethics of intercultural communication).

In this section, we will briefly review systems of ethics at odds with the premise of universal, absolute standards for ethical decision making. First, we will consider *situational ethics*, which holds that no one can predict the factors in every situation that arises and so one must do what seems the right thing at the time. Second, we will look at moral relativism or cultural relativism, which is based on the idea of accepting culturally different standards for that which is considered right or wrong.

Remember that deontological systems of ethics rely on two conditions: (1) they are based on rules; and (2) they are universal. Situational ethics provides guidance that could be universal but lacks hard-and-fast rules. Ethical relativism or cultural relativism may have rules, but the rules are not universal but differ from one group to another.

Situational Ethics

The cases of lying to criminals or to avoid insulting someone in the examples above are cases of applying different ethical standards depending on the situation. Does this make all these cases instances for applying situational ethics? Perhaps or perhaps not—it depends on the motive or intention. One may deceive or lie to others in these examples because one believes in utilitarian ethics, looking to achieve the greatest good for the greatest number of people. This system is discussed in the next chapter. The intention under this system is to achieve certain consequences. Situational ethics is less concerned with calculating outcomes while more concerned with achieving something for the individuals involved in an encounter, not necessarily for the abstract greatest number.

This may seem confusing at first, but may be clearer if we turn to one of the foremost proponents of situational ethics in the last century. Dr. Joseph Fletcher was a professor of theology and Christian ethics at the Episcopal Theological School in Cambridge. Later, he became a professor of medical ethics at the University of Virginia Hospital in the United States. Fletcher described his beliefs in a book, *Situation Ethics*, published in 1966.[9] At first, you may be surprised to find a professor of theology arguing for situational ethics, seemingly against the theory of divine command described earlier in the chapter.

He maintains that the real-life situations that confront people are too varied and complex for any one set of universal rules, even religious rules, to apply in every case. Rather, he argues, one must adhere to the single principle of love, in the sense of *agape*, or love that is spiritual and selfless. If one always acts out of this kind of love, Fletcher reasons, one will be led to do the ethical or the right thing in most circumstances. It is possible according to Fletcher to actually harm another person, treat them in a nonloving way, by strictly following the rules in some cases. It is a question of the first premise, or the beginning point, in our reasoning about ethics, he would say. The rules should bend to the underlying values we hold, rather than let the rules cause unnecessary pain or suffering. This may seem like ethical relativism, but Fletcher points out in another article, some may be worried that "relativity lies at the normative level, but that at the substantive level the overarching value, loving concern, is not relativized."[10] One could say that Fletcher proposed replacing all the rules with the one overriding value placed on unqualified love for the other. He continues in the same article, "Another way to put this might be to say that the overall or prime (cardinal) virtue (value) of love can sometimes be subverted if a moral agent blindly follows an ordinarily or usually pertinent normative principle." Furthermore, situational ethics suggests that it is very difficult for one person to understand the full context in which another person acts. This reasoning leads to the Christian directive that one should not judge another person, meaning that we should not condemn the ethical decisions of another person, since we as finite beings cannot really understand the full picture. In fact, acting from Fletcher's principle of *agape* love, we must not judge or condemn another person.

Fletcher's proposed system of ethics has been controversial among church leaders and clergy, as one might suspect. They fear that his system is too subjective, allowing one to rationalize any departure from the standard norms of conduct on the claim that the violation was done out of love. In short, if the rules against lying can be broken on an individual's decision that she was doing the lying out of love, one begins down what logicians call a *slippery slope.* Perhaps the lie did not do much harm, but lying can still be wrong, although the force of the lie, as a sin, may be mitigated by the circumstances. Aquinas, after all, allowed for *jocose lies* (joking, in other words) and lies that do no harm. In other words, there may be degrees of the wrongness of lying in a certain case, but it is still lying, and still to some degree wrong, they would say. So, according to this view, lying in a particular situation may avoid greater harm or benefit people for the value of love, but that does not make the lying right or ethical. Lying in such a case is wrong but perhaps not terribly wrong.

Situational ethics, thus, argues that context determines the ethical action in a given situation. A set of rules cannot cover all situations, so it is preferable to rely on the single principle of love for other people to decide the right thing to do in each case.

Cultural Relativism

In Chinua Achebe's classic novel of Africans' confronting the experience of European colonialism, *Things Fall Apart*, the cultural values and traditions of the Igbo people of southeast Nigeria are carefully described chapter by chapter in the first part of the book. Achebe realized that some of the traditions would meet with the approval of Americans and Europeans and some would not. The Igbo's sense of community, equality, and family loyalty are generally praised by Westerners. On the other hand, such things as polygamy and the rights of men to beat their wives and children are often not approved in the West. One of the practices that may raise the most serious objection outside the culture was the practice of throwing newborn twins into the bush, since the birth of twins was believed to be an evil omen. Even in the context of the culture, however, as presented by Achebe, some of the Igbo questioned the rightness of this practice as well. The son of the protagonist, a boy named Unoka, began to question the values of his culture and traditional religion because of this practice and the ritual slaying of a boy taken as a hostage to placate his clan, preventing a war.

In a lecture, Achebe maintained that the Igbo people fear extremism and follow the proverb, "Where one thing stands, another thing can stand also."[11] The meaning of this proverb, explained by Achebe, is that there can always be two points of view. The Igbo people, he is saying, abhor absolutism and prefer toleration of different ideas and practices. Cultural relativism takes the position advocated here by Achebe, that where one thing stands another thing can stand also. Ethical standards are not absolute and universal for all people but are dependent on the cultural values and beliefs of different human cultures. All human cultures are equally valid and moral within their own systems. No one culture is better or more moral than another. What is said to be moral in one society is an expression of the accepted view based on the customs of that particular culture. Ethics are based on human conventions and traditions, not on a universal code.

The case for cultural relativism in ethics was advanced by American and European anthropologists in the last century to counter the tendency to compare traditional societies unfavorably to European ones. This tendency was manifested as ethnocentrism, the belief that one's own culture or ethnic group is superior to all others and those cultures and people who are different are therefore wrong or backward or primitive.

The practices of one culture cannot be judged against the standards of a different culture, according to this view. Hence, each human society may have a set of ethical rules, but they are not universal. This point of view at first seems compatible with most Americans' sense of tolerance and *live-and-let-live* ideas about human rights. But, how far are we willing to go along this road? We may not want to allow polygamy in our nation, but many people would be willing to allow that it is all right for others. After all, Islam does allow for a man to have up to four wives, although under very restrictive conditions. What permits us to judge people in another country or culture, we may ask. On the other hand, how do we feel about the practice of infanticide, killing twins at birth? Most people would not allow their tolerance to go this far. Now consider cases of human slavery—should that be allowed if it is acceptable in a particular culture (as it was in the United States before the Civil War)?

It appears that there are moral strictures that do go beyond cultural boundaries in some areas. Before the U.S. war against the government of the Taliban in Afghanistan, there was a great deal of revulsion against that government's treatment of women, not allowing them to go to school or work outside the home. Moral condemnation of certain practices, which are allowed in a different culture, does seem to be justified in such cases.

Supporters of ethical cultural relativism are probably willing to concede that there are limits to the practices or values that are to be tolerated. International conventions, such as the Geneva Conventions on the treatment of prisoners of war, and those against torture and genocide suggest nearly universal acceptance of some limits. In 1948, the United Nations adopted the *Universal*

Declaration of Human Rights, setting forth at least the minimum standards for members of the international body for the moral and proper treatment of people everywhere.[12] The Declaration explicitly speaks against such things as torture and slavery and upholds the rights of freedom of speech, religion, education, and human dignity. So, while tolerance and acceptance of the beliefs and cultural traditions of other cultures is generally seen as a good thing, there appears to be a general acceptance of limits on such tolerance and relativism.

In our discussion of evolutionary ethics earlier, we made the point that biology may explain why we do something, but does not necessarily tell us whether it is good or bad. Some may argue the same point about cultural differences: it is true that in some cultures certain things are permitted that are not in others. This is a descriptive statement, like Achebe's description of the killing of twins, telling us what some people do; but it does not tell us whether killing twins is a good or a bad thing. That value judgment is sepa-rate from the description of the facts. The advantage of cultural relativism is that it serves as a corrective to our tendency to denounce practices or beliefs that are different from our own (our ethnocentrism), but it does not mean we should suspend all judgments. There are practices such as slavery or the subjugation of women that most people of most cultures today would judge to be wrong, regardless of an attitude of cultural tolerance on most other matters.

In the specific field of communication practices, are there differing cul-tural standards regarding ethical practices? While truth-telling is generally considered morally required in most cultures, there are limitations regarding to whom one must tell the truth, under what conditions, and on what sub-jects. Often it is considered right to withhold certain kinds of information from specific classes of people, such as children. We have already mentioned the reluctance of people in certain Asian cultures to give someone a negative response face to face. On the other hand, Westerners, particularly Americans, feel there is an ethical value to being open and candid. Cultural practices in communication often take on a moral component, because what we do to get along in our culture takes on a sense of universal rightness. So, when some-one with whom we are communicating violates a cultural expectation, we feel wronged somehow. We will cover these aspects of cultural norms of com-munication in more detail in Chapter 8, dealing with intercultural communi-cation. The point is that we need to be sensitive to the possibility of cultural differences in expectations about communication practices.

A second version of ethical relativism is somewhat different from the cultural version we have been considering. In our classes on ethics, students will sometimes become frustrated in the discussion of an ethical dilemma, throw up their hands and say, "I have no right to judge whether what another person does is right or wrong." They may continue that they are responsible for their own actions and beliefs, but should not judge those of another.

Essentially this form of relativism states that ethical principles are subjective and relative to each individual. This position is illustrated by old story. A student in a philosophy class says to the professor, "You're just going to try to make me believe that what you think is right is what I should think is right. You're just imposing your beliefs on me. There are no real or objective standards for saying what is right or wrong."

"If you believe that, then I will have to lower your grade or flunk you," says the professor.

"You can't flunk me for my beliefs," retorts the student.

"Why not?" asks the professor.

"It just isn't right," responds the student.

"Where did you get that notion of what is right? That is just your personal opinion," responds the professor. At some level, the student wanted to claim there were objective standards to back his claim that he should not be flunked because of his personal beliefs.

Of course, there are two different interpretations to these situations. The first interpretation holds that a person does not feel qualified to judge the actions of another. People may not feel they have all the facts to understand the reasons a person behaved in a certain way or they may feel they lack the experience or knowledge to make ethical judgments of the sort required. So, the first student says she does not have the right to judge another. That is not really the same as ethical relativism, however; one could still believe in universal ethical rules (not be a relativist) while still maintaining they lack the right or information to apply those rules to another person. The interchange between the student and the professor better illustrates the meaning of ethical relativism in the claim that there are no universal standards.

The question becomes, then, whether or not ethical beliefs are like tastes in food. I don't like the taste of beets, but you do. There is no right or wrong about how we respond to the taste of this particular root vegetable. In stating an ethical judgment, according to this view, a person is merely reporting a subjective response, indicating how he or she feels about an action. Ethics is a matter of subjective feelings, in other words. (This position is also sometimes referred to as *emotivism*, because it is based on feelings or emotions, or as *intuitionism*, because it is based on individuals' intuitions about what is right and wrong.) It may happen that most people share these subjective responses to certain behaviors, so that most people accept that murder is wrong, although killing in a war is all right. Again, ethics comes back to judgments that are relative to individuals or to groups of people.

In this section, we have considered alternatives to the view of universal rules of ethics. The contrasting views maintain that there should be no absolute standards for making ethical decisions or ethical judgments of the actions of others. In the next section, we look at a contemporary attempt to bring together these conflicting points of view.

Modern Trends: Jürgen Habermas and Discourse Ethics

Jürgen Habermas, a German philosopher and public intellectual, was born in 1929, growing up during the rise of Hitler and the Nazis in his country. He was only fifteen when World War II ended and when he, like so many other young Germans, began to confront the enormity of the evil of those days. His father had been a passive supporter of the Nazis, and he had even been enrolled in the Hitler Youth in the last days of the war. It seems probable that his revulsion against the Nazi era led to his desire to find an intellectual foundation for reason and rationality in political life. He was a philosophy student in college and went on to graduate work in both philosophy and sociology. He became a highly successful professor in these fields and became associated with the Institute for Social Research, making him part of what is called the *Frankfurt School. School* used in this sense refers to a group of like-minded academics, interested in working on similar projects. The Frankfurt School is noted for developing what is called *Critical Theory*, an effort to apply the critical analysis of philosophy to the practical life of politics with the goal of furthering democratic life and freedom from all sorts of domination (including economic domination by corporate or wealthy elites). Their general view that capitalism represents a form of economic domination at odds with true freedom for all people has led to their being identified with a neo-Marxist interpretation of history and society (*Neo-*, that is, new, in the sense that they do not necessarily accept Marx's original analysis of class warfare and eventual revolution by the working classes to overthrow the capitalistic system).

As a public intellectual, Habermas is hard to pigeon-hole. He has at times been criticized as a radical leftist, while at other times he has been criticized by the radicals for his stands in support of the Allied interventions in Serbia and Kosovo in the 1990s as well as support for the first Gulf War against Iraq. He is often listed with contemporary European figures known as post-modernists, while he himself is concerned with justifying the *modern* ideals of reason and science against the attacks on modern rationality posed by the postmodernists. He retired from active teaching in 1994.

Our interest in Habermas lies in his effort to construct a basis for rationality that would reestablish the purposes of the Enlightenment and Kant in particular. The goal is to develop a rational basis for universal principles of knowledge, ethics, and politics. He therefore delved into communication theory, with a major two-volume work, *The Theory of Communicative Action*.[13] He continued to try to develop a method for justifying universal principles for ethics, as Kant had tried to do two centuries earlier. His method is known usually as *discourse ethics*.

Although his goal is the same as Kant's—to find a foundation for universal ethics based on reason—he departs from Kant on the particular method of the categorical imperative. Recall that to use the categorical imperative, an individual worked out logically the meaning of applying the rule for her immediate action as if it were a universal rule. (What would it mean if everyone followed the same rule I am following at this point in time?) We saw for example that one would decide lying was wrong because one could not want lying to be the general rule for everyone to follow in all similar situations. The individual, according to Kant, could reason this out for herself, because the laws of logic were the same for every rational person. Here is where Habermas differs from Kant. He believes it is preferable to test the validity of the imperative in communication with other people, instead of relying on the logic of a single person. That is the reason for calling his system *discourse ethics*. He replaces the term *ethical rules* with the term *norms*, so that his claim is that valid ethical norms (rules) are those which all in open communication can agree to. So, instead of one person figuring out the rules on lying or deception for himself or herself, the rules are to be agreed to by consensus of all affected by the rules.

How do people arrive at this consensus? Habermas proposes that special conditions for the discussion have to be set, conditions that he calls *communicative action*, or the *ideal speech situation*. Let's see how he distinguishes communicative action from other sorts of communication and debate. Most of the time in the *real world*, he recognizes, arguments are presented with *strategic* intent rather than *communicative* intent. He is using the word *strategic* here in a special sense to mean communicating in such a way so as to manipulate the response of the other person by the use of verbal stratagems rather than good reasons. As he puts it, "Whereas in strategic action one actor seeks to *influence* the behavior of another by means of the threat of sanctions or the prospect of gratification in order to cause the interaction to continue as the first actor desires, in communicative action one actor seeks *rationally* to *motivate* another. . ."[14] The use of *strategic* communication (given his definition) results in what Habermas calls *distorted communication*, distorted because it misleads another or intentionally relies on partial or slanted information. The ideal, however, is cooperative argumentation, in which all involved use arguments to test their validity with other people (the emphasis is on arriving at the most valid form of an ethical rule rather than winning a case).

Attaining this ideal speech situation would be very difficult. Habermas indicates the conditions that must be present for such a cooperative discussion to take place.

The four most important features are: (1) that nobody who could make a relevant contribution may be excluded; (ii) that all participants are granted an equal opportunity to make contributions; (iii) that the participants must mean what they say; and (iv) that communication must be freed from external and internal coercion so that the *yes* and *no* stances that participants adopt on criticizable validity claims are motivated solely by the rational force of the better reasons.[15]

In laying down the conditions for undistorted communication, Habermas describes not only what must be present for reaching agreement on universal principles of ethics, he also sets forth his prescription for ethical, cooperative communication. Such an ethic requires full and free access of all to the public platform. No one can be cut off or denied this opportunity, regardless of wealth, status, or position. All speakers must proceed in the spirit of cooperation rather than competition. And, everyone must have the opportunity to agree or disagree.

One may object at this point that Habermas' conditions are so idealistic that they are not realistic. He appears to believe that the conditions should be those present in a truly democratic society, in which there was a desire to arrive at valid conclusions regarding what ought to be the norms of a society. One can see something partly analogous to the ideal he proposes in cases such as the Truth and Reconciliation Commission that completed its work in post-Apartheid South Africa near the end of the twentieth Century. While the objective of this commission was not to establish ethical norms, it did display many of the conditions and characteristics of communicative action. Instead of instituting a process of accusation and defense, a sort of war-crimes trial, to bring to justice people who had committed crimes or atrocities on both sides of the trial, the *TRC* was set up in the spirit of cooperatively exorcising the evils done during the Apartheid years in South Africa. Most observers agree the process was successful in averting violent reprisals or even civil war. It may be taken as an example of the sort of process Habermas believes could work as ethical *communicative action.*

The ideal may be extremely difficult, almost impossible, to achieve, but it may be worth the effort.

CASE STUDY: OSKAR SCHINDLER, THE *RIGHTEOUS GENTILE*

In 1982, the Australian writer, Thomas Keneally, completed his book, *Schindler's List,* later made into the highly regarded film by Stephen Spielberg (if possible, we recommend viewing the film as part of the study of this case).[16] Years before, Keneally reports having come into contact with *Schindlerjuden* in a luggage store in California. Beginning from this point, he researched and put together the remarkable story of the German who saved 1,100 Polish Jews from certain death during the Holocaust.

Schindler was born in the Czech area of what was then known as the Austro-Hungarian Empire. After the defeat of Germany and Austria in World War I, the new country of Czechoslovakia was carved out of the old empire and the Schindler family found themselves now living in this new country as a minority among the Czechs. Apparently, when Hitler appealed to the Germans living in Czechoslovakia to support his call for occupation of their land, Oskar embraced the Nazi cause. Having been brought up in privileged circumstances, he was accustomed to having his way and to ignoring many of the rules of society. As a free-wheeling, pleasure-seeking young man, not above using bribes, he easily won over many of the Nazi functionaries in Krakow, Poland, where he had gone to seek his business fortune after the outbreak of World War II.

He was able to acquire an enamel factory in Krakow, benefiting from its confiscation by the German authorities from its former, Jewish owner. Directed by self-interest, he relied on a Jewish accountant, Itzhak Stern, to organize his business. Through his contact, Schindler was able to arrange financing from Jewish businessmen who have managed to keep secret their money from the occupiers. He also came to rely on the expertise of Polish-Jewish workers, many recruited by Stern, to run his factory.

Gradually, Schindler became aware of the fate the Nazis had in mind for the Jewish population of Poland—certain death in the ovens of Auschwitz, Bergen-Belsen, and other camps. Still the Germans relied on the labor—essentially slave labor—of able-bodied Jews with needed skills. Schindler was able to get his workers designated as essential workers for the German war effort (he supplied cooking utensils for the army and, later, munitions). In that way, he was able to protect many of them from being sent to the death camps. Still, at one point, he had to make a rescue of several of the women who had been sent to the huge Auschwitz complex.

We can apply a deontological analysis to several of Schindler's actions during the War.

QUESTIONS FOR ANALYSIS OF THE CASE

1. First, was Schindler being ethical in portraying the Jewish workers as entirely essential for his factory and for the German war effort? Can it be established that he used subterfuge or deception in keeping his Jewish workers in his factory? What would a Kantian analysis suggest about the ethics of his actions?

2. Was he acting from self-interest or from a sense of duty in protecting the Jewish workers? In other words, was his behavior the result of highly ethical principles or the result of the coincidental overlap between his interests and the rescue of the Jews?

3. Consider the ethical stance of a Kantian, of one who follows divine command theory, and of one who believes in natural law. What would each say about the ethical principles of Oskar Schindler? Was he truly a *righteous* person?

Chapter Summary

One who practices the ethics of duty (deontological ethics) believes that the reason for acting is the only important consideration. The outcomes of the action are irrelevant to the judgment of whether one's behavior was ethical or not. This rather strict stance seems to be in line with the way many people, at least at first, think about morals and ethics. We should do what we should do, without regard for the consequences. On the other hand, in real life we find the unbending demands of Kant that one should never lie under any circumstance, not only difficult but even undesirable.

Today, most ethicists seem to have moved away from the hard-and-fast stricture of Kant on lying, but his categorical imperative, as a method for thinking through ethical issues, still has some appeal. After all, one could reformulate the *maxim* concerning lying in such a way that the general rule was "Never lie except to avoid greater harm." Of course, Kant would point out that in so doing, the reformulation has left open the possibility of self-serving subjective judgments creeping in. His strict interpretation removes the potential of self-delusion about the greater harm being something you particularly want to avoid.

The second formulation of the categorical imperative, "treat all people always as ends in themselves and never simply as means to an end," provides excellent guidance for other ethical systems as we shall see in the next chapter. The idea of the inviolability of the individual human being does seem to be an ethical polestar accepted by many. This principle also underlies much of thinking about how to treat others in our communication and interaction with them.

Two other approaches to deontological ethics covered in this chapter include the religiously based theory of divine command and the sometimes related theories based on natural law or human nature. For many people in the world, religion provides a foundation for ethical beliefs and practices. It may not be clear whether there is an independent concept of right and wrong, which allows us to know that the divine authority is always right. Nonetheless, many people are comfortable with the motivational and clarifying principle that religion provides. We recall that in some forms of situational ethics, love as a religious commandment can trump strict religious duty, at least in the interpretation of some.

Situational ethics and relativism, especially cultural relativism, serve as alternatives to duty-based universalistic systems. It is hard to deny that some universal systems apparently deny the values of cultures different from a dominant one. Does respect for cultural differences lead to the conclusion that there are no universal standards of right and wrong? It does appear that there are some basic moral principles, such as those against slavery, torture, human sacrifice, and the like, to name some extreme examples. It becomes difficult to sort through the different communication practices and norms of a culture and see some as decidedly right or wrong from a universal perspective. This issue comes up again in the chapter on intercultural communication.

The *discourse ethics* of Jürgen Habermas represents an effort to rebuild a universal system of deontological ethics. The difference with this system is that it does not formulate or prescribe the content of such a universal ethical code, but rather tries to reason out the process to be followed to achieve consensus on ethical norms in practice.

QUESTIONS AND TOPICS FOR DISCUSSION

1. Is it ever right to lie? What are the conditions you believe it may be acceptable to not tell the truth?

2. Can one ethically avoid lying by ambiguous statement or withholding part of the truth? For example, someone asks you how their performance was in the play the acted in last night. You respond, "You should have seen it from the audience" (which could mean, things would have gone better if you had been in the audience instead of in the play).

3. What do you think of Kant's claim that you should tell the truth even to a murderer hunting down a victim, someone whose hiding place is known to you? What would Kant say about the people who protected Anne Frank and her family in Amsterdam during World War II?

4. Do you feel more comfortable with situational ethics or ethical relativism? Discuss the conditions under which you think situation or cultural context do make a valid difference and those in which they might not.

5. Does Habermas' *ideal speech situation* seem like a possible eventuality? How could the conditions for such an ideal situation be used to help reconcile two opposing sides of a debate, such as the debate over a right to end one's life when facing a painful, terminal illness.

NOTES

1. *Sports Illustrated* SI.com, "O'Leary out at Notre Dame after One Week," at http://sportsillustrated.cnn.com.college.news,2001/12/14/oleary_notredame/ (accessed July 3, 2004).

2. Immanuel Kant, "On a Supposed Right to Lie from Philanthropy (1797)," in *Immanuel Kant: Practical Philosophy*, ed. and trans. Mary J. Gregor (New York: Cambridge University Press, 1996), pp. 605–615.

3. Immanuel Kant, *Groundwork of the Metaphysics of Morals* (1785), in *Immanuel Kant: Practical Philosophy*, ed. and trans. Mary J. Gregor (New York: Cambridge University Press, 1996), p. 56.

4. Kant, *Groundwork*, p. 72.

5. Kant, *Groundwork*, p. 80.

6. *Internet Encyclopedia of Philosophy*, at www.utm.edu/research/iep/n/natlaw.htm (accessed July 3, 2004).

7. Sharon Begley, "In Explaining How We Got this Way, Beware of the Just-So Story," *The Wall Street Journal,* June 25, 2004, p. B1.

8. Sharon Begley, "Researchers Seek Roots of Morality in Biology, With Intriguing Results," *The Wall Street Journal,* June 11, 2004, p. B1; see the online survey information at http://moral.wjh.harvard.edu.

9. Fletcher, Joseph, *Situation Ethics* (Philadelphia: Westminster Press, 1966).

10. Joseph Fletcher, "Naturalism, Situation Ethics, and Value Theory," in *Normative Ethics & Objective Reason,* ed. George F. MacLean (Washington, DC: PAIDEA Publishers, 1996), online at www.ajgoddard.net/Writers/Joseph_Fletcher/joseph_fletcher.html#Con (accessed July 6, 2004).

11. Chinua Achebe, Lecture sponsored by the Change and Tradition Program (Indianapolis, IN: Butler University, 1994).

12. Adopted and proclaimed by General Assembly resolution 217 A (III) of 10 December 1948; at the United Nations web site, at www.un.org/Overview/rights.html (accessed July 7, 2003).

13. Jürgen Habermas, *The Theory of Communicative Action, Volume 1: Reason and the Rationalization of Society,* trans. Thomas McCarthy (Boston: Beacon Press, 1984); Jürgen Habermas, *The Theory of Communicative Action, Volume 2: Lifeword and System: A Critique of Functionalist Reason,* trans. Thomas McCarthy (Boston: Beacon Press, 1987).

14. Jürgen Habermas, *Moral Consciousness and Communicative Action,* trans. Christian Lenhardt and Sherry Weber Nicholsen (Cambridge, MA: MIT Press, 1990), p. 58, italics in original.

15. Jürgen Habermas, *The Inclusion of the Other: Studies in Political Theory,* ed. Clarian Cronin and Palble De Greiff (Cambridge, MA: MIT Press, 2001), p. 44.

16. Thomas Keneally, *Schindler's List* (New York: Simon & Schuster, 1982).

4 Consequences

Does the end justify the means? The question is so familiar that it is essentially a cliché, and people often imply the answer in the way they ask the question. When one considers ethics in terms of duties, as in the previous chapter, there is no concern for the outcomes or the consequences. One following deontological ethics has no hesitation answering the question with an emphatic, "No!" From that perspective, the end can never justify the means—one must do one's duty and let whatever happens happen. We might say that deontological ethics is input based rather than output based. In this chapter, we will now look at the other side of ethical reasoning, the side that considers the outcomes of actions rather than what motivated them.

When the Allies in World War II were preparing for the famous D-Day invasion of Normandy on the French coast, they developed a plan to mislead the German commanders so that they would think the attack was coming further north, near the French city of Calais. Few people doubt that in warfare, in which thousands of lives may be at stake, such deception is ethically warranted. On a less serious level, deception is a major, usually ethically neutral aspect of many sports and games. A key element in most sports lies in deceiving your opponent or *faking* him or her out. Imagine what a game of poker would be like if every time you tried to *bluff* (act as if you had a better hand than you in fact do have), you were required to tell the truth if an opponent asked whether you were indeed bluffing.

There do seem to be limits, however, on how much deception is acceptable even in such cases. During the fall 2003 National Football League season, when the Denver Broncos quarterback suffered a shoulder separation early in the game, the coaching staff announced that the injury was a concussion. The coach said that he lied because he feared that if the quarterback had to return to the game, the other team would know that he could not throw the ball and therefore look for running plays only.[1] League officials considered the coach's deception controversial, because he may have broken rules concerning accurate reporting of injuries. In college sports, The NCAA (National Collegiate Athletic Association) considers deception about the academic standing of players or concealing payments to college players' serious infractions. Deception in poker cannot include palming higher cards into your hand or dealing *seconds* from the deck in order to deceive people about the actual value of your hand.[2] When deception becomes *cheating*, there can be severe consequences. Las Vegas casinos, for example, put millions of dollars into security and surveillance to catch and prosecute such forms of deception.

If the duties approach to ethics places strict limits on deceptive communication, the approach based on consequences seems more flexible. In this chapter, we will discuss two kinds of systems concerned with consequences, *utilitarianism* and *egalitarianism*. In the first, the aim is to arrive at actions that will result in the most *utility*, the best outcomes for the largest number of people (or all sentient creatures, some would add). The second, as its name implies, aims at obtaining equal or, at least, fair outcomes for as many as possible. These kinds of theories fall under the general label of *Consequentialism*, since they focus on the consequences of actions.

Utilitarianism

In utilitarianism, the ethical or right action is the one that results in the *greatest good for the greatest number*. Rightness or wrongness is determined by totaling the positive and negative outcomes of an action, and the one that produces the highest score of positives over negatives is the most ethical, or right thing, to do. Whether lying is wrong depends on the outcomes, who is benefited and who is harmed. The most famous proponent of this theory of ethics was the nineteenth-century British intellectual, John Stuart Mill, although he is not the originator of it. Nearly all the advocates of utilitarianism have been British or at least English speaking, and even the major contemporary advocate is the Australian Peter Singer, who now teaches in the United States. Utilitarianism, based on the notion of utility or usefulness, appears to be a very practical philosophy, and Americans, as well as others who share an economic and political heritage from Britain, seem quite at home with things practical and useful. We find as teachers that American students readily understand the point of utilitarianism and readily accept many of its tenets as sensible.

Foundations of Utilitarian Ethics

There is a certain mathematical logic to utilitarianism, since one should be able to count and total the benefits versus the costs and calculate the number of people affected. The Englishman considered the *founder* of utilitarianism, Jeremy Bentham, in fact presented his theory in just this way. He developed a very elaborate system for calculating the quantities of pleasure in terms of their duration, intensity, certainty, remoteness or nearness in time and place, and on and on. Bentham, hence, used the quantitative and objective methods he associated with the scientific method in developing his theory. Next, in determining the number of people benefited or harmed, he laid down the rule that every person is to count as one, the happiness of a farmer in a distant land received the same weight in the calculations as your mother or lover. The counting was to be impartial. Bentham was thus concerned with maximizing the total happiness in the world. Therefore, in your calculations about whether or not to lie to someone, you cannot consider only the advantages for you and your immediate family or associates, but everyone everywhere.[3]

Bentham and Mill were reformers, who wanted to improve the conditions of British citizens and workers by following scientific principles. The desperate conditions of the English working class in the early stages of the industrial revolution, described so vividly in the novels of Charles Dickens, were of special concern to these reformers. They believed that the application of utilitarian principles in government, education, and social life in general would lead to public policies that would eliminate most of the evils of industrialized living. Utilitarian ethics, as originally conceived, seem to be most applicable in matters of public communication, in which there are likely to be effects on a whole community. We believe that it is therefore more difficult to apply utilitarian ethics in matters of interpersonal communication, for which dialogical ethics seems more appropriate (as explained further in the following chapter).

Bentham's formulation of utilitarianism, particularly the extreme quantification principles, seemed unwieldy. His effort to come up with a precise numerical weight for each kind of pleasure was quixotic and unrealistic.

A second major criticism of Bentham's theory lay in his claim that all pleasures were essentially equal. To be as scientific and as objective as possible, he did not feel one could start making subjective judgments about whether one kind of pleasure was better than another kind. His critics pointed out that this scheme reduced human beings to animals, implying that there was no difference between the pleasures of a pig (enjoying food and rest) and those of a great artist or philosopher or religious leader.

Bentham was a close friend of James Mill, who was the father of John Stuart Mill; for that reason, a close relationship developed between Bentham and the younger Mill. John Stuart Mill became the principle head of the utilitarian movement, as he improved on the system developed by his older mentor. First, Mill replaced the quantitative approach attempted by Bentham with a more reasonable emphasis on the quality of pleasure or happiness. Secondly, he maintained that there were important differences in the quality of kinds of pleasure as well. Pleasures related to the *higher faculties* of human beings, particularly pleasures of the mind and of contemplation, were superior to pleasures derived from satisfying bodily appetites.

John Stuart Mill thus formulated the foundation of utilitarianism in the following way:

> The creed which accepts as the foundation of morals, Utility, or the Greatest Happiness Principle, holds that actions are right in proportion as they tend to promote happiness, wrong as they tend to produce the reverse of happiness. By happiness is intended pleasure, and the absence of pain; by unhappiness, pain and the privation of pleasure.[4]

Notice that Mill intends this principle to be the basis for morals. The statement therefore serves the same function in utilitarianism that the categorical imperative serves in Kant's system of ethics.

Immediately following this formulation of the basic principle, Mill deals with the criticism that naming pleasure the only touchstone for morals and human happiness reduces people to their lowest appetites. First, he makes a clean break with Bentham's insistence that quantity or sheer amount of pleasure is all that matters: "It is quite compatible with the principle of utility," he maintains, "to recognise the fact, that some *kinds* of pleasure are more desirable and more valuable than others."[5] In this section, Mill anticipates the more modern and quite influential theory of motivation developed by Abraham Maslow in the 1950s, which held that those things that motivate people could be placed in a hierarchy. The lower levels of Maslow's hierarchy include food, shelter, and security, while the higher levels include esteem, self-respect, and what Maslow called *self-actualization*.[6] Mill places human pleasures in a similar hierarchy, leading to perhaps the most famous statement in his work on utilitarianism: "It is better to be a human being dissatisfied than a pig satisfied; better to be Socrates dissatisfied than a fool satisfied."[7]

Mill may not have realized that in breaking with Bentham's principle of quantification of pleasure he introduced an apparent inconsistency in the theory of utilitarianism. Clearly, there needs to be some criteria outside the one of utility alone to determine which are the higher and which the lower kinds of pleasures. He appears to be relying on some theory about human nature or some sort of intuition about what are higher and lower pleasures. At any rate, he has abandoned the strictly objective and scientific method envisioned by Bentham and Utilitarians in general. The inconsistency lies in the conflict between the principle of utility as the final arbiter or what is ethical, on the one hand, and the principle that there must be some standard for judging the value of various pleasures outside applying the utility rule, on the other.

Implications of Utilitarian Ethics

This difficulty remains an important criticism of utilitarian ethics. The determination of what is the greatest good (the highest or best principle of happiness or pleasure) is a subjective matter. A person can therefore justify an action as ethical, along utilitarian lines, based on his or her own definition of what is the *greatest good* in any situation. To take an extreme example, Hitler and his Nazi cronies could have justified to themselves the mass murder of millions of people in the Holocaust because of their contention that such murder was necessary for the greatest good. We reject this justification outright as wrong, but the basis for judging mass murder for any purpose wrong lies outside the strict boundaries of utilitarianism as formulated by Mill. We feel certain that such mass killing is wrong because of a belief in the sanctity of human life; a principle derived more from deontological ethics than from consequentialism. It would also violate principles of egalitarianism, as we shall see, because it does not accept every person as equally valuable.

Returning to our basic method for reasoning about ethics introduced in the first chapter, we maintain that determining what is the *greatest good* in any situation requires proving a proposition of *value*, rather than a proposition of *fact*. Bentham and then Mill had hoped to structure their ethical system in a way that allowed these issues to be matters of *fact* rather than matters of *value*.

The strict application of the utilitarian method also appears to lead to other outcomes that we feel are somehow undesirable. For example, we may feel that wrongfully accusing one person or group of people with a crime in order to prevent panic may bring about the greatest good for the greatest number. To most of us, the sacrifice of the few for the benefit of the many in this kind of situation seems wrong but it also appears to be in line with utilitarian ethics. The classic film, *Jaws* (and its many sequels), presents a situation in which the town leaders, especially the mayor, feel it is better to cover up the dangers of the lurking *great white* shark than to sacrifice the

overall economic benefits for the townspeople. We in the audience are supposed to feel that the mayor is ethically wrong. A utilitarian may feel he is
wrong about his calculation of benefits in the case (confronting the problem
of the shark openly could result in greater benefit); while others might feel
he is wrong to use a strictly utilitarian calculation in the first place. One is
reminded of the feeling that one gets when realizing that the categorical
imperative of Kant requires one to reveal the potential victim's hiding place
to the inquiring potential murderer. Following the rule strictly seems to lead
to some unexpected or at least uncomfortable results.

Let us here introduce another technical distinction developed by utilitarian philosophers to help deal with this sort of problem: *act utilitarianism*
versus *rule utilitarianism*. The situation envisioned by Bentham and Mill
suggested that each separate act be judged by the utilitarian principle; hence,
it is called *act utilitarianism*. The strict application of act utilitarianism seems
to lead to some of the seemingly undesirable results, such as sacrificing an
innocent person for the benefit of the many. Rule utilitarianism sets up a
slightly different principle. It looks to whether the application of a *rule*
of conduct in a given case results in the greatest good for the greatest number in all similar kinds of cases. The sacrifice of the innocent to bring about
some benefit may not seem best, as a general rule, since such a rule would
not generate the general benefits of respect for justice and protection for
individual rights. Respect for justice and human rights may make for a better
society in the end and therefore, as rules for action, serve better to promote
the greatest good of the greatest number. Therefore, although in a specific
case, sacrificing the innocent for the many seems best for that situation, people should reject that option because we would not want the rule applied
generally.

Using rule utilitarianism allows us to avoid some other questionable
results as well. For example, say that a large corporation deceived a small
number of workers about whether the plant was going to relocate their jobs
overseas. Fearing that the workers would leave prematurely if they knew the
plans, and knowing it would be hard to replace them for exactly that reason,
the company chose to make them think their jobs were permanent and
secure. We have seen people apply a utilitarian analysis to this case and determine the deception was ethical. Let us see how this answer was justified. First,
they claim that the greater number of people involved (the *stakeholders*) are
the other employees and stockholders of the company, who outnumber the
few employees. The deception resulted in greater good for the greater number. Second, they did not feel they had to investigate the consequences for
people beyond the corporation and stockowners. The reasoning is faulty,
especially when applying rule utilitarianism. The question is, would the greatest amount of overall happiness result from this localized deception? First,
people beyond the corporation and the specific plant under consideration
could suffer harm from this action, especially if the local economy depended

on the economic benefits of the plant's being in the town. Second, this action could damage the reputation and credibility of the corporation, eventually causing loss of confidence in its stock. Third, if this sort of deception were widely practiced by similar firms, the results could be harmful for the economy as a whole. Furthermore, the theory of utilitarianism holds that the results should be the best possible, rather than merely better than an alternative course of action; it must be better than all alternatives (the *maximization principle* implied by the phrase, *the greatest good*). One might ask would it be more ethical for the company simply to keep its intentions a secret rather than positively assuring the workers of their security? The answer to this question may be debatable. One could take the position that the best course of action would be to communicate with the workers about the possibilities, assure them of some sort of consideration and assistance with replacement, perhaps in the company, or something of the sort. Alternatively, one could argue that secrecy may be best to prevent competitors knowing of the company's plans, if such knowledge could be used to the serious disadvantage of the company, employees, and stockholders. Still, the force of rule utilitarianism is to force one to take account of the overall effects of any action beyond the effects on those most immediately involved.

Even by replacing act utilitarianism by rule utilitarianism, we still may not overcome this problem of distorting the calculations of benefits and costs: determining what is best for the greatest number requires some subjective judgments. Only one U.S. president has resigned before completing his term of office and only one Attorney General of the United States has ever served actual jail time. Both cases resulted from the national scandal referred to as Watergate over thirty years ago. The events that led to the cover-up known as Watergate suggest the problems of subjectivity in deciding "the greatest good for the greatest number." The Attorney General involved in the case was John N. Mitchell, who had been a long-time adviser to former President Nixon after Nixon had joined his New York law firm (several years before Nixon's first term as President). Mitchell ultimately admitted that he approved funding for the clearly illegal Watergate break-in and burglary, but did not tell the president about it during the 1972 campaign. When he was questioned about how he had got himself involved in such a scheme, Mitchell explained, "In my mind, the reelection of Richard Nixon, compared to what was on the other side, was so important that I put it in exactly that context."[8] In other words, Mitchell applied a utilitarian rule to the situation and concluded that the illegal act was justified because the president's reelection represented a greater good for the greatest number of people. The analysis led him, first, not to communicate his role in the burglary to the president, and, second, to participate in denying the Administration had any role in the Watergate affair (the cover-up, or *stonewalling*). Probably he really believed he was acting for the greater good of the American people at the time. At least he no doubt convinced himself of that. On New Year's Day 1975, the jury in the federal trial of Mitchell and five other Watergate defendants found him guilty of conspiracy and lying under oath. He was sentenced to 2 ½ to 8 years, but a judge reduced the sentence to 1 to 4 years. He served nineteen months in a minimum-security facility before being paroled.

Attorney General Mitchell applied what he felt was an appropriate utilitarian standard to determine what action would produce the greatest good. The consensus at the time, as well as of the jury, was he had figured wrongly. He had let political self-interest distort his reasoning about what was the ethical course of action.

When we apply consequential reasoning to our own ethical judgments and actions, we need to be aware of this sort of danger. Some ethicists have reasoned that a way to reduce such dangers is to focus on what may be clearer to each of us than the *general* good, our own self-interest. We will consider this particular variant system of consequential ethics next.

A Variant on Utilitarianism: Ethical Egoism

Can we do the best for everyone by doing what is best for us as individuals? This is the fundamental question leading to this theory. Ethical egoism holds that one can determine the ethical action in a given case by always doing what is best for the individual's own interests, without regard to the interests of others. This theory differs from what is called *psychological egoism,* which maintains that people *do* always act from their own self-interests (as a matter of *fact*). Ethical egoism thus upholds a *should* proposition, while psychological egoism advances an *is* proposition. The position of the ethical egoist is one *should* do exactly those things that are in the individual's best interests, without regard to the interests of others.

Ethical egoism takes two forms: in one sense the theory purports to show why ethical behavior is self-interested (an explanatory function); and in the other, it prescribes how one ought to behave, how one ought to make ethical decisions (a prescriptive function).

The theory claims that when someone behaves in a way people praise as selfless or altruistic, he or she is really only acting out of self-interest. It may appear that someone acted in a selfless manner by sacrificing so that another may benefit. In reality, the ethical egoist says, the sacrifice satisfied the person's need for approval or the praise of others; perhaps it satisfied some inner need of the person him or herself for self-approval. People who appear to be self-sacrificing paragons of virtue, such as Mother Theresa, appear to be putting the needs of others before her own. In reality, the ethical egoist would say, Mother Theresa was really sacrificing her health and life, putting others first in order to fulfill some personal need she had for this apparent altruism. Therefore, according to this view, that which seems to be altruism may actually be really egoism. The problem with this reasoning is that the definition of what is in one's own interest becomes empty of meaning. No matter what someone does, for whatever reason, the ethical egoist can claim it is really done out of self-interest. How do we know the act was done from self-interest? Because they did it, and anything anybody does is from self-interest—so the circular reasoning goes. The argument can never be lost, because the proponent can fall back on the claim of psychological egoism as a mantra. Someone to justify taking an ethical egoistic position, by claiming it is natural or, even, unavoidable, advances this sort of argument. Evolutionary psychology also puts forth the claim that the selfishness of the organism (or the *selfish gene*) explains seemingly altruistic behavior. People may sacrifice themselves for others in order to perpetuate relatives, who share the same or related genes, or to secure the survival of the species in the end.

Ethical egoism has roots in the British reform movement and the related movement known as *British empiricism*, as did utilitarianism. Empiricism is the philosophical position that knowledge comes from experience or from physical sensations. John Locke, about whom we have more to say, is one of the major founders of the point of view. If all our knowledge of the world comes through physical sensations and experiences, it stands to reason that pleasure and pain will play central motivating roles in utilitarianism and related theories. This major thrust of utilitarian thinking led to the assumption that maximizing pleasure was the primary end people should aim at.

At about the same time the utilitarians were developing their theories, Adam Smith and other early economists such as David Ricardo were developing the new science of economics. Smith believed that if every individual were to act, in the economic marketplace, to further his or her own best interests, the overall effect would benefit all. As some observers put it at the time, the butcher does not sell you meat because he likes you (although he may in fact like you), but to make money for himself. Regardless of his lack of altruistic motive, you still benefit by getting the meat, and because the other butchers have the same aim as yours, you probably get it for a lower price. He still makes a profit and you still get your roast—everyone benefits. This type of classical economics represents the foundation of capitalism in the idea of the *invisible hand*, operating in the market to allow everyone to maximize their wealth. When each performs some act to do nothing other than advance his or her own best interest, the result appears to come out in favor of everyone's interest.

Mill's successor as leading exponent of utilitarianism was the British professor of philosophy, Henry Sidgwick, who died in 1900. Sidgwick concluded that both classical utilitarianism and ethical egoism seemed to be in accord. If everyone did look only to their own selfish interests, the result would generally be the same as if everyone followed the utilitarian principle. The rub is that not everyone is always able to discern his or her genuine interests or needs. John Mitchell may have thought he was furthering his own interests in lying about Watergate, but, as the eventual result demonstrated, his real interest lay in coming clean from the start.

In the twentieth century, the major proponent of the position of ethical egoism was the Russian-born writer, Ayn Rand. Her background may provide some context for her influential ideas. She was born in St. Petersburg, Russia, in 1905, before the Russian Revolution of 1917, daughter of a pharmacist. Her family suffered financially in the Revolution, because the Soviets confiscated the father's business. Although she completed college in St. Petersburg (then called *Petrograd*), she harbored the desire to be a writer and, to achieve her goal, a desire to get out of the Soviet Union. After enrolling in the State Institute of Cinema Arts to become a screenwriter, she was able to defect to the United States in 1925, on a visit to relatives. She went out to Hollywood, where a chance meeting with Cecil B. DeMille led to her becoming an extra in a movie and there to meeting her husband. She finally became a film writer in the 1930s and published her first novel, *We the Living*, about life under the Soviets, in 1935. She published her most famous works *The Fountainhead* and *Atlas Shrugged* in 1943 and 1957 respectively.

The two novels, especially *Atlas Shrugged*, attracted a large following, who responded to the books' strong philosophical advocacy of individualism and self-reliance. As a result, her emphasis turned more and more to nonfiction writing, developing her ideas into a philosophy she called *objectivism*. Among her admirers after *Atlas Shrugged* were economists such as Milton Friedman and Alan Greenspan, later Chair of the Federal Reserve.[9] In describing the ethical principles of *objectivism*, Rand maintains that every person is an end in himself or herself. People should not sacrifice themselves for others nor expect others to sacrifice for them. "The pursuit of his own rational self-interest and of his own happiness is the highest moral purpose of his life."[10]

The key point here is the notion of *rational* self-interest. Doing what is in your best interest is not the same as doing whatever you want, since we often do not know what is truly in our best self-interest. In fact, gaining what is in your rational best interest may require discipline and self-denial, as an athlete must force herself to suffer long hours of rigorous training to obtain her objectives. Rand is not espousing a hedonistic philosophy of pleasure seeking, but a possibly strenuous effort at self-discipline and concentrated reasoning.

What are the implications of ethical egoism for our everyday communication behaviors? Can we apply the principle of always following our own self-interest to make ethical decisions? If we start from the premise that the only good decision is one that furthers our own good, will we automatically behave in an ethical fashion? This does seem to be the basis for our economic life as well as many aspects of our political life as well. The idea of the social contract implies that when each person recognizes it is in their own self-interest to surrender some freedom to the state or society, everyone benefits from the resulting security and regularity. We all agree to stop at red lights and go at green ones to avoid the hassle of road accidents and injuries.

The weaknesses of the position, however, reveal themselves through exercises such as the *prisoner's dilemma.* You may be familiar with this puzzle, in which everyone following their own self-interest does not result in the best consequences for themselves and others. Here is an updated version of the exercise. Imagine that two students, Avery and Beth, are working on a class exercise like a presentation or a term project. Avery has a lot of work for his other classes, and so does Beth. Each realizes that it would be preferable if he or she does as little research as possible on their joint project, concentrating on their individually graded assignments. For Avery, the best outcome occurs when Beth does all the research for the project, so he gets a good grade on it, while avoiding the effort at working himself. The same, of course, is true for Beth. When they finally get together to put the presentation together, they discover neither has done any advance preparation. If they both slack off on the project, seeing that as their best individual choice, then they will both achieve the worst possible outcome, a shared low grade or failure.

Another version of this kind of criticism of ethical egoism is the *free rider* syndrome, in which an individual benefits from the efforts of others on a joint project or responsibility. When you see a fund-raiser for public television, you often see this criticism used to make people, who are not contributing to public television, feel guilty about their benefiting from the sacrifice of others, going along for a free ride. If you can take advantage of a service, for free, that others are willing to pay for, isn't that in your own best interest? A second variant of this line of reasoning is, "the law of the commons." This view points out that if everyone shares a resource, each appears better off by taking care of his or her own property instead of the common property, in the hope that someone else will take responsibility for it.

Our intuition that something is wrong or unethical about free riders implies a weakness in the position of ethical egoism. Of course, one can argue that the free riders, or Beth and Avery, simply misunderstood what was in their genuine self-interest. However, as with the explanation of psychological egoism, then anything or everything could fall within the definition of self-interest, so that the concept ends up explaining very little. If no matter what someone does, if it works out well, we say it was in self-interest; if it doesn't, we say it was not. One knows only after the fact; the principle hence provides no useful guidance.

Lies or cover-ups of wrongdoing often seem in the self-interest of individuals, leading to some of the major scandals in public and political life. President Nixon's fall from office began with a decision to cover up the role of the White House in the Watergate affair, presumably because that course of action seemed to be in his own best interest at the time. Former President

Clinton nearly lost his office when he lied about his relationship with a White House intern. At the time, covering up that relationship seemed in his self-interest, to avoid difficulties in his own marriage, let alone national scandal.

Would a tack opposite to ethical egoism work? Instead of acting only out of self-interest, could we always act or always prefer to act only in the interests of others? This approach is *ethical altruism*, and says that we should always do the best we can for other people, even to sacrifice our own interests and ourselves. This approach suggests an extreme form of the *Golden Rule*, always do for others, period. Ethical altruism may also suggest the notion of *servant leadership*, as advanced by Robert K. Greenleaf and Larry C. Spears.[11] Who would be the leader should serve other people rather than himself or herself. One problem with ethical altruism is that the purpose behind the altruism may always be some sort of self-satisfaction. One may hope, perhaps not consciously, for praise from others or for a sense of inner satisfaction or even pride. Occasionally, ethical altruism has a religious connotation, as one believes that by putting others first, one will gain ultimate salvation. Still, as Kant pointed out many years earlier, people who do something for others in order to achieve some reward, including a reward in the hereafter, are not acting from selfless motives. Of course, someone espousing either psychological or ethical egoism would agree with Kant on this score.

Highlights of Utilitarian Ethical Systems

Utilitarians answer the question, about the end justifying the means, by calculating the ends in terms of how much total, overall happiness, for how many people, the means bring about. If the end represents a maximization of overall pleasure or happiness for the largest possible number, the means are ethical. The calculation requires us to project the probable outcomes to the best of our abilities. Utilitarianism has a certain democratic and well-intentioned sense. Many people feel that it provides a practical guideline.

The founders of the utilitarian principle, Jeremy Bentham and John Stuart Mill, hoped it would have a scientifically objective feel to it as well. Despite those hopes, predicting the quality and the quantity of pleasure to result from an action remains a subjective exercise. People can never fully know what all the significant ramifications of a particular decision might be. Additionally, we easily mislead ourselves concerning those costs and benefits by considerations of our own selfish interests and desires, even when such considerations are unintended or out of our awareness. For those reasons, utilitarianism can seem, to some, to be a form of rationalization for doing what we want to do in the first place (regardless of genuine ethical concerns).

In more recent times, utilitarians have developed two forms of the principles: act-utilitarianism and rule-utilitarianism. The development of rule-utilitarianism allows one to avoid seeming injustices to individuals in certain cases by requiring the application of the rule for the act for all time and all places. One thus asks whether following the *rule* results in the greatest good for the greatest number.

Ethical egoism, as well as ethical altruism, provides alternatives to the utilitarian need to project effects for huge numbers of people and society. The ethical egoist holds that if one acts always from self-interest, the best consequences will come about. We have seen that looking exclusively to self-interest, while perhaps *natural,* has some unwanted consequences as well.

In the next section, we turn to the issue of equal treatment intended to bring about outcomes that, if not the best, are at least equitable and fair for all involved.

Egalitarianism

The utilitarian principle of ethics aggregates or totals the interests of all individuals to determine right and wrong. Those who emphasize fairness and equal treatment are more likely to concentrate on the effects of actions on people as individuals. They wish us to consider the effects on each person, so that no one is called on to make undue sacrifices in the interests of the greater number. You might think of the familiar lifeboat example, in which there are so many survivors in the lifeboat that unless some are thrown overboard, the boat will sink and all will be lost. For the majority, who are saved (assume rescue vessel or pleasant island landing eventually), the sacrifice of the few for them seems acceptable. To the ones drowned, the outcome may not seem as pleasant. It may seem that we are back to Kant's duty of respect for every individual as an end, not merely a means. We do recognize that some theorists consider the theories in this section to be deontological, or duty-based, rather than consequentialist. We place these theories here with consequentialism, however, because they do look to outcomes in terms of whether they are fair or equitable.

Background to Egalitarianism: The Social Contract

In November of 1620, a small ship anchored in the waters off the coast of what is now Massachusetts. On board was a group of religious separatists from the Church of England, intending to found a colony in the *New World,* where they could practice their faith without fear of persecution. Because the coast on which they were going to settle was beyond the boundaries of the English colony of Virginia (which in those days was assumed to stretch as far north as Long Island), there would be no royal charter to serve as a basis for their own government in the new colony. Dissent among factions on board was already evident, and so the leaders of the expedition decided to draw up an agreement, signed by all the male heads of households among the colonists. This agreement, known later as the *Mayflower Compact*, committed the settlers to the following contract:

> [to] covenant and combine ourselves together into a civil Body Politick, for our better Ordering and Preservation, and Furtherance of the Ends aforesaid: And by Virtue hereof do enact, constitute, and frame, such just and equal Laws, Ordinances, Acts, Constitutions, and Officers, from time to time, as shall be thought most meet and convenient for the general Good of the Colony; unto which we promise all due Submission and Obedience.[12]

The notion that people could agree to their own form of government goes back to the revolutionary and democratizing era we have already described in the time of Kant and the Utilitarians. When the basis for legitimate government was no longer the *divine right of kings*, philosophers felt the need to come up with something justified by rational or scientific principles. If everyone were equal and no kings or nobles were naturally better than anyone else was, then what did scientifically observed nature say about government and the state? What leads us to give up some of our rights to do whatever we want for the good of all? We have already referred to the concept of the *social contract*, in noting why we generally stop at red lights. We agree, as if by contract, to give up our right to drive through intersections however we like in order to prevent the chaos of unregulated traffic. The theories we discuss in this section are for this reason referred to as *contractualism*.[13]

The idea of the social contract is one that you may have encountered in other courses or other texts. You may know the idea is mainly associated with two British philosophers, Thomas Hobbes and John Locke, and a French philosopher, Jean-Jacques Rousseau. Hobbes and Locke were active in the 1600s and Rousseau in the 1700s. Hobbes reasoned that in a *state of nature* all human beings would be in constant competition with each other, as well as with other creatures, resulting in a constant state of chaos and individual warfare. People discovered that they could all survive and better protect their lives, families, and property if they got together and agreed on a cooperative organization, the early beginnings of human government. Locke did not envision humans in the state of nature being quite so combative, but he reasoned that they discovered they could further their interests more efficiently and safely in the sort of cooperative arrangement called a *social contract*. Rousseau, an intellectual precursor of the French Revolution of 1789–1795, was even more at odds with Hobbes, in that he imagined the state of nature to have been a sort of ideal lost when people began to claim land and property. To uphold their claims, Rousseau also assumed people had to come to some contractual, cooperative arrangement to prevent the competition getting out of hand.

None of these writers claims there actually were primitive meetings at which people worked out all the arrangements of the contract, as the pilgrims did on board the *Mayflower.* They are saying, rather, most people accept the legitimacy, the rightness, of basic political organization, rights, and limitations on rights because it is *as if* they have signed such a contract. If you enjoy the rights and protection of a state, you have *tacitly agreed* to such a contract. The contract is therefore a kind of thought experiment, helping us to understand why we accept the restrictions of cooperative life and government. On the other hand, those political arrangements that could not be justified on the grounds of being like a fair contract are deemed to be illegitimate. If the officials or rulers in a state act in such a way that appears to violate a reasonable contract, they give up their right to rule.

In short, the ideas of contractualism arose from efforts to explain arrangements that were primarily political, rather than ethical. The ethical principle derived from this thinking is that if we were to deliberate as a society or social group on how we wished to be treated and how we should treat others, we would come to a similar kind of social contract. We would not want to be treated any worse than anyone else is, and we would therefore have to agree not to treat anyone else worse than we want to be treated. Morality therefore requires treating each person fairly rather than allowing differences in treatment, as in utilitarianism, aimed at some greater good for the group as a whole. The two major proponents of this sort of reasoning today are John Rawls and Thomas Scanlon, whose theories we will discuss next. A third contemporary major contractualist, or contractarian, is David Gauthier, who was a professor of philosophy at the University of Toronto in Canada for many years and then at the University of Pittsburgh.

Rawls: The Ethics of Social Justice

In the musical, *Oklahoma,* often performed by school groups, there is a rollicking number with the chorus beginning, "Oh, the farmer and the cowman should be friends." The plot, to the extent there is one, tells the story of a cowboy, Curly, and the beautiful farm girl, Laura, who of course fall in love and presumably live happily ever after. The song and the plot remind us of the major problem in any large, complex society: how people with different beliefs and backgrounds can get along and cooperate.

John Rawls, a distinguished professor of philosophy for many years at Harvard University, focused his efforts on this particular problem. After graduating from Princeton University in 1943, he served in the infantry in the Pacific, fighting against the Japanese in World War II. His experiences led him to conclude that some way must be found for people with different, strongly held systems of beliefs, such as religion, to collaborate peacefully in building a just society. Another philosopher says about Rawls, who died in 2002, that he is a person "whom it is now safe to describe as the most important political philosopher of the twentieth century."[14]

As so many others have done, Rawls devised a thought experiment to work out how to construct such a just society. He realizes that it is quite difficult for people, even when they are trying their best to be fair, to forget their real-life circumstances and put themselves into the place of someone else. To help us think about this problem, Rawls came up with what he calls *The Original Position.* In the first part of the original position, he imagines that there are people, fully rational and interested in doing as well for themselves as possible, essentially equals in their abilities of speech and reason. These people meet to work out the principles on which to build their society and their relationships in that society. As with the case of the social contract, it is assumed that these people can better meet their needs by cooperating than by doing it alone or by competing with each other.

The second part of the original position holds that these people do not know at the time of this discussion how they will be situated in their lives in the society. They do not know whether they will be male or female, Christian or Muslim or of some other religion or atheist, able-bodied or having some disability, rich or poor, and so on. As Rawls puts it, they are to be behind a *veil of ignorance* about what their actual lives will be like. Rawls came up with the idea of the veil of ignorance because he thought it would be a good way for people to imagine how to be genuinely impartial in thinking what the future arrangements of life should be. Picture yourself in this situation. Since you are rational and want the best for yourself, you will be careful to ensure that no one would be particularly disadvantaged, because that could affect you. You would not want to risk that the good things in life could be denied to any particular category of persons, since you could be in the jeopardized category. As a rational person, you would want to be sure that everyone had equal rights and access to equal justice.

This situation Rawls envisions is similar to the old story about two children, say a brother and sister, arguing over how to divide a piece of cake. One feels that if the other person does the cutting, he or she will make the cut so that he or she will get the bigger piece. The mother has a wise solution to end the bickering. One child is to do the cutting of the pieces and the other one gets to choose which piece to eat. You can be sure that the one doing the cutting will be especially careful to make the two pieces as equal as possible. In other words, a person divides the goods, in this case the cake, without knowing in advance which piece will be his or hers. That is the situation Rawls has in mind for the original position behind the veil of ignorance.

The third part of Rawls' conception of the original position deals with the inevitability of some inequality in the distribution of the wealth or other goods of the just society. He therefore introduces the *Difference Principle*. The difference principle allows him to suggest that there could be differences in the distribution of the good things in life. These inequalities can be justified only when they meet two conditions: they must work to the benefit of those most disadvantaged in the society; and, they may provide compensation for offices or positions, which are clearly open to anyone (no one can be precluded from holding such an office). Any other inequalities, such as in rights or liberties, must similarly be to the benefit of those who would otherwise be the worst off. Again, he assumes that rational people in the original position would prefer these principles in case they end up in one of the most disadvantaged or least well off groups.

In sum, Rawls' model for devising impartial principles for justice includes three main concepts:

1. People in the *original position*, to work out the principles of justice that will govern their lives (all are rational and of equal ability).
2. People behind the *veil of ignorance* about what role or position they will occupy in life.
3. Acceptance of the *difference principle*, allowing for some inequalities as long as they are to the benefit of the least well off or most disadvantaged.

How could we apply Rawls' principles to issues of communication practices? In Chapter 9, dealing with ethical communication and people with disabilities, we will see that once you place yourself in the original position, behind the veil of ignorance, you may think more carefully about how you communicate with another person who may have a disability, which you do not have. The exercise of the original position should force you to place yourself in the position of any other person you may harm or influence by your messages. When you consider withholding information from others, for example, the exercise should allow you to imagine how those other people feel about their being left in the dark.

A typical kind of relevant case could be that of a physician trying to decide whether to give an honest but grim prognosis to a patient. Many doctors, as well as other professionals, wrestle with just such problems. How would the doctor herself want the issue handled if, from behind the veil of ignorance, she did not know whether she was the doctor or the patient? The answer may not be clear, even then, because other factors should be weighed—the state of mind of the patient, the wishes of others such as family members, and so on. The idea is, however, that the exercise provides a useful way for a professional to think through the real issues involved in these kinds of decisions. Too often, it is easy to avoid unpleasantness by glossing over dire news one has to give. Placing oneself, hypothetically, in the original position becomes a way to focus on the viewpoints of others involved in the matter. In short, Rawls' method intends to highlight empathic reasoning about our ethical choices and their impact on other people.

Additionally, we feel that the theory put forth by Rawls is most applicable to situations involving public communication, such as political communication, organizational communication, mass communication, and the like. After all, he intended to construct principles for a just society, with emphasis on the principles of equal rights and a just distribution of goods and opportunities. For these reasons, Rawls' approach sheds the most light on procedures for determining the range and possible limits (if any) on freedom of speech and the press in society, on speech that not only tolerates but respects differences in beliefs, and on the nature of and fair practices in political, corporate, and religious communication. His position will therefore serve as a reference point for our later discussion of these genres of communication.

Scanlon and Reasonable Obligations to Others

A film we often use in our class on communication ethics is *The Emperor's Club*. This film describes the relationship between a beloved teacher of classics at a private prep school and a particularly troublesome student, the son of a prominent U.S. Senator. The teacher, Mr. Hundert, believes that he can redeem the rebellious, even obnoxious, student, named Sedgwick, by inducing him to study so that he can compete in the premier contest of the school—a sort of quiz show over Roman history. The students earning the three highest averages on a series of examinations will be contestants in the all-school event. The ploy seems to work as the student turns around and shows dramatic improvements in his test scores. He just barely misses the final cut, until Mr. Hundert reviews his paper a second time and decides to award it an A+ instead of an A−, thereby putting him in the contest, and excluding the student who would otherwise have been third. The student thus excluded is bitterly disappointed because his father had been a winner of the contest when he was at school and expected the same of his son. After many twists and turns, in which Mr. Hundert discovers sedgewick cheating during the contest in school and again in a later setup of the original contest at a reunion many years later, the teacher finds he must confront the student who would have been third and explain his actions.

Thomas Scanlon, in his important book, *What We Owe to Each Other*, suggests a method, in some ways similar to that of John Rawls, for thinking through ethical obligations we have in our interactions with other people.[15] He provides a way for thinking about the sort of situation Mr. Hundert confronted—how could one justify his actions to another person affected by those actions. One authority describes Scanlon's book as "surely one of the most sophisticated and important works of moral philosophy to have appeared in many years."[16] Scanlon suggests making ethical decisions in a way that the principles we follow could be justified to others so that they could have *no reasonable basis for objecting.* In other words, Scanlon envisions a thought experiment in which we find ourselves deciding whether a particular action is ethical or not. To carry out the experiment, we try to picture ourselves explaining and justifying the action we have decided to take to those other people affected by what we do. We can imagine there is something we would like to do, but realize we cannot really justify it to some other person affected by our action, because we know he or she could reasonably object to it. In such a case, we should conclude that the action might be wrong. If we can determine, however, that their objection really would not be reasonable, then the action would not appear to be wrong. In sum, Scanlon claims his notion of contractualism "holds that an act is wrong if its performance under the circumstances would be disallowed by any set of principles for the general regulation of behavior that no one could reasonably reject as a basis for informed, unforced general agreement."[17]

One of the differences between the approach devised by Scanlon and that of Rawls is that Scanlon does not place people behind a veil of ignorance in an original position. You are to picture yourself, just as you are, making your case to other people similarly real and embedded in their actual-life circumstances. Secondly, the principles that guided your decision are subject to their acceptance without serious, reasonable objection. Notice that Scanlon does not require that you all agree on acting in a certain way, but that at least no one involved can have a serious objection to the grounds for your action. They may choose to act differently in a similar case, but your approach is not ruled out on any reasonable basis, that is, on ethical grounds. A third difference between Rawls and Scanlon is that *What We Owe to Each Other* is more about morality or personal ethics than it is about politics.[18] As we have already noted, Rawls' theory seems more applicable to public communication than to interpersonal communication.

You no doubt notice that Scanlon uses the word *reasonable* to designate the kind of objections people may have to unethical behaviors rather than an alternative, such as *rational*. Scanlon believes that in our interactions with others the standard for judging our actions is their *reasonableness*. How does being reasonable differ from being rational? Rationality implies a cold calculation of the costs and benefits to an individual or group, but may not result in an action that another person might consider *reasonable*. Scanlon says for us to imagine that we are farmers involved in a debate about water rights in our county.[19] One landowner controls the major source of water in the vicinity, a river running right through his property. There is no rational reason that he need share with any of the rest of us. Still, the rest of us could object that he is not being *reasonable*. In our interaction with other people, there is an expectation of reasonability used in this sense. To live together in a just society, the landowner really should take into consideration the needs of fellow farmers, even though there is strictly no legal compunction to do so. In a sense, this is what ethics is about: doing something not because it is required but because it is the right thing to do. If we have no choice in our behavior, because of laws and other requirements, there is no ethical issue. Good reasons for justifying our ethical decisions, therefore, ought to be those that others could agree are reasonable, or are an acceptable way to behave (or, in Scanlon's formulation, they could have no reasonable *objection* to our behavior).

Let us see how Scanlon's formulation of a contractual way of reasoning affects our thinking about the ethics of communication. His method calls for a principle of *justifiability*. In deciding whether a particular communicative act was ethical or not (a proposition of value), we need to be able to justify to others that there are no grounds for reasonably rejecting it as ethical. When deciding how to act, we need to imagine having to explain or justify the reason for our act to all others potentially affected by that act. A second way to think about this method is to ask how we could publicly justify the action in front of others. Scanlon contends, "A moral person will refrain from lying to others, cheating, harming, or exploiting them, 'because these things are wrong.'"[20] Why are they wrong? Such behaviors, he believes, undermine the basis for our relations with other people. A person suffers a sense of loss—loss of unity, loss of pleasure and comfort in the support and community of other people—when he or she treats others in a way to which they could reasonably object.[21] The loss cannot be outweighed by some larger good for a majority—we justify our behavior to each person as an individual. Scanlon thus places his theory in opposition to utilitarianism. Harm to one person is not balanced by some general advantage.[22]

Living with other people—whether they are family members, friends, colleagues, fellow professionals, fellow workers, or whatever—implies accepting a social contract. Your duties to these other people spring from your obligations to maintain the standards of this implied agreement. Erving Goffman, one of the most important sociologists of the twentieth century, concentrated on the *rules* by which people communicate in relationships. Many of the rules of communication he discovered in his research are compatible with the reasoning followed by Scanlon. For example, he maintains that when we enter into interpersonal communication with another person, we assume an obligation of involvement or engagement. When we fail to do so, we become "alienated from interaction," in his terms.[23] From a contractualist point of view, this becomes an ethical obligation. Goffman also writes about the importance of maintaining one's own *face* in an interaction while protecting the *face* of the other person. In a sense, Goffman postulates we create a contractual relationship when we communicate with others. Successful face-to-face communication requires our knowing and following the rules of interaction. Scanlon adds the further notion that we should test the rightness or wrongness of how we meet the obligations of such relationships by thinking how we would justify our actions to the others involved.

Let us return to the situation the teacher, Hundert, confronted because of his original deception in the grades for the quizzes leading to the all-school prize. The facts of the case are that after completing the grading of the final examination, Hundert discovered his *special project*, the difficult student, had just missed placing third and getting into the contest. He raised the grade from an A− to an A+, which required merely drawing a vertical line through the minus sign already in ink next to the A on the test book cover. A question of fact would be whether he in fact reviewed the test itself and determined he had marked it incorrectly in assigning the original grade. We do not see him rereading the test book; after sitting back and pondering the circumstances, he changes the minus to a plus. It would appear, therefore, that the change was made arbitrarily, for reasons other than the actual quality of the exam answers. The student denied third place because of this action was a very sensitive boy, whose father had been a winner of the contest prize when he was a student. The boy appears in the next scene to be crushed by his failure to make the contest. We see that the result has caused him some pain.

To determine whether Hundert's action was right or wrong, from Scanlon's perspective, we begin by asking whether he could justify his action on a principle to which the aggrieved student could not object. What could such a principle be? Hundert might argue that the boy denied the place in the contest had many other opportunities to excel, in ways that were not available to Sedgwick. He may try to explain to the boy that Sedgwick had special needs that were somehow more important than his needs. We discover later that Mr. Hundert wrote for this boy a glowing recommendation letter instrumental to his admission to the U.S. Military Academy. Does this show that Mr. Hundert found other ways, perhaps more important ways, to boost the career and self-esteem of this student? We probably would reject this interpretation, because we have the suspicion that the recommendation could have been the result of guilt feelings stemming from the incident. Do time and the outcome diminish the hurt felt by the boy at the time of the incident? Again, this rationalization seems to deny the validity of the boy's feelings at the time. In the end, Mr. Hundert finds he cannot justify his action to the boy who was hurt, but can only ask for his forgiveness.

Highlights of Egalitarianism

This set of theories holds that the results of ethical actions depend on equitable, if not exactly equal, outcomes for all involved. In this way, these theories run counter to the basic principles of utilitarianism. The ideas behind these theories derive from the notion of contractualism, in which our obligations to others find their basis in a *social contract*. The contract is implied or hypothetical. To participate in social or political life we tacitly accept the rights and constraints implied.

Rawls' theory of social justice requires us to place ourselves in an original position, behind a veil of ignorance about what our station in life will be, to come to a consensus about what the rules for a just society would be. Because we are rational and self-interested, we will arrive at arrangements as fair as possible so that no one will have any arbitrary advantage over another. Any inequalities should be justified only to the extent they benefit those otherwise least well off. Ethical communication is hence that which accepts and treats all people equally, regardless of situation, race, religion, ethnicity, perceived disability, age, sex, appearance, or any other such characteristic.

Scanlon's principle for social life is that we can justify our behavior to others in such a way that they would have no reasonable grounds for objecting to what we did. The standard for justifying the rightness or wrongness of ethical behavior is reasonableness, rather than a standard such as rational calculation. A justification is reasonable to the extent that others will accept it as fair and considerate of the position and needs of others involved. Goffman and other communication theorists have noted the contractual obligations one assumes in entering into interpersonal communication with others. These obligations are similar to the grounds of ethical judgments formulated by Scanlon.

CASE STUDY: SURVEILLANCE AT SIZGIE CORPORATION

This case study asks you to consider the methods used by a fictitious corporation to discover whether competitors were making contact with some of their key employees. The communication issue lies in a decision not to disclose to the employees involved the steps taken to find out what people were talking about in supposedly private areas, although still on company property. As you read the facts of the case, think in terms of the tests for ethical communication provided by utilitarian theories and then by the egalitarian theories.

The upper management team of Sizgie Corporation had been worried for some time about contact between executive and professional staff members and competitors during work hours or on company property. In their industry, there tends to be high level of competition for the brightest and best professional staff and, consequently, there is a lot of turnover. People often move from one firm to another in the industry. In order to deal with this potential problem, the senior management team has had installed various electronic monitoring devices in the informal spaces used by employees. The reasoning behind locating the devices in these places is the assumption people may be more likely to let their guard down in such places. There are therefore secret monitoring devices in areas such as the following: exercise areas, locker rooms, and lounges, where people often use their cell phones for private calls.

This is not an unlikely scenario. Between two-thirds and three-fourths of all major corporations reportedly engage in monitoring or surveillance of employees and staff. Much of the electronic monitoring involves reading emails on company computers, using software to keep track of keystroke and internet browsing, listening in on phone conversations, storing and reviewing voice mail, as well as placing hidden video recorders in various places around the workplace. Miniaturization in electronics allows such video cameras to be extremely unobtrusive and often undetectable.

Senior management has learned, as well, that some of their strongest competitors have been using misleading offers, which occasionally are conveniently *forgotten* once the person has committed to one of these firms (and when it is too late for that person to take back their resignation from Sizgie). For this reason, management feels they have some responsibility to protect not only the corporation, and its maintaining of the best possible staff, but to protect staff members from these kinds of abuses. They justify to themselves their intrusion on their employees' privacy in this way.

If that were not enough, the senior management people also feel they have reason to believe that one of the firms has been slandering executives at Sizgie, implying they may have even engaged in criminal or civil improprieties. This belief leads them to think there is good reason for them to use the secret surveillance techniques to protect both themselves as well as the rest of the staff.

QUESTIONS FOR ANALYSIS OF THE CASE

1. How would you apply a utilitarian analysis to this case? Is the monitoring justified based on utilitarian considerations? Consider the question from the perspective of both act utilitarianism and rule utilitarianism. Where does the *greatest good* lie? Who is harmed, and who is helped?

2. Based on this analysis, should the management continue to keep the secret monitoring in place?

3. Consider the issue of secrecy itself: would it be all right to continue the monitoring as long as everyone was informed about it? How would full disclosure change the case, or would it?

4. Consider the case from the point of view of a contractualist analysis. Is any implied contract or agreement being violated?

5. Can one apply the principles of Rawls' original position and veil of ignorance to the case? What would the issues be following these principles? Would your judgment of the ethics of the secret surveillance be different from your conclusions based on utilitarianism?

6. Describe how Scanlon would approach this case. Can the secret surveillance be justified to all involved without anyone having a *reasonable* objection to the principle of the surveillance?

Chapter Summary

When does the end justify the means, if ever? From the perspectives of character and duties, one does not consider the results, the ends. When using consequences to judge the ethics of an action, the ends become central.

The most famous of the consequentialist theories of ethics is utilitarianism, based on the principle of achieving the greatest good for the greatest number. Although the early utilitarians, such as Bentham, had hoped to find a quantifiable, concrete basis for the *greatest good*, achieving this goal has been elusive, and probably must remain so. Mill therefore preferred a qualitative definition of the *greatest good*, emphasizing the *higher* pleasures of rationality. Many people attempting to use a utilitarian calculation for making ethical decisions tend to forget that in counting the number of people affected, everyone is to count equally and the same.

When act utilitarianism seemed to lead to undesirable outcomes, such as irreparably harming a few for the benefit of the many, some utilitarians turned to the alternative of rule utilitarianism. The question then became whether the application of the rule used in a particular case did benefit the greatest number when that rule was used in other cases. Ultimately, it became clear that there was a nagging subjectivity about judgments made concerning the good and the greatest number, even under Rule Utilitarianism.

Some writers, notably Ayn Rand in the twentieth century, have put forth ethical egoism as a more plausible form of consequentialism in ethics. In ethical egoism, the ethical thing to do is what is in the self-interest of the individual, without regard for the effect on others. Few philosophers have accepted this position, partly because of the lack of clarity regarding exactly what rational, best self-interest means. Ethical altruism seems to suffer from the same limitations.

Instead of maximizing the good for the majority or the greatest number, egalitarian theories emphasize the worth of each individual. Each person is valuable and therefore all should be treated fairly or nearly equally. The two most famous programs under these contractualist theories are those of the philosophers John Rawls and Thomas Scanlon. Both of their systems rely on a hypothetical situation for working out rationally what is accepted as fair to each person concerned. Rawls' theory is especially suitable for thinking about social and public issues of justice and fairness. Scanlon tries to work out a system for determining what each person owes to another in mutual interaction. The contractualist theories posit the implied existence and acceptance of a set of rules for communication and interaction. When we engage in relationships with other people, we are considered rational and effective when we show that we are aware of and competent in the use of such rules. Following these rules of interaction, hence, is a mark of ethical competence as well.

QUESTIONS AND TOPICS FOR DISCUSSION

1. Most people consider that they practice some form of utilitarianism in thinking through their actions. Do you agree with this statement? Are the results of behavior all that really matter? If things work out the best for nearly everyone involved, regardless of the intent, is that a problem?

2. Consider the approaches for thinking about ethical behavior advanced by Rawls and by Scanlon. Does either of them seem practical? How could you use one or the other technique for making ethical decisions?

3. Think of the implications of ethical egoism. Does the system of private enterprise and economics assume people should be motivated solely by self-interest? What do you think about the claim by Gordon Gecko that *Greed is good* in the film *Wall Street*? In the final analysis, is he right? Can we be expected to behave in any other way than to put our own needs first? Are there instances when you have put (or feel you should have put) the interests of others ahead of your own?

4. Consider the case of the doctor having to face a patient who does not have a very hopeful prognosis. What do the various theories covered in this chapter suggest as guidance for how the doctor should proceed in talking to the patient about this situation?

NOTES

1. ESPN.com web site, "Denver coach lied about Plummer's injury," at http://sports.espn.go.com/nfl/news/story (accessed July 20, 2004).

2. *Dealing seconds* means dealing the card second from the top, rather than the top card, as a way of gaining an advantage over another player.

3. Alasdair MacIntyre, *A Short History of Ethics*, 2nd ed. (Notre Dame, IN: University of Notre Dame Press, 1998), p. 234.

4. John Stuart Mill, *Utilitarianism, Liberty, and Representative Government*, intro. by A. D. Lindsay (New York: E. P. Dutton & Co., 1951, orig. pub. 1861), p. 8.

5. Mill, *Utilitarianism*, p. 10, emphasis in the original; *recognise* is the British spelling.

6. See Abraham Maslow, *Motivation and Personality* (New York: Harper, 1954).

7. Mill, *Utilitarianism*, p. 12.

8. *The Washington Post* online, "John N. Mitchell, Principal in Watergate, Dies at 75," at www.washingtonpost.com/wpsrv/national/longterm/watergate/stories/michobit.htm (accessed July 22, 2004); story dated November 10, 1988.

9. *Internet Encyclopedia of Philosophy*, "Ayn Rand," at www.utm.edu/research/iep/r/rand.htm.

10. Ayn Rand, *Introducing Objectivism* (Objectivism Home Page, 1962), at www.anyrand.org/objectivism/io,html (accessed July 6, 2004).

11. Robert K. Greenleaf and Larry C. Spears, *The Power of Servant Leadership: Essays* (San Franciscon: Barrett-Koehler Publishers, 1998).

12. *The Mayflower Compact*, at the Avalon Center at Yale Law School, web site, updated spelling, www.yale.edu/lawweb/avalon/amerdoc/mayflower.htm (accessed July 27, 2004).

13. The term *contractarianism* is also used, but often refers more to the political philosophy, especially that associated with the British Seventeenth-century philosopher, Thomas Hobbes.

14. Thomas Nagel, "Justice, Justice, Shalt Thou Pursue: The rigorous compassion of John Rawls," in *The New Republic Online*, 1999, at www.thenewrepublic.com/archives/1099/102599.

15. T. M. Scanlon, *What We Owe to Each Other* (Cambridge, MA: Harvard University Press, 1998).

16. R. Jay Wallace, "Scanlon's Contactualism," *Ethics* (2002), 112, 429.

17. Scanlon, *What We Owe*, p. 153.

18. Thomas Nagel, *One-to-One*, London Review of Books online, 1999, at www.lrb.co.uk/v21/no3/nage01.html (accessed October 3, 2002).

19. Scanlon, *What We Owe*, pp. 192–193, describes this example.

20. Scanlon, *What We Owe*, p. 162.

21. Scanlon, *What We Owe*, pp. 165–166.

22. Nagel, *One-to-One*, 1999.

23. Erving Goffman, *Interaction Ritual: Essays on Face-to-Face Behavior* (Garden City, NJ: Anchor Books, 1967).

5 Relationships

The *Game*: Survivor

At the height of the popularity of television *Reality TV*, the concluding episode of a series called *Survivor All-Stars* featured a debriefing conversation among all of the competitors. On stage were not only the winners of the contest, but also every contestant who had previously been eliminated ("The Tribe Has Spoken," as the host liked to proclaim.) This season's finale had a new twist, however, in that the woman who finished first and the man who finished second due largely to their *alliance* throughout the series had just announced their upcoming wedding to the national audience.

The cast's on-air discussion eventually focused on the tactics used by the man who finished second. What seemed to upset many of the other contestants was how he entered *alliances* with several of them, only to break those agreements when the time for voting contestants off the show rolled around. Many of the contestants expressed feelings of betrayal and anger and felt they had been manipulated and lied to by the runner-up, who was simply doing whatever he could to advance his own interests.

Finally, when everyone had expressed their opinions, the man on the *hot seat* declared that he had indeed made alliances that he did not ever intend to keep. And, yes, he did in fact lie to others in order to promote his own chances of surviving. Of course he sabotaged trusts and set others up to be voted out of the competition. "It's a *game*," he declared. "I got to the Final Two because I played the game better than anyone else. It's not real life, people. It's a *game*!" Some of the other contestants nodded in agreement with this assessment. Others remained miffed about the way they were treated. The man's fiancée, who actually won the big money in part due to her strong alliance to her newfound love, did not comment on her fiancée's lying or breaking agreements. We wonder if somewhere in the back of her mind lurked a concern that the ease in which this man could lie or break covenants might one day spill over into her upcoming marriage to him.

The notion of *Playing the Game* introduces the possibility that lying and deception are acceptable if not necessary when advancing one's own interests. And, it's just not on Reality TV where these tools are used, either. Recall from Chapter 1 the advice one of our seniors gave to another senior who was in a quandary about whether she should withhold from a prospective employer the fact that she intended to work only for one year and then go to graduate school, even though she knew the company wanted someone who would be on the job much longer. "You *lie*," he advised. "It's how the Game is played." Many other classmates nodded in agreement. Playing the *Game* is the way we get ahead. It's how we gain an advantage over others. The further away we get from direct interaction, the easier it is to play the *Game*. Email, text messaging, and voicemail have made it much easier for us to be less than direct in our dialogue with others. We often *talk* with our keyboards, Palm Pilots, and Blackberries rather than in direct, eye-to-eye proximity, where we have to be fully *present* to the other person.

Many prefer playing the *Game* of indirect, nonintimate, impersonal communication over the more direct, honest, and personal dialogue-driven interactions. It seems far easier to manipulate people or situations than it is to *engage* them honestly and openly. "Games are sandwiched, as it were, between pastimes and intimacy," wrote psychiatrist Eric Berne in his 1964 bestseller *Games People Play*, in which he continues:

> Intimacy requires stringent circumspection . . . in order to get away from the ennui of pastimes without exposing themselves to the dangers of intimacy, most people compromise for games when they are available, and these fill the major part of the more interesting hours of social intercourse.[1]

People may believe it much safer to play the *Game*. Intimacy requires our presence and full attention to another person. In a truly intimate relationship, the methods we use to communicate are far more important than whether our personal, individual needs are advanced. When we play games, the outcome is settled by a *winner* and a *loser*. In a committed relationship, it is the process and not the outcome that matters. How we talk to and with each other is the heart of dialogical ethics.

Dialogical Ethics

The previous chapters show that we can view communication ethics through many theoretical lenses. In addition, we find that many colleges and universities offer courses on ethics in virtually every area of academic discipline. It is common in academia to offer courses in medical ethics, business ethics, and ethics of law, among others. Some colleges and universities have developed programs of Ethics-Across-the-Curriculum in which every student must have some ethics education. Many of these ethical systems are built on the foundations of psychological or biological development of the individual, or the socio-political or religious framework of the community or society. In this chapter we will show that *dialogical ethics* provides an excellent way to understand ethics from an experiential, everyday point of view. In other words, our personal ethics are formed by, and demonstrated in, the ways in which we *dialogue* with others.

Dialogical ethics is a system in which ethics can be judged by the attitudes and behaviors demonstrated by each participant in a communication transaction. Key to this definition is the willingness and ability of each participant to surrender (during the communication event) self-interest in favor of experiencing the views, beliefs, and convictions of the other. One is not required to forego one's own beliefs or values, but one must be willing not to promote one's own attitudes or views while involved in a communication transaction. Each person in a dialogical exchange is accepted as equal, unique, and having value and worth.

In face-to-face interaction one participant is tempted to use words and actions to mislead the other person. What we mean by *dialogue* in this section is different from this manipulative and often competitive sort of conversational transaction. The old adage, "Words are meant to conceal as well as to reveal" is particularly applicable to this form of communication masquerading as dialogue. At our Friday night poker game, I may look you squarely in the eyes and say to you, "I'll see your quarter and raise you fifty cents," hoping to persuade you that my hand is superior to yours. In fact, I may have a certain losing hand. But if my words convey enough confidence and strength to cause you to *fold*, then my *bluff* was effective interaction and I gained from it.

When people engage in face-to-face interaction outside of structured games as if it were ideal dialogue to advance their own interests, others may feel hurt and betrayed, as we demonstrated in the *Survivor* example.

Think about an important relationship in which you are involved. Perhaps your best friend comes to mind, or maybe you think of a boyfriend or girlfriend with whom you can say anything. Maybe it's a parent, spouse, or trusted older person with whom you have such a relationship. In this mental exercise, ask yourself how you know for certain that you can trust this person. How can you be sure they aren't playing the *Game* with you to advance a personal agenda? This special person may play the *Game* every day in his or her business life. He or she might not hesitate to be less than forthcoming with a colleague or customer or another student, but you just *know* that he or she is always honest with you. How does this happen?

Our understanding of dialogue applies to not just interpersonal relationships but to virtually every other type of communication we do. As we will demonstrate throughout this book, dialogical ethics apply to political, religious, health, and most other areas in which people communicate with each other.

Dialogical ethics provides us a *Firewall* to ensure that, no matter how our loved one may treat others in his or her daily activities, when it comes to our relationship, the *Game* ends and intimacy becomes the foundation of who we are together. As we will illustrate, it is that *Firewall* that both protects us and allows us to trust our communication with others.

An Ethical *Firewall*

We believe that the *Game* ends at *I and Thou*. The use of the phrase *I and Thou* evokes the theories of Martin Buber, one of the leading theorists of dialogical ethics. Simply put, it is intimacy that provides our most important relationships with the *Firewall* between the self-promoting *Games* and the self-sacrificing dialogue, in which there is a desire to be attentive to and present for each other. We are secure in the knowledge that there may be that one person in our lives with whom we can speak what is in our hearts without fear of rejection or judgment. We know that at the end of the day there will be a moment when we set aside the frustrations of our own day's experiences and make ourselves fully present to someone else as they tell us about theirs. We know, because we have committed to the other that no matter how we respond to the world in our daily interactions, with each other our style of response is *different*. With each other, communication is unguarded. With each other, our dialogue is free and unrestricted.

"In dialogue, we penetrate behind the polite superficialities and defenses in which we habitually armor ourselves," claims public opinion expert Daniel Yankelovich. "We listen and respond to one another with an authenticity that forges a bond between us."[2]

Not only does dialogue forge a bond between people, it becomes the *Firewall* that ensures us that the *Game* of daily activities and interactions has been suspended. We will examine this *Firewall* from four different twentieth-century perspectives as we dig more deeply into the grounds of dialogical ethics.

We began this section with a reference to *I and Thou*. Many theologians and ethicists will instantly recognize this reference to Martin Buber's foundational work on the nature of dialogue and relationships. Imagine a world in which we were free, unrestricted, and completely open in our dialogue with others. What if everyone were unfettered in his or her dialogue with everyone else? Chaos! Dialogical ethics is hence quite unlike the other systems of ethics we have discussed. We suggest dialogical ethics is more than an interpersonal relationships principle, but that it also functions as an effective means to end the *Game* of self-promotion to engage to the fullest possible level the person Buber describes as *Thou*, and Emmanuel Levinas calls the *Other*.

Foundations of Dialogical Ethics

Martin Buber: *I and Thou*

In an historic meeting between two great dialogical theorists, Martin Buber made this simple yet profound statement to Carl Rogers, "I think no human being can give more than this. Making life possible for the other, if only for a moment."[3] This brings us to the theories of Buber, born into an Austrian Jewish family in Vienna in 1878. He found his spiritual journey took him through both Zionism (the movement to return Jews to their homeland, Israel) and Hasidism (a mystical Orthodox Jewish movement which began in the 1700s in Eastern Europe). Eventually, he settled on the study of relationships of people with people as well as their relationship to the world around them. Buber was a professor of Jewish and Religious Studies in Frankfurt, Germany, after World War I, but fled to Jerusalem when the Nazis took power in Germany in the 1930s. It was there that Buber began to write intensely about dialogical communication and interpersonal relationships.

Buber's foundational work in dialogical relationships is the classic *I and Thou* (*Ich und Du*, 1923). Buber maintained there is a significant difference between engaging the world, and manipulating it for one's own ends:

> The capricious man does not believe and encounter. He does not know association; he only knows the feverish world out there and his feverish desire to use it. We only have to give use an ancient, classical name, and it walks among the gods. When he says You, he means: You, my ability to use! And what he calls his destiny is merely an embellishment of and a sanction for his ability to use.[4]

Buber's use of the phrase "his feverish desire to use it" is significant historically.

Remember that Buber fled Germany during the rise of Adolph Hitler and the Nazi Party. Buber saw firsthand the *feverish* world of his time, and must have been dismayed and frightened by the *feverish desire* of the Nazis to use the world for their own purposes.

For Buber, the ways we engage in dialogue (the turning to one another in truth, without need to forward one's own agenda, and with complete regard for the *other*) with each other, with our world, and with God encompass all of human experience. According to Buber, a person adopts two approaches to the world: *I–Thou*, or *I–It*. In the *I–It* relationship, we perceive others as objects. That is, one views oneself not as a part of a unified creation, but rather as one set apart from that creation and viewing others as differentiated from him or her. For example, a student who views members of a certain fraternity as *all jocks* or a sorority as *all party girls* is objectifying these individuals and adopting the *I–It* position. In conversation with another person, when one focuses more on one's own thoughts and feelings, or if one is not fully listening to what is being said by the other, one is not engaging them in an *I–Thou* manner, but in the form of *I–It*. The individual is *standing apart* from the other person rather than *leaning in* toward him or her, Buber would say.

On many occasions, when we argue with another person, we use the time when the other is talking to strategize how we will respond once he or she stops. When that happens, it really doesn't matter what he or she is saying. What matters is how we will counter his or her points, and strengthen our own. That is typical *I–It* dialogue. It's not necessarily a bad way of communicating, and it's sometimes fun to outduel the other person in an argument. But such dialogue is not conducive to relationship building. It is designed to promote one's own wishes, plans, or opinions. By contrast, if we were to spend the time actually listening and encouraging the feelings and opinions of the other person instead of planning our next response while he or she is speaking, we would be approaching the *I–Thou* concept of dialogue.

One can easily understand that there are many instances when a simple *I–It* dialogue is not only acceptable, but preferable. One could argue that most everyday conversations are not designed for full *engagement* with the other person. When one places an order at a fast-food restaurant, or requests directions to a classroom from a stranger in the hall, there is no reason to engage in dialogue that is anything other than purpose driven. Such dialogue is meant to be fast with no need to fully attend to the other.

Implications of Buber's Ethics of Dialogue.   In our sound byte–driven world, where quick and impersonal communication is so often used, many people do not want to engage in any meaningful dialogue with one another, either face-to-face or in less direct modes. It has reached the point that one who sees LOL, or BBL, or SWF23, or 3BR2BALoft, instantly translates what has been said and that is all the engagement one needs. Sports and talk radio thrive on *smack talk* where fans of one team are *called out* and *trashed* by fans of another. Communication then becomes the *Game* that has been discussed earlier in this chapter.

While the *I–It* approach to dialogue is common and easy to achieve, dialogical ethicists believe this approach exacts a tremendous price from us, leading us to become the sort of people we would not want to be. In objectifying and marginalizing others, we lose the ability and opportunity to become intimately engaged with people around us. Buber, as a theologian, believed that such dialogue is even moving humankind further from God. If the *I–It* approach represents an ethical "means to an end" stance, then there needs to be a dialogue that is an end in itself. When we relate to a *Thou* in *It* terms, we invite all kinds of misunderstandings, hurt, and deceit into a relationship that has value and meaning to us. One only has to experience losing the trust of the other because of a lie to understand the devastating results of using an *I–It* approach to a Thou.

Earlier in this chapter we made the statement that the *Game* ends with *I and Thou*. Unlike the subject-versus-object approach in the *I–It* relationship, *I–Thou* is the deeper, more intimate, way in which subject converses with subject. In Buber's view, all of human existence is defined by the way we dialogue with one another and with God. In the *I and Thou* position, we relate and dialogue with the other as a complete being, rather than as an objectified person for whom we notice the features, peculiarities, or small details. Your relationship with that important person you pictured earlier, a relationship that encourages unfiltered, unedited dialogue, is representative of the *I and Thou* position.

Essentially, this perspective requires that we treat the other person as someone wholly unique. This person does not represent any sort of *type*. When we categorize someone (even to say the other person is *he* or *she*), we have placed them in a category with other people and therefore are no longer treating them as a completely unique person, completely unlike any other person.

The ethics *Game*, as we have described it so far cannot be played on the *I–Thou* field. The *Game* ends at that point, because the nature of our relationship in an *I—Thou* mode demands that I neither seek any gain for myself nor suspect that you are doing the same. Even this brief and rather cursory journey into the thoughts of Martin Buber should indicate to us that while we may understand the concept of communicating from an *I–Thou* perspective, it is not always easy to do so.

The requirement that one shed one's ego, personal needs, and individual desires to communicate ethically with another person is difficult and demanding. Other theorists who recognized the importance of dialogical ethics can help us better understand how to engage others in meaningful and ethical dialogue. One such theorist was a psychotherapist named Carl Rogers, a younger contemporary of Buber.

Carl Rogers: Unconditional Positive Regard

> . . . it seems to me that . . . when another person is really expressing himself
> and his experience and so on, I don't feel . . . different from him. That is . . .
> I feel as though in that moment his way of looking at his experience, distorted
> as it might be, is something I can look upon as having equal authority, equal
> validity with the way I see life and experience. And it seems to me that that
> really is the basis of helping . . . [5]

Born in 1902, Rogers was initially trained in theology at Union Theological Seminary in New York, but his career as a psychotherapist gave him
his fame. Rogers believed in a *nondirective* style of therapy, in which the
therapist was to be *fully present* to the patient, allowing the patient to truly
and openly express his or her own pain, feelings, desires, and so on. Instead
of analyzing and explaining the meaning of a client's feelings when he or
she might say, "I am feeling terribly depressed and lonely lately," Rogers
might simply reflect the statement back to the client. "You're struggling
with feelings of depression, and feel that there is no one there for you." This
dialogue, Rogers advocated, permitted the client to then elaborate on those
feelings rather than having to respond to the interpretations of the therapist. Contrary to the generally accepted traditions of therapy up to that
time, in which the therapist carefully guided the patient to ends the therapist thought helpful, Rogers allowed the patient to deal with what he or she
considered important, and at his or her own pace.

Thus was *Client-Centered* therapy, a term associated with what became
widely known as *Rogerian Therapy*, born. Rogers reveals some striking
similarities to Buber's *I–Thou* approach to relationships. By making the
doctor–patient relationship a mutually respectful, mutually responsible
partnership, Rogers saw the healing value in a setting in which neither person was playing a *Game*, advancing hidden or self-serving agenda. While
this approach to therapy was popular in the 1970s and 1980s, insurance
issues affecting long-term therapy and a general shift in the delivery of psychotherapy eventually caused what became known as *Rogerian Therapy*
to give way to a more strategic, systemic, interventional, and prescriptive
approach to psychotherapy. But what Rogers gave to the field of therapy, as
well as to the study of communication ethics, is the belief that *Unconditional
Positive Regard* is the most ethical form of dialogue between people. To
give a client or any other person our full, caring, undivided attention without judging or evaluating them is the key to reaching our full potential as
human beings. Rogers believed that any form of conversation that permits
others to have different values, different beliefs, different feelings, or different goals than I might have is a powerful and healing approach to communicating ethically.

Carl Rogers was a major contributor to the field of communication
ethics. In the field of psychotherapy, Rogers is considered to be the most

influential psychotherapist of the twentieth century. He was responsible for revolutionary ways of conducting the practice of therapy. For example, it was Rogers who introduced the term *client* when referring to the person whom he was treating. Until that time, people in therapy were considered *patients*. Rogers was the first person to record and publish complete cases of psychotherapy, and was the first to assert that clients needed to give their permission to be recorded in therapy.

Rogers is best known for principles of Congruence (honesty and genuineness), Empathy (feeling *with*, not *for*, the other), and Respect (unconditional positive regard). Rogers was known as a bit of a rebel in the therapy field, and he received a great deal of notoriety for his belief that the *experience* of relating to the other, rather than strategy or treatment plans, is what is transforming. "Neither the Bible nor the prophets; neither Freud nor research; neither the revelations of God nor man can take precedence over my own direct experience," wrote Rogers.[6] In this experience, dialogical ethics suggests, the true nature of *being present to the other* begins.

Clearly, Rogers' person (or client)-centered approach to therapy relies on dialogical ethics. As with Martin Buber, and as we will explore next with Emmanuel Levinas, at the heart of Rogers' *experiential* approach to therapy is the act of subjugating the therapist's agenda to the unconditional acceptance of the other.

> The counselor says in effect, 'To be of assistance to you I will put aside myself–the self of ordinary interaction–and enter into your world of perception as completely as I am able. I will become, in a sense, another self for you–an alter ego of your own attitudes and feelings–a safe opportunity for you to discern yourself more clearly, to experience yourself more truly and deeply, to choose more significantly.'[7]

The success and popularity of the Rogerian style of therapy is due to several factors. Clients tended to appreciate being clients, and not patients. Just the change in terminology gave to many the sense that the therapist is working with and not on them. The dialogue between therapist and client was ethical in that the focus was on the client's agenda, and not the therapist's. In the ideal Rogerian therapy, the client might often experience an *I–Thou* relationship rather than the *I–It* nature of the doctor–patient model. In addition, many therapists became *Rogerian* because they appreciated the sense of being liberated from the constraints of interpretation and analysis before knowing the client and the need to be directive in therapy sessions. Ethically, many Rogerian therapists believe, it is better to empower the client to explore his or her own psychodynamics than it is to manipulate the client to accept the therapist's analysis or diagnosis.

Both Buber and Rogers regard dialogical ethics from both theological and therapeutic perspectives. We now shift our focus to the discussion of dialogical ethics from the perspective of one of the most influential twentieth-century philosophers to write on the subject of ethics. Emmanuel Levinas believed that what we have described as this *Firewall* from the ethical *Game* is anchored in the way we communicate with the *Other.*

Emmanuel Levinas: The *Other*

> But behold! The emergence, in the life lived by the human being (and it is here that the human, as such, begins–pure eventuality, but from the start an eventuality that is pure and holy), of the devoting-of-oneself-to-the-other. In the general economy of being in its inflection back upon itself, a preoccupation with the other, even to the point of sacrifice, even to the possibility of dying for him or her; a responsibility for the other. Otherwise than being! It is this shattering of indifference–even if indifference is statistically dominant–this possibility of one-for-the-other, that constitutes the ethical event.[8]

This quotation reveals the passion and the fire that underscore Levinas' beliefs. Born in Lithuania in 1906, and becoming a French citizen in 1930, Levinas studied phenomenology in his early twenties under Edmund Husserl and Martin Heidegger (twentieth-century German philosophers who were pioneers in the study of *phenomenology,* a twentieth-century philosophical movement dedicated to describing the structures of experiences as they present themselves to consciousness, without recourse to theory, deduction, or assumptions from other disciplines such as the natural sciences). In other words, phenomenology refers to the approaching of an issue with no predetermined philosophical system to influence the one who approaches. His first major publications appeared when he was twenty-four, and he was an important resource for the influential French existentialist philosopher Jean-Paul Sartre. In the 1950s Levinas began his work on ethics, influenced in part by the work of Buber, basing his theories on what he called the *face-to-face* relation with the *Other.*

The above powerful and passionate quotation is pretty easy for us to understand in light of our own relationships. We remember that dialogical ethics requires a willingness to sacrifice the forwarding of our own agenda for the sake of the other person. How many times have we heard someone say, "I love him (or her) so much, I would die for him (or her)?" For Levinas, ethics does not reside in a universal set of *oughts* (Kant) or in the will of God (divine command.) Rather, Levinas posited that ethics begins first and foremost in person-to-person contact. Not only are we to respect, and pay attention to, the other person, believed Levinas; we are to indeed become *preoccupied* (or in Rogers' terminology, *setting aside oneself*) with that other being. When such preoccupation is not present, the *other* may begin to feel a void or gap in the relationship. The following may be an all-too-familiar example of how this might happen.

Tammy and Jeff, students whom both of us taught in a few classes, met in their junior year of college. After dating exclusively for a few months, Jeff proposed marriage after graduation. Inseparable during their senior year, Tammy and Jeff shared everything with each other. Jeff was even heard to say that he would "give everything I have to make Tammy happy." The couple wed a few weeks after graduation and moved to another state so that Jeff could begin graduate work. We lost contact with the couple until early winter of that same year, when Tammy dropped by the university office during a visit back home to see her family. After some preliminary conversation, we asked her how things were going with Jeff. "Jeff has changed," said Tammy. "It's like he's forgotten how to listen anymore. When I talk to him about my day, it's like he's just waiting for me to finish so that he can get on with his day. And when I try to tell him about problems I'm having with whatever, he comes back with how bad *his* problems are. He talks about everything to his friends at school, and it's like he's tired of talking by the time he comes home. Meanwhile, I've met this guy at work who actually *wants* to know what I'm thinking, and who is always asking how I am. I need that right now, you know?"

The difficulty with dialogical ethics, given its constant emphasis on the needs of the other, is that it has to be maintained, according to Levinas. It's not enough to be preoccupied with the other occasionally, or when we have the energy or inclination to do so. For Buber, Rogers, and Levinas, dialogical ethics is based on a *life stance* that requires us to respond to the other in a consistent and sacrificial manner. This is where Jeff in the above story has slipped up. His engagement of Tammy's *Otherness* worked very well in their courtship period. She fell in love with him because of that. And, when she perceived he was no longer engaging her in that way, she felt a sense of longing for the way things used to be. The danger to this relationship, of course, is that Tammy met another man who gave the appearance of being willing to engage her in the manner that Jeff once did.

As Levinas discovered in his work, the more one sacrifices oneself for the other, the more he or she becomes preoccupied with the other, the more we realize that the other has some power over us. "To recognize the Other is therefore to come to him across the world of possessed things, but at the same time to establish, by gift, community and universality," wrote Levinas. "Language is universal because it is the very passage from the individual to the general, because it offers things which are mine to the Other. To speak is to make the world common, to create commonplaces."[9] The dialogue between me and the *Other* is the intentional sharing of the gifts of acceptance and mutuality. Ethical dialogue, Levinas would argue, creates a common ground on which there is no recognition of status or balances of power.

Perhaps the loss of a sense of *I–Thou* is what happened to Tammy and Jeff. Perhaps, as their world expanded dramatically after the *bubble* existence of college life, Jeff began to offer his *gifts* to multiple *others* instead of just to Tammy, and the commonality of their shared life was lessened for her.

For Levinas, dialogical ethics is a matter of responsibility to the other. A careful look at the word *responsibility* illustrates what Levinas means. Our conversations with the *Thou* (Buber's term) requires a *response-ability*, calling us to set aside ego and power, and to see ourselves in the *other*. It gives us a common place (Levinas) that permits us to engage someone else in the most ethical of ways. In that common place the ethical *Game* no longer is played.

Buber's *Thou*, Roger's *Unconditional Positive Regard*, and Levinas' *Other* reveal a significant common theme in our study of dialogical ethics. In theology, psychology, and philosophy, these theories represent the transformative power of communicating ethically. Before presenting a case for your consideration, we will visit one more ethical arena where dialogical ethics are valued. We will explore a significant contributor to the field of education who was a strong advocate for dialogical ethics.

Paulo Freire: The Ethics of Empowerment

> Through dialogue, the teacher-of-the-students and the students-of-the-teacher cease to exist and a new term emerges: teacher-student with students-teachers. The teacher is no longer merely the one-who-teaches, but one who is himself taught in dialogue with the students, who in turn while being taught also teach.[10]

Paulo Freire, the Brazilian educator and contemporary of Buber, Rogers, and Levinas, left an indelible mark on educational practices. The word *dialogue* appears twice in this quotation from his landmark work, *Pedagogy of the Oppressed,* published in 1970. When we dig more deeply into Freire's philosophy of education, we quickly discover his kinship with the other dialogical ethicists discussed in this chapter. Freire believed learning should be a dialogical, or conversational, process between student and teacher. Dialogue, Freire argued, requires respect between one person and another. Education involves people working *with* each other, rather than acting *on* each other. From early grade school through university and even graduate work, we tend to gravitate toward those teachers who know how to talk with us rather than lecture at us. We are able to understand difficult subject matter or concepts more readily if the teacher shows us respect and is willing to dialogue with us about the material.

One colleague of ours recently lamented that he was born much too late. How he would have loved the way higher education used to be in the *good old days*, students rising to their feet as the professor entered the classroom, and them sitting in their seats and saying nothing unless asked directly by the professor. He said he would have loved lecturing for an hour, challenging the students to figure things out for themselves instead of begging him for answers. And then, when class was over, he wanted the students again to rise in applause as he gathered his notes and exited the classroom. Fortunately, only a few still long for those antiquated days when teachers talked, and students shut up and listened. Our colleague probably prefers the method of *acting on* his students rather than *engaging with* them. Today's classrooms are much more fluid and interactive, where the most effective education occurs in the give-and-take between faculty and students.

Freire believed that dialogue is a cooperative activity, at the heart of which was mutual respect. This stance requires a genuine caring for the student on the part of the educator. In what sounds a lot like *Thou* language (Buber), Freire wrote, "My openness to caring for the well-being of my students has to do with my openness to life itself, to the joy of living."[11] This caring, believed Freire, was the way in which the teacher shows respect to students, engendering respect in return. Freire provides us with a nice foreshadowing of an *Ethics of Care*, which we will discuss in detail in Chapter 6. As Freire might explain to our *born-in-an-earlier-century* colleague, true respect is not manifested in the applause of students, or in the public display of courteous manners. Rather, true respect and hence true education lie in the nature of the relationship between teacher and student, in the commonality of respect. Respect and caring, according to Freire, were demonstrated in the dialogue between the parties.

Freire, like Buber, Rogers, and Levinas, advocated an ethical system of dialogue with others. Our summary of these four philosophies illustrates a common thread in dialogical ethics. Buber, a German Jew, developed dialogical ethics in his concept of "*I–Thou*." Rogers, an American psychotherapist, called it *Unconditional Positive Regard*. For Levinas, a French philosopher, giving oneself to the *Other* was the foundation of dialogical ethics. In the mind of the Brazilian educator, Freire, dialogue is not only sound educational practice; it is—in his own words—liberating:

> It is to the reality which mediates men, and to the perception of that reality held by educators and people, that we must go to find the program content of education. The investigation of what I have termed the people's 'thematic universe'—the complex of their 'generative themes'—inaugurates the dialogue of education as the practice of freedom. The methodology of that investigation must likewise be dialogical, affording the opportunity both to discover generative themes and to stimulate people's awareness in regard to these themes. Consistent with the liberating purpose of dialogical education, the object of the investigation is not persons (as if they were anatomical fragments), but rather the thought—language with which men and women refer to reality . . . [12]

As we think about the *Game* discussed throughout this text, we might understand that Buber, Rogers, Levinas, and Freire are providing a *Firewall* from the lies, deceptions, and self-serving behavior in our daily relationships and interactions. When we dialogue with the *Other* (Levinas)—or *Thou* in Buber's terms—we are leaving the *Game* and its potentially destructive consequences, and are instead participating in that rarest of relationships: the *engagement* of another person in honest and selfless dialogue.

Practicing engagement, present-ness, self-sacrificial relationships, and game-free dialogue is not easy to do, however. Even people we trust to listen to us and to be honest with us sometimes let us down. Were dialogical ethics easy to do, we wouldn't have all the books (including this one) and theories trying to explain the concept. Dialogical ethics may be easy to understand on paper, yet much more difficult to master in our daily lives. Even well-meaning friends or loved ones may think they are being *present* to us, but in fact they may be relating to us out of their own *agenda* when we communicate with them. We began this chapter with a discussion of the *Reality TV* series *Survivor*, featuring the exploits of various people in a remote location competing to gain the most advantage from their situations, thus *winning* the grand prize.

CASE STUDY: THE ISLAND STORY

In our ethics course, we tell a story to our students which also features people stranded on two islands. This story (origin unknown) challenges the listener to evaluate from an ethics perspective the dialogue and behaviors of the five characters on these two islands.

Once upon a time, there were two islands in the middle of a vast ocean. The islands were close enough so that the occupants of each could see and shout across the waters to each other. But there were killer sharks in the water, so swimming back and forth between islands was out of the question.

Stranded on one island was a beautiful young woman named Anna, her mother Bertha, and an old sea captain named Carl—no relation to the two women. Stranded on the other island were two brothers: a young, handsome man named David, and his older brother, Ed.

David and Anna had become fond of each other, and often shouted back and forth across the distance, professing their undying, unconditional love for one another, and their mutual desire to one day hold and kiss and make love together. So intense did the desire become that David begged Anna to find a way to come to him, and after a time her love for David was so great that Anna agreed to find a way to get there.

Swimming was out, of course, because of the sharks. But Anna was not without resources. On the far side of her island lived old Carl, a man with a boat, albeit an old, dilapidated boat. The rotting vessel could possibly make the crossing with a little luck. But old Carl kept to himself, and said very little to the women on the rare occasions when their paths crossed.

Anna, burning with love and desire for David, approached Carl one afternoon and begged him to ferry her across the water to David's island, where she just knew she could live out her life fulfilled and happy. Carl, who had been everywhere and seen just about everything, thought about the lovely Anna's request. Carl agreed to take Anna on his boat to meet her David on the following morning's tide. But Carl explained that there would be a *price* for this service. Money was useless on the island, of course, and Carl wasn't much interested in money, anyway. His offer was as follows: Carl would take Anna to David's island first thing the next morning *if* Anna consented to have sex with Carl that night and remain with him until morning.

Anna was angry and frightened, and ran off without giving Carl her answer. She immediately sought the advice and wisdom of her mother, Bertha. After listening to the plight of her frightened but lovesick daughter, Bertha said, "Anna, you are a grown woman, and you no longer need me to tell you what to do. It is up to you—not I—to make this choice." Anna went off by herself to consider her situation.

Carl was asleep in his hammock when Anna returned with her decision. She woke him up and told him she would agree to his offer as long as he took her to her beloved David the next morning. Carl and Anna had sex that night, but all Anna could think about was finally being in David's arms.

The next morning, as agreed on, Carl took Anna to David's island, and returned to his own immediately. Just a few feet from his home pier, the creaky old boat finally sank, and Carl had to wade ashore.

Anna and David rushed into each other's arms, their meeting joyful and passionate. Anna was overcome with emotion and pledged her undying devotion to David. In fact, so excited was Anna that she even told David everything she had to go through in order to get to his island. She told him *everything*, because she just knew that their love was real, and that honesty was the cornerstone of their relationship.

When David heard Anna's story, he froze in her arms. He removed his arms from around Anna and looked her in the eyes. He said, "Anna, after what you have done, I can no longer love or trust you. Your behavior disgusts me. I shall have nothing to do with you from this point on." David walked away, leaving a broken Anna in tears on the beach. True to his word, he had nothing more to do with her.

Ed, having seen and overheard all that had taken place, approached the crying woman and said, "Hey, Anna, I don't love you, either. But I do have certain needs here on this island. If you will cook for me, give me sex when I want it, clean my hut, wash my clothes, and make no trouble for me, I will take you in since you cannot return to your island.

Anna went with Ed.

QUESTIONS FOR ANALYSIS OF THE CASE

Although the case of the imaginary islands is an artificial situation, the ethical issues raised by the interactions and dialogue between the participants are real and germane to our everyday lives. Consider and discuss the following questions based on the Island Story:

1. From Martin Buber's *I–Thou* perspective, how would you assess the dialogue between Anna and her mother? Between Anna and David?

2. In your opinion, did any character in this story *not* play the *Game* as described throughout this chapter?

3. How would you reconstruct Bertha's response to Anna's dilemma to reflect the *Firewall* discussed in this chapter?

4. When Ed offered to *rescue* Anna from her loneliness and pain, was he showing her what Carl Rogers would call *Unconditional Positive Regard*?

5. In your opinion, would Emmanuel Levinas praise Anna for her *preoccupation* with, and willingness to sacrifice everything for, David? Was Anna being true to Levinas' concept of the Other?

6. Re-create this story using whatever criteria you wish, but keep the basic facts and characters the same. Make everyone act ethically in their dialogue and behavior. How does your story turn out?

Flip the Script

When we asked the off-handed question of the men and women in our ethics class "Would your opinion of the ethical dialogue and behavior of each character change if we changed the gender of all the characters?" the response surprised us. Most of class agreed that, yes, it would indeed change the way we view this story.

So, let's take the liberty of changing the scenario so that each of the characters in the Island Story is the opposite gender. We'll keep the plot the same as the original story. Let's suppose that a young handsome man named Adam lived on an island with his dad, Barney. On that island also lived an old woman named Carla, who owned a dilapidated boat. Carla lived on the far side of the island and kept to herself. On the second island were two sisters, the beautiful young Diane and her older sister, Elise.

If it were Adam who slept with Carla in order to get to his lovely Diane, how would you feel about him? If Barney took the attitude "A man does what he has to do," when his son Adam asked him for advice, would you have thought him supportive, or uncaring? What would you think of Carla when she was able to convince Adam to sleep with her? When Diane *dumped* Adam after all he went through to get to her, would your opinion of her rise, or fall? Failing to get one sister, did Adam *luck out* when Elise made her offer to him?

If we changed the race of some of the characters, might you reevaluate your feelings about them?

Finally, are we inclined to view *I–Thou* or the *Other* through gender-specific or even race-specific lenses?

Chapter Summary

By studying the theories of Martin Buber, Carl Rogers, Emmanuel Levinas, and Paulo Freire, we have attempted to situate dialogical ethics as one of the foundational ethical platforms for Communication Ethics. In Chapters 1–4 we have discussed other major foundational theories of ethical communication. As we teach the course every semester, *tweaking* the material based on what we ourselves are learning, we realize that ethics for many of our students is strictly theoretical, almost without shape or form in their understanding. We believe that dialogical ethics gives our students (and ourselves) a clearer, more understandable platform on which we can judge ethical behavior.

Dialogical ethics is a cornerstone of communication ethics, because it provides a method by which we can engage and be engaged with the world around us. Dialogical ethics can help us comprehend why some of our relationships are not working, or why so many people in society have been marginalized, or why countries choose war to resolve conflicts. Dialogical ethics may also be the most easily understood of the foundational platforms of ethics. We may not understand the *Veil of Ignorance* immediately, and the definition of postmodernism might be something with which we need to struggle before we grasp it, as we will see in the following chapter. Kant's universal maxims might elude our understanding on first reading. But we can understand the concept of trust, because we all have trusted someone at one time. We can understand empathy because we have both given it to and received it from others. We can relate easily to the opinion of Finnish psychiatrist Eero Riikonen, who said, "A genuine dialogue is a form of joint action, and all participants have responsibilities for its results. The responsibility for all participants is in essence the same: be alive, be trustworthy, and be human."[13]

Although dialogical ethics may be easy to comprehend, actually behaving ethically is a much more difficult task. As mentioned earlier, not only must we be willing to open ourselves to honest, non-self-serving dialogue with others, we must also be able to sustain it over the course of a relationship. That is to say, if we are open and engaged with our *Other* (Levinas) during the first fifteen minutes of a conversation, we can not allow our attention to waiver when the NFL Monday Night Football game comes on television. Dialogical ethics requires repeatable, honest, and unselfish behavior for the duration of the exchange, and not just when we feel like listening.

Dialogical ethics also is difficult because, as Levinas pointed out, it can cause the other person to truly have power over us. When we turn ourselves over to the Other, or to the Thou (Buber), we surrender our own self-interests to those needs of the other person. The hope, of course, is that the other person is doing the same thing with us, and not manipulating the relationship for his or her own ends. Rogers' concept of Unconditional Positive Regard demands that we set aside our goals and wishes so that the other person may flourish. There is no guarantee that we will be afforded a similar response, but if there was such a guarantee, it really wouldn't be an ethical issue at all. As we think back to young Tammy and Jeff, we can hope that this new man in Tammy's life is showing interest in her only for her own growth and benefit, since she is, after all, a married woman. We can hope that he has no hidden agenda where this emotionally vulnerable young lady is concerned. Perhaps some of us read the story and thought, "Yeah, right. We know exactly what this other guy is after! Anyone can see where this is heading."

For Tammy and Jeff, for Anna in our case study, for all of us: being open to a Thou guarantees us nothing in return. The ethics involved in dialogue happens when we choose to be open and honest as we engage others, and to seek those who equally engage us as well.

We find it very revealing that four theorists from three different continents representing four disciplines all end up on almost the same page with dialogical ethics. And to our students who believe that one must *play the Game* when it comes to ethical issues, we say this: "just be careful that the *Game* doesn't play you." In our lives, the time will come when we need that *Firewall* from the harmful effects of unethical people. As we stated at the beginning of this chapter, the *Game* ends with *I and Thou*. Dialogical ethics provides us with an effective way of communicating ethically.

QUESTIONS AND TOPICS FOR DISCUSSION

1. How realistic is the expectation that we can *really* put aside our own agenda in order to dialogue ethically with someone else?

2. Can you think of a time when you and another person had a conversation during which time both of you were totally engaged with the other? How did that go?

3. What are the risks involved in an *I–Thou* relationship?

4. Using the principles of dialogical ethics as a guide, what do you think happened to the relationship between Tammy and Jeff?

5. If you are a student: Can you identify professors or teachers in your school who exemplify Paulo Freire's approach to education? Do you think students really *want* to engage in meaningful dialogue with their teachers?

NOTES

1. Eric Berne, *Games People Play* (New York: Grove Press, Inc., 1964), pp. 171–172.
2. Daniel Yankelovich, *The Magic of Dialogue* (New York: Simon & Schuster, 1999), p. 15.
3. Rob Anderson and Kenneth N. Cissna, *The Martin Buber–Carl Rogers Dialogue* (Albany: State University of New York Press, 1997), p. 65.
4. Martin Buber, *I and Thou*, trans. W. Kaufmann (New York: Simon & Schuster, 1970), p. 109.

5. Anderson and Cissna, *The Martin Buber–Carl Rogers Dialogue*, pp. 40–41.

6. Carl Rogers, *On Becoming a Person* (Boston: Houghton Mifflin Co., 1961), p. 24.

7. Carl Rogers, *Client-Centered Therapy* (Boston: Houghton Mifflin Co., 1951), p. 35.

8. Emmanuel Levinas, *Entre Nous: Thinking-Of-The-Other*, trans. M.B. Smith and B. Harshaw (New York: Columbia University Press, 1998), p. xii.

9. Emmanuel Levinas, *Totality and Infinity*, trans. A. Lingis (Pittsburgh: Duquesne University Press, 1969), p. 76.

10. Paulo Freire, *Pedagogy of the Oppressed*, trans. Myra Bergman Ramos (New York: Continuum International, 1993, orig. pub. 1970), p. 80.

11. Paulo Freire, *Pedagogy of Freedom*, trans. Patirck Clark (Lanham: Rowman & Littlefield, 1998), p. 125.

12. Paulo Freire, *Pedagogy of the Oppressed*, p. 97.

13. Sheila McNamee & Kenneth J.Gergen, *Relational Responsibilities; Resources for Sustainable Dialogue* (Thousand Oaks: Sage Publications, Eero Riikonen, contributor, 1999), p. 148.

CHAPTER

6 Contemporary Challenges

What is more up-to-date than *modern?* Are we not living in the *Modern Age?* Not, according to some writers and authorities. They would characterize current times as *postmodern.* To understand what is meant by *postmodern,* we need to begin with defining what we really mean by *modern.*

One of us begins a class with an exercise in which the students think of the word, *modern,* and then write as quickly as possible as many terms or items that come to mind associated with that word. The exercise is often slow going at first, as students have trouble putting a meaningful frame around the exercise. Everyone knows what *modern* is—it is right now, this minute, the times we are living in. Before the modern was the past, and after the modern comes the future—and that is it. After some prodding, we get to questions such as what is it about a nation or a time that allows us to say it is modern? How can you tell a modern society from one that is not? What are the characteristics of a modern society? Then we begin to get answers including terms such as the following: *science, industry, technology, democracy, mass media, mass market,* and so on. In other words, people begin to see something different between modern and not modern in terms of ways of life, not just the calendar.

It is thus possible to think that some people are living in a modern way at the same time that others are not. The idea of *modernization* captures this notion. In the 1950s and 1960s, economists occasionally talked about the newly independent countries of Africa and Asia by saying these countries should begin to *modernize.* This modernization was part of the process of *development,* and people would speak of these new nations as *underdeveloped,* or *undeveloped.* To become *modernized* or *developed,* they would undergo *industrialization,* and start to look more like the United States or Western European countries, in their politics as well as their economies. Some people described areas of the world that were not *modernized* as *backward,* or *traditional.* In this way, *modern* became a value-laden concept (and it probably still is).[1]

At the same time, the term modern developed different connotations when, as an adjective, it modified the arts. Especially in the twentieth century, people began to designate certain works as *modern art* or *modern music.* New art museums came on the scene to display the modern form of art. The Museum of Modern Art opened in New York City in 1929 with the mission of bringing together all forms of modern, visual art, including painting, sculpture, photography, architecture, design, film, and video (now of course there are other such museums for modern art, such as the one opened in San Francisco in 1935 and the Tate Modern in London). Modern art was often abstract, a move away from photographic realism. Modern music was atonal, and to traditionalists did not sound like music at all. When Stravinsky's *Rite of Spring* debuted in Paris, reportedly there was a near riot in the audience hall. "The audience responded to the ballet with such a din of hisses and catcalls," one commentator notes, "that the performers could barely hear each other."[2] Today, postmodernism seems to be just as jarring to modern people as Stravinsky's groundbreaking music was in 1913, when it was introduced.

In any case, *modern* has come to denote a way of life—characterized by science, technology, bureaucratic organization, institutionalized education, and so on—or to denote a sort of artistic movement. *Not modern,* therefore, could be anything that maintained the traditions of an earlier way of life or art. The notion behind the concept of *postmodern* suggests a different way of being *not modern,* a way that is neither like what came before nor like *the modern* either.

In this chapter, we consider some of the contemporary challenges to the various ways of thinking about ethics we have outlined in the first five chapters. These challenges flow from questioning some of the basic premises of the whole enterprise. Back in the first chapter, we stated our belief that you can reason about ethical issues, that you can follow a systematic procedure for such reasoning. *Postmodern* approaches to ethics question this claim. Although there could be different starting points or assumptions for the reasoning process, we did not doubt that one could use reasoning that would be acceptable to appropriately rational people. We assume some universal validity to the reasoning process and its relation to reality. Much in *postmodernism* rejects the notions of universal validity and its relation to reality, as we shall see.

Feminist ethical theory represents a second trend challenging reasoning about ethics exemplified by modernists such as Kant, utilitarians, and consequentualists. In Chapter 2, we referenced feminist ethics in showing its relationship to aspects of virtue ethics. You will recall that an *ethics of care* differs from an *ethics of duty* in that personal relationships become centrally relevant to ethical decision making. Philosophical *reasoning* and argumentation about ethics seem to emphasize objectivity, rationalism, impartiality, and impersonal analysis of issues, all associated with a distinctly male perspective, feminist theorists maintain.[3] The requirements of impartiality and objectivity require that we do not consider our own personal involvements with people when making ethical decisions. An *ethics of care*, on the other hand, stresses relationships, nurturance, and the actual human circumstances in which people find themselves.

Some consider feminist theory, particularly feminist ethical theory, as postmodern, others do not, while admitting some overlap in interests. Often, the feminist movement is associated with postmodernism, as are other initiatives that have a strong interest in emancipation of otherwise oppressed groups. Other related movements sometimes embracing a postmodern stance include those calling for racial equality, homosexual rights, peace, anti-globalism (especially in economic and trade matters), and *green* environmentalist groups.[4]

Postmodern Perspectives

> It was six men of Indostan
> To learning much inclined,
> Who went to see the Elephant
> (Though all of them were blind),
> That each by observation
> Might satisfy his mind.

So begins the famous poem by the nineteenth-century American poet, John Godfrey Saxe, about the blind men and the elephant. In the poem, each man touches a different part of the elephant and therefore comes away with a decidedly different *view* of what an elephant is like. One happened to fall against the side of the animal, and therefore determined that an elephant is *very like a wall.* A second, grasped one of the tusks and decided the elephant was like a spear (*so very round and smooth and sharp*). The next man felt the trunk and so asserted the elephant was like a snake. The fourth man took hold of the leg around the knee, and so believed it to be like a tree. The one who felt only the large ear claimed the elephant was like a fan, while the last, who felt only the tail, asserted it was like a rope.

The six men began to argue loudly among themselves:

> *And so these men of Indostan*
> *Disputed loud and long,*
> *Each in his own opinion*
> *Exceeding stiff and strong,*
> *Though each was partly in the right*
> *And all were in the wrong.*

Saxe gives the moral to his poem, with a call for religious toleration:

> *So oft in theologic wars,*
> *The disputants, I ween,*
> *Rail on in utter ignorance*
> *Of what the other mean,*
> *And prate about an elephant*
> *Not one of them has seen.*

Saxe based his poem on a folktale told and retold many times in different versions in Hindu, Buddhist, and Islamic traditions. The moral is quite clear in the Buddhist version. Some disciples or monks have come to the Buddha bewildered because they have heard quarreling and wrangling among devotees of different sects about the soul, immortality, and other beliefs. The Buddha responded to the followers with a parable about a king (a *rajah*), who one day had all the men in his town who had been blind from birth brought before him. He presented to them an elephant and had each feel a different part of the animal. In this version, those who feel the head say it is like a jar; those who feel the ear, like a basket; those who feel the tusk, like a plow; and so on. The blind men fell to fighting with their fists over their differing claims, causing the king much laughter. Although each has only very limited knowledge about the elephant, each is ready to fight the others to force his limited view on them.

In the Sufi version in the Muslim tradition, as told by *Rumi*, the leading Sufi poet, some Hindus are exhibiting the elephant in a dark house, so dark it is impossible to see all or much of it. Like the blind men, they gather their impression of the animal from the sense of touch. One feeling the trunk declares it is like a water pipe; one feeling the leg says it is like a pillar, and so on. One of the points of the Sufi version is that one cannot rely on physical senses alone to know what eternal or sacred matters are like. Our senses can give us only partial data, subject to interpretation from a particular point of view.

Those who argue for a postmodern perspective would embrace the parable of the blind men and elephant, especially the latter version of the Sufi mystic. No one is in a position to see all of reality; each person can see only part and only from his or her own point of view. The ideal of modernism, on the other hand, holds that there is a single, true reality the same everywhere. These two views constitute the clash in the debate between the *modern* and the *postmodern*. We hope that sharpening the nature of that clash will help you understand how postmodern thinking challenges standard ethical systems.

Modern versus Postmodern

Postmodern can be a fashionable, *with-it* label. One uses the word to describe all sorts of events, ideas, and even people today. One author observes, "Postmodernism is not a theoretical option or a stylistic choice; it is the very air we breathe."[5] He feels that postmodernism is ubiquitous and therefore unavoidable when discussing culture or society. This very ubiquity, however, makes it also difficult to pin down. It is not easy to define or explain just what it means to be postmodern. One writer on the postmodern observes that it "refers to a diffuse set of sentiments rather than any common set of doctrines—the sentiment that humanity can and must go beyond the modern."[6] We began this chapter by defining the postmodern by negation, by what it is not. Now, let us go into a little more detail in an effort to explain a postmodern view of ethics.

A key point in the clash between modern and postmodern lies in domination versus emancipation. Modern institutions began in the hope of liberating people from the oppressive state of feudalism, superstition, and the tyranny of monarchy. Somehow, according to the postmodernists, the ideal got lost along the way in the developments that we now think of as modern. The ideal got lost through a series of steps something like the following. Again we emphasize that there is no single representative of postmodernism (by the very nature of the perspective) and that this summary does not claim to represent the viewpoint of all those who may be considered postmodern in their views.

Modern science begins with the *scientific method*, associated with Galileo. This method required careful observation of what was actually in nature, using new instruments like telescopes that allowed Galileo to see that actually there were moons around Jupiter and rings around Saturn. The microscope allowed Leeuwenhoek to see creatures and detail unimaginable before. Science dispelled the notion that mysterious spirits guided matter and life—there appeared to be *natural causes* for what happened. There appeared a regular, repeatable structure to the natural world. The scientists revealed an impersonal and material universe operating without magic or supernatural intervention. Such knowledge permitted beneficial cures in medicine, more effective techniques in chemistry, and very useful tools, machines, and technologies in general.

The scientific revolution preceded and prepared the way for the Enlightenment, already introduced in Chapter 3. Philosophers began to hope they could apply the methods of observation and mathematical analysis, so useful in the new sciences, to all aspects of life. They could think of people as *units*, that is biological units, and study them in that way. Under this new social microscope, kings and aristocrats were no different from ordinary human beings, and certainly they were no better. There was no divine nature or cosmic law decreeing some people were better than others were. The whole of society or the nation could be a sort of machine and thus set up and operated like a machine. In this way, the idea of the modern bureaucracy took shape—a mechanical organization, with replaceable parts (with the difference that the parts could be people). And, thus, the French Revolution and then other revolutions replaced the older, feudal regimes with political systems aiming to be democratic (in which each human unit counted the same as any other).

The Industrial Revolution grew out of applying new machines and energy sources, derived from the scientific revolution, to the production of goods. Workers became units in large, bureaucratic factories, such as the textile mills in England in the early nineteenth century. The popular novel and later the movie, *Holes*, suggests the nature of such regimented work places, as Stanley Yelnats IV, along with his fellow detainees like Hector, Squid, and Armpit, must dig holes in the desert for no apparent reason day after day, under the watchful eye of *Mr. Sir.* Following the Industrial Revolution, the new science of economics was born, around the time of the founding of the new United States of America.[7] The new economists envisioned a vast, self-regulating machine that ran on its own logic, the democracy of the marketplace. Most aspects of modern life took on the structure of a bureaucratic machine, or institution.

Education moved into institutional schools, with students organized by age into standardized units of instruction (first grade, second grade, and so on; in England the grades were even referred to as *standards*). Charles Dickens begins his novel, *Hard Times*, describing such a modern school and institutionalized education: "Now, what I want is, Facts. Teach these boys and girls nothing but Facts. Facts alone are wanted in life." He continues, "The scene was a plain, bare, monotonous vault of a schoolroom, and the speaker's square forefinger emphasized his observations by underscoring every sentence with a line on the schoolmaster's sleeve."[8] The children are arranged in rows in an *inclined plane*, which after all is one of the elementary tools. Asked to give a definition of a horse, one of the boys, named Bitzer, responds with the correct form of the answer, "Quadruped. Graminivorous. Forty teeth, namely twenty-four grinders, four eye teeth, and twelve incisive. Sheds coat in the spring; in marshy countries, sheds hoofs, too. Hoofs hard, but requiring to be shod with iron. Age known by marks in mouth. Thus (and much more) Bitzer."[9]

Before education took on this bureaucratic aspect, the modern army virtually became a machine. Not only was the modern army organized as a hierarchical bureaucracy, but it also relied more and more on industrial technologies and weapons. The weapon of choice by the close of the 1800s was the *machine* gun. The industrialized armies and navies became the technology for projecting the power of the modern states (i.e, the modern European states) into those traditional lands, the ones considered not-modern, traditional, or *backward*. The modern world began to colonize the rest of the world, and colonialism thus became another-ism in the progress of modern times.

The age of the machine also became the age of the mass, which is an aggregation of individuals, of units. In large industrial nations, people became a mass market for the mass consumption of standardized goods. The new mass media informed as well as propagandized the public through mass communication. Mass consumption and mass markets required an emphasis on the public (or publics, with the coming of *demographics* in marketing) over the individual. As Rick says in the movie *Casablanca*, "Ilsa, I'm no good at being noble but it doesn't take much to see that the problems of three little people don't amount to a hill of beans in this crazy world. . . . Someday you'll understand that." World War II, the setting for *Casablanca*, brings us to the culmination of this purported trend in modernism, with its mass invasions, mass battles, and industrialized mass death in *factories* such as Auschwitz, Buchenwald, and Treblinka. Steven Best and Douglas Kellner, in one of their studies of postmodernism, conclude, "Yet the construction of modernity produced untold suffering and misery for its victims, ranging from the peasantry, proletariat, and artisans oppressed by capitalist industrialization to the exclusion of women from the public sphere, to the genocide of imperialist colonization."[10]

Domination versus Emancipation

If modernism leads to a deadening sense of unitization, loss of individuality, consumerism, and standardization, then postmodernists reject such a model of society and culture. "Thus, there was a turn away from modern discourses of truth, certainty, universality, essence, and system," two commentators on the postmodern outlook observe, "and a rejection of grand historical narratives of liberation and revolution."[11] Truth is what appears to be true from some particular, human perspective. Scientific truth relies on fictitious entities, such as atoms, quarks, gravity, inertia, species, and genera, as much as earlier traditional systems relied on spirits, genius, or

A *Post*-It Note

Not only has the term *postmodernism* become fashionable over the past two decades or so, but also so have many other terms following the construction of the prefix *post-* plus some other term. Consequently, in addition to postmodernism and postmodernity, we have poststructuralism, postcolonialism, postfordism, postindustrialism, posthumanism, postMarxism, and so on. These various post-isms have some familial resemblance one to the other. Such terms seem to signify the end of some widely accepted consensus.

Perhaps closest to postmodernism is poststructuralism. Structuralists believed that many aspects of human behavior, in language, culture, economics, and so on, could be explained in terms of underlying structures or patterns. Most modern structuralists took their cue from theories of descriptive linguistics, developed by the French-Swiss founder of modern linguistics, Ferdinand de Saussure. He postulated that all natural languages worked because of units, common to all, such as phonemes and morphemes could be combined and recombined by a set of rules into comprehensible language. The specific language, whether Tagalog or English, and the content, a novel or a shopping list, did not matter; the units and rules were the same. The Marxist, as a structuralist, claims that the structural basis of production determined history, not the decisions or actions of human beings. As structuralism relied on objective, universal explanations, the same kind of criticisms we see applied to modernism in this section undercut it as well.

Postcolonialism similarly rejects the theories or ideologies that justified (or still justify) the colonization of the non-Western world by Europeans. Postcolonial studies extends the criticism to cultural and art forms in which the models of the colonial countries—such as the modern novel, film, or music form—are held up as superior to *primitive*, or traditional art forms.

Postfordism and postindustrialism are conceptual *cousins*, as they both maintain that modern forms of mass production, with their emphasis on the assembly line and centralized industries, are being replaced by dispersed modes of production. The new economic globalism is an aspect of the postindustrial world. New words in our vocabulary mark this era, words such as *outsourcing* and *offshoring.*

---

humors. The rejection of a *grand narrative* became a hallmark of the postmodern perspective. A *grand narrative* is an all-encompassing system intended to explain everything. Thus, behaviorism, for example, aimed to explain human motivation and psychology. Scientists, following Einstein, sought a unified field theory that would explain all natural, physical laws. Certainly, modern thinkers held to the notion that the world was knowable, and that objective observation and analysis would eventually reveal the nature of everything.

Without objective reality as the bedrock of certainty, modernists might lament with the poet Matthew Arnold:

Ah, love, let us be true
To one another! For the world, which seems
To lie before us like a land of dreams,
So various, so beautiful, so new,
Hath really neither joy, nor love, nor light,
Nor certitude, nor peace, nor help for pain;
And we are here as on a darkling plain
Swept with confused alarms of struggle and flight,
Where ignorant armies clash by night.[12]

Many postmodernists believe that the modern quest for certainty and objective truth—for light, for certitude, for peace, for help for pain—is not just doomed to fail, but is wrongheaded as well. That which is certain or, simply, common sense is determined always from some point of view, they claim. The powerful, who maintain control and dominance over others in a society, get to dictate what is *common sense* or what is *natural.* We know what the elephant is like, they say, but those other people have some strange ideas about the creature. Defining reality and common sense is a source of power.

The postmodernist is quick to point out there is no such *thing* as an elephant at all. There are various instances of large beasts, which look much alike to us, and so we have come up with the abstract concept of a species, for which we have created the arbitrary sound-unit *elephant.* Buildings, human beings, airplanes, Brazilians, unicorns, and so on are all abstract categories we have created for our own convenience. Deep down, we know there is no such *thing* as a building, but rather a single instance of something that we agree to refer to as a building. The powerful get to decide which things will be designated in such categories. There is an unlimited number of ways to slice up reality, the postmodernist suggests.

The modernist replies, "Yes, but we have to start somewhere in order to be able to carry on with our lives and communicate at all."

"That's true," replies the postmodernist, "but you tend to forget that all you are doing is creating a frame of reference for your own convenience, not representing actual reality. After a while, you begin to treat your arbitrary categories as facts." Let us emphasize this point—the categories become *facts.* These so-called facts take on a taken-for-granted legitimacy, which makes the assumptions behind them very difficult to challenge.

The intention of *critical theory* (as represented by Habermas) is to provide a *critique* of the hidden assumptions that lead to people's accepting as *common sense* the normality of their own subjugation. For example, critical theorists argue that the function of mass entertainment is to divert the public's attention away from the restrictions on their true range of freedom of action in the modern, corporate world. People accept as *normal* the limitations on their freedom of choice (in the ways they can actually choose to live) because of the apparent overwhelming choice of consumer products in the shops, malls, and Internet shopping sites. Just look at all the different kinds of bottled water available in this day and age—no one in any other time has had such variety available to them. Although Habermas himself rejects the label of postmodernist, and maintains that he is trying to fulfill the original ideals of modernity, his critical theory, as well as that of his colleagues is often seen as contributing to the postmodern analysis of domination versus emancipation. The idea of *playing the game*, that we have been developing in these chapters so far, takes on a more *sinister* aspect in the view of critical theory and postmodernism. One must play the game by the rules laid down by the power structures of the corporate, educational, and cultural world. In the next section, we will see that feminists also question the legitimacy of the assumptions that are taken for granted within these modern systems as well.

The *French Connection*

Many of the most famous proponents of the postmodern in the fields of philosophy, sociology, and culture in general have been European, particularly French. A list of the names often associated with postmodernism include Michel Foucault (although he did eschew that designation himself), Jean Francois Lyotard, Jacque Derrida, Gilles Deleuze, Jean Baudrillard, Jacques Lacan, Paul Ricouer, Roland Barthes, Alain Badiou, Pierre Bourdieu, and Georges Bataille. Many would also include the influential feminist scholars, Luce Irigaray (although born in Belgium), and Héléne Cixous. Bear in mind that *postmodernist* is a very slippery term, and arguments can be made for excluding some or all of these people at various times and of including many others. Of course, there are many thinkers who are not French who are counted among postmodernists as well.

Most of the members of this generation of French academics and intellectuals share several commonalities. They were born early in the twentieth century around the time of or just after World War I. Most of them completed their advanced education right after World War II and then became active in the universities of France, especially in Paris. Many of them espoused or were sympathetic to Marxist or radical politics, especially prior to the 1960s. Most reported they were significantly affected by the events in Paris around May of 1968. The 1960s represented a decade of upheaval, not just in the United States, where opposition to the U.S. involvement in Viet Nam came to a head in 1968 at the Democratic Party Convention in Chicago. The earlier part of the decade saw the March on Washington and the other civil rights demonstrations that preceded the passage of the Civil Rights Act of 1964. In Europe, students and workers were similarly engaged in various kinds of public protests. France had just ended its occupation of the country of Algeria, which had been rocked throughout the 1950s by the guerrilla war of

(continued)

(continued)

Algerian nationalists against the occupying French military. Many of the intellectuals, led by Jean-Paul Sartre, had opposed France's involvement in Algeria just as strenuously as some American academics were to oppose the U.S. role in the Viet Nam conflict.

In May 1968 several student strikes at universities and even some high schools resulted in clashes between students and police in the streets. Many French academics (many from our list above) actively supported the students. When the French government responded with more force, the situation was even more inflamed. In June, however, the workers' unions and the French Communist Party withdrew their support for the demonstrations, and the movement died out. Many French students and professors felt betrayed, especially by the Communists, and began to question their own ideological views. This moment was therefore a turning point for many of the academics.

Other similarities include an intellectual debt owed to the nineteenth-century German philosopher, Friedrich Nietzsche. Before going mad near the end of his career, Nietzsche developed a philosophy questioning all the certainties of the Western tradition. His rejection of certainties, not just in religion but in science as well, foreshadowed the kind of criticism the postmodern thinkers were to level against the *grand narratives* of modern philosophy and culture.

In addition, these writers tended to move in the same or similar circles, and either influenced one another, or were themselves influenced by the same intellectual leaders, such as Sartre. The surrealist writer, Georges Bataille, for example, edited some of the early work of Foucault and Derrida for journals he worked on; his first wife later married Jacque Lacan, a psychoanalyst and teacher who also influenced Lyotard. Bataille also had an important influence on Hélène Cixous. Deleuze was a friend of Michel Foucault; and both Deleuze and Foucault taught at the same university with Cixous. Luce Irigaray was also a student of Lacan. And so on the connections go.

Implications for Communication Ethics

What does this all mean for ethics and specifically for the ethics of communication? We saw in the previous chapter that to practice dialogical ethics, one must strive to overcome the tendency to treat people as classifiable, countable, objectified units. In fact, Levinas, identified with Dialogical Ethicists in that chapter, is often counted among postmodern ethicists, as well. The modernist perspective did attempt to generalize about people and to categorize them for various purposes. The postmodern view attempts to avoid such generalizations, such *totalizing narratives*, to use a postmodern term. Instead, they begin with the notion that the *Other* does not fit into any theory or science. This means that each communicative event, particularly the face-to-face, interpersonal event, is a unique and fresh experience. Generalizations that applied in the last encounter do not apply in the new one.

The direction taken by the postmodern is therefore against universal tendencies, including efforts to uphold universal systems of ethics. Any attempt to construct a systematic theory about ethics is seen as misguided from the postmodern point of view. The postmodernists contend there is no sameness, no overall uniformity in our experiences—rather there are only *differences*. Each person is different and each encounter is different from any other. There can be no general rules. Alain Badiou represents this position in holding, "There can be no 'ethics in general', no general principle of human rights, for the simple reason that what is universally human is always rooted in particular truths."[13] In other words, there can be no system of rules for ethical conduct or ethical decision making.

First, the critics of postmodern ethics, however, charge that postmodern ethics ultimately relies on *relativism* or even *nihilism*, a term we will explain in a moment. In regard to relativism, postmodernists could deny they rely on ethical rules that change from one culture to the next, since they deny the universality of rules even within a given culture or time. If anything, postmodernism seemingly advocates a type of situational ethics. In order to behave in an ethical fashion, one needs to address each situation from a certain point of view, or with a certain attitude. Levinas implies that the attitude lies in having full regard for the *Other*, altruism taken to its logical limit. Foucault, in his later work, came to describe ethics in terms of a sort of *care for the self*, in which the person behaves ethically by acting in a way that provides for the nurturing of the self. This nurturing of the self should not evoke ethical egoism, however. Foucault's care for the self is closer to the virtue ethics of Aristotle, in which one tries to live the best possible life to achieve fulfillment. It calls for self-mastery and self-control while striving to live *an examined life*.

A second charge leveled against postmodern ethics is that of *nihilism*. The Russian novelist, Ivan Turgenev, coined the term, *nihilism*, in the nineteenth century. His most famous character was Bazarov in his masterpiece, *Fathers and Sons*. Bazarov, returning home from college as a young student, informs the older generation that he is a *nihilist*, that is, someone who accepts no authorities.[14] As his best friend's father surmises, nihilism is derived from the Latin term *nihil*, meaning *nothing*. Their purpose is to tear down all existing social or intellectual structures. Jacques Derrida's principle of *deconstruction* seems at times similar to this nihilistic program.

Derrida shows that through the practice of *deconstruction*, one can take apart (deconstruct) any kind of text to reveal no fixed, single meaning of any work—a basic premise of the postmodern project. Similarly, one can deconstruct any justification of an ethical principle. The utilitarian says the ethical action is the one that results in the greatest good for the greatest number. But, we have already partly deconstructed this formulation by questioning who determines what is the *good* and who is to constitute the *greatest number*. Furthermore, who says this is a basic principle of right and wrong anyway?

Or, who is to say that Kant's categorical imperative of logical consistency is the basis for right action? Who has determined that Rawls and Scanlon are correct in holding that people should be treated fairly and equitably? Why are fairness and equity hallmarks of moral action? The nihilist and the postmodernist seem to undermine the very basis for moral reasoning. In fact, many of them seek to uphold the value of emancipation from domination by the powerful in modern societies. In that sense, their intentions are more like those of Bazarov, who maintained in the novel that his goal was to *clear the ground* for the eventual creation of a better, freer society.

Ethical communication from a postmodern perspective, therefore, cannot be predicated on the application of systems or rules. Rather one approaches the communicative encounter with another person each time as a new experience, as a *different* experience. One is guided by an attitude of openness to the different experience and a desire to avoid any sort of manipulation or domination of the other person. In considering ethical decisions involving communication with other people, one tries to *deconstruct* conventional standards of behavior, to be alert to subtle ways in which such standards might undermine the full humanity of the other person.

Postmodernism can also provide a lens for examining corporate and organizational communication. One can analyze the case study of the Sizgie Corporation, in which the managers decided to use technological surveillance techniques, as an example of *modern* control and domination over the communication of employees. Such monitoring technologies surface in many *modern* institutions such as prisons, the military, hospitals, schools, modern factories, and similar institutions, and are therefore suspect to the people following a postmodern approach. These practices lead to the technologizing of personal space and private life. We take for granted this *colonization* of our lives by modern corporations and institutions. The intrusions become commonplace, a *normal* part of *playing the game.*

The postmodern criticism of modern life is that these practices are not *normal*, since no activity or practice is *normal* in and of itself. People, usually those in a dominant position, define for their own benefit what is *normal*. Take for example the observation that nearly everyone today in the modern world seems to carry a cell phone and pager everywhere. This technology, together with the laptop connected anywhere to the Internet, means one is always accessible to a workplace or similar organization. The electronic ankle bands worn by felons on home detention are only slightly different from these electronic connections to employers or supervisors, the postmodern critic maintains. The modern person, according to postmodernism, is thus fettered to organizations and institutions, not necessarily for her own benefit, but for the benefit of some more powerful, institutionalized group.

The postmodern critique of conventional ethical systems attempts to replace their decision-making processes with ways of thinking or living. The critique fears that rational systems, born during the modern age, are inhospitable to human freedom and dignity, because the rationality surreptitiously maintains the dominance of one group over another. Next, we turn to a similar challenge to modern systems of ethics, feminist approaches to ethics.

The Feminist Challenge

In this section, we see that feminism, like postmodernism, can have a wide range of definitions and meanings. There are many different kinds of feminists and there are, consequently, varieties of feminist ethics. Chapter 2 provided a brief introduction to the feminist ethics of Nel Noddings and Carol Gilligan, as the ethics of care, as well as those of Martha Nussbaum, in her emphasis on universal capabilities. We will expand on these ideas here as well as introducing other feminist theories that challenge the conventional approaches reviewed in Chapters 2–4. Dialogical ethics, presented in Chapter 5, seems to us foundational to ethics of communication and may be more compatible with both postmodern theories and feminist perspectives.

Overview of Feminist Positions

First, we should be clear about the basic position of feminism, which is based on the following principles:[15]

- Women are the equals of men.
- Oppression of women is wrong.
- The categories of male and female, as well as all others related to gender and gender roles are *socially constructed*.
- The male perspective has dominated the *social construction* of these categories, and, therefore, male virtues have been taken to be *normal*, or the standard.

The principle that gender is socially constructed is significant. The statement *socially constructed* means that these things are not given by nature, but rather are formed and shaped by human beings. It means that our meanings for gender and gender roles could very well be different from the way they are. The emphasis on the artificial and arbitrary, that is, socially constructed, nature of gender, gender roles, and norms draws a connection between the postmodern enterprise and the feminist perspective.[16] Seyla Benhabib of Harvard University observes a "paradigm shift to postmodern feminisms which occurred in the middle of the eighties," a shift which she notes was influenced by the French intellectuals such as Foucault, Derrida, Lyotard, Irigaray, and Cixous.[17] She further observes that feminist theorists "also discovered an attractive ally in these positions for their concerns" at that time.[18]

It would be misleading to say that feminism represents a monolithic movement, as already noted; different emphases and approaches fall under this general heading. All the versions are of course *women-centered*, and hold generally to the four basic principles outlined previously. The *ethics of care*, associated with Gilligan and Noddings, represents one strain. A second strain appears in what some call *Maternal Ethics*, associated with Sara Ruddick, for example, which emphasizes the special ethics of an unequal relationship between parent and child. Femin*ist* ethics, with more of an emphasis on the -*ist* suffix tends to be much more political in its tone and program.

Within this feminist wing, there are various branches.[19] *Liberal Feminists* aim at bringing about political and institutional changes that will end discrimination against women in regard to political, legal, and economic rights. They work to support equality of opportunity in pay and hiring, support equal educational opportunity, in programs such as Title IX, affirmative action. They also work to implement policies against domestic abuse and sexual harassment. *Marxist Feminists* stress the function of class and economic forces in creating and maintaining women's subordination to men in society. They would feel that the liberal feminists are somewhat naive in their belief that political action through the existing class and capitalist structures can ultimately be successful. *Radical Feminists* take a further step, contending that our very assumptions about biological and cultural roles of men and women hinder women's ultimate liberation from domination. In other words, they would place the issues beyond the political realm and move it into every aspect of culture and human society. *Lesbian ethics* focuses more on what should be ethical norms for a specific group of people in society and their right to choose their own way of life.

Feminists, especially outside the United States and Europe, take issue with what they see as a Western or Eurocentric bias in the concerns of these feminists. *Multicultural, postcolonial,* or *global* feminists would all affirm that liberals, Marxists, and many radicals do not take sufficient note of ethnic, racial, or national factors. They often charge that American and European feminists focus too much on the cultural and political situations in their own countries. For example, they might find U.S. feminists' concern about date rape and the glass ceiling as understandable in their situation but not as relevant to the experience of women who face genital mutilation in Africa, assassinations of daughters-in-law in India, the helplessness of women to avoid infection from HIV, denial of basic access to education and health care, and so on. In fact, global feminists may find some of the liberal feminist program insensitive to the cultural needs and experiences in their own countries. As Alison Jagger points out, women in some Third-World cultures may feel Western feminists are outsiders, attacking aspects of feminine life essential to the defense of those cultures, "especially as these are manifest in traditional practices of marriage and sexuality."[20]

So there are many varieties of feminism and feminist ethics. In one way or another, most of these systems of feminism reject the universal, rules-based approach, based on impersonal, rational calculations of duties or utility. They tend to reject the impersonal nature of ethical decision-making favored by the standard ethical theories.

The Ethics of Care

Most of the systems of ethics we have considered are based on *justice*, according to feminist critics, and therefore more compatible with a male perspective than a female one. The difference can be demonstrated by the sort of illustration developed by the Australian utilitarian philosopher, Peter Singer. Imagine that you come on a small child of about three years old drowning in a retention pond along the roadway. If you rush into the pond to save the child, you will soil your good clothes, resulting in a dry-cleaning bill and some inconvenience. Despite that, most people agree they would save the child. Now imagine that you come home from that walk and find a mailing from a reputable charity group soliciting you for $10 (about the same as the cleaning bill) to help feed a starving child in the Sudan in East Africa. Many people would discard the mailer without thinking much about it. According to a strict utilitarian, such as Singer, the two situations are identical: your duty to save the child in the Sudan is exactly as strong as your duty to save the drowning child in front of you. If all human life is valuable and not one life can be said to be more worthy than any other, then justice demands equal treatment for both children. Singer puts the case this way: "It makes no moral difference whether the person I can help is a neighbor's child ten yards from me or a Bengali whose name I shall never know, ten thousand miles away."[21] Presumably, the egalitarian views of contractualism present a similar argument. An ethics based on care and relationships would draw a distinction between the two cases, based on the real, human connection created in the face-to-face situation of the drowning child. Nel Noddings maintains that ethics from the feminine view "is very different from the utilitarian practical ethics of, say, Peter Singer."[22]

Carol Gilligan became the leading figure advocating a distinct feminine ethics of care contrasted to the masculine ethics of justice. After completing her Ph. D. in social psychology at Harvard University in 1964, she joined the faculty at that school and began to work with some of the most famous authorities in developmental psychology, notably Erik Erikson. But while doing research with another well-known psychologist there, Lawrence Kohlberg, she began to develop her ideas of gender differences in moral development.

Kohlberg's main research project consisted of presenting children and adults with cases involving moral dilemmas and then analyzing their reasoning for the answers they gave to the dilemmas.[23] The studies were longitudinal, which means conducted over time, and cross-cultural. As a result of this research, he claimed to discern six stages of moral development, as one matured from childhood into adulthood, although he points out that only about 5% of adults reach the highest stage of moral reasoning, Stage 6.[24]

Kohlberg's six stages are grouped under three levels:[25]

The Preconventional Level

> Stage 1. Obedience to authority and avoidance of punishment and physcial consequences.
>
> Stage 2. Instrumental exchange, emphasizing the practical benefits of behaving well, such as reciprocated favors.

The Conventional Level

> Stage 3. Social conformity, behaving well results in the approval of others, *good intentions* become significant in moral judgments.
>
> Stage 4. Social duty, behaving well maintains the proper social order and represents your social obligation.

The Postconventional or *Principled* Level

> Stage 5. Rights and the social contract, in which behaving well derives from a critical, rational examination of social responsibility.
>
> Stage 6. Universal ethical principles, based on one's deep reflection.

Gilligan and other feminists note that Kohlberg's original study's subjects included eighty-four boys and no girls. In his later studies, women as well as men were included. According to these studies, women tended not to progress beyond Stage 3, which concerns interpersonal relations and pleasing and helping others. But, Gilligan and others contend, the tendency for males to progress to the higher stages more than females is a result of the scale, which has been skewed to reflect values of male experience and psychology: the scale is biased in that way. The male definition of mature reasoning and judgment, as represented by Kohlberg's stages, is not superior to women's take on these matters, but is simply different. "Given the differences in women's conception of self and morality," Gilligan explains, "women bring to the life cycle a different point of view and order human experience in terms of different priorities."[26]

Men tend to perceive ethical *duties* in terms of individual rights and consequences. Women, she argues, experience morality and ethics in terms of their role embedded in a network of human relationships. The highest, or principled, stage of moral development for women hence lies in responsible caring for the self and for others with whom one has a concrete relationship. Ethical decisions are made in a *context* of caring and nurturing relationships, in real life, not in an abstract process in which context is incidental. Noddings explains, "What we do depends not upon rules, or at least not wholly on rules—not upon a prior determination of what is fair or equitable," but upon the conditions at a given time as seen by the two parties in the relationship, the one-*caring* and the *cared-for*.[27] Noddings also maintains that there is a difference between *caring about* and *caring for*. Men might well care *about* principles in ethical thinking, but women care *for* some specific person. So, she is really talking about an ethics of *caring for*, when she speaks of an *ethics of care.*

Gilligan and her colleagues would contend that women are horrified by the Biblical story in which Abraham is depicted as willing to sacrifice his son, Isaac, for a principle. Ethical systems developed from the masculine point of view emphasize universal application of principles in an impartial manner; women's ethics cannot be divorced from the real-life situation as it presents itself to one's actual experience. Abraham in this context represents the detached father-figure, while the woman cannot imagine responding except with horror to the command to kill her own son.

One can draw a distinction between the views of Gilligan and Noddings, however, on the following grounds. Gilligan maintains that there is a fundamental difference in the psychological makeup of women and men. Noddings allows that the ethics of care typically arises from the experiences of women, "which is not to say, of course that it cannot be shared by men, any more than we should care to say that traditional moral systems cannot be embraced by women."[28]

As we have seen, virtue ethics, as described in Chapter 2, and dialogical ethics, in Chapter 5, seem compatible with the viewpoint of feminine ethics as an ethics of relationships and caring as well. As in dialogical ethics, the attitude with which one approaches the other person in a relationship determines one's ethical responsibilities, rather than an abstract set of principles. This attitude reminds us of the *I–Thou* relationship of Martin Buber, as Noddings points out in describing the caring relationship as *engrossment* in the other. This attitude also evokes the ideal of the response to the Other as envisioned by Levinas. As a former teacher and for many years a professor of Education at Stanford University (now *emerita*, or retired), Noddings, along with Freire, stresses the teacher's approach to her craft. She, like Freire, working in the field of education, favors *pedagogical caring*, developed from an "analysis of caring itself and not from the formal requirements of teaching as a profession."[29] We will now turn to a discussion of the ethics of care, which will provide a foundation for points about ethics of interpersonal communication and communication and diversity. These issues are taken up in the second part of the text, when we return to issues of gender and feminism in regard to these communication settings.

Responses to the Ethics of Care

Despite the pop psychology claim that "men are from Mars" and "women are from Venus," it is probably closer to the truth that they are both from planet Earth.[30] Even for those philosophers inclined to be sympathetic with the project begun by Gilligan, some doubts surface. Rita C. Manning in her book, *Speaking from the Heart*, as the title itself implies, defends the notion of an ethics of care.[31] She finds, however, through some of her own empirical research, that gender is not the only variable that affects the extent to which individuals adhere more to an ethics of justice or an ethics of care. Manning finds that socioeconomic class, occupation, age, ethnicity, and race are also significant factors in the moral decision making and the justifications people give for their judgments. Manning admits that her findings should be considered preliminary and that she had an especially small sample of African Americans (more Asians were in her study). Gender may not be as strong a factor as Gilligan contends, Manning concludes, but it is still present as one of the major determinants.[32] And, furthermore, in her follow-up questions regarding how people justified their answers to moral dilemmas, those using what she called a *justification of care* offered the most nuanced responses and considered a wider range of viewpoints.

A more sharply critical response comes from feminists who fear that emphasizing the value of an ethics of care is counterproductive to the struggle for women's emancipation. One feminist expressed this fear in a symposium at the State University of New York at Buffalo, pointing out that women represent the values of caring more than men because they are in a subordinate position.[33] It benefits men and allows them to remain in control in society as long as women are identified as valuing, above other virtues, their caring for others. Gilligan's response was that this claim requires one to accept the language and values of domination and power in describing the situation. The criticism does not directly refute the possibility of genuine value in an ethics of care, nor does it damage the claim that we would be better off if it were more highly valued than it is. Nonetheless, one can see how many feminists would be worried about implications of the position that women should be seen as the caregivers in society. By holding up the ethics of feminine caring as exemplary of women's moral development, they fear proponents of the ethics of care may be undermining the struggle for full equality and autonomy for women.

Another serious criticism of the ethics of care questions the science on which the case is based. Critics in this vein point out that Gilligan's conclusions are based on a small set of cases and have not been peer-reviewed in the normal course of social science.[34] Diane Romain finds Gilligan's methodology confusing in that she listened to women talk about ethical problems, such as whether or not to have an abortion, and then interpreted their talking.[35] She finds many of the transcribed words of the women interviewed ambiguous and unclear, so it is also unclear how Gilligan came to the conclusions that she did. Others have disputed the notion that there are different *communication cultures* for men and women, and in fact one recent study concludes that both men and women are in fact quite similar regarding their value of relationships and relational support in their interpersonal communication.[36] Such criticisms argue against the notion that there are irreducible and inherent differences among people traceable to sex or gender.

A supporter of Gilligan and Noddings could respond to these charges that the basic claim—that there are differences in the way women in general view ethical decision making and the way men in general do so—is not refuted by these points. Those espousing an ethics of care do not claim that men and women are not similar and do not respond fundamentally as human beings in the first place. Rather, they are claiming that there are differences in emphasis in how men and women approach many of these moral questions. They do not deny, either, that there are other important factors, such as class or ethnicity, which will influence what one emphasizes or attends to when facing an ethical dilemma.

Along these lines, we can point out that Kohlberg himself did address the issues raised by Gilligan concerning his initial research and corresponding conclusions.[37] He believes that she is quite justified in identifying an ethics of care that does represent a mature, moral outlook, one that is not incompatible with the mature ethics of justice. He feels that some confusion may arise from the use of the concept of *moral* in two related but distinct ways. One concept of the *moral*, he points out, places its emphasis on universal obligations grounded in impartiality. A second concept, the one elaborated by Gilligan, places its emphasis on caring and personal responsibility. The ethics of care arises in the particularities, the specifics, of actual personal relationships, especially family relationships. In these cases, Kohlberg maintains, the sense of personal responsibility to a specific *Other* supplement and add to one's reasoning about what is just in a given situation. We have already had occasion to refer to Plato's dialogue, *The Euthyphro*, which raises a similar issue. In this dialogue, Socrates confronts a young man hurrying into court to lodge a charge against a criminal. When Socrates inquires who the alleged criminal is, he learns it is the young man's own father. Socrates is disturbed by this revelation, feeling it is not right, not moral, for a son to prosecute his own father. In this case, personal responsibility changes what is seen to be justice. There is still an ethics of justice, but with considerations of care and relationship added in the mix.

Implications for Communication Ethics

First, the basic principles of feminist ethics require that women and men be treated equitably in communication. Communication practices that imply that women do not have as important a role as men in society, organizations, or relationships are clearly unethical according to these principles. A related implication is that people have an ethical responsibility to bring subtle (or not so subtle) discriminative practices of communication to light. The difficulty in doing this is that the practices of *normal* discourse and interaction have been shaped by long-held assumptions which need *deconstructing*, to invoke a principle from postmodern methods. We need to be alert that the *male* is assumed to be the *normal*, or the expected, and so is not *marked*. When something seems to go against long-held assumptions, it becomes *marked*, so that we say *woman* doctor, while we might never say *man* doctor. We have heard people speak about a *male* nurse, but we have not heard the term *female nurse*. The implications of these problems in communication surface in interpersonal, organizational, and cross-cultural settings, as we further explore in Part 2.

Second, the ethics of care has broad implications for practices in communication. The issue of whether women are *hard-wired* to think differently about ethics than men—a controversy not really settled at this point—should not distract us from the profound values of thinking about communication in terms of valuing care for others and valuing real, human relationships. One is less likely to approach an encounter with the intent of asserting one's rights (seeking justice), for example. A parent, a child, a friend, or a lover deserves special treatment and consideration. It would be considered unethical, if not even unnatural, to treat those standing in a special relationship with us impartially, as some rational systems, such as utilitarianism, demand.

Third, emotional responses arising from relationships are as important as or more important than logical reasoning in making ethical judgments (or, one could argue that there is no real separation between these types of reasoning). Rita Manning in her book, *Speaking from the Heart*, reminds us, "We don't live in a caring world," which she further explains as meaning, "not everyone recognizes his or her obligation to care."[38] Her point implies that we have an ethical obligation to make others aware of this need for caring. People may appear to treat others in a caring manner in order to fulfill legal obligations or in order to avoid being sued. We have become a litigious society and so our treatment of others may often be calculated in just those terms. The result can be a minimalist approach to what we owe another person, rather than an approach based on compassionate care for the other. But, this approach based on calculation and minimum duties, as Benhabib points out, "neglects that the moral self is not a moral geometrician but an embodied, finite, suffering and emotive being."[39]

Remember that in virtue ethics, the ethical act is what the virtuous person would do in similar circumstances. Applying an ethics of care to communication implies framing this guideline as follows: the ethical act is what the *caring* person would do. One's emotional attachments, consequently, should be legitimate matters of concern. Martha Nussbaum makes the case for the legitimacy of emotional considerations in her thorough treatment of the subject in *Upheavals of Thought: The Intelligence of Emotions*.[40] At one point in the book she compares the ethical implications of acting from the emotional responses of compassion or empathy with the system advocated by John Rawls, which we have studied in Chapter 3 in this book. Rawls, you may recall, bases his principles for ethical judgments on relying on rational self-interest together with the ignorance of people's actual, real-life conditions in the *original position*, behind his *veil of ignorance*. Concern for the least well off in society (the disadvantaged such as those people with handicaps, conditions of poverty or illness, and so on) is generated out of concern that the individual might herself be in such a position. Rawls feels his approach is safer than relying on the compassionate judgment of people fully aware of their real-life conditions. People will be less likely, he believes, to rationalize their advantages and minimize the disadvantages of others in such a case. Nussbaum, however, points to the fact that the *original position* is wholly hypothetical and that in fact people do know their actual circumstances in life. It would therefore seem more effective to generate emotional compassion for the least well off than to rely on abstract hypothetical situations to generate the kind of altruistic care for others that would make for ethical treatment of other people.[41]

This principle does not necessarily imply that you should ignore your obligations of care to all others except those with whom you have special bonds. Let's return to the example used earlier involving the film *The Emperor's Club*. The teacher, Hundert, changed the exam grade of the difficult boy, the one in whom he had taken special interest. One could argue that Hundert was moved to act against the rules in this case because of his care for the boy. The boy's father, a powerful U.S. Senator, had neglected his son's need for affection and attention. Hundert identified with this situation, because his own father had been so busy as a scholar and academic that he had similarly neglected Hundert. As a caring person, did Hundert have an obligation of care to break the rules for Bell, the Senator's son? At first, we may say that he did. We should remember, however, that as a teacher, he had an obligation to be caring for his other students, particularly the boy who was denied his rightful place in the final contest as a result of Hundert's changing of the exam grade. A caring person would have to take his responsibilities to both boys into consideration. The implication is that developing the ability or the awareness for sympathetic understanding of the conditions of others leads to more ethical behaviors. The ethical responsibilities of care require us to consider the complexities of each particular case, to see each case as different from all others. Again, we return to the notion of *difference*, as developed by those in the postmodern camp, as well as the virtues of flexible judgments emphasized by an attitude of care, compassion, and empathy. This attitude of care must take account of real-life circumstances, including our special responsibilities resulting from the other person's specific relationship to us. This attitude therefore rejects calculations based on abstract rules or universal ethical duties, which are the same for all people in all places for all times.

CASE STUDY: THE PRODIGAL CHILD

There were three children in a family: the oldest, a daughter, then a son, and the youngest, another daughter. As the children grew into adulthood, the two oldest stayed in the same city, Atlanta, as their parents, while the youngest child, Vickie, completed an advanced degree and moved to San Francisco, where she had a wonderful professional career. Mary and John were somewhat older than Vickie, and due to the financial situation of their parents at the time they reached college age, they got neither the advanced degrees nor professional training afforded to Vickie, who benefited from improved circumstances at the time she reached college age. As the parents aged, Mary and John found they were shouldering the major responsibilities of taking care of the mother and father as the health of both declined.

Vickie made it to Atlanta only a couple of times a year, usually around holidays or her birthday. After the father died, the mother increasingly made it clear, despite her best efforts, that Vickie was her darling and her favorite. John and Mary, talking to each other, developed feelings of resentment toward Vickie, feeling that she had been favored with special education and benefits they could never have. They had to curtail their own activities and divert some of their attention from their own families in order to take care of their mother, who needed more and more care every year. They loved their mother, of course, but they found her demands were becoming heavier, especially as she seemed to blame them for her growing unhappiness in her health situation. When Vickie breezed into town (as they would put it), she was treated royally by the mother—everything must stop so that Vickie will receive all the mother's loving attention. When Vickie was not in town, most of the year, the mother extolled Vickie's virtues and how wonderful it was to have her in town, if only for a few short days.

John and Mary began to form the idea, in their conversations with each other, that Vickie was getting off scot-free in San Francisco, enjoying the cosmopolitan city and the success she had achieved. They had to stay near the home in Atlanta and dutifully take care of the mother, who seemed not to show them the gratitude they felt they deserved for their sacrifices (they assumed that had they had the same opportunities as Vickie, they would be having the same kind of professional success). They decided that they should ask Vickie to provide financial support for the care of their mother in place of the hours and work that John and Mary were providing. Vickie enjoyed a far higher income than they did and was free of the major responsibilities of caring for their mother. Further, they wanted to suggest to their mother that the two of them should receive a larger proportion of the property and other inheritance that will come their way when their mother died. After all, they reasoned, that seemed the only fair and equitable way to deal with the unequal burden of parent care.

They met to decide how they should communicate all this to, first, Vickie, and second, to their mother.

QUESTIONS FOR ANALYSIS OF THE CASE

1. Determine what you feel are the ethical issues involved in this case. Have all the parties engaged in what you would consider to be ethical conduct in their interactions with each other?

2. What would various systems of ethical decision making say about the case? Is this a case in which justice demands fair treatment and distribution of burdens and benefits among the siblings? How do the relationships among the various parties affect this determination?

3. A postmodern analysis might suggest that there are hidden dimensions of social control and dominance underlying the major problems revealed in this case. What are the hidden social or cultural assumptions leading to the pattern of relationships and feelings represented in this case (if any)?

4. A feminist analysis might also suggest that there are unstated cultural assumptions being made in this case leading to the hurt feelings and desire for justice— what might those be?

5. How could you apply the principles of an ethics of care in this case? Who has caring responsibilities for others in this situation? Has the mother acted from an ethics of care in this situation? Has she been just? Does Vickie exhibit a pattern of caring for others, including her siblings as well as her mother?

6. How would you counsel John and Mary to communicate their concerns to Vickie and their mother if they were to act in accord with an ethics of care?

Chapter Summary

In this chapter, we have explored two significant and related challenges to the major systems for ethical decision making, especially the systems of deontological or universal ethics, utilitarianism, and contractualism. These challenges take issue with the universal claims of validity made by those who follow these types of ethical philosophies. Postmodern and feminist critics of these rationalistic systems feel their claims to universality are misleading, because the details of each specific case, as actually lived and experienced, are too complex for the supposedly cut-and-dried rules of such systems.

At first it seems surprising to say we are now living in something called *postmodern times*, because of the everyday assumption that the modern refers to the present, to contemporary life. But, postmodernists see the *Modern Age* as a particular period in history, with an approximate beginning and end. This period began with the European Enlightenment, represented by thinkers such as Kant, and events such as the French Revolution. The Modern Age also is seen as beginning in the Scientific and Industrial Revolutions, as people sought objective and practical solutions to problems of understanding and production. The Modern Age also brought in a tendency to create uniform categories, and to place people in categories, like so many units of production or elements in a chemical process. The *modern* thus came to mean uniformity, conformity, and institutionalized regulation of work and life.

During the period of modernism, a particular way of thinking was given special privilege. That way of thinking stressed generalized laws that could cover all possible cases in a given realm of activity. The chemical laws, such as Boyles' or Charles' Laws of Gases, operated the same everywhere; similarly, the laws of human behavior should be equally the same everywhere. These universally applicable systems of thought are called by postmodernists *Grand Narratives*. The postmodern view rejects the possibility of such *Grand Narratives*. One's perspective determines reality; and no one perspective is better or truer than any other. In stating this point, we must remember that there is no one definitive theory or philosophy that we can call *postmodern*. There are many different varieties of views and theories that are labeled *postmodern* today.

The modern culture tended to lead to losses in freedom and therefore a need for emancipation from the bureaucratic sameness represented by modern institutions. Those taking a postmodern view, therefore, believe that a major purpose of their project is to emancipate people everywhere from the deadening pigeon-holing so common in modern life. There has been a strong reaction against the tendencies of postmodernism, however, because of the fear it represents relativism or nihilism, the belief that nothing is necessarily true or good. In terms of ethics, postmodernism holds that there are no universal systems of ethics nor uniform rules or principles for ethical decision making. To some, a major danger of postmodernism is that it rejects religious systems of ethics and morals as it rejects other such all-encompassing *narratives*.

The interpersonal theories of dialogical communication, as represented particularly by Levinas and Buber, seem close to the tenor of postmodern views on ethics. Dialogical ethics is based on taking a particular attitude toward the other person in communication, rather than setting forth a set of principles or rules to be followed in various situations. In place of a rational system of argumentation, postmodernists as well as dialogical ethicists put a perspective or a way of acting toward the other.

Feminists in a similar way tend to reject rules-based, universal systems of rationalistic ethics. As with the postmodernists, we must remember there are many different kinds of feminists, and that representatives of the different branches would not all agree on the points we are making here. Many feminists outside Europe and the United States, for example, would reject some of the programs of Western feminists as culture-bound or at least culturally insensitive. A generally accepted tenet of the feminist view is the concept of the social construction of reality, especially social reality. Reality, particularly the reality of relations among the sexes and gender roles, is not given by nature but is created and has been created over the years in human interaction.

Of special interest for the ethics of interpersonal communication is the ethics of care as represented by Gilligan and Noddings. Gilligan and feminists following her views maintain there are inherent differences between the way women and men think. Patterns of thought about ethics differ between the sexes in that men tend to emphasize justice and rules while women emphasize caring for others and relationships. The scientific basis for such inherent differences may not be clear, but Noddings and others point to the value of upholding an ethics of care on its own terms. There are feminists, as well, who worry about the emphasis on an ethics of care because they fear it perpetuates or even seems to legitimize a subordinate role for women.

In the end, an emphasis on an ethics of care leads one to ask, when making ethical judgments, what would the *caring* person do given the circumstances before us. The ethics of care, therefore, rejects the rationalistic calculations based on systems of rights, rules, and impartiality. As with Levinas, one takes the position of focusing on the other person in a real-life relationship (not a hypothetical one); in that sense, one becomes *engrossed* in the other person. On the other hand, Noddings and others such as Manning would remind us that in the mature stage of ethical caring development, one must also take account of the need for care of the self as well. Foucault also came to stress the need for care for oneself in order to live a flourishing kind of life. An ethics of care requires one to consider all who might be affected by one's actions. When we focus entirely on one person in one relationship, we may overlook considerations conducive to making the world, or at least our part of it, more caring.

Postmodernists and feminists force us to think carefully about the assumptions we make about our views about people and society. When we assume something is *natural* or *normal*, are we really able to justify such a view? We are forced to become conscious of the unstated premises that underlie our tendencies to accept what has become the *modern* or the rational way of doing things. People need to be aware of the traps they lay for themselves when they place people and events in categories and take it for granted that those categories represent reality. When we communicate with others, we may unwittingly imply they are somehow superior or subordinate to us or that they are a *type* rather than an individual with a difference.

QUESTIONS AND TOPICS FOR DISCUSSION

1. How does the idea represented by the postmodern view challenge your own view of the world? Are you comfortable with living in the modern age and would you really rather not give it up? What *grand narratives* are important to your understanding of the world and how people should relate to each other?

2. Can you think of hidden assumptions we make everyday that pigeon-hole people into categories and determine how we treat them? Are these assumptions warranted? Are there cases in which treating people as types rather than individuals makes good ethical sense? Apply the same questions to assumptions about sex and gender roles.

3. What do you think about the claims of the postmodernists that modern life has led to dehumanizing tendencies? Do some postmodernists go too far in condemning the trend toward modern institutionalizing of life? What are some institutions resulting from modernization that have been mostly beneficial?

4. Do you feel that postmodernism represents relativism, so much so that people are left with no basis for judging any acts as either right or wrong?

5. In what ways do you believe that women and men are inherently different in the way they think about ethics? What do you think accounts for the differences that you observe?

6. What would be different in our everyday lives if people practiced an ethics of care? Do you feel there is a difference between ethics emphasizing rights and justice, on the one hand, and an ethics of care, on the other?

NOTES

1. Steven Best and Douglas Kellner, *Postmodern Theory: Critical Interrogations* (New York: Guilford Press, 1991), p. 2.

2. NPR Online, 1999, NPR's Performance Today: Milestones of the Millenium, Igor Stravinsky's *Rite of Spring* with Thomas Kelly, at, www.npr.org/programs/milestones/991110.motm.riteofspring.html. (accessed July 29, 2004).

3. Eve Browning Cole and Susan Coultrap-McQuin, eds, "Toward a Feminist Perspective of Moral Life," in *Explorations in Feminist Ethics* (Bloomington, IN: Indiana University Press, 1992), pp. 2–3.

4. "Postmodernism," in *Wikipedia, the Free Encyclopedia*, at http://en.wikipedia.org/wiki/Postmodern.

5. Steven Shaviro (1995–1997), at www.dhalgren.com/Doom/ch00.html.

6. David Ray Griffin, "Introduction to the SUNY Series in Constructive Postmodern Thought," in *Postmodernism and Public Policy*, ed. John B. Cobb (Albany, NY: SUNY Press, 1999), p. xii.

7. Adam Smith's *The Wealth of Nations* first appeared in print in 1776.

8. Charles Dickens, *Hard Times for These Times*, ed. David Craig (London: Penquin Classics, 1985, orig. pub. 1854), p. 47.

9. Dickens, *Hard Times*, p. 50.

10. Steven Best and Douglas Kellner, *The Postmodern Turn* (New York: The Guilford Press, 1997), p. 3.

11. Best and Kellner, *The Postmodern Turn*, p. 6.

12. Matthew Arnold, *Dover Beach*, 1867.

13. Peter Halliward, "Translator's Introduction," in *Ethics: An Essay on the Understanding of Evil*, trans. Alain Badiou (London: Verso, 2001), p. xiv.

14. Ivan Turgenev, *Fathers and Sons*, trans. Rosemary Edmonds (London: Penquin Classics, 1975, Orig. pub. 1862).

15. Rita C. Manning, *Speaking from the Heart: A Feminist Perspective on Ethics* (Boston: Rowman & Littlefied Publishers, Inc., 1992) p. 2; Cole, and Coultrap-McQuin, Explorations in Feminist Ethics p. 2.

16. D. Lynn O'Brien Hallstein, "A Postmodern Caring: Feminist Standpoint Theories, Revisioning Caring, and Communication Ethics," *Western Journal of Communication*, 63 (1999):1.

17. Seyla Benhabib, "From Identity Politics to Social Feminism: A Plea for the Nineties," in *Philosophy of Education*, accessed at www.ed.uiuc.edu/EPS/PES_Yearbook/94_docs/BENHABIB.HTM, 1994, p. 3.

18. Benhabib "From Identity Politics to Social Feminism," p. 2–3; see also O'Brien Hallstein, *Western Journal of Communication*, 32.

19. The *Stanford Encyclopedia of Philosophy* provides a very helpful overview of many of these positions; available online at http://plato.stanford.edu/entries/feminism-ethics/.

20. Alyson M. Jaggar, "Globalizing Feminist Ethics," *Hypatia*, 13 (1998):2, p. 1–2.

21. Peter Singer, *Writings on an Ethical Life* (New York: HarperCollins, 2000), p. 107.

22. Nel Noddings, *Caring: A Feminine Approach to Ethics & Moral Education* (Berkeley, CA: University of California Press, 1984), p. 2.

23. Lawrence Kohlberg, *The Philosophy of Moral Development: Moral Stages and the Idea of Justice* Vol. 2 (New York: Harper & Row Publishers, 1981).

24. Kohlberg, *The Philosophy of Moral Development*, Vol. 1, p. 192.

25. Kohlberg, *The Philosophy of Moral Development*, Vol. 1.

26. Carol Gilligan, *In a Different Voice: Pyschological Theory and Women's Development* (Cambridge, MA: Harvard University Press, 1982), p. 22.

27. Noddings, *Caring*, p. 13.

28. Noddings, *Caring*, p. 8.

29. Noddings, *Caring*, p. 17.

30. Rosalinde C. Barnett and Caryl Rivers, "Men Are from Earth and So Are Women, It's Faulty Research that Sets Them Apart," in *The Chronicle of Higher Education Review*, September 3, 2004, pp. B11–B13, is the source for this reasoning.

31. Rita C. Manning, *Speaking from the Heart: A Feminist Perpective on Ethics* (Lanham, MD: Rowman & Littlefield Publishers, 1992).

32. Manning, *Speaking from the Heart*, p. 56.

33. Benhabib, "From Identity Politics to Social Feminism," p. 1.

34. Barnett and Rivers, *The Chronicle*, p. B11.

35. Diane Romain, "Care and Confusion," in *Explorations in Feminist Ethics* (see note 3), pp. 27–37.

36. Erina L. MacGeorge, et al., "The Myth of Gender Cultures: Similarities Outweigh Differences in Men's and Woman's Provision of and Responses to Supportive Communication," in *Sex Roles: A Journal of Research*, 2004, 50, 143–186.

37. See Kohlberg, *The philosophy of Moral Development*, Vol. II, pp. 224–236, for the reasoning in this paragraph.

38. Manning, *Speaking from the Heart*, p. 73.

39. Benhabib, "From Identity Politics to Social Feminism," p. 50.

40. Martha C. Nussbaum, *Upheavals of Thought: The Intelligence of Emotions* (Cambridge, UK: Cambridge University Press, 2001).

41. See Nussbaum, *Upheavals of Thought*, pp. 338–342.

PART TWO

Issues, Settings, and Applications

One can use several perspectives to analyze ethical situations and to make ethical judgments and decisions. These perspectives have been presented in the first part of this book under these key headings:

- Character
- Duties
- Consequences
- Relationships.

In addition, we have pointed to additional considerations that may be relevant by discussing challenges to the prevailing standard models of ethical decision making:

- Postmodern perspectives and feminist ethics.

We suggest that these perspectives can provide a procedure for thinking through the ethical judgments and decisions facing us when we practice communication with others in a variety of settings.

Each perspective provides a lens for looking at the factors in a situation:

- What does a particular action say about one's character? What would a person of exemplary character do in this situation?
- Are there specific duties or obligations that bear on us in making this decision?
- What are the consequences of this action or decision? Will it enhance the most good for the most people? Will people be treated equitably as a result of this action?

- What does the action or decision say about our relationships with other people? Will the action affirm the full humanity of the other person or people involved?
- Are there hidden assumptions behind the values and actions involved in this situation? Do these assumptions lead to the subjugation of certain people or groups? Does the action lead to emancipation of subordinated groups?

Furthermore, we believe that one can follow a systematic approach to thinking through ethical decisions and judgments by following steps in a process for developing arguments. These steps suggest that we look at the following kinds of issues that usually present themselves:

- The *facts* in the case.
- The *values* relevant to this situation and these people.
- The *actions* (decisions) to follow in this case.

In the second part of the text, we move to applications for thinking about communication ethics in various settings. The first part of the text has focused attention on what philosophers call *normative ethics*, meaning that we discussed general principles for establishing norms for ethical conduct and decision making. In the second half, we take up various kinds of settings, focusing on communication in interpersonal relationships, organizations, politics, mass communication, and others.

Applied and Professional Ethics

In the second part of the book, we give more attention to what philosophers and ethicists might call *applied ethics* or *professional ethics*. Let us explain these terms in a little more detail.

When doing applied ethics, we use the principles of a general ethical theory or perspective for analyzing a specific issue or controversy. These issues often involve matters of public policy, such as whether or not cloning human beings should be permitted, whether euthanasia should be practiced, or whether or not animals should have the same rights as human beings (and so experimenting on animals would be wrong). It is not necessary, however, that the applications be in the realm of public policy.

In Chapters 7, 8, and 9, for example, we turn our attention to applications of communication ethics in ongoing human relationships, including relationships among diverse others, and involving people with different abilities and with disabilities. Chapters 10 and 11, on the other hand, deal with mass and political communication, where the issues are more closely tied to public policy. In the chapters on organizational communication and communication technologies there is a mix of public and interpersonal issues.

Professional ethics, a subset of applied ethics, concerns how people conduct themselves—as professionals—in their professional practices, such as law, medicine, journalism, consulting, and so on. Most recognized professions have established professional organizations or associations. Nearly all these bodies have written standards and rules for the practice of their professions, often including a code of ethics. These codes of ethics differ in the extent to which they are enforceable. The American Medical Association (AMA) indicate their code of ethics represents "not laws, but standards of conduct which define the essentials of honorable behavior for the physician." The federal and many state governments, on the other hand, have ethical codes that can be enforced with legal sanctions on governmental employees and officials.

These professional codes of ethics deal almost entirely with behavior of the individual while in the active conduct of professional duties and not with behavior outside their professional practice. Professional ethics, therefore, may overlap with but not entirely coincide with one's personal ethics. Professional ethics, with codes of ethics, are applicable in many of the fields we will discuss in the second half of the book, in the mass media, political activities, and organizational communication. Many professionals in information technology, computer programming, and other communication technologies also belong to professional associations with written ethical codes. We will refer to the code of ethics, a *Credo* (a statement of belief), adopted by our own professional organization, the National Communication Association, in our wrap-up in Chapter 14.

You will notice overlap in the discussion of issues in several of these chapters—that is unavoidable. When discussing issues in political communication, it is hard to avoid talking about the ethical implications of advertising, public relations, broadcasting, and other branches of mass communication. In discussions of both mass media and political communication, we will have to talk about the effects of computerized or digitalized forms of communication, such as web sites, blogs, the use of the Internet, email, and so on. Even our discussions of interpersonal communication will take us to some issues arising from the use of various communication technologies.

Chapter 14 intends to draw together many of the threads developed throughout the book. This chapter looks forward as well as back at the developing perspectives on communication ethics.

7 Ethics in Interpersonal Communication: Relationship and Character

. . . And let there be no purpose in friendship save the deepening of the spirit. For love that seeks aught but the disclosure of its own mystery is not love but a net cast forth: and only the unprofitable is caught.

And let your best be for your friend.
If he must know the ebb of your tide, let him know the flood also.
For what is your friend that you should seek him with hours to kill?
Seek him with hours to live.
For it is his to fill your need, but not your emptiness.

*And in the sweetness of friendship let there be laughter, and
sharing of pleasures.
For in the dew of little things the heart finds its morning and is
refreshed.*

—Khalil Gibran, *The Prophet*[1]

We visited a neighborhood bookstore just to browse. On our way to the
books on ethics, we happened to pass by the section titled Self Help. It was
one of the largest sections in the store, and our curiosity caused us to stop
and peruse the titles in that section. To our mild surprise, we found that a
major proportion of the titles focused on relationships with others, and that
self help really meant "help me deal with other people in my life." To be sure,
there were a few books on subjects like memory improvement, time management, and dressing for success. But what caught our attention were the
cleverly titled and colorful books dealing with the way we treat—and are
treated by—others.

While we doubt that men and women are really from different plan-
ets, or that our relationships are determined by our planetary alignment at
the moment of our birth, we realize that people are seeking real answers to
their concerns about relationships. For decades people have searched for
the answers to questions involving the way we treat one another. Self-help
gurus have become wealthy writing books offering strategies for dealing
with the significant people in our lives. Surf the television or radio channels
during daytime, and you will no doubt come across *talk-show* hosts who
parade for our entertainment people who can't live with (and apparently
without) the parent, child, friend, husband, wife, girlfriend, or boyfriend
with whom they are in daily contact. The history of movies demonstrates
Hollywood's attempts to explore how people both handle and mishan-
dle meaningful relationships in their lives. From the classic *Casablanca* to
When Harry Met Sally, we watch in fascination the creation, destruction, and
resurrection—Hollywood style—of relationships and the communication
between people.

Since childhood, we have been taught how to communicate. We were
influenced by how parents and then others communicated with us. In our
formative years (see the discussion of Kohlberg's Stages of Moral Development in Chapter 6) parents tell us how to speak, how to address others, how
to play fairly, and how to get along. We tell our students that if they ever
want to see people truly practicing strict deontological universal ethics, they
have only to observe the raising of young children. Parents routinely tell
children that "Lying is always wrong," and then confuse them later when
the child answers a phone call from someone and hears the parent whisper,
"Tell her I'm not home." Adults instruct children how to treat others, how to
communicate respectfully, and how to treat friends. And children do so
because they have been told that is their duty. William Bennett writes:

And, consequently, home is the place where we receive our first instruction in the virtues. It is our first moral training ground, the place where we can come to know right from wrong through the nurturing and protective care of those who love us more than anyone else. Our character takes shape under the guidance of the *do's* and *don'ts*, the instructions, the exhortations we encounter around the house. . . In the familiar world of home and hearth, we learn the habits of virtue that will fortify us when we venture into the world.[2]

While *home and hearth* may, indeed, fortify us, they do not guarantee us a life free of uncertainty, doubt, and the continuing need to rethink the early lessons we were taught as children. As we get older the *how to's* of treating others become increasingly fuzzy. We learn that in some cases it might be better to not be entirely forthcoming with a loved one (for example, "Honey, don't you think I'm a really good dancer?", "Sweetheart, does this dress make my thighs look fat?"). In some situations, we rationalize, perhaps it might be better if we do *not* share with others (regardless of what the Good Book says, are we *really* ready to give of our bounty to help the poor?). Life becomes more complex as we grow older. Decisions become more difficult to make. We realize that not everyone shares our values. We make new friends, fall in love, some of us marry, start families, begin to deal with aging parents, and come to grips with our own mortality.

Much of the foundation of this chapter took shape in Chapter 5 (dialogical ethics.) As we have stated earlier in this book, we believe that it is in dialogue with others that we begin to shape our ethical beliefs about communication. As the lessons learned at age three begin to clash with our adult perspectives, interpersonal relationships highlight the ethical concepts of character and relationships. We turn first to an explanation of what we mean by interpersonal communication and then further explore its foundation.

The Nature of Interpersonal Communication

Interpersonal communication has developed into a field within the discipline of communication studies. This field studies how communication occurs in situations in which one person talks with another person. For our purposes in this chapter, we will designate three characteristics typically used in defining what we mean by interpersonal communication:

1. It is *face to face*. The encounter is unmediated and immediate. There is no delay in communication, and nonverbal cues can be observed by both participants.

2. It is *dyadic*. There are only two people involved in the communication event. When a third person is introduced into the mix, the communication begins to take on the characteristics of a small group interaction.
3. It takes place in an *ongoing relationship*. The relationship has a sense of continuity. In contrast, interaction between one and the person at a roadside fast food joint, a person with whom he has no relationship and will likely never see again, is not interpersonal communication.

For users of the Internet, this definition of interpersonal communication may seem limiting. While many of us spend hours engaged in Instant Messaging, chat rooms, or exchanging email, we are not actually involved in interpersonal interaction. All these forms of communication depend on a computer with online access, and are thus *mediated*. The lack of immediacy can be seen in the following possibilities. We may be virtually anyone we want to be online, may become more beautiful, taller, younger, or older, with more hair, richer, or *unattached* relationally. No one knows the difference, because our *words* are electronically mediated and not presented face to face. We can't see the look in the eyes of the one with whom we are Instant Messaging, nor can we hear the *tone* in which messages are sent. We can read *LOL*, yet never hear the sound of the other's laughter. Interpersonal communication occurs only in *real-time*, personal contact. However, we fully understand that many people who grew up with the Internet and other mediated communication have a hard time seeing face-to-face communication as any different from mediated communication. We understand and respect differing opinions about the nature of interpersonal communication. For purposes of this chapter, though, we are limiting our discussion of interpersonal communication to face-to-face interaction.

There may be occasions when these three characteristics are not fully realized. Sometimes an interpersonal exchange can take place with more than two people in a setting in a short-term relationship. A work team or task group, for example, may throw together acquaintances, people who share no ongoing relationship. While the team is functioning, the communication may take on interpersonal dynamics. But when the stated goal or task is achieved, the purpose and function of the team (and in many cases the need to be in personal contact) ends, and communication often ceases. Some aspects of online interactions occur within the context of an ongoing relationship and may thus exhibit the features of interpersonal communication. There are of course always various kinds of exceptions.

The features of interpersonal communication bring to the fore some ethical dimensions. In our interaction with another person we have the chance to assess and evaluate the ethics of communicative behavior. We can imagine guidelines for how to communicate ethically and morally, and in the physical presence of the other we can quickly see the impact of our message. The ongoing nature of the relationship ensures that we will have a *yardstick* to measure how well we are communicating with one another and an opportunity to make adjustments in that communication along the way.

The Ethics of Dialogue in Interpersonal Communication

Dialogical ethics, as discussed in Chapter 5, provides some basic principles for evaluating the ethical nature of our communication with others. The principles of Martin Buber's *I and Thou*, Emmanuel Levinas' concept of the *Other*, and Carl Rogers' *Unconditional Positive Regard* maintain that dialogic thinking is the key to ethical interpersonal relationships. In our dialogue with the other person we engage him or her in the relationship. This engaged dialogue is a fluid, ever-changing process. It requires listening and being listened to while sharing thoughts and feelings. Ethical dialogue in interpersonal communication is not tied to personal agenda and strategic ends. There it exhibits a give-and-take quality, which can often change focus in the middle of the interaction.

Dialogue creates and shapes meaning for the relationship. The nature of our interaction with the other person in an ongoing relationship determines the *meaning*, as we use the term here. This is significant because our trust in and investment with the other person can only take place over time. We may immediately like a person on meeting him or her, but the trust and engagement will come only as our dialogue continues.

To illustrate what we mean in the above paragraph, reflect on the following:

1. Who is your closest friend?
2. How long have you known this friend?
3. What makes this person your *closest* friend?
4. Do you talk differently with this person than you do with others?
5. How is your dialogue different with this friend than it is with a person not as close to you?

Your answers to the above questions probably reflect the *meaning* you and your closest friend have created through the way you talk with each other. In other words, you *trust* him or her, *listen* more carefully to him or her, and are more *open* to that person because the relationship has been tested and found strong because of the way you communicate with that friend. There is a mutual *investment* which requires that the dialogue is free, open, and, as a result, ethical.

How can we know that our dialogue in interpersonal relationships is, indeed, ethical? When we talk with our friend, spouse, or parent, does the conversation always have to be *deep* or philosophical? Does the conversation have to last for a long time in order to be considered ethical communication? Does the subject matter of our dialogue even have to be serious, or can it be playful or trivial? What constitutes genuine ethical dialogue raises important issues, and we will explore them here. We begin with some qualifying assumptions about dialogue from an ethical perspective.

Principles from Dialogical Ethics

In this section, we will discuss the application of principles from Chapter 5. First, the principles of dialogical ethics require that interpersonal communication takes place in truth. Words we use with the other person are designed not to conceal, but to reveal. This means that ethical dialogue does not allow us to hold back from the other person those things which we perceive to be true. The environment of truthful dialogue establishes and nurtures trust, allowing the relationship to continue. We tell our boyfriend or girlfriend, "I can handle anything that happens between us, just don't lie to me." We are asking that they always speak the truth to us, no matter what. Truth telling is the first requirement of ethical dialogue.

Second, principles of ethical dialogue require that both participants be *fully present* in our engagement. People approach dialogue with each other in such a way that they are not distracted by anything physical or psychological. Do you remember the last time you tried talking to your best friend, or your boyfriend or girlfriend, but they were doing something else while you were talking? Did you feel at the time that he or she was truly *present* and attentive to you? Perhaps he or she was wrapped up in a movie, or reading the last few pages of a mystery, or still depressed about flunking a test earlier that day. For one person in a relationship to fake attentiveness and interest in what the other person is saying goes against this principle of ethical dialogue. Feigned engagement often leads to confusion and hurt feelings. Ethical dialogue requires that both individuals select a place and time in which both can focus and pay attention to the needs of the other.

Third, in ethical dialogue both participants should focus on *you* rather than *I*. Just as a first-year communication student learns that a good speech is audience centered rather than speaker centered, the student of dialogical ethics realizes that interpersonal communication works best when each person is focused on the other, rather than on self. Martin Buber, the Jewish philosopher and teacher featured prominently throughout this book, expressed the concept of the dangers of *I* dialogue:

In the atmosphere of genuine dialogue, he who is ruled by the thought of his own effect as the speaker of what he has to speak has a destructive effect. If, instead of what has to be said, I try to bring attention to my *I*, I have irrevocably miscarried what I had to say; it enters the dialogue as a failure and the dialogue is a failure.[3]

Many of us have had the experience of being in a conversation—more often than not an argument—with a friend or other person close to us, when anger and frustration escalate. The disagreement often begins with a small issue, and then builds with each ensuing exchange until a much larger issue explodes. We remember a conversation overheard a few years ago. A husband and wife, married for twenty years, replayed an argument from that morning:

"Honey, you forgot to put the cap back on the toothpaste—AGAIN—and I accidentally set my coffee cup on the tube and got toothpaste all over the place."

"I was in a hurry, and forgot to put the cap back on. I overslept because you snored all night. Did you clean it up?"

"Yeah, but I shouldn't have had to, damn it! YOU left the cap off."

"Don't start! If you knew how many times over the years I have cleaned up after you, mister. I'm not your mother!"

"My mother would never have left cap off the toothpaste, DEAR. She was a little more conscientious about that stuff than you are."

"Well maybe you would rather go back to your mother. You never appreciate the things I do around here! Everyone takes me for granted!"

And so it went. Although they laugh about it years later, at the time it happened they did not find it amusing. Like those which so many of us have experienced, this interaction was not about regard for the other. In fact, as one was talking, the other was busy planning his or her retort. The exchange quickly became a runaway verbal fight. What started with a misplaced toothpaste cap very quickly became a conflagration of hurt feelings and accusations. The conversation was more concerned with me and my feelings than with you and your needs. Buber would claim that this dialogue had failure written all over it.

A fourth criterion, or *litmus test*, for the ethics of dialogue concentrates on the unspoken component of communication. Listening—truly listening—is an important part of ethical dialogue. Listening attentively, focusing on the other and what he or she is saying, and giving feedback assuring he or she is being heard are indicators of ethical interpersonal communication. A good listener is everybody's friend. Everyone wants to feel heard and understood. Carl Rogers revolutionized therapy by being an active and reflective listener to his clients. As you may remember from the earlier discussion, being a good listener frees one from being judgmental or opinionated.

In view of dialogical ethics as a foundation for interpersonal communication, we turn to an application of these principles by considering how we handle interpersonal conflict.

Conflict in Interpersonal Communication

The very nature of interpersonal communication suggests that there are bound to be difficulties and rough spots in communication with others. Remember that interpersonal communication is face to face, dyadic, and ongoing. There are going to be differences of opinion in any ongoing relationship. People are going to get angry or frustrated, and are going to knowingly communicate in ways that will trigger an argument. Regardless of how it comes about, there is nothing unethical about conflict. Conflict is a condition of relationships. It happens.

The myriad self-help books as well as textbooks on interpersonal relationships are chock full of theories and strategies to deal with conflict. We will not discuss those strategies here, but rather we will approach conflict and its resolution from an ethical perspective. Specifically, we will apply dialogical ethics in considering managing conflict in interpersonal relationships.

Interpersonal conflict occurs when our needs or desires are thought to be at odds with the needs and desires of the other person. As the earlier discussion indicates, this conflict arises when we are unable to keep our focus on the needs of the other, or they are unable to reciprocate. A mutually agreed on solution cannot be reached, and perhaps feelings of anger and frustration are rising. In this phase it becomes difficult to honor the *Thou* (Buber's term, Chapter 5) in the other person. *Unconditional Positive Regard* (Roger's concept, Chapter 5) has faded when we become embroiled in a *Win/Lose* contest. It is at this stage that the *Game* begins, and people begin getting hurt.

Our ethics usually become evident by the way we treat—and are treated by—each other. We can directly and immediately observe our interpersonal relationships and our communication in them. We can have a verbal exchange with another person, and immediately come away thinking, "I don't think I treated her very well just then." Our interpersonal *filter* gives us instant feedback on how the dialogue went, and whether the exchange felt ethical. Of course, the situation can be reversed if we sense the other person has not treated us very well. Many of us have experienced the feeling of being marginalized or dismissed after a conversation with another person.

As we have noted, conflict in interpersonal relations is inevitable. Even people in the best of relationships must learn to communicate ethically when conflicts arise. Dozens of self-help gurus, authors, coaches, counselors, talk-show hosts, and amateur advice-givers will gladly suggest *can't-miss* strategies to improve interpersonal communication. Being aware of, and using, the principles of dialogical ethics in our relationship by honoring the *other* and remaining honest and engaged can allow the conflict to be more manageable. Interpersonal ethics reside, then, in the nature of our relationship— the trust, honesty, covenants, and availability of each person—as well as in the character of both parties involved in that relationship. That is to say, how we conduct ourselves in our interpersonal relationships is largely determined by the ethical quality of our very character. How we respond to the conduct of the other person often depends on the ethical quality of their character. For that reason, we now turn to a discussion of character.

Ethical Communication in Interpersonal Relationships: Character Counts

An examination of our ethical behavior in interpersonal communication does not only have a relational dimension, but a character dimension as well. Recall from the section on virtue ethics (Chapter 2) that we can evaluate our ethical behavior on the basis of what a virtuous person would do. In our everyday interactions and interpersonal communication we may strive to *communicate as a virtuous person would communicate.* We should, as people of character, treat others the way we ourselves wish to be treated. Traits like integrity, honesty, compassion, and empathy are character virtues, and as such are foundational to our communication in interpersonal relationships. In his book, *Integrity*, Stephen Carter writes:

> Indeed, one reason to focus on integrity as perhaps the first among the virtues that make for good character is that it is in some sense prior to everything else: the rest of what we think matters very little if we lack essential integrity, the courage of our convictions the willingness to act and speak in behalf of what we know to be right. In an era when the American people are crying out for open discussion of morality—of right and wrong—the ideal of integrity seems a good place to begin.[4]

During the administration of former President Bill Clinton, a story was leaked regarding his alleged inappropriate relationship with a former intern and the then current legislative affairs employee named Monica Lewinsky. As the scandal unfolded in the press, the president initially denied having any relationship with the young woman. The accusations and denials continued until the president finally said the following to a national audience on August 17, 1998:

> As you know, in a deposition in January, I was asked questions about my relationship with Monica Lewinsky. While my answers were legally accurate, I did not volunteer information. Indeed, I did have a relationship with Miss Lewinsky that was not appropriate. In fact, it was wrong . . . my public

comments and my silence about this matter gave a false impression. I misled people, including even my wife. I deeply regret that. I can only tell you I was motivated by many factors. First, by a desire to protect myself from the embarrassment of my own conduct.[5]

With this admission, and with the memories of the Watergate scandal during the Nixon administration still embedded in the national psyche, the issue of *character* began to dominate public conversations. From talk shows to the tabloids to the national media, the question "Does character matter?" was discussed and debated on a regular basis.

As we have established in several chapters throughout this book, character most definitely *does* matter. And while the approaches are somewhat different, the various ethical systems we have discussed rely on the issue of character. In Kantian ethics (Chapter 3), we learn that the person of character will see it as an absolute duty to act in such a way that wills that everyone else could also act in a similar manner. Bentham and Mill, both utilitarians (Chapter 4) believe that the person of character would always act for the greater good for the greatest number. The person of character for Rawls would stand behind the veil of ignorance (Chapter 4) and affirm the concept of justice as fairness. For Aristotle, the person of character was the person of virtue (Chapter 2) who exemplifies moral excellence by performing in a way that a person of character would perform.

In interpersonal communication, the person of character is the person who attends to the concepts of dialogical ethics and holds the *other* in such high regard that his or her needs and ego become secondary to the other. When that full positive regard is not present, when the relationship loses mutuality, it becomes vulnerable to the *Game*, as we discussed in Chapter 5. When the *Game* is being played, the *Firewall* is removed, and the people in that relationship are put in harm's way for issues of trust and manipulation to arise.

Trust and Manipulation in Interpersonal Relationships

Anyone who has been lied to knows that trust takes a long time to establish and that in just an instant it can be destroyed. A deception, or cover-up, or breach of confidence can destroy a lifetime of intimacy and confidence built up in a relationship. Like intimacy, *trust* is a term that we use constantly in our relationships, yet it is a concept that is often difficult to comprehend. We trust or mistrust a government official because of policy or his or her track record on issues. We trust or mistrust the salesperson who is telling us that the fifteen-year-old car will run just like new. We trust our doctors to have the expertise to know that the prescription will safely relieve our pain.

But the issue of trust in interpersonal relationships is much more complex, due mainly to the very definition of the term. Remember that an interpersonal relationship is dyadic, face-to-face, and ongoing. As such, establishing and maintaining trust involves a much more *fluid* process, because the nature of the relationship is always changing. When we meet someone and begin to fall in love, we trust him or her more after our sixth or tenth or twentieth encounter than we did after our first or second. As our communication with the other person deepens and becomes more meaningful, we also begin to allow ourselves to be more vulnerable to that person. It is during this development that we begin to establish what Martin Buber calls the *I–Thou* relationship, and what Levinas describes as the engagement with the *Other*. The level of trust we place in the other person, and they in us, depends almost entirely upon how we judge their truthfulness; a term Sissela Bok describes as *veracity*. Bok writes:

> Trust as some degree of veracity functions as a *foundation* of relations among human beings; when this trust shatters or wears away, institutions collapse . . . The function of the principle of veracity as a foundation is evident when we think of trust. I can have different kinds of trust: that you will treat me fairly, that you will have my interests at heart, that you will do me no harm. But if I do not trust your word, can I have genuine trust in the first three? If there is no confidence in the truthfulness of others, is there any way to assess their fairness, their intention to help or to harm? How then can they be trusted? *Whatever* matters to human beings, trust is the atmosphere in which it thrives.[6]

It is in that *atmosphere* of trust that the foundation of dialogical ethics is established. Trust, as in the *I–Thou* relationship, or Levinas' *Other*—involves great risk. When we put our trust in a friend or lover, when we disclose our deepest fears or hopes, we entrust that person with custodial rights to our innermost thoughts and feelings. When we sense that he or she is doing the same with us, the level of trust deepens, and the *Thou*-ness of the other takes on even more intimate dimensions. When we risk being vulnerable to the other, we trust him to be open and nonjudgmental of our self-disclosure. When we accept and hold in trust the self-disclosure of the other, we are demonstrating the very essence of dialogical ethics—that of unconditional acceptance. When trust is high in an interpersonal relationship, communication is more ethical and intimate. There is a mutual desire to deepen and enrich the dialogue of the relationship. Problems and issues are more readily identified, diagnosed, and resolved because of the level of trust.

A student of ours—we'll call her Jenny—came back from a Spring Break trip and announced that she was immediately deactivating her sorority membership and moving off campus as soon as she could find a place. As we talked, we learned that the spring trip had been a disaster for Jenny, causing her to believe (in her words), "I will never trust another person as long as I live." Jenny and her best friend and roommate joined several other sorority sisters for what was to be five days of fun in the sun, and a break from the rigors of studying and college routine. According to Jenny, all went well until their last night before catching a plane for the return to campus. By agreement, all the girls met together for dinner and drinks as a last celebration of what had to that point been a wonderful trip. As the drinks continued to come, and conversation became louder and less inhibited, Jenny's trusting and secure world fell apart. Her roommate, a very close friend of four years, had too much to drink. She began to share with all the girls at the table all the things that Jenny had had to *overcome* to become the "sweet girl she is today." In the next ten minutes, everything that Jenny had trustingly confided to her friend tumbled out in a drunken rush. Everyone at the table learned of Jenny's abortion at the age of seventeen. They learned that Jenny had been in therapy for two years. They discovered that the reason Jenny had switched majors was because she had failed two key courses in her first major. The group drank to Jenny's courage, and Jenny ran from the room in tears. Her roommate stayed and drank with the rest of the girls. When they returned, Jenny left the sorority house and lived with an acquaintance while she looked for another place. Despite months of apology and efforts to resolve things by her roommate and former friend, Jenny never again spoke to her. Three years later, Jenny had not dated or attempted to form another friendship. The next person to become Jenny's friend, or the next person she dates, will need to be very patient and willing to allow her some extra time to begin to form trust again.

Jenny's experience demonstrates the risk. When we trust others, we can be hurt. Sometimes that hurt comes from friends who may not be trying to hurt us. Words may *slip out* or intimacies may be unintentionally revealed during normal conversation. If we are the one unintentionally betraying a trust, we feel terrible about it, and try as we may, we might not be able to regain that person's trust again. If we are the one whose trust is being unintentionally compromised, we may decide either to forgive, continue trusting, or pull back and be very careful before we ever risk trust again.

The real damage happens when we are intentionally deceived—when someone we trust takes that trust and uses it for his or her gain, and then moves on to the next trusting person to come along. Sometimes we are the victim of manipulation, of people who gain our trust only to use it against us somewhere along the line. Often, this manipulation takes place over matters financial. An elderly person, for example, might put trust in a person selling impossibly cheap insurance, or retirement planning, or financial management. When the manipulator has gained that person's trust, the scam is nearly complete. Once money changes hands, the manipulator leaves for parts unknown while the trusting person is left with broken trust and, often, no money.

Sometimes, manipulation of our trust happens in the workplace. We may trust a supervisor or a colleague to treat us with respect, only to find out that the person we trusted was really acting only for his or her benefit or advancement. There are many ethics stories of inter-office affairs, where the balance of power and influence in the relationship often means that the person with power often gets the romance and sex he or she wants, while the person in the inferior position usually gets fired.

In interpersonal relationships, the instances of manipulation are often manifested in trusting someone in a loving relationship. We hear students complain that they met someone whom they initially trusted, only to discover that the other person was a *serial lover* who played the *Game* of pursuit and conquest and later left when the discussion turned to intimacy and commitment.

The point we made in our discussion of dialogical ethics in Chapter 5 is worth repeating here. Ethical communication is an excellent way to measure and evaluate our personal ethics because it gives us measurability as to how we are progressing in a relationship. However — and this is the point — deciding to engage someone in an *I – Thou* relationship is risky because we may get hurt. Any time we allow another person's feelings and values and agenda to be greater than our own — even if for a moment — we make ourselves vulnerable. We can know the exhilaration of trusting and being trusted, but with it comes the risk that we may be hurt by someone who is manipulating the interpersonal relationship for his or her own benefit. We can prevent becoming manipulators of others with whom we have an interpersonal relationship by always self-disclosing our interests, biases, and wishes. This disclosure allows the other to make the decision to engage us around those issues, or not. We can trust that the other person will be equally self-disclosing, thus giving us those same choices, but we cannot control the unethical practices of the manipulators of that trust. We can hurt and feel betrayed, but we can always decide to trust again one day.

The Ethics of Self-Disclosure

In order to us to be able to trust enough to allow an *I – Thou* relationship to develop, we must have a good idea what the other person is about. In order to establish an ethical relationship with the *Other* (Levinas), we must have a sense of the other's needs, wishes, and desires. For the other person to make the same decisions in an interpersonal relationship with us, we must first allow him or her to *see* us through as clear a lens as possible. For there to be an ethical relationship with ethical dialogue, a framework of trust and self-disclosure must first be established. Self-disclosure is the act of revealing things about ourselves to other people in our lives. In an interpersonal relationship that depends on ethical dialogue, we must first be able to assess the other person's self-image as well as share our own with him or her. Much of our dialogue with that person helps shape our (and his or hers) self-image.

The Ethical Dilemma of Self-Disclosure

Of course, there is risk in self-disclosure, too. Jenny learned this lesson the hard way. The issue of ethical self-disclosure presents us with a bit of a dilemma. It is rather easy to understand that in order for an interpersonal relationship to grow and deepen, our communication must have a mutual commitment to self-disclosure. The importance of self-disclosure in the maintenance and ethical development of interpersonal relationships has been repeatedly documented in self-help books and communication texts. Trust is enriched when we have spoken our deepest thoughts and are still held by the other in an *I–Thou* relationship. We breathe a sigh of relief when our closest friend or lover declares, "You now know all my secrets. There is nothing I am holding back from you." It is safe to say that no relationship or meaningful communication can be judged as ethical without mutual self-disclosure.

And yet, there is the dilemma. Most of us can reasonably agree that self-disclosure is crucial to the success of communication. We can reasonably understand that dialogical ethics, from Buber to Levinas to Rogers, has at its core the component of trusting mutual self-disclosure. But the question arises: how much do I disclose about myself? Does my *Thou* need to know everything about me? Are there some things better left unsaid in a relationship, while still being ethical?

Interpersonal communication expert Joseph DeVito reflects on this dilemma:

> At times it may be expedient to omit, for example, past indiscretions, certain fears, and perceived personal inadequacies if these disclosures may lead to negative perceptions or damage the relationship in some way. In any decision to self-disclose, possible effects on the relationship should be considered. But it is also necessary to consider the ethical issues involved, specifically the other person's right to know about behaviors and thoughts that may influence the choices he or she will make. Most relationships would profit from greater self-disclosure of present feelings than details of past sexual experiences or psychological problems. The sharing of present feelings also helps a great deal in enabling each person to empathize with the other; each comes to better understand the other's point of view when these self-disclosures are made.[7]

It is at this point in the discussion that the question of what we *ought* to do, versus what we *choose* to do needs to be raised. Note that DeVito suggests that one take the *expedient* route while at the same time considering ethics. In reality, most of us do exactly as DeVito describes. We balance the ethics of self-disclosure with what we believe the other person needs to know. For example, if you got suspended in school for two days when you were in the 9th grade for cheating on a U.S. History test and lying about it when confronted, does your fiancée need to know about it fifteen or twenty years later? Is an indiscretion of youth part of what needs to be self-disclosed in order for you to be ethical? Certainly, DeVito advocates the disclosure of *present* feelings as the ethical standard for interpersonal communication. Many people in relationships today adopt the stance that everything that has taken place since they met is open for discussion and ethical consideration, but things that happened before they met really are not relevant to their friendship, or marriage, or partnership unless there were legal or medical ramifications resulting from it. We would certainly disclose a prison term in our past. We would be ethical if we disclose a history of a sexually transmitted disease, for instance. These self-disclosures would be necessary information for the other person to have, so that he or she can make decisions and choices in our relationship. How we resolve the ethical dilemma of self-disclosure is a matter of choice. It depends on the level of trust and intimacy the two people have established.

We may look at this issue of self-disclosure through deontological, duty-based ethics and ask if we should always tell the truth no matter how obscure or seemingly unimportant the event. Or we may look at the issue through the lens of virtue ethics, and wonder if we should disclose of ourselves as a person of virtue would. But we are proponents of dialogical ethics as an effective platform on which to measure ethics. As such, we believe not only that the *I–Thou* relationship requires the trust and intimacy necessary to self-disclose everything necessary for the continued growth of the relationship, but also that we hold the other's self-disclosure as sacred. There are times when the decision to share or withhold information is not clear-cut or simple for us. When that decision involves someone close to us, as it will in the following case as well as it did with the story of Jenny, it can affect the future of our relationships.

CASE STUDY: SHOULD SHE TELL?

Deandra and Shay are lifelong friends. Born in the Midwest, they met each other as young girls in the fourth grade, and were inseparable through high school and college. When Deandra went to graduate school in New York, Shay got a job in Manhattan and moved with her. The closest of friends through the usual dating woes and even with the breakup of Shay and her fiancé a year earlier, the two women were always there for one another as support and comfort. Men entered and exited the lives of one or both of the women for the first two years in the city, and still the bonds of friendship between the two remained strong. Deandra received her graduate degree and decided to remain in New York. She had met someone at school, and had shared with Shay that she felt that, for the first time in her life, she was in love. For Shay, this news came as a bit of a surprise. Deandra had not mentioned this developing relationship much at all over the past few months. Shay's surprise turned to shock when Deandra revealed that her new love interest was a woman named Beth. Beth was younger, just out of college, and living on her own for the first time. Unlike the studious Deandra, Beth was a self-described "party animal" who loved being with people and living a life of play.

As the months went by, Shay found it harder to maintain the level of relationship she and Deandra had enjoyed for so many years. Beth was spending more time with them now, she and Deandra had announced that they were now exclusive, and Shay was beginning to feel more and more relegated to the sidelines as Deandra fell deeper in love with Beth. Still, as her friend of so many years, Shay remained supportive of Deandra despite her own personal reservations that Beth was going through a *phase* and would soon move on to someone else.

One evening, as Shay and a group of coworkers met for happy hour at a neighborhood pub, something happened that would change the long-time interpersonal relationship between Deandra and Shay forever. As she went to the bar to order another round for her group, Shay saw at a corner table a familiar face. As she watched in horror, Beth and a man were locked in a passionate embrace, kissing and touching despite the public setting. After a while, Beth and the man left the tavern, arm-in-arm, and walked into the night. As the initial shock subsided, Shay realized that her best friend was being *played* and that she was going to get hurt badly. Nobody else had witnessed the encounter between Beth and her male companion, and Shay began to weigh her options as to how she would handle what she now knew.

The authors now invite you to consider three possible options that Shay was considering. Use what you know about ethics, interpersonal relationships, disclosure, and the *I–Thou* position of engaging the *Other*. We will not suggest a *correct* way for Shay to handle this situation, because ethics and communication and relationships do not very often come with a guarantee of correctness. We ask only that you form your reasoned opinion based on what you are learning about your ethical approach to relationships.

Shay's first thought was that she would say nothing to Deandra about what she had seen. This would allow the relationship between Deandra and Beth to take a natural course without interference from her. Shay would be there to pick up the pieces for Deandra when she discovered (and Shay was sure that Beth's betrayal would be discovered) that she had been manipulated by the woman she loved. Shay would then appear to share the shock and pain of her friend as if they were learning about what happened for the first time to Deandra. Despite the pain of Beth's unfaithfulness, Deandra would realize that Shay had always been there for Deandra as a friend. Not revealing what she knew certainly had its advantages, Shay thought.

On second thought, Shay reasoned, maybe she should go to Deandra immediately and tell her exactly what she had seen. Deandra is her best friend. They tell each other everything. They have a history of always being truthful with each other, and what better time than now to be completely truthful? What she has to say to her friend will be painful at first, but she will stay with Deandra and support her and allow her to grieve when she hears the news. While she hated the thought of being the bearer of such painful information, honesty really is the best policy, figured Shay. Yes, she would go and speak the truth of what she had seen to Deandra.

Unless maybe there is an even better way to handle this, thought Shay. Rather than say nothing to Deandra ("Isn't that kind of like lying or something?" wondered Shay) and allowing her to find out from someone else, or rather than just blurting out the painful news to her best friend, perhaps there is a third way. What if Shay went directly to Beth and confronted her with what she had seen? As she played it out in her mind, Shay envisioned the dialogue going something like this: "Beth, I saw you with that guy in the bar. I was shocked and angry, but even worse is what this is going to do Deandra. I am not going to permit you to manipulate her and cheat on her. So here's what we're going to do: either *you* tell Deandra what happened, or *I* will. You have 24 hours to tell her the truth and if you don't, then I will have to." This strategy put the onus on Beth to confess her dalliance while at the same time removing Shay from being in the middle. And, if Beth didn't tell Deandra herself, then Shay still had the other ways of handling the situation.

QUESTIONS FOR ANALYSIS OF THE CASE

That's the case. We have given you three options to consider. How do you think Shay should handle this information that affects her closest friend? Consider first the option of Shay saying nothing to Deandra of what she had witnessed. We raise the following questions about this first option:

- Is there an ethical justification for saying nothing?
- Does the possibility that Shay misinterpreted what she had seen warrant the decision to not tell Deandra?
- Might there be some hidden reasons why Shay would opt to wait until Deandra finds out on her own?

Shay's second option was to immediately tell Deandra what she had seen:

- Is there an ethical justification for speaking up immediately?
- Is bringing pain to a friend worth full disclosure of what Shay believes to be the truth?
- If you were Shay, what words would you use to tell Deandra?

Shay's third choice was to directly confront Beth:

- Does this strategy constitute manipulation on Shay's part?
- If self-disclosure is forced (on Beth), is it truly ethical?
- Is it moral to set into play something that will affect not just one, but two, relationships (Deandra and Beth; Deandra and Shay)?

Is there an even greater question here? Deandra has made a significant life change. Should Shay raise with Deandra the sexuality question? How ought she raise the issue with her friend?

One more question to consider is whether this case would have additional ethical issues if the relationship Deandra had developed was a heterosexual one. If so, what might those new ethical issues be? If not, why not?

Chapter Summary

Our interpersonal relationships test and exercise our communication ethics every day. Our relationships provide the stage on which not only our communication skills but also our character are formed. As we have suggested throughout this text, we believe that dialogical ethics is the most applicable system of ethics system for this kind of setting. As we have seen, the formation, development, and enrichment of our meaningful relationships happen in the way we learn to manage dialogue with one another. Chapter 5 is foundational for this study of our relationships and how we communicate in them. In the communication ethics within our interpersonal relationships perhaps we understand a little better why there are so many self-help books written on the subject. Maybe we can see more easily why so many of us are focused on—and confounded by—the nature of intimate relationships. Many of us understand how important ethical communication is in our interpersonal relationships, but still we find that the answers to the ethical questions are not simple ones.

We have seen, in the story of Jenny, how risky self-disclosure can be in interpersonal relationships. And yet, without the trust and ability to be more open and revelatory to one another, how can we become more intimate? If moving to *I–Thou* is so ethically sound, why can't we all just do it?

As Shay in our case study is about to discover, there is no easy way to resolve the ethical dilemma in which she finds herself. There is often risk involved in disclosing what we know, and sometimes lifelong relationships can be damaged even though our intentions may be good ones.

Still, communication ethics remains the best platform from which we can evaluate the depth of our relationships. Even though it is risky to be ethical in our communication with significant others in our lives, we must take that risk if our important relationships are to grow and flourish.

QUESTIONS AND TOPICS FOR DISCUSSION

1. In your most meaningful relationship, are there things about yourself that you have chosen to withhold from the other person? By what criteria did you make that decision?

2. How does the concept of dialogical ethics affect the way you communicate with people in significant interpersonal relationships?

3. Can you imagine a circumstance when manipulation might be considered an ethical response to a situation?

4. In your opinion, is there a difference in the ways men and women communicate in interpersonal relationships?

5. In your relationships, do you handle conflict well? Can you imagine an ethical approach to communicating in interpersonal conflicts that might help you manage conflict more satisfactorily?

NOTES

1. Kahlil Gibran, *The Prophet* (New York: Alfred A. Knopf, 1977), pp. 58–59.
2. William J. Bennett, *The Moral Compass* (New York: Simon & Schuster, 1995), p. 19.
3. Martin Buber, "Elements of the Interhuman", in *The Knowledge of Man*, trans. M. Friedman and R.G. Smith (New York: Harper & Row, 1965); John Stewart, in *Bridges Not Walls* (New York: Random House, 1986) p. 388.
4. Stephen L. Carter, *Integrity* (New York: Harper Perennial, 1996), p.7.
5. "Clinton's Speech to the American Public, August 17, 1998", at www.coffeeshoptimes.com/clinadd.html (accessed October 28, 2004).
6. Sissela Bok, *Lying* (New York: Vintage Books, 1999), p. 31.
7. Joseph DeVito, *Messages*, 3rd ed. (New York: HarperCollins College Publishers, 1996), pp. 301–302.

CHAPTER

8

Ethics and the Communication of Diversity

The *USA Today* on September 30, 2004, reported that *minorities* are becoming a majority in more and more parts of the United States.[1] In 280 counties out of 3,141 in the country, whites who are not Hispanic are no longer in the majority. As a state, California has not had an ethnic majority for several years, and Texas is rapidly approaching or may already have joined California in that designation. Major cities such as Denver and Detroit do not have a specific racial or ethnic majority either. Furthermore, the so-called *demographic upheaval* means that the majority—minority divide is no longer a simple black-and-white affair, giving the growing populations of Asian and Hispanic background. As part of this trend, we may soon find that the word "minority," used as a demographic category, will no longer be used or even considered acceptable. Concerning the ethics of labels for people, many people now object to the term "minority" anyway as implying diminished importance or status.

Elements of Diversity

Advertising specialists today stress the importance of the *Demographics*. In fact, you can have your own, as when someone asks, "What are your demographics?" The word *demographics* begins with the same, classical Greek root as the word, *democracy*. We would therefore be right if we guessed that *demo-* (from the Greek word, *demos*, the people in their *demes*, the traditional *tribes* of Athens) had something to do with people. You may not realize that the suffix *-graphics* has to do with writing about or the study of something (hence the lead in your pencil is called *graphite*).

The demographics are therefore the study of the people, specifically dividing them into groups or categories for determining what sorts of messages, products, or advertising they might be interested in. This notion of demographics is at the heart of understanding what people tend to mean by diversity, as well. The demographics shows us all the different ways that people can be divided into categories, by religion, race, sex, and so on.

Diversity has become a matter of central concern in the United States, especially in regard to education, employment, media, and culture in general. A look at headlines from a typical issue of *DiversityInc.com*, will indicate the range of topics and issues covered by the area of concern:[2]

- *Gay, Lesbian "Economic Walkout" Friday* (a woman calls for an economic action similar to the type used during the Civil Rights Movement).
- *L'Oreal Settles Age Discrimination Case* (case involved a fifty-eight-year-old woman who had sued the cosmetics manufacturer over a denied promotion and her firing).
- *Racism Conference Removes References to Arabs, Jews, and Christians* (conference in Suriname decides that specific reference in regard to crimes against black people in the past was divisive).
- *Poll: 1 in 4 Americans Holds Anti-Muslim Views* (after the September 11, 2001, attack many Americans quickly developed negative views toward Muslims).
- *Arnold's Vetoes Anger Latinos* (story refers to Arnold Schwarzeneggar, Governor of California, vetoes of legislation seen as favorable to Latinos in that state).

We see, therefore, that there are many kinds of diversity, or ways that people can be categorized. For example, here is a list of possible elements in human diversity in a modern society:

Sex or gender	Ethnicity
Age	National origin
Race	Citizenship

Parental status	Health status
Work, occupation, or profession	Region or local origin
Sexual orientation	Athletic ability
Social status	Disability
Education	Personality
Religion	Interests
Weight or body type	Language; monolingualism or
Height	bilingualism.

And this list is by no means complete or thorough. One can easily add other categories. Much of our concern about how we as a society deal with diversity is bound up with communication. In our personal relationships, organizations, institutions, and businesses, the issue of diversity revolves around how we talk to and about one another.

In the field of communication studies, the subfield of *intercultural communication* provides theoretical and research background for interactions among diverse people. Admittedly, not all of these types of diversity are markers of cultural differences or even subcultural differences, but many of the basic concepts from the study of intercultural communication are applicable. The field of intercultural communication can therefore provide a paradigm for thinking about the ethics of communication between people from diverse background.

Intercultural Communication

The notion of *inter*-cultural communication combines two elements: the prefix *inter-*, suggesting between or among; and cultural. We are therefore talking about communicative interactions between at least two people, each from different identifiable cultures. Much of the communication theory discussed so far has dealt with *intra*cultural settings or what could be termed *mono*cultural settings. The cultural difference between the two parties thus becomes an additional factor or variable affecting the course and possible outcomes of the parties' interactions. The term *intercultural communication* typically is distinguished from related subfields of study, such as cultural studies, cross-cultural studies, and international communication. The first term usually applies to studies of communication practices in a particular culture, often different from the culture of the investigator. Cross-cultural studies usually involve making comparisons of communication practices between two cultures. For example, one might study how aspects on nonverbal communication differ from one culture to another. International communication usually deals with mass or mediated communication, and so would deal with global communication issues or even diplomatic communication. In this chapter, we are mainly concerned with settings featuring interpersonal communication, face to face, with usually two participants, each from a different culture or subculture (or coculture).

The Concept of Culture

We need first to consider the idea of culture and what makes a factor cultural. We are using culture here in an anthropological sense, referring to distinct patterns of living characteristic of an identifiable group of people. These patterns of living have a quality to them that we call *out-of-awareness*. By this we mean that people often take for granted the cultural assumptions they make and expectations they have regarding encounters with other people. Our culture provides us with a set of engrained rules directing us how to behave in various circumstances. In that sense, culture gives us our notion of what is *common sense*. People who violate these rules are vaguely seen as being in error or in some way transgressing against us, because they are acting against *common sense*. They are not behaving *normally*. Culture is not inherited and is hence not in our genes, but is learned as a result of being brought up in a particular culture.

As our list of potential categories of diversity at the start of this chapter shows, there are different ways to subdivide large cultural units into smaller ones. For example, the United States represents a large cultural unit. We can speak of people from that culture interacting with people from, say, the Japanese culture. Yet we know that within the national culture of the United States, there are many variations in communities that share certain culture-like patterns of behavior that differentiate them somewhat from the larger culture. At times, these smaller communities are termed *subcultures*, and at other times, *cocultures*. The first term, *subculture*, suggests a smaller community within the larger culture that exhibits some significant and systematic variations from the larger culture. Hence, one might speak of an African American or a Latino subculture within the larger American culture of the United States. The term *coculture* implies that one is simultaneously a member of two cultures. The second term can therefore be, for some, an alternative to subculture, or it can imply something slightly different, as when one speaks of the Deaf Culture existing alongside the American culture. As we discuss in Chapter 9, people with certain disabilities may also see themselves as constituting a coculture within national cultures. The sociolinguist, Deborah Tannen, among others, holds that men and women represent two different cultures (or cocultures in the larger American culture), who speak two different *genderlects*. Many of the categories used to represent diversity can be considered examples of subcultures or cocultures. In doing so, however, we should bear in mind that we may be stretching the anthropological concept of culture a bit to call smaller and smaller units separate cultures.

To further elucidate the effects of culture on communication, we need to consider why there is such a thing, that is, why human beings have cultures in the first place. Perhaps the most important function of culture is to reduce uncertainty in our everyday lives and interactions with others. When we go out and meet someone on the street, we can assume some basic givens, which reduce the range of uncertainties about such a meeting. Usually you know what language to speak, for example. Language is considered to be one of the most important elements in setting a culture apart from others, but many other patterns of living are involved as well. We know what sorts of clothes to wear, how to behave on the street, how to greet others, whether strangers, family, or friends. We can assume that certain gestures and other nonverbal signs have fairly standard meanings and interpretations. Our culture thus serves to reduce the sheer number of decisions we would otherwise have to make to get through a normal day. Because we know the rules and can presume that others know them as well, the rules provide a solid base for understanding what is going on around us.

Cultural Rules of Communication

One serious problem with these kinds of cultural rules is that we can know them in the sense of knowing how to follow them without knowing that there even are such rules. This is what we mean by saying that culture largely operates *out-of-awareness*. For example, many people are not aware of the expectations they have concerning how far to stand from another person in an interaction. There is a distance that just *feels right*. If someone stands closer than that, they are *breaking the rules*, but we are not sure how. Another kind of rule that people in North America may not be aware they are using has to do with eye contact during conversations. While a person is *holding the floor* in the conversation (continuing to speak), she typically looks up and away from the other person at the start of her contribution, continues occasionally looking away and then back to signal she is not yet finished, and then concludes by maintaining fixed eye contact when she is finished and waiting for a reply. The person who is temporarily *listening* in this culture is expected to maintain fairly constant eye contact without the occasional looking away (if they are not looking at us, we say they are "not listening"). When the listener is ready to say something, he looks up and away briefly to signal the start of his turn, then looks back at the other person.

There is nothing given by nature that dictates what the *correct* conversational distance should be (within a range) nor is it given how to signal turn-taking in a conversation by using eye contact. It can be hard for people to grasp that these rules are merely conventions, that could be or probably are different in other cultures. It is especially difficult when we are not consciously aware there is a rule that we are following (and someone else is breaking). These cultural rules or expectations in this way come to have emotional value placed on them. We feel comfortable when people follow the rules, uncomfortable when they don't. Therefore, there is a tendency to respond emotionally when people seem not to follow our rules.

If communication is mutual sense-making, a definition we find appropriate, then when two people conversing share many of the same assumptions, symbols, and meanings for things, the mutual sense-making should go more smoothly. The further apart people are in these basic assumptions and rules, presumably, the more difficult it will be for them to arrive at a common, shared sense of understanding about what is going on. The more people share in common in terms of language, symbol-meanings, assumptions about the world, norms for behavior, and so on, the easier it should be to arrive at a common understanding through communication. The further apart they are on these factors, the more difficulty they will have arriving at common understanding.

To recap the effects of culture on communication, first, note that many of our cultural expectations about how to communicate are held out of our conscious awareness. Secondly, we tend to respond emotionally when these expectations are violated, even though we are not quite sure why (given the out-of-awareness factor). We therefore may find ourselves reacting with frustration when the person from the other culture is not behaving the way we think they ought to.

Reservations about Cultural Rules of Communication

Three further characteristics of culture need to be taken into consideration when analyzing the difficulties of intercultural communication:

1. Culture is not static, but fluid.
2. Culture applies to people in general, not in specifics.
3. People can belong to or switch identities among different cultures.

The first point reminds us that it would be a mistake to assume that the elements and rules that constitute a culture are set for all time, or that they are static. Just as language is constantly undergoing change, so too are cultures. In the early days of field work, cultural anthropologists essentially tried to take *snapshots* of cultures they were working in. The danger is that people could be led to make timeless statements such as "the Yanomamo are fierce, warlike people" (although it is certainly questionable whether such characterization was ever true). People describing the San people of southern Africa, for example, might say that they are hunter-gatherers, who have practiced this way of life for generations. It could be, however, as later indications suggest, that these people have been driven to this way of life because of encroachments on their traditional lands by the occupations of white settlers as well as other African peoples. We may not be seeing a continuation of a much older way of life. Unfortunately, these people have become so marginalized in the nation of South Africa today that their language, characterized by its famous *clicks*, is not even one of the eleven official languages of that nation. One must therefore be cautious when making generalizations about cultural practices and patterns on the assumption that they are timeless. Fred Casmir puts the problem this way: "It needs to be stressed here that we may have hindered progress by overly simplified models of cultures as more static, much more fixed than they are."[3]

The second point reminds us that cultural descriptions should not become stereotypes. When we say that a culture is collectivist, for example, we mean there is a general tendency for members of that culture to prefer the collective good over the individual benefit. But, within that culture, one expects to find individuals who themselves reflect the whole range of preferences from extreme individualism to extreme collectivism. Cultural patterns are characteristic of an average rather than of any particular individual. So, more people in that culture will tend to cluster in their preferences around collectivist values rather than individualistic ones. In the so-called *individualistic cultures*, there will still be some individuals with quite collectivist ideals. Furthermore, each individual has his or her own idiosyncratic way of performing culturally influenced behaviors. None of us speak our native language in exactly the same way as anyone else. So, there are individualized differences in carrying out what could be thought of us cultural performances. If we go into an encounter with a person from another culture and expect him or her to behave exactly in line with our general expectations about that culture, we will probably be disappointed or surprised.

The third point is that individuals can also choose to identify with one culture at one time and with another at a different time; just as there is *code-switching* in languages, so is there *culture-switching*. This practice of switching among cultural systems is probably most prevalent among people from immigrant communities in various nations. Often the children, the *second generation*, will find themselves communicating in terms of a dominant or majority culture away from home, while returning to the norms of their parents' culture when at home. Sometimes one's economic or business roles bring one to enact different cultural identities from time to time. One of the most famous examples in the anthropological literature was an African sharecropper in South Africa. This man, known usually by the name Kas Maine (but also several variations on this name as well), lived from 1894 to 1985. He was a master farmer, who, because of the land ownership laws of South Africa, never was able to farm his own land. As he occasionally told the author of the study, giving the book its title, "The seed is mine, the oxen are mine, the plow is mine, but the land was never mine." He thus described the tragedy of the South African situation all his long life.[4] It seems at various times in his life, he lived as a *Tswana* man and at other times, identified himself as a *Sotho* (both groups are closely related ethnically and linguistically in South Africa).

At still other times, he lived, dressed, and spoke as an *Afrikaner*, the white community descended from primarily Dutch settlers in South Africa. There was recurrent fluidity to his cultural self-identification and practices depending on the stages in his life. Presumably, such fluidity was not unusual on the agricultural plateaus of northern South Africa at that time. The Nobel-prize-winning author V. S. Naipaul represents such flexibility in his own life, as a member of a Hindu Indian community from Trinidad holding a British passport and writing in English. He once remarked about sitting next to an Indian man on an aircraft, as they both tried to decide whether to have an *Asian conversation* or an *English conversation*. In an *Asian conversation*, one would expect to move quickly into what would be considered issues too personal or private for an *English conversation*. Both persons seemed capable of operating from either cultural norm.

Ethical Stance on Intercultural Communication

We hope that you notice the ethical implications already implied by these three characteristics of culture. One of the ironies of training people in intercultural communication is a danger of overgeneralization. Often such training consists of instructing people on the various dimensions of culture that make the other culture distinct from one's own. In the first place, this approach implies that other cultures are to be interpreted in terms of one's own and observed through the lens of our own *common sense*. In a way, this is similar to teaching pronunciation of sounds in another language by giving a student a supposed equivalent sound in his or her own native language. To a certain extent, of course, this is unavoidable as a beginning point. Still, it is difficult to avoid assuming that one's own culture is the standard, which represents general human nature, and that the other culture is a variation on that standard. As Edward Said, the culture and literary critic, has pointed out, this point of view can lead to an assumption of cultural superiority *vis a vis* the person from the other culture.[5]

In the second place, there is an implication that each individual you meet from the other culture will display the same values, norms, and behaviors as everyone else in that culture. If culture is not static and if individuals vary in their own practices from the hypothetical cultural mean, as we have maintained, then one would be mistaken to assume that dimensions learned for a given culture in general apply necessarily to a particular individual. One needs to be careful to avoid treating the other person as a *stereotype*, or as a representative *token* of his or her culture. We expect people we meet from our own cultural community to exhibit all sorts of different behaviors, even quirks. When we meet someone from a different cultural community, in the same way, we should not expect them to behave according to an almost rigid set of expectations. There is value in educating people about cultural rules of communication, as long as these reservations are borne in mind.

Dimensions of Cultural Communication

An important step in training people for intercultural communication is to make them aware of culturally determined differences in how people communicate in the new culture. Becoming aware of the different expectations and norms about interpersonal communication in cultures other than one's own should help prepare one for intercultural experiences. As we have said, however, the danger is to assume a static nature about such cultural norms and to treat the person from the other culture as a stereotypical representative of all the rules one has learned from the training.

That being said, our ethical stance regarding intercultural communication begins with a recognition of the importance of expecting differences in the *rules of communication* when one talks with someone from a culture different from one's own. Also bear in mind that research or education in the other culture, while important, is usually not enough to prepare someone completely for the experience and often not always possible (if one is unable to predict or prepare for the encounter). Nor does such training necessarily address the question of ethics in communication.

The discussion of cultural factors in communication often begins with a summary of the points made by the anthropologist, Edward T. Hall, who may himself have coined the term *intercultural communication*. Hall first described how people in different cultures have developed distinctive norms concerning various kinds of nonverbal communication (and so he said, "Space Speaks," and "Time Talks.").[6] In formulating the ideas of *proxemics* and *chronemics* he made us aware that in different cultures different rules have been developed for how we communicate by our use of space and time. Proxemics reminds us that cultures differ in terms of how comfortable people are with how close we stand to one another when interacting—what is conversational distance, formal distance, intimate distance, and so on. How we spend time and how we decide when being on time is important or not, similarly, are culturally determined features of communication rules. Keeping someone waiting may show disrespect, for example. Communicating with two people at the same time may be perfectly appropriate in one culture and disrespectful in another.

Hall goes on to describe the out-of-awareness effects of other nonverbal communication systems, such as eye contact (*oculesics*), gestures and movement (*kinesics*), the use of objects (*objectics*), and touch (*haptics*). Each system has its own code that differs from culture to culture as language differs from culture to culture.[7] Because people in a given culture have learned to take nonverbal communication for granted, these differences often result in misunderstanding or, as we said before, frustration in intercultural encounters.

Hall is also responsible for developing the idea of differentiating cultures and communication in cultures along the line of *high-context* versus *low-context*.[8] By this terminology, Hall indicates that in some cultures, the context, usually the nonverbal elements and events surrounding a communication episode, is more important in interpreting the intended message than the actual words being used. These cultures give high importance to the context and are, thus, *high-context* cultures. In *low-context* cultures, what is said, the content, takes precedence over the nonverbal elements accompanying the message. One would say, in these cultures, what one says is more important than how she says it or when or where she says it. The culture of the United States, he believes, is mostly *low-context*, in that we focus on the *bottom-line*, meaning the words that are said, the verbal content. Asian cultures, for example the Japanese, Hall feels, represent high-context cultures, in which the words can be interpreted only in terms of the setting, background, and other elements surrounding the communication event. One often hears of the importance of saving or giving *face* in such cultures. To avoid saying no to someone face to face, and thereby taking something away from that person's *face*, one strives to hint at or talk around the negative response, assuming the other person will pick up the real message from nonverbal aspects of the meeting.

Scholars as well as trainers in intercultural communication also find the distinction between individualist and collectivist cultures useful. Researchers differentiate large national cultures from each other on this scale. In general, northern European cultures and North American culture tend to be more individualistic, meaning that people think of themselves first as individuals; while people in collectivist cultures tend to think of themselves first as members of a community or a group. It would appear that there is often a correlation between a culture being high context and falling on the collectivist end of the continuum as well.

A collectivist standard can have an impact on the formulation of ethical thought for a given culture. Among the Akan people of West Africa (for the most part, related ethnolinguistic groups in Ghana and the Ivory Coast), ethical standards are derived from the ethos or the character of one's family (rather than from the individual himself or herself). A Ghanaian ethicist goes so far as to write, "What can be called the first and foremost ethical standard among the Akan is what I would call the family standard."[9] The writer continues to point out that whatever an Akan person does is said to reflect directly on his or her family. Should he or she behave badly or unethically, it brings discredit on the entire family, not just on the individual. This point of view appears to be in contrast with the American or Western view that one is responsible for one's own conduct, which does not reflect on one's family.

Geert Hostede and his colleagues, carrying out research in cultural dimensions of communication, have isolated three other factors that appear to significantly differentiate cultures along lines important to communication.[10] These other dimensions developed by Hofstede include the following:

1. Uncertainty-avoidance; this means people in some cultures tend to be very uncomfortable with high levels of uncertainty in their lives. People in agricultural societies, for example, may understandably fear the uncertainties of weather or of changing crops. Other societies may be more open to risk taking, more likely to experiment and explore; these would be low on uncertainty-avoidance.
2. *Masculinity* (the term does not necessarily connote gender, but an orientation); a culture high on the masculinity scale would be one in which people are very work oriented and career oriented; family concerns are subordinate to professional life. In addition, there is an assumption that work and family roles are gender specific.
3. Power distance; in a culture high on this dimension, it is expected that there will be very large gaps between people at the top of the social or political structure and the mass of people; democratic states tend to be low on the power-distance scale.

As we have said, some education or background on these factors affecting intercultural communication may be useful prior to an intercultural encounter. For example, you might be able to predict that in your message to someone from a culture high on uncertainty avoidance, appeals to security and tradition would be more effective than appeals to the thrill of the new. One could predict that appeals to authority could be effective in a culture high on power distance. In a society low on masculinity, as defined in Hofstede's terms, one could expect that persuasive appeals based on getting ahead in your business would be less effective than appeals to the importance of family life. One could go on and build similar kinds of implications for creating messages for people in individualist or collectivist cultures, and so on. These factors, together with expectations regarding nonverbal and contextual factors of communication, could help us think about how to formulate effective messages or, at least, to avoid the most ineffective messages, in preparing to communicate with someone from a culture different from our own.

In other words, this kind of information can be useful for developing *effective* messages, but may not necessarily bring out the ethical implications of the encounter. A desire to be sensitive to the cultural expectations of the other person not only can have an ethical component to it, but can also spring from a strategic desire to come up with the most persuasive message. Strategic considerations are not themselves unethical, of course, and they can be ethically neutral in themselves. Understanding another culture, on the other hand, does not guarantee ethical communication. So, what does all this tell us about an ethical stance in regard to intercultural communication and, by extension, communication involving diverse participants?

An Ethics for Intercultural Communication

We believe that there are several approaches to interpersonal communication in general that can be especially relevant in intercultural interactions. These approaches spring from the attitude one takes going into an encounter with another person, rather than specific strategies based on cultural factors of communication. We believe that the following three approaches provide useful ways to think through ethical issues of interactions with diverse others: the theory of Coordinated Management of Meaning, as developed by Barnett Pearce and Vernon Cronen; the dialogical ethics of Martin Buber; and the Third-Culture Building model of Fred Casmir. We see some compatibility among these three theories or models stemming from their common idea that in an interaction, in communication together, two people co-construct a new meaning. This new meaning or understanding is not contained in the original understandings or intentions of the interactants, and is not therefore a result of combining their contributions to the discussion. Rather, together the two participants have created something new and unanticipated, which grows out of the interaction itself.

Coordinated Management of Meaning Theory. The theory of Coordinated Management of Meaning, or CMM, has evolved into a practical theory for improving the quality of one's interactions with others and for conflict resolution.[11] Let us start from the point of view that intercultural communication is a face-to-face interaction between two people, each from different cultures or groups with distinctly different understandings of their experiences. They share this interaction in common and are thus bound in some form of shared experience. The theory of CMM holds that together these two people are creating their own new reality, which is this shared experience and understanding. Although they each begin from a different set of cultural givens or *common senses*, they are in effect creating a new set of givens applicable to just their relationship. In other words, they are striving (or should be striving) to develop some coordination in how they go about giving meaning to their interaction. The relationship, assuming it continues, develops its own set of rules, norms, and expectations, negotiated from the stock of rules, norms, and expectations each brings from his own cultural background.[12]

In effect, the theory holds that how people communicate with each other is as important, or more important, than the actual content of what is said. On this point, the CMM theory draws from basic concepts associated with the perspective known as *Relational Communication*. We do not intend to over-complicate this discussion, but it is important to understand this point of view as it relates to both interpersonal and intercultural communication. The theory of relational communication goes back to the work of Gregory Bateson and his colleagues, such as Paul Watzlawick. Bateson first pointed out an idea picked up later by Watzlawick and his colleagues: a communication both reports that something has happened (a message has been sent) and indicates how that message is to be understood (what he called a *command* function). Watzlawick similarly contended that every message communicated carries both content (what is said) and relationship components. In other words, no message has just content, but every message implies something about the human relationship existing between the two people in communication. If one looks only to the content of what is said, while ignoring how the message shapes the relationship between the communicators, one will not be able to interpret the full meaning of the interchange.

The context—in terms of what came before and will come after, as well as the physical setting, perceived status of the interactants, and so forth—provides the basis for interpreting the relationship component of messages. For example, if one says to you, "Let me put this as simply to you as I can," he may be implying that you are too simple to understand him if he speaks in his accustomed fashion. Or, if you say to him, "What I am asking you to do is really in your own best interest," it may imply that you are in a superior position, better able to understand his needs than he does himself. The overall meaning of the interaction can be interpreted only by understanding how the content is embedded in the larger context.

This context for interpreting meaning places the content of the message within a series of larger levels of meaning in a sort of hierarchy, according to CMM. First, the content is said to be part of an *episode*, which is a piece of experience that we can label as *lunch, a date, a business conference, a conversation at a party*, and on and on. Note that one's culture can lead to different labels and meanings for the *episode* in which the interaction is taking place. This suggests the first level for misunderstanding in intercultural communication (although the two people hardly need to come from different cultures for there to be misunderstanding on this point—is this studying together or a date, for instance?).

The episode has meaning because of the nature of the *relationship* each person perceives existing between the two people. Do we come to the meeting with already formed stereotypes concerning people from the other culture represented? Are we trying so hard to overcome the stereotype that, in over-compensating, we appear to be condescending toward the other? It may be possible that there are cultural expectations about certain kinds of relationships taken for granted by each of the participants. For example, if you are older than the other person, it may be that in his culture you must be shown deference even though you want both of you to be equals. In some cultures, there may be similar constraining rules for communicating with people of a different gender. In other words, unstated cultural factors may determine, at least partly, how each person does or can define the nature of their relationship.

The episodes and relationships that constitute our lives are shaped by our own self-identity, or the *life-script* that we have come to adopt for ourselves. I see myself as this kind of person or that kind of person and therefore expect to communicate with others in terms of that identity or life-script. Again, the nature of such self-concepts and life-scripts are influenced by the culture from which one comes.

The final level for interpreting meaning is culture, the general values and norms that are inculcated in people brought up in a certain culture or society. Obviously, at this level, the influence of culture is evident by definition. The theory of CMM thus tries to help us understand what is going on when two people communicate with each other by revealing all the factors of context that we bring to bear to give meaning to our communicative experience.

The theory is useful in pointing out potential points at which the two people from different cultures may need to negotiate what things mean. We say that the two people often need to *meta-communicate*, which means to step back from the ongoing conversation and communicate about how they are communicating. They may need to explore together what each thinks is the *episode* in which they are engaged. What is the meaning for each of those kinds of episodes? Are they seen as positive, negative, or neutral? Is this kind of episode appropriate in each culture, or does it cause discomfort to one or the other of participants? At another time, it may be necessary to stop and explore the meaning each has for the relationship thought to exist between the two. How is this relationship different as seen from one point of view or the other? Are the differences significant enough, again, to cause discomfort, let alone misunderstanding?

Mindfulness, a concept used by theorists of intercultural communication, provides a quite useful concept for illuminating what we mean. To be mindful requires one to consciously bring to mental awareness the assumptions and preconceptions one brings to an encounter. It means to work at being aware of how one habitually defines the episodes, relationships, and self-concept and life-scripts. The opposite of this mind-set is, of course, *mindlessness*, which means that one just willy-nilly goes on acting in the encounter as if everyone interprets life and experience in exactly the same way.[13] Bringing these assumptions and preconceptions to awareness often requires joint work, as the two people engaged in the relationship help each other to expose their taken-for-granted expectations.

Dialogical Communication.   In later versions of the theory, Pearce has turned to the dialogic communication of Martin Buber, in order to provide the ideal for coordinating meaning between two people. As we said above, Buber's theories as well as the general perspective of dialogic communication provides an ethical basis for intercultural communication. This view suggests that each person in the interaction is to take the attitude of full regard for the *Other.* If each person listens to and responds to the other as a unique individual, rather than as a representative of a group, subculture, or culture, the pair is more likely to arrive at a more complete sense of a shared meaning. In terms of the CMM theory, they are more likely than otherwise to successfully coordinate their meaning. We have already discussed the dialogic communication ethics represented by Buber, as well as Levinas, in Chapter 5 and in the previous chapter on interpersonal communication.

Third-Culture Building.   Taking this sort of ethical attitude into an intercultural encounter would also make more likely the kind of productive sense-making that Fred Casmir refers to as *third-culture building.* Casmir postulates a serious need for improved approaches to intercultural communication in the world today, because, as he puts it, human beings "must find a way to resolve conflicts."[14] Such an approach, he further maintains must recognize this point: "Second, the process of human communication ultimately is based on and deals with the establishment and maintenance of relationships."[15] Such a process implies the sort of mutual and cooperative creating of a common basis for making sense of interactions similar to what we have been describing for CMM and dialogic communication. New rules can be created or negotiated when cultural rules are different for the two people engaged in an interaction.

The point is that much training for intercultural communication stresses communication between people from different cultures rather than the necessity for creating a third-culture, which would be a new cultural understanding specific to a particular, direct human relationship. The result of such traditional training for intercultural encounters is still, in a sense, based on *cultural* communication rather than *inter*cultural communication. Operating from within the system of my culture, I hope to find ways to influence you—to get you to agree with me—by learning how to rely on your cultural values or expectations in rhetorically composing my arguments to you. In that sense, I am not aiming at a new, unanticipated understanding, but *your acceptance* of *my* point of view. Third-culture building advocates, on the other hand, the goal as well as the necessity of jointly negotiating a new basis for our communication. The result should hence be the creation of new meaning shared by the participants. Casmir believes this approach is different from one based on the idea of integration, because integration seems to imply that people from one group need to adopt the cultural norms of the other group in integrating into or with the other group (usually representing the larger or more dominant culture).[16] Third-culture building thus maintains that the two people engaged in an encounter, when each comes from a different cultural background, together work out a new, negotiated set of communication norms—this becomes the *third culture.*

As in the CMM theory of communication, this approach sees interpersonal communication as an ongoing process of negotiating meanings. In this case, there is the added factor of the cultural differences between the participants. In any interpersonal encounter, of course, there are degrees of difference between the two people interacting. Bear in mind that we are saying that the degrees of difference can be more or less. When the differences become more pronounced, as we engage people from outside the group with whom we have become most familiar, we are getting closer to intercultural communication. And, as the differences become more pronounced, our care in negotiating a *third way*, or a *third culture*, must also become more mindful. The need for such care is most obvious when the two people are from distinctly different national cultures, such as the case of an Akan man conversing with an American woman. More subtle differences in expectations and norms are more difficult to bring to awareness. Go back to the list of categories of diversity at the beginning of this chapter. When people from one of these groups converses with a person from another one of these groups, to what extent is the conversation an intercultural one? In each case, the answer is probably one of more or less. An ethics of communication among people from diverse backgrounds calls for mindfulness and alertness to potential *cultural* misunderstandings when the interchange does not appear to be going well. Deborah Tannen, as we have said, goes so far as to contend that men and women, otherwise in the same culture, are from two different cultures, represented by their genders.[17] When men and women do not seem to understand each otherwise, she would claim, they need to become aware of differences in the communication rules for each gender (*genderlects*).

In summary, ethical intercultural communication, therefore, seems to us to be based on the attitude with which one approaches interaction with diverse others rather than rules of interaction based on studies of cultural dimensions of communication. An *ethical stance* regarding communication with diverse others is therefore based on the principles of dialogic communication, as implied by the theories of CMM, Buber's approach of *I–Thou* communication, and Casmir's Third-Culture Building model. While all four of the major ethical perspectives can have some application for ethical judgments related to intercultural communication, relationships seem to provide the most useful lens. In the next section of this chapter, we turn to examples of applications involving intercultural communication or communication involving people from diverse backgrounds.

Applications: Tolerance and Diversity

Racism, ageism, sexism—these are all ways of communicating that intentionally or unintentionally signal one's sense of superiority over entire classes or groups of people. Because these forms of communicating can clearly be harmful, they raise ethical issues. We note at the outset that legal issues may be involved in some of these cases as well. For example, sexual harassment is proscribed by law in many institutions in the United States. Communication, particularly speech, that creates a hostile environment, due to the use of sexually demeaning or offensive messages, is against the law or can legally be the basis for lawsuits in these cases. We have been making a distinction between what is legal and what is ethical, although there is often overlap between these categories. What we wish to do is discuss these issues in relationship to ethical standards rather than legal ones.

Especially on college campuses, there has been a growing concern with intolerant speech, speech that denigrates others on the basis of their membership of some particular group. Such intolerant speech is often termed *hate speech*, and several campuses have specific codes against it. The issue of *hate speech* raises a series of related topics and controversies: *political correctness*, *multiculturalism*, and *affirmative action*, among others. What is interesting from a communication standpoint is how these terms have acquired positive and negative connotations to the extent that they can be flashpoints for divisive controversy—not just on campuses but in other institutions as well.

The first term mentioned as a related topic is *political correctness*, sometimes abbreviated as *PC*. Especially in the abbreviated form, PC has become almost a rallying cry for some political commentators and politicians. If you enter either the long or the short version in an Internet search engine, you will invariably pull up, early in the list of *hits*, several politically and religiously conservative sites, which clearly see the label as negative if not downright dangerous. *Multiculturalism* not only is slightly more neutral as a term, but also has been attacked as part of a conspiracy to undercut the values of family and education by some of the same groups. Obviously, there are strong feelings on both sides of the conflict involving the use of these terms. The third of the terms, *Affirmative Action*, also leads to acrimonious debate by those who support it and those who denounce it as a policy for government, business, or education. One side feels that affirmative action redresses the disabilities placed on certain groups of people in the past—and so it would meet the standard of the *difference principle* described by Rawls (more on that follows). On the other hand, opponents have maintained that affirmative action does not treat all people equitably and so violates principles of egalitarianism.

How can we sort out the ethical issues involved in these topics? Before turning to the approach advocated in the previous section of this chapter, we consider the various ethical systems that might illuminate these matters.

The debates that often swirl about the issues of speech codes, hate speech, and intolerance in institutions seem to imply that there are competing goals or ends involved. On the one hand, it is said, these institutions are communities, small societies, in which respect for one another is required for the full and effective functioning of the organization. On the other hand, some maintain that speech codes, as attempts to uphold *politically correct* speech and multicultural diversity, work against the robust and open debate required for well-reasoning decision making. Both these positions suggest that utilitarianism and a concern for consequences provide the ethical yardstick for analyzing the relevant issues. The first position holds that messages that denigrate whole groups of people are unethical because they do not meet the standard of leading to the greatest good for the greatest number in that institution. The other side contends that the best ends are realized by allowing more open and perhaps contentious even hurtful speech. This argument, however, can cut both ways. A member of a slandered group can claim that her free speech has been denied and that she does not feel free to enter into the debate, because of the derogatory attacks on her group inhibits her own speech. The hateful speech can thus serve to undermine others' freedom of expression. Those on the other side of the debate may respond that the codes are often worded so vaguely that what is only the cut and thrust of vigorous discussion can be wrongly condemned as demeaning speech and sanctioned by the code.

The implementation of speech codes on college campuses often brings out just these arguments. Campus speech codes are typically embedded in university documents, such as student handbooks, intended to govern conduct, including communication, on campus. Such codes usually attempt to balance freedom of expression with freedom from harmful or harassing messages and conduct. A code in effect at the University of Pennsylvania in the 1990s, for example, guarantees students the right of freedom of expression together with the right to be free from discrimination. The handbook continues as follows: "The University condemns hate speech, epithets, and racial, ethic, sexual and religious slurs."[18] Speech can be open and free as long as it does not seem to be harassing or demeaning toward a specific group identified by race, ethnicity, gender, religion, or, in many cases, sexual orientation. Other universities similarly attempted to implement such policies in their handbooks. In many cases, various courts struck down the policies and their sanctions, which could include expulsion, on the grounds of vagueness as well as violations of the U.S. First Amendment and its guarantee of the right of free speech.

As we have already indicated, however, it is not the legality of these attempts but their ethical implications that interest us at this point. In the debate described above both sides take their positions, as we have seen, from considerations of *consequences*, and specifically the idea of utilitarianism. Those who debate both sides of the issue of strong, potentially demeaning language have tried to give us the touchstone of the greatest good.

A second approach under the umbrella of *consequences* seems also relevant to this discussion: egalitarianism, as represented by the ideas put forward by Rawls and Scanlon. The major concern in this perspective has to do with ensuring equal outcomes for individuals rather than the best outcome for a majority. From the point of view of Rawls' *original position*, in which one is behind the *veil of ignorance*, it would seem likely that you would want everyone to be treated in a fair and respectful manner by everyone else. In that sense, egalitarianism seems to support the advocates of speech codes, as they are saying that hurtful or demeaning speech denies some people respect and prevents their free participation in the communication and life of the university. Recall, specifically, the *difference principle* added by Rawls to his theory: any differences in the distribution of the goods of the society are to benefit those who would be otherwise least well off. If we look at the *goods* in this case as the rights of free debate and respect, this principle implies that the restriction of the *good* of free speech for some people is justified as it benefits those who have traditionally been discriminated against—those who would otherwise be least well off.

If we consider the issues from the point of view of *duties*, specifically the Kantian ideas about ethics, we will come to some similar judgments. One form of the categorical imperative, which seems most relevant in this regard, is that you should treat others always as ends, and not merely as means. This requirement is that one should always uphold another person's human dignity. Kantian duties would seem to require, therefore, that treating others in a respectful manner is the best way of ensuring that they are valued as ends in themselves rather than opponents to be defeated in a debate or argument. Again, this principle could conceivably cut both ways as well. Those opposed to speech codes might maintain that they are the ones denied equal respect and dignity when they have to fear their candid speech could be misrepresented or misconstrued by someone else as in violation of the code's directives.

Do the qualities of *character* and the virtues enter into a consideration of the points in contention here? Does the use of speech that is perceived by others to be denigrating affect or say anything about the character of the one so speaking? The question then becomes whether someone of exemplary character would use such language. The other way of putting the questions asks whether there are important virtues upheld or violated by the use of such language. First, consider the virtues of courage or courageous speech, as represented by the virtue of *parrhesia*, as explained by Foucault (see Chapter 2). Does the use of strong language that could be heard as demeaning of a group still be acceptable as having the virtue of courageous speech? The answer appears to be probably not, because such fearless speech was seen as courageous only when the speaker put himself or herself in some danger from offending a more powerful authority. One could argue that the administration of the university is the powerful other in this case. But, it is more likely that we would look to the power held by the group that has been offended. Assuming that they have been the weaker group in the general society as well as historically, fearless speech as a virtue may not apply in this case.

Putting aside the consideration of legal or institutional punishment—such consideration is outside the ethical analysis we are attempting here— attacking a group often discriminated against in the past would not seem to meet the test of fearless speech. Tolerance and fairness in the treatment of others, however, have typically been seen as virtues in most cultures. The use of communication that seems threatening or harassing or demeaning to members of specific groups of people would not seem compatible with these virtues.

Postmodern or feminist perspectives would probably suggest that the free speech being debated in these cases has worked in a way to exclude certain *muted groups*. In the past, seemingly open debate, they would argue, has occurred in an environment in which women and groups such as African Americans did not feel they had a voice. The danger some postmodernists may see, however, is that the new speech codes could similarly be enforced in a way that maintains the dominance of particular power elites. Global or radical feminists could claim that the individuals empowered shared characteristics, such as education and privilege with the former dominant groups.

The considerations of *relationships* seem to us most relevant for working through the issues represented by the debates over strong or demeaning language, especially on college campuses. The question then becomes what communicative behavior and interaction is most likely to result in improvement of the human relationships between or among the people involved? If we approach communication with the other person from the point of view of full regard for the *Other*, as advocated by Levinas, we will want to avoid communication that denies them that full regard. The legalities and the sanctions of a speech code are not germane to such considerations. Let us look at the issues as they might be seen from the perspective of Coordinated Management of Meaning or Third-Culture Building. Communication would then involve engagement with the other person in a cooperative process of together negotiating a mutually acceptable and mutually constructed reality. Language meant to antagonize or alienate the other person (or people) would fall outside the ethical spectrum delineated by these models. The question becomes one of asking whether the desirable or ethical situation to be sought is one of conflict or cooperation. The result of such consideration, however, is not a decision that speech codes are a good or bad thing on campuses or elsewhere. It would appear that an effort has been made to resort to such rule-books because of a sense that conditions conducive to an ethics of relationships is not present on many of today's campuses or in many institutions. Ethics is concerned with what ought to be rather than with what is. Our intent in this section is to help develop an analysis of the ethical implications rather than to offer a legal or policy recommendation.

Let us consider one of the related topics discussed above, political correctness. In communication between people from different cultural backgrounds, we have noted, it is important to cultivate an attitude of *mindfulness.* This attitude implies that as people encounter frustration or discomfort in their interaction, they will proceed to metacommunication in order to bring to the awareness of each participant what the problem might be. Both then proceed to a negotiation concerning their own rules for communicating in a way that neither could reasonably object to (echoing a principle from Scanlon, discussed in Chapter 4). Note that both people go beyond simple toleration, in which you appear to accept the other person's different way of doing things while still adhering to your own norms. The goal, rather than this kind of toleration, is a meshing of both people's norms and expectations for that particular relationship. One does not therefore adhere to an almost bureaucratic list of politically correct terms, because one has adopted an attitude which values the full worth of the other person. "Being PC," in the way of mentally consulting a list of words, comes across as condescending toward the other person in the dialogue. And condescension will undermine the relationship.

In the wake of the events of 9/11 (the attacks on the New York Trade Center Twin Towers and the Pentagon on September 11, 2001), and the American military actions in Afghanistan and Iraq, a relatively new form of intolerant communication has appeared in the United States. The fears and emotions created by the wartime footing in the United States have led some people to be overly suspicious of anyone whom they perceive as Arabic or Muslim. Both on and off college campuses people have been singled out or even attacked for any kind of supposed resemblance to these groups: a perceived shared ethnicity or nationality and members of a religious community. An online news service covering diversity issues reports, "About one in four Americans holds anti-Muslim views, such as a belief that the religion teaches violence and hatred, according to a survey an Islamic advocacy group released Monday [October 4, 2004]."[19] The survey reported here indicates that anti-Muslim and anti-Arab feelings surged after the attacks in 2001. The ethics of the situation revolve around treating people as stereotypes or as unique individuals, as called for by dialogic communication. The situation is made more difficult because of the new sense of threat following the terrorist attacks in 2001. One is reminded of the blanket judgments made about Japanese-Americans during World War II.

Strong feelings, as these examples show, can cloud our processes of ethical decision making. New conditions can bring to the fore new *target* groups. What has been called *hate speech* can be directed at the new targets. As a consequence, debates may continue about hate speech, speech codes, extending *politically correct* speech, and affirmative action for members of these new groups.

Communication between and among people from the majority culture and those perceived to be members of *target* groups calls for increased mindfulness and willingness to engage the other from the ethical stance of dialogue.

CASE STUDY: SECURITY AND TOLERANCE

Longacre State University is a regional state campus in one of the Midwestern states. The Administration has prided itself on what they perceive as a fairly successful program of equal opportunity and affirmative action, aimed at raising the percentage of women and minorities among their faculty and staff. The college is located in a medium-sized city, one of the largest in the state, and a former center for manufacturing. The area around the campus has undergone a depression in home and property values over the last decade or so. In the immediate vicinity of the campus, there have been a growing number of vacant homes and businesses that have been on the market for some time.

University officials have worked with neighborhood associations to try to shore up the livability of the surrounding community. Still, there have been some growing concerns about crime, particularly property crime in this part of the city.

Evelyn Vygotsky was in her second year as faculty member in the Sociology Department, concerned about keeping up with her class prepara-tions, grading, and her fledgling scholarship, which she saw as of central importance to her progress toward a tenured position at Longacre. As she occasionally did, that Sunday afternoon she had come to her office on campus in the social sciences building to catch up on grading and do some work on a convention paper she hoped to submit for a national conference in a couple of weeks. Longacre was largely a commuter campus, which means that on the weekends the campus tends to feel a little deserted, in contrast to the liveliness of the typical weekdays. Evelyn knew that there had been warnings about thefts from cars in the campus parking lots. On that Sunday, the old social sciences building felt a little more deserted than usual, but she welcomed the quiet, providing some solitude for her work.

Dan Wilson was in his first year on the faculty in political science with a joint appointment in Longacre's new Center for African, Caribbean, and African-American Studies. Dan was from Chicago and he had to admit he was a little apprehensive about moving out to a conservative, largely white Mid-western city in the Great Plains. He hoped that the new creation of the Center at Longacre indicated a new atmosphere, which would be more welcoming of people from minority groups, especially African Americans. After early morn-ing church with his family, Dan had gone for a workout in the campus new recreational center. Still in his old sweatpants and Chicago Bulls tee shirt, he decided to stop by his new office in the political science department to pick up blue book exams he wanted to grade before Monday.

At about the time Dan was coming into the social sciences building, Evelyn was going down the hall, on the same floor, to warm up some of Friday's coffee still in her mug in the microwave in the faculty lounge. Suddenly, she spotted an African American man coming in the doors near the lounge; Dan, remember, was a new faculty member, and Dan and Evelyn had been in some of the same faculty meetings but did not really know each other. She panicked, rushed back to her office, slammed the door behind her, and immediately called campus security. Within minutes, a campus security officer confronted Dan in his office, demanding to see his faculty ID. Dressed for his workout, in his sweats, Dan had no wallet or identification with him. There was a period of awkwardness and discomfort while the campus security staff tried to contact Dan's department head to get the whole matter straightened out. Matters were finally resolved when the department head called back to confirm Dan's legitimate status.

That night Dan, feeling outraged by the incident, had contacted the few other members of the African American caucus at Longacre to tell them what happened. He felt that Evelyn, who was identified as his accuser by the campus security officer, acted the way she did out of racial prejudice. On Monday morning, Dan demanded and was granted a meeting with the Dean of Social Sciences at Longacre to lodge a complaint against Evelyn for what he saw as racial discrimination, even harassment. She had seen him at faculty meeting, he declared, and she ought to have recognized him. It was only because of her overreaction to his skin color and appearance, he felt, that put him in such a bad situation. Hearing about the accusation, the members of the caucus of women faculty and staff members rallied to Evelyn's side. A woman alone on campus, during the time of a crime alert, had every right to react as she did, they claimed. Women are not treated with respect, they contended, when they express legitimate concerns about their personal safety on campus.

Both the African American caucus and the women's caucus were demanding an immediate audience with the dean. Both groups feel that Dan or Evelyn was owed an apology and that some sort of action should be taken in view of what each side saw as discrimination against them.

Q U E S T I O N S   F O R   A N A L Y S I S   O F   T H E   C A S E

1. How should the dean proceed? What communication strategies should she adopt to deal with this volatile situation?

2. What are the facts in the situation? To what extent do you believe that this problem involves a problem of *intercultural communication*?

3. What are the perceptions that could have led to the emotional responses on both sides?

4. What are the ethical implications of how each individual in the case study have communicated? With the dean? With each other? With their supporters?

5. What sort of ethical perspective or stance would you recommend the dean follow in this case? Consider particularly approaches based on consequences, duties, and relationships. Develop scenarios for how various attempted solutions might play out, using each of the three ethical lenses suggested here.

Chapter Summary

The United States as well as most other nations are becoming increasingly aware of the significance of diversity in most aspects of social and economic life. Diversity refers to the situation in which people from markedly different backgrounds interact with one another. Elements marking diversity can be classified in many different ways: race, gender, ethnic background, age, occupation, religion, national origin, citizenship status, and on and on. In the next chapter we will take up separately ethical issues involved in communication between people with different abilities and disabilities. Conflicts among such diverse groups may represent one of the most important threats to human life and well-being over the next several decades.

We believe that a useful way to think about communication between diverse others is provided by research and training in the field of intercultural communication. Many of the variables which can make communication tricky among people from diverse backgrounds are similar to the sorts of variables studied by those working in the area of intercultural communication. For example, concepts from intercultural communication help explain why intergroup communication can be difficult. The problem is that culture provides us with a necessary set of assumptions that are *taken-for-granted*, that allow us to get on with our everyday lives. Many of these assumptions give us norms or rules for communicating with others that are not within our conscious awareness. Because these rules provide stability in our lives, we tend to respond emotionally or with frustration when our *common sense* rules appear to be violated.

Studying about rules for communication in other cultures, however, can also be misleading as we enter into communication with diverse others. First, we must be aware that these cultural factors of communication are not static but constantly changing. Second, we must remember that individuals are not necessarily representative of the average for the whole group. And, third, we need to bear in mind that individuals may be able to switch from one culture or subculture to another.

An ethical stance toward intercultural communication, and, by extension, communication with diverse others, begins with being aware that there will be these kind of out-of-awareness factors in communication. Attention to these variables or dimensions of cultural communication, however, cannot substitute for an ethical approach to such encounters (since the cultural dimensions describe what *is*, rather than what our ethical stance *ought to be*). Knowledge of cultural variables may allow us to develop more effective strategies for communication but may not necessarily lead to ethical intercultural communication.

We suggest that an ethical approach to intercultural encounters may be grounded in a dialogic approach to communication, as represented in recent versions of the theories of Coordinated Management of Meaning, dialogic communication, and Third-Culture Building. The basis for such an ethics is to approach the encounter with the other with an attitude of positive regard for the other and an openness to negotiate a set of norms for the new relationship, distinct from specific norms of either culture or group. The approach is similar to the perspective toward ethics we have labeled concern for Relationships in Part One.

We have discussed ways to deliberate about ethical situations, such as those arising from concerns about *hate speech*, speech codes, especially on campuses, political correctness, multiculturalism, and affirmative action. While considerations of character, duties, and consequences can all illuminate ethical thinking about such encounters, we conclude that the dialogic approach based on concern for relationships may be the most satisfying.

QUESTIONS AND TOPICS FOR DISCUSSION

1. Discuss the meanings and particularly the connotations of the word *diversity*. Is it a positive, negative, or neutral term?

2. Look over the list of categories of diversity early in the chapter. Do all the items on the list make sense? Which ones are probably more relevant to the problems of your society today? What important terms or categories have been left off this list? Which categories might you eliminate? Why?

3. Discuss with others the intercultural encounters you have had. Were the circumstances involving travel, service work, job-related functions, or study abroad? What parts of these experiences made you feel uncomfortable or frustrated? Why was that so?

4. In a group, see how many out-of-awareness rules for communication you can come up with. Did people suggest rules for communication that seemed surprising to you? Have you had experiences in which violation of these rules caused some sort of breakdown in communication for you or another person?

5. Does your school or place of work have a special anti-discrimination policy? Is it based on equal opportunity or affirmative action (find out if your organization considers there to be a difference between these terms). Does your school or employer have specific rules against speech or communication (such as in emails) that denigrate other people because of their membership in an identifiable group? Are the policies enforced? Have they been debated in this organization?

NOTES

1. "Minorities Majorities in More Areas," *USA Today*, September 30, 2004, p. A1.
2. *DiversityInc.com*, at www.diversityinc.com (accessed October 7, 2004).
3. Fred L. Casmir, "Ethics, Culture, and Communication: An Application of the Third-Culture Building Model to International and Intercultural Communication," in *Ethics in Intercultural and International Communication*, ed. Fred L. Casmir (Mahweh, NJ: Lawrence Erlbaum Associations, Inc., 1997), p. 99.

4. Charles van Onselen, *The Seed Is Mine* (New York: Hill & Wang, 1996).

5. Edward W. Said, *Culture and Imperialism* (New York: Vintage Books, 1993).

6. Edward T. Hall, *The Hidden Dimension* (Garden City, NY: Doubleday & Co., 1966); see also, Edward T. Hall, *The Silent Language* (Garden City, NY: Doubleday & Co., 1959).

7. Hall, *The Silent Language*.

8. Edward T. Hall, *Beyond Culture* (New York: Doubleday, 1976).

9. C. A. Ackah, *Akan Ethics* (Accra, Ghana: Ghana Universities Press, 1988), p. 121.

10. Geert Hofstede, *Culture's Consequences* (Beverly Hills, CA: Sage Publications, 1980); see also Stella Ting-Toomey, *Communicating across Cultures* (New York: The Guilford Press, 1999), pp. 66–74.

11. W. Barnett Pearce, *Interpersonal Communication: Making Social Worlds* (New York: HarperCollins, 1994).

12. W. Barnett Pearce and Vernon Cronen, *Communication, Action, and Meaning: The Creation of Social Realities* (New York: Praeger, 1982).

13. Stella Ting-Toomey, *Communicating across Cultures* (New York: The Guilford Press, 1999), pp. 45–54.

14. Fred L. Casmir, "Third-Culture Building: A Paradigm Shift for International and Intercultural Communication," *Communication Yearbook 16* (Newbury Park, NJ: Sage, 1993), p. 407; see also Casmir, *Ethics in Intercultural and International Communication*.

15. Casmir, *Communication Yearbook*, p. 408.

16. Casmir, *Ethics in Intercultural and International Communication*, p. 101.

17. Deborah Tannen, *You Just Don't Understand: Men and Women in Conversation* (New York: William Morrow, 1990); Tannen, *Talking from 9 to 5* (New York: William Morrow, 1994).

18. *The Pennbook 1994–95: Policies and Procedures Handbook,* University of Pennsylvania, cit. in Kenneth A. Strike and Pamela A. Moss, *Ethics and College Student Life,* 2nd ed. (Upper Saddle River, NJ: Prentice Hall, 2003), pp. 38–39.

19. "Poll: 1 in 4 Americans Hold Anti-Muslim View," *DiversityInc.com*, at www.diversityinc.com/public/9146.cfm (accessed October 7, 2004).

9 Communication Ethics and Disabilities

"Yes, I am in a wheelchair. And yes, it takes me longer to say what I want to say. You may not understand me at first, and I may seem strange to you until you get to know me. What I want most of all is for people to understand that, no matter what my body looks like . . . my mind is sharp. My accident did not destroy my ability to think, or to have informed opinions. I have feelings, and dreams, and goals. I have intelligence. I can make music. I can conceptualize. I can make people laugh."

"Talk to me, and not to my wheelchair."

—From a friend with a disability

Ethical Considerations: Our Story

A request came to our university Communication Lab (a tutoring service staffed by students for the purpose of training peers to research and present speeches) to make a presentation to a group of people with disabilities on *communication*, and we jumped at the opportunity. The organization making the request often gets requests from schools and civic organizations to have people with disabilities make presentations on how to live with disabilities and the people who have them. We were asked to assist these presenters in sharpening their communication skills. And, oh, did we prepare! We were the communication *experts*, after all, and we had much to teach these folks about communication. Armed with overhead transparencies, PowerPoint slides, handouts, and myriad *How To* tips, we headed for the facility. In the car, we talked about predicted outcomes, how we would get small group involvement, and in what order we would present.

What we didn't talk about was just how we communication *experts* were going to *teach* our discipline's time-honored organization skills to people who, for example, have no mechanism for short-term memory. We never thought of that. Nor did we think about how our audience would look, or how they would talk. We never anticipated that they might even interrupt our ordered, well-structured presentation.

As it turned out, we really hadn't prepared very well at all. We *did our thing* anyway, and we were politely received. It was clear that our structured presentation—always successful in our classrooms at the university—completely and utterly missed the mark. Our learning process was about to begin. Our teachers had arrived.

In communicating effectively with persons with disabilities, the *experts* were in the audience, and not up front with the charts, slides, and handouts.

Communication is about language, the way we describe others, and the way we frame our communication with those who are both similar to and different from us. The discipline of communication studies should speak directly to the ethics of communicating between people with disabilities and those without. As we began to write this chapter, we found ourselves challenged by the lack of a good vocabulary or language for discussing these issues. If we were discussing, for example, intercultural or interracial communication, we would have an existing frame for exploring these relationships. But there is no word to go with the prefix *inter* when speaking about the presence or absence of physical or other disabilities. A possible term could be *differently abled*, but that term seems awkward and not very clear. We think it is instructive for ethicists of communication that one must struggle to find appropriate language that would be both neutral and inclusive in discussing this major form of potential discrimination in our society.

In this chapter, we will investigate the often overlooked situation of communication between people with disabilities and those without. In so doing, we hope to make clear that this type of interaction is common in most societies but often not understood, especially by those who feel they are *normal*. Of course, no one is really normal or typical, and that kind of understanding is essential first as we consider this topic. People are people and physical characteristics or abilities ought not to enter into the equation. But, they do—and so we feel it necessary to address this issue in this chapter. We begin with an overview of the ethics of this issue, followed by a discussion of one solution called *people-first language.* The idea is to focus on using communication that does not limit, that in fact allows for empowering the other person with or without a disability. This statement is reminiscent of the tenets of dialogical ethics, introduced in the Chapter 5 of this text. We believe that dialogical ethics offers one of the best ways to think about ethically communicating with people in the kinds of interactions featured in this chapter. In addition, we feel that other ways of thinking about ethics are applicable in this situation as well: the *Ideal Speech Situation* of Habermas, the egalitarian approach of contemporary social justice, and the deontological imperative of Kant. We apply each of these perspectives in the following sections. Finally, an extended case study involving a major telethon for raising money for those with disabilities allows us to explore some of the ethical implications of these issues.

Ethics and Communication Involving Persons with Disabilities

With the steady advances in science, life expectancy is lengthening, and people are living longer. At some point in all our lives, the concept of thinking about people with disabilities being a separate group with its own sense of *otherness* will change. The authors maintain that there is virtually no difference between those with disabilities and those who will one day be a person with a disability. The tendency to view this issue as an *us and them* matter is one that both people with and people who have not yet been diagnosed with disabilities tend to fall into. It is our strong belief that the issue of the ethics of communicating with people with disabilities is an inclusive and shared issue. There is no *otherness* in our thinking about this important issue (although the concept of *Other* – capital *O* – will be discussed later.). Blindness or visual impairment, deafness or hearing impairment, mobility impairment caused by illness or accidents, decreases in mental capabilities affecting memory, logic, and ordered thinking—these and numerous other changes can await anybody. In this section we attempt to address both people with—and people who are not yet diagnosed with—disabilities as members of this text's audience.

Fortunately, attitudes toward people with disabilities have changed dramatically. In the past, there were schools for the *Retarded*, or people with disabilities were pushed into a *mainstream* status ("Let *them* join *us*—under controlled circumstances, of course"). Only recently has the attitude shifted to an acceptance that "The disabled ARE us." It is sobering to realize that those of us not classified as having a disability, who in our daily lives don't think much about disability, are just an automobile accident away from a life in a wheelchair. It shakes our narrow perception and beliefs about life when we realize that the next birth in a family, the next accidental tumble one takes, the next vision or hearing test, can make the realities of disability very present and personal to anyone. The curtain that separates people with disabilities and those not yet diagnosed with disabilities hangs by a gossamer thread.

People-First Language

The most effective (and ethical) way to communicate with one another is to establish a language that avoids the tendency to precede a person with his or her disability or other incidental characteristic. In the community of people with disabilities, such communication is called *People-First* language. Many of us remember hearing about *The Disabled*, or even *Wheelchair People*. We know of the *blind man* who sells brooms on the street corner, or the *deaf kid* in our daughter's scout troop. To describe it differently, to talk about "the man who is blind" or "the kid who is deaf" seems awkward at first. But when we actually *say* or read it, using *people-first* language makes sense.

We often in our daily lives talk about people and issues without giving much thought to the labels we are using. In casual conversation, it is common to talk about the "blonde who sits in the seat in front of me," or the "bald professor who teaches the evening class." We use the descriptor first: *blonde* or *bald*. This kind of exchange is *label-first*, rather than *people-first* language. We hear friends comment, "Her excuse was so *lame*," or "Her new boyfriend is so *retarded*," and we think nothing of it. No deliberate disrespect is being demonstrated. But looking at this communication through the lens of ethical consideration involves the use of emotionally charged language with negative connotations.

The word *handicapped* carries similar connotations. For years, people with disabilities have been burdened with the label of *handicapped people*. The word itself has been a part of our lexicon for a very long time. There are clearly marked *Handicapped* spots in the parking lot at the supermarket. Some establishments claim, "This restaurant is *Handicapped Accessible*." Although no doubt well meaning, these signs reinforce a stereotype. Let's consider the derivation of this terminology. The word *handicap* is derived from an old beggar's phrase, *cap in hand*. When one envisions someone with *cap in hand*, one pictures a person in the act of seeking charity. By using label-first language, people with disabilities are relegated to a state of dependency, incapable of supporting themselves.

From the Ohio Public Images/Public Images Network come these guidelines for using language that empowers, rather than limits:

> Think *people first*. Say "a woman who has mental retardation" rather than a "mentally retarded woman."
>
> Avoid using words like *unfortunate*, *afflicted* and *victim*. People with disabilities are just people, and not tragic figures.

A disability is not a disease. Words like *symptoms, patient* or *treatment* is the language of illness, and not of disability.

Use common sense in word choice. Labels like *cripple, deaf and dumb, lame* or *defective* carry negative and judgmental connotations.

Never refer to a person as *confined to a wheelchair.* Using a wheelchair allows people to *escape* confinement by being mobile.

Describe people without disabilities as *typical* rather than *normal.*[1]

Fortunately, recently signs signifying access for people with disabilities now display the universal symbol of a wheelchair. These symbols have become more and more prevalent in parking lots, restaurants, and other public places, replacing the label of *handicap.* Eventually, with the adoption of *people-first* language, the stereotype of the *Handicapped* will go the way of other antiquated descriptors.

Applications of Ethical Perspectives

Dialogical Ethics Applied to Disabilities

We have heard the questions from some colleagues who wonder if communicating with people with disabilities is nothing more than a matter of insensitivity or prejudice, and not really an issue for communication ethics. As they explain their opinions, our friends sometimes assert that it is more a matter of respect than ethics when it comes to communicating with people with disabilities.

It is a question well worth answering and we would respond this way: *respect is an ethical matter.* So are insensitivity and prejudice. Treating people fairly is a communication ethics issue. When we communicate to a person with a disability the message that "I recognize you as a complete human being equal to or superior to myself," we are ethically communicating with her. We call your attention back to Carl Rogers and his concept of Unconditional Positive Regard (Chapter 5) as a basis for this contention. As we will illustrate in Chapter 14, the Code of Ethics of the National Communication Association begins with the sentence, *Questions of right and wrong arise whenever people communicate.* We believe that one cannot separate respect or insensitivity from the judgment of communication ethics.

As mentioned earlier, the ethics of communicating involving people with disabilities is based on an ethic of the *Other.* Dialogical ethics (see Chapter 5) is foundational to the study of communication ethics. Emmanuel Levinas, a twentieth-century philosopher who bridges the gap between modern and postmodern philosophy, and who also established ethics as that which orients philosophy, wrote poignantly in *people-first* language when he claimed,

> You turn yourself toward the Other as an object when you see a nose, a forehead, a chin, and you describe them. The best way to encounter the Other is not even to notice the color of his eyes.[2]

Were he writing today, Levinas would likely have added "... *or his and her disability.*" To see beyond the physical and commune with the Other's humanity, rather than with the other's disability, is the goal of communicating ethically with people with disabilities. The ability to see past one's limitations, to ignore the wheelchair in favor of the person who sits in it, finds a comfortable home amidst the ethics of the Other.

> Ordinarily one is a 'character': a professor at the Sorbonne, a Supreme Court justice, son of so-and-so, everything that is in one's passport, the manner of dressing, of presenting oneself. And all signification in the usual sense of the term is relative to such a context: the meaning of something is in its relationship to another thing. Here, to the contrary, the face is meaning all by itself. You are You. . . . the relation to the face is straightaway ethical.[3]

Levinas asks us to communicate with the face of the person rather than with the person's *presentation*. His ethical position is to see beyond one's physical limitations. Levinas' point regarding our communication with the Other *outside* of his *context* (e.g., being in a wheelchair or using a machine-enhanced speech device) is important to our understanding of how persons with disabilities become frustrated in everyday dialogue. What may be common and familiar word choice for people who have no disabilities can be problematic for those people who happen to have a disability. Communication is one of the most commonly mentioned problems voiced by people with disabilities. Hearing, sight, thought, and mobility disabilities all require more focused and patient communication on the part of the communicator with people with disabilities. For example, consider a conversation between a person who has a speech disability, and one who does not. People who don't share a speech disability often lose patience when waiting for a person with a speech disability to complete a thought. In today's society, instant communication is the coin of the realm. It's all about the sound byte and *headline news*. Waiting for someone to get to the point when it takes him or her several minutes to finish a sentence demands a great deal of patience and respect for ethical communication.

Patience and respect for the communication process are central to the understanding of this process. One is obligated to relate to the Other at his or her own pace, not ours. As discussed earlier, a key tenet of dialogical ethics is to be *Person-Centered*. To gain such a position, one first must become *present* to the other person—a concept that is beautifully developed by Martin Buber (Chapter 5).[4] Losing focus or patience while listening may be common, but it is not an ethical way to communicate. Dialogical ethics require a nonlabeling, nonjudgmental, unconditional positive regard of the Other. As Levinas urges us to "not even notice the color of (the Other's) eyes," truly ethical communication is maximized when we allow each other to communicate at our own pace, and cherish each other throughout that process.

Martin Buber, one of the most influential religious ethicists of the twentieth century and the guiding spirit of dialogical ethics, gave us a road map for coming to grips with communication involving people with disabilities (see Chapter 5.) His magnificent work, *I and Thou* (1923), illustrates a phenomenological approach to dialogue as a living, ever-changing, event in the lives and culture of people. His dialogical theory is at the heart of ethical communication in the area of disability. Buber posited the theory that all relationships exist in the form of dialogue. Buber believed that ethics are centered in and reflected by the way we dialogue with others. The promotion of mutuality and self-development, and of being present for the Other in an inclusive, nonmanipulative way are all keys to Buber's approach. Buber's warrant is that ethical dialogue is not determined by any fixed *code* or system. Dialogical ethics is the perfect platform for communication involving people with disabilities. If one understands his *I–Thou* philosophy, one knows that dialogue is a concrete, real-time process, and not something that is governed by a universal system of ethics (I–It.) Remember that Buber's concept of I and Thou involved a dialogue based on a true meeting of souls. It is almost a holy, pure style of communication. Conversely, Buber believed that an I–It relationship is one in which we give technical or everyday information. Communication with people with disabilities has at the center Buber's thesis that we enter into dialogue from the situation itself, and not from a rule-based system.

> The idea of responsibility is to be brought back from the province of specialized ethics, of an *ought* that swings free in the air, into that of lived life. Genuine responsibility exists only where there is real responding.[5]

To the people who are active in the area of advocacy for ethical communication with people with disabilities, dialogical ethics speaks clearly to their mission (and it is why the authors advocate its inclusion into serious study of communication ethics.) Consider a recent proclamation by one such group. In the next few paragraphs, we will show one example of how some people with disabilities attempt to marry the theory and practice of dialogical ethics.

The Association for Persons with Severe Handicaps (TASH)—an international association of people with disabilities, their family members, advocates, and allied professionals—is actively involved in raising awareness of (among myriad other issues) ethical considerations in communication with people with disabilities. The acronym admittedly does not reflect *people-first* language. It is interesting to note how even professional organizations in the field of persons with disabilities continue to monitor the ways they communicate their values and ethics in the names they use. Nancy Weiss, then executive director, wrote in the March,

1998, TASH newsletter this explanation of how the acronym does not reflect the values of the organization:

> When TASH was started in 1974, it was called the American Association for the Education of the Severely/Profoundly Handicapped and went by the acronym AAESPH. In 1980 the name was changed to the Association for the Severely Handicapped, reflecting TASH's broader mission. The name was changed to The Association for Persons with Severe Handicaps in 1983 but the acronym, TASH, continued to be used. In 1995, the Board voted to maintain the acronym because it was so widely recognized but to stop using the full name of the organization as it didn't reflect current values and directions.

A list of over thirty resolutions was published by TASH, which are position statements designed to create dialogue around issues of disability. Prominent among those resolutions was the TASH Resolution on the Right to Communicate, which maintains,

> Where people lack an adequate communication system, they deserve to have others try with them to discover and secure an appropriate system. No person should have this right denied because they have been diagnosed as having a particular disability. Access to effective means of communication is a free speech issue.[6] The resolution goes on to advocate an "ethics of access" (our term). This may include the involvement of allies, advocates, and communication partners before and after meetings, and may also include the involvement of a *communication ally* during the course of the meeting.[7]

The TASH resolution promotes considered and focused communication with people with disabilities as a *free speech issue*. The authority of the First Amendment forms its spine. We assert a more fundamental warrant: becoming *communication allies* with persons with disabilities is a clear ethical position for any student of communication studies.

Now we shall turn to three other systems or perspectives that allow us a way for thinking about the issues raised in this chapter.

Habermas: The *Ideal Speech Situation* and Disabilities

The ethical warrant for the approach advocated here finds support beyond dialogical ethics. Jürgen Habermas, the twentieth-century German philosopher, was the primary exponent of critical theory, and one of modern Germany's most influential thinkers. We recall Habermas' description of the *Ideal Speech Situation* and find relevance to the communication issues raised in this chapter. In nearly perfect harmony with the TASH resolutions, Habermas describes the *Ideal Speech Situation* as occurring when there are no restraints on communication or discussion. There are no *power plays* or restrictions of access to a platform of communicating. The elements of Habermas' *Ideal Speech Situation* are clearly outlined in the following:

> Rule (3.1) defines the set of potential participants. It includes all subjects without exception who have the capacity to take part in argumentation. Rule (3.2) guarantees all participants equal opportunity to contribute to the argumentation and to put forth their own arguments. Rule (3.3) sets down conditions under which the rights to universal access and to equal participation can be enjoyed equally by all, that is, without the possibility of repression, be it ever so subtle or covert.[8]

We highlight two other major theorists' contributions in the field of ethical communication with people with disabilities. One such leading thinker is John Rawls (see Chapter 4.) We will show you how his theory of social justice speaks directly to the issue.

Rawls: Contemporary Social Justice

Perhaps no ethical system speaks more clearly to the issues of disabilities than does Social Justice, embodied in the theories of John Rawls. Rawls' theory of social justice is the concept of fairness and reciprocity. Equality in a communication setting requires at its core the conditions of equal opportunity. Rawls' concept of the *veil of Ignorance* requires us to assume the *original position* behind the veil of ignorance. From behind the veil, we have no knowledge of who will be a person with disability and, thus, our thinking about the ethics of communication is free from our prejudices and biases. From that position, no one is advantaged or hindered in the achieving of one's own ability to fairly communicate. The *original position* of Rawls permits the establishment of a fair, unprejudiced, and nonbiased stance for communication involving people with disabilities. The very presence of the veil means that we do not know whether we will be with or without a disability. The Veil of Ignorance blinds us from any particular knowledge of the personal characteristics or status we will have in life, compels us to listen equally and patiently to all voices in society—especially those voices which come from a slow-talking, wheelchair-seated fellow member of society.

Rawls believed that as self-interested rational people, we desire the means to pursue happiness and fulfillment, each in his own way. From behind the veil of ignorance, we communicate without knowing whether or not we have a disability. We have no knowledge of our race, sex, physical or mental disabilities, or generation. We would not want to belong to a society in which discrimination is possible, or to be a person with a disability in a society where we are treated with no respect or dignity. Nor would we wish to be excluded or patronized because of any difficulties we may have in the ways we communicate. Rawls' veil of ignorance provides us with the framework from which we can construct our mental models of communication. As Rawls establishes in his work *A Theory of Justice*, the principles which are at the heart of our position of advocating a clear, meaningful ethical protocol for communication between people with and without disabilities are as follows:

> First Principle. Each person is to have an equal right to the most extensive total system of equal basic liberties compatible with a similar system of liberty for all. Second Principle. Social and economic inequalities are to be arranged so that they are both: (a) to the greatest benefits of the least advantage, consistent with the just savings principle, and (b) attached to offices and positions open to all under conditions of fair equality of opportunity.[9]

We may note that nowhere in this discussion of justice-based ethics is the claim that all citizens must be equal contributors to society in order to lay claim to equal and fair ethical treatment. All members of society are due the same ethical considerations regardless of how, where, or how often they contribute to the overall well-being of the society. We will look at this specific issue, and provide an ethical framework a little later in this chapter.

Let us look at how these concepts are applied to more practical, *how to* situations in ethical communication. We will find that—what appears to be simple, common sense suggestions—each of these suggestions has a clear connection to Rawls' theory. These components of Rawls' theory of social justice are highlighted in the following *Ten Commandments for Communicating with People with Disabilities*.[10]

1. Speak directly rather than through a companion or sign language interpreter who may be present.
2. Offer to shake hands when introduced. People with limited hand use or an artificial limb can usually shake hands and offering the left hand is an acceptable greeting.
3. Always identify yourself and others who may be with you when meeting someone with a visual impairment. When conversing in a group, remember to identify the person to whom you are speaking.
4. If you offer assistance, wait until the offer is accepted. Then listen or ask for instructions.
5. Treat adults as adults. Address people who have disabilities by their first names only when extending that same familiarity to all others. Never patronize people in wheelchairs by patting them on the head or shoulder.
6. Do not lean against or hang on someone's wheelchair. Bear in mind that disabled people [sic] treat their chairs as extensions of their bodies.
7. Listen attentively when talking with people who have difficulty speaking and wait for them to finish. If necessary, ask short questions that require

short answers, a nod, or a shake of the head. Never pretend to understand if you are having difficulty doing so. Instead, repeat what you have
understood and allow the person to respond.

8. Place yourself at eye level when speaking with someone in a wheelchair or on crutches.

9. Tap a hearing-impaired person on the shoulder or wave your hand to
get his attention. Look directly at the person and speak clearly, slowly,
and expressively to establish if the person can read your lips. If so, try
to face the light source and keep hands, cigarettes, and food away from
your mouth when speaking.

10. Relax. Don't be embarrassed if you happen to use common expressions
such as "See you later," or "Did you hear about this?" that seem to
relate to a person's disability.

At first glance, this list looks like simple common sense. And yet, when we
consider how we interact with people everyday, with no real thought about
how we are communicating, the suggestions above are not only helpful,
they also put communicating with people with disabilities into an ethical
frame.

There is one final theorist we wish to highlight in this discussion of ethical communication with persons with disabilities. We have applied the theories of people-first language, dialogical ethics, the *Ideal Speech Situation*, and
contemporary social justice in specific ways to the issue of ethical communication. We now turn to a more universal, rules-driven, duty-bound perspective to complete our study.

Kant's Deontological Ethics and Disabilities

The final ethical system we will consider when communicating with people
with disabilities is perhaps the easiest to understand. It responds to the questions of rights and ethical considerations in the communication with and
among people with disabilities.

Recall (Chapter 3) that Kant's deontological approach to ethics is
always to treat others not simply as a *means*, but always at the same time as
an *end*. All people are ethically due the support and honest communication
of all of us on the sole criterion that they are fellow human beings. They are
deemed to have *intrinsic worth*, and thus are to be afforded our best efforts of
communication and consideration. In other words, if we ourselves wish to
be treated as people with value and worth, we are compelled to accord
everyone the same treatment. This, of course, includes the ways we choose
to communicate. The following case study—one which continues to cause
controversy among some people with disabilities—provides us with an
interesting platform from which to understand these Kantian principles.

CASE STUDY: ETHICS AND *JERRY'S KIDS*

It is Kant's second formulation of the categorical imperative that leads into an issue that still rages in the community of people with disabilities. The issue we highlight is that of Jerry Lewis' Telethon, aired every year during the Labor Day holiday. As we explore the ethical considerations of this issue, one that ignites the passions of so many people with disabilities, let us keep as a *baseline* Kant's imperative to "Act in such a way that you always treat humanity, whether in your own person or in the person of any other, never simply as a means, but always at the same time as an end."

> The singers croon. The eyelids droop. The money pours in. The firefighters, the Boy Scouts, the business executives, the neighborhood kids, all tiredly smiling proud smiles, carry in their collected funds, in jars, in boots, in oversize checks. The camera rolls. The host smiles. The money pours in. The Poster Child gives awkward answers to inane questions. The host smiles. The Poster Child smiles. The host cries. The money pours in.[11]

Some members of the community of disabilities feel very strongly about the Jerry Lewis Telethon to benefit the Muscular Dystrophy Association (MDA). Although they speak with no *official* voice for all persons with disabilities, these activists and friends of the protesters have very clear objections to the long-running and hugely successful fundraising campaign spearheaded by Lewis. The vehement protestations against—and the ethical communication implications of—the Telethon controversy are fascinating as a study in the ethical treatment and communication to and about people with disabilities. There seems to be no question of the effectiveness of the Telethon. Annually, the Telethon enjoys viewer numbers rivaling those of the World Series or the Academy Awards. And, the Telethon has continued to raise huge amounts of money for the MDA. In 2002, the Jerry Lewis Telethon netted $58.3 million for the MDA.[12] Assisted by celebrities from all walks of entertainment, Lewis said of those celebrities who participated in the record-setting event,

> I asked for their talent and their energy, and they brought it all out on that stage for me and *my kids*. This was the most successful show we've ever done, and I couldn't have done any of this without them.[13]

Let us analyze this controversy to see how some view the ethical issues played out in an ostensibly positive campaign. The issues for our consideration are how the protesters, on one hand, and the Telethon, on the other, communicate their positions and beliefs, especially in light of the ethical systems we have discussed in this book. One of the concerns of the Telethon protesters is that Lewis and the Telethon employ the use of pity to appeal to the emotions of the viewers, with the hope that this emotional appeal will help open checkbooks. Laura Hershey, a contributor to the *Spectacle* article cited earlier, writes:

> Pity is a complex and deceptive emotion. It pretends to care, to have an interest in another human being . . . Pity paves the way for paternalism, for the attempt to control people on the basis of disability. I have lived with the implications of this reaction, this assumption that I am less able to, have less of a right to run my own life.[14]

The ethical issue here is the perception that as far as the Telethon is concerned, people with disabilities are being used as a means (to raise money) rather than an end (being accorded the respect, communication, and dignity as people with value *as they are*). There is anger and discomfort by being labeled *Jerry's Kids*.

It appears that it was a segment from an interview with Jerry Lewis on the CBS Sunday Morning Show, May 20, 2001, which triggered the *pity* issue among activists in the community of persons with disabilities. Lewis said, "If it's pity we'll get money. I'm just giving you facts. Pity? You don't want to be pitied you're a cripple in a wheelchair? Stay in your house!"[15]

This issue of using pity for any segment in society as a means to raise money (no matter what the cause) is a fundamental one to the study of ethics in communication.

As we learned from Kant, ethical communication demands that we always view the person as an end, and not as a means to an end. Hershey voices the concerns of many activists among people with disabilities when she writes:

> I don't necessarily enjoy attacking another person's motives, but I hear defenders saying, 'Jerry Lewis is trying to help so many people. How dare you criticize his methods?' This means-justifies-the ends argument has a long and despicable history, which I don't need to go into here. Even more dangerous is the attitude that people who are *being helped* have no right to say HOW they want to be helped, or treated, or thought of. This is paternalism at its worst. By being the object of charitable efforts, do we thereby waive our right to respect, and to free speech?
>
> With the stated goal of *helping* his *kids*, Jerry Lewis is helping to keep alive the most pernicious myths about people who have disabilities. He ignores our truth, substituting his own distorted assumptions.[16]

Q U E S T I O N S   F O R   A N A L Y S I S   O F   T H E   C A S E

1. Consider the idea of *The means justify the ends*. In your opinion, does the fact that the Telethon for *Jerry's Kids* has raised over sixty million dollars—and drawn considerable attention to the issues of disability—somehow soften the ethical issues raised by the Telethon protestors?

2. Isn't *emotional appeal* a long-accepted persuasive device in the field of communication? Is it really such a bad thing to make me feel just a little guilty or make me cry a little if it means I will also pick up the phone and call in a pledge? Isn't "There but for the grace of God go I" a perfectly valid and desired response if you are trying to persuade me to spend money on your cause?

3. What, if any, changes would you make to the way the MDA Telethon is conducted?

Chapter Summary

The arguments will continue, and issues will be raised regarding the perception of, and ethical communication with, people with disabilities. As we have established, the need for ethical, considered, and respectful communication between people with and without disabilities is supported by nearly every established major ethical system.

The implications of this case study are clear for anyone trying to come to grips with communication ethics. To our readers who do not have a disability, we ask this: When we recall the last time we had a conversation with someone who exhibited some disability, the issues become more relevant, don't they? Remember that person who stuttered? Weren't we tempted—in the interest of time—to complete her sentences for her? Didn't we find ourselves wishing that she would just *get it out,* so that we could move on? Aren't we tempted to simply look past the person in a wheelchair because he looks differently than we do? If he says something that we can't understand, isn't it easier for us to simply smile and nod—pretending to agree or understand in order to not have to truly listen and engage in communication?

To our readers who do have a disability, we ask: isn't it easy to get frustrated with people without disabilities when they don't seem to pay attention to us? Don't we sometimes tend to just dismiss them as being uncaring or not interested in what we have to say? If we wish people without disabilities to be patient and *present* with us, isn't it ethical for ourselves to be patient and *present* with them?

As we have established, virtually every major theory of communication ethics applies directly to communicating with people with disabilities. They address the question of what we owe (in terms of our communicating) people who have disabilities. We have shown that, as our society ages and the potential for each of us to become a person with disability increases, ethical communication with people with disabilities is *our* issue and not an issue merely for intellectual consideration.

The men and women who have disabilities, as well as the staff who works with them, have been patient with us as we are learning what it means to be ethical in our communication with persons who have disabilities. As in any communication situation, when the barriers are lowered and people choose to engage at a meaningful and ethical level with one another, rich and poignant interaction takes place. Our students who now regularly interact with persons with disabilities are keenly aware that the differences between them and the people with disabilities with whom they communicate are miniscule. An auto accident tonight, a slip on an icy sidewalk, a tumble down the dormitory stairs, a traumatic injury in a recreational game, and that gossamer thread has snapped and we ourselves now have become a person with a disability. This sobering possibility has caused us to shift our communication from that of communicating *to* the other, to that of communicating as if we *were* the other.

Because we are.

QUESTIONS AND TOPICS FOR DISCUSSION

1. Are the ethical concerns raised by the protestors of the Jerry Lewis Telethon valid ones?

2. Which of the major communication ethics systems (Dialogical, Social Justice, Kantian,) gives us the best framework when considering the issues of ethical communication between people with and without disabilities?

3. Is there a person with a disability in your family? Do you and the rest of your family communicate differently with that person than you might with a classmate or a coworker? Do you find that you resent how others communicate with him or her?

4. Does the *people-first* language found in the literature of disabilities change the way you think about how you talk about persons with disabilities? Is it OK to talk about *lame* excuses, or a friend who is so *retarded* sometimes? Are there ethical considerations there, or is it simply innocent talk among friends?

NOTES

1. Public Images Network, Ohio Public Images, Inc. "Think 'People First'" at www.publicimagesnetwork.org/first.html (accessed June 29, 2004).

2. Emmanuel Levinas, *Ethics and Infinity*, trans. Richard A. Cohen (Pittsburgh: Duquesne University Press, 1985), p. 85.

3. Levinas, *Ethics and Infinity*, pp. 86–87.

4. Martin Buber, "Elements of the Interhuman," in *Bridges Not Walls: A Book About Interpersonal Communication* (Chap. 11), ed. John Stewart (Menlo Park, Calif.: Addison-Wesley Publishing Co., 1973), p. 109.

5. Martin Buber, *Between Man and Man*, trans. Ronald Gregor Smith (London: Kegan Paul, 1947), p. 16.

6. TASH (The Association for Persons with Severe Handicaps), "TASH Resolution on the Right to Communicate" at www.tash.org/resolutions/res02communicate.htm (accessed June 29, 2004).

7. TASH web site (accessed June 29, 2004).

8. Jürgen Habermas, *Moral Consciousness and Communicative Action*, trans. Christian Lenhardt and Shierry Weber Nicholsen (Cambridge: The MIT Press, 1996), p. 89.

9. John Rawls, *A Theory of Justice* (Cambridge: Harvard University Press, 1971), p. 302.

10. *The New York Times*, June 7, 1993.

11. *Spectacle*, Spring/Summer 1997, Pachanga Press, Burlington, MA. *Spectacle* is a semiannual print and online journal of essays and articles.

12. Muscular Dystrophy Association home page, at www.mdausa.org (accessed June 29, 2004).

13. Muscular Dystrophy Association, USA, web site (accessed June 29, 2004).

14. *Spectacle*, n.p.

15. A web site for Jerry Lewis Telethon activists at www.stoppity.org (accessed June 29, 2004).

16. *Spectacle*, n.p.

10 Ethical Issues in Mass Communication

Wherever we are, the environment washes us with a constant flow of potential information—from the hum of the air conditioner or heater or from the processor of our personal computer. In public, we overhear snatches of conversation all around us. Moreover, people are subjected to all sorts of mediated messages—usually electronic media. Increasingly, we live in a mediated environment, certainly much more so than was the case for parents or grandparents. There is little doubt the *Media* (pictured as a single, monolithic entity) have powerful influences over the way we experience and think about our lives today. This power implies the need for ethical accountability. Whenever people or a group of people have power to influence the lives of others, ethical obligations arise.

Media messages range from quite mundane to very profound or important. Striking, singular events demand our attention, broadcast over television, radio, the Internet, or cell phones. Media bring momentous events directly into our lives, as when we all watched in growing horror the effects of the earthquake and tsunami that devastated people around the Indian Ocean at Christmas time in 2004. At other times we get caught up in less important events, such as following the various votes on the *Reality TV* shows, such as Survivor. Or, we are riveted to our screens or monitors for the latest courtroom developments in a sensational murder or crime, such as the cases of JonBenet Ramsay or O. J. Simpson case or the murder of Lacey Peterson in California.

We depend on these sources to be accurate and fair. After all, the press is granted a special status by the First Amendment of the U.S. Constitution (referring to the freedom of the press) and fulfills a special function as watchdog against abuses by the powerful in government. We are therefore shaken when award-winning journalists working for respected journals such as the *New York Times* or *The New Republic* are caught fabricating or plagiarizing their stories. The cases may be less clear-cut than outright fabrication or lying, as when Dan Rather on *Sixty Minutes* admits that a memo featured in a story questioning President Bush's National Guard service had not been thoroughly checked for veracity or accuracy. That this report came during the closing stages of the very heated presidential campaign of 2004 reinforced the seriousness of this breach of sound journalistic practice.

Those involved in the mass media face many issues that raise serious ethical questions. For example, following the attacks of 9/11 in the United States, broadcasters were faced with the question of whether or not to run on the air videotapes from, purportedly, Osama bin Laden, the head of the *al-Qaeda* network, which had taken responsibility for the attacks. The issues resided in whether or not broadcasting the videotapes would benefit or serve the purposes of terrorists planning more attacks. Decisions about what messages to transmit thus become ethical matters. Even decisions about what part of a news event or story should be broadcast or printed can also raise an ethical question. For example, the case of alleged rape in 2002 involving the famous professional basketball player Kobe Bryant presented the dilemma of balancing the alleged victim's right to privacy against the public right to know the name of the accuser. In most jurisdictions, rape victims are usually shielded and are not identified publicly in media.

The press and the broadcast media have the ability to shape and frame our understanding of what is important in the current events. Institutions as pervasive as the mass media hold great potential for harm or benefit, and so the field covering the ethics of mass communication is very broad and complex.

In a single chapter, we cannot hope to cover what is a major subdiscipline of the field of communication itself. There are entire college courses on journalism ethics, broadcasting ethics, and the ethics of mass communication. Our goals in this chapter are therefore *limited* to providing a context for thinking critically about the ethical issues that arise in mass communication and an overview of significant ethical issues that do arise in this field.

The Field of the Media and Mass Communication

The word *medium* (plural, *media*) refers to something in the middle, between two things or two or more people. It is the same as the Latin root for many related words in English, such as middle, moderate, median (both in math and in super highways), and mediator. In communication, a medium refers to a device or physical channel that carries message signals back and forth between communicators, typically when the two are not present at the same place at the same time. The medium (or media) is thus in the *middle*, between the communicators. Mediated communication therefore differs from interpersonal communication, in which two or more people communicating are typically face to face, without a medium of communication between them. A telephone is hence a medium of communication, allowing two people to bridge the distance between them so they can communicate with each other.

Defining Mass Media and Mass Communication

Not all mediated communication is *mass* media, just as not all communication is *mass* communication. Emails, phone calls, some fax messages, and personal letters (*snail mail*) represent mediated communication but not mass media. The word mass implies a large number of recipients of the same message. The number is much larger than the people who could be physically present as an audience for a live performance or public speech. Mass communication reaches a much wider audience than those who can be present at one place and one time. In the past, such a medium was probably in the form of print publication. Books and newspapers were disseminated to vast audiences over great distances. Many historians date the beginning of the modern age to the time of the French Revolution, when the widespread publication of political pamphlets kept revolutionary fever high during 1789 in Paris and the rest of France. The ideas of the European Enlightenment, especially as spread through the medium of the first-ever mass-produced Encyclopedia, created the intellectual atmosphere fueling the Revolution.

Mass communication is the product of the mass media. Mass communication is primarily one-way, in contrast to most forms of interpersonal or face-to-face communication. The roles of sender and receiver are more differentiated, and receivers tend to be passively involved in the process. Any feedback from receivers to sender is delayed and often indirect. As a result of these factors, it is usually difficult to determine the effects of the messages of mass communication. The sources of messages are typically institutional or organizational, rather then individual. The messages seem impersonal, certainly more impersonal than most forms of interpersonal or face-to-face communication. At times, the source or sources may be nearly impossible to identify with certainty, and so it is also difficult to hold any particular individuals accountable for the messages in mass communication.

Categories and Types of Mass Media

We can further delineate the nature and functions of the mass media by listing the various categories or areas of study associated with the media:

- Journalism or the Press
- Public Relations
- Advertising and Marketing
- Entertainment.

And, one could add others, such as Educational Broadcasting or Religious Communication.

Journalism aims (or is supposed to aim) at creating or maintaining an informed public while holding public officials accountable—so informing and criticizing are its main communication functions. The practice of public relations is concerned with influencing public opinion and creating or changing public beliefs and attitudes. Advertising and marketing are, obviously, more like public relations, in that their main function is to sell products, usually by creating favorable beliefs among the public about a product or a company. While entertainment aims at providing diversion and relaxation for a public audience, it seems clear that advertising and selling products are central to their functioning as well, especially in a market-based economy. These divisions are arbitrary and not clear-cut: news outlets rely on an entertainment format to increase the numbers of readers and viewers (and thereby sell advertising). The growing use of *product placement* in entertainment shows illustrates the blurring of the lines. For years, movies and shows had actors using certain brands of cigarettes or soft drinks presented so the viewers would clearly see the brand name. Once, General Motors gave away Pontiacs to all the audience members at an Oprah Winfrey show, an unusually expensive form of *free samples*. College football bowl games now rely on product names for their contests (our favorite was the Poulan Weedeater Bowl). Public relations and advertising certainly rely heavily on entertaining people to get and hold attention. In practice, it is actually difficult to clearly distinguish among these four categories of mass communication. Thus, a news broadcast will juxtapose *hard news*, say a story about a war or natural disaster, with *news* about the network's *Reality* TV show, as the news anchor reports which participant was voted off in the most recent episode.

These categories may not necessarily correlate with any particular medium of communication. Journalism and the press employ print publications, broadcast, and hyperspace media. Most large newspapers and broadcasting stations now distribute their content over the Internet as well as in print. Obviously, public relations and advertising use a variety of types of media. Entertainment is equally diverse, disseminated through radio, television, Internet, video games, CDs, DVDs, cell phones, and so on.

Overview of Ethical Problems in Mass Communication

Before proceeding to a summary of the major ethical issues involving mass communication, we will begin with an overview of the three fundamental sources of ethical dilemmas often facing those in *the Media*.

Fundamental Ethical Issues in Media Ethics

Mass Communication is directed at a public audience, even though their messages are often received by individuals, in private, sitting alone at home in front of a television set or in front of a computer screen. The first major source of ethical problems in mass communication is that given its public nature, there is a presumption the mass media are to serve society or the public at large rather than individuals. Utilitarianism, which holds that the ethical action is that which provides the greatest good for the greatest number, usually becomes the basis for ethical judgments regarding mass communication. The good of the many seems therefore to trump the good of the individual. Making ethical judgments in the field of mass communication hence often pits *the rights of the individual against the good of the public or society* at large.

A second major source for ethical problems in mass communication lies in the mixed purposes and goals of those engaged in the field. Many of the institutions providing mass communication are for-profit businesses. *The good of the public at large, therefore, is often perceived as pitted against the economic interests* of those running or employed by the mass media corporations and institutions. This problem is growing in significance given the increasing consolidation of media ownership by a small number of corporate conglomerates. Today about 90 percent of daily newspapers in the United States are owned by corporate chains compared to only about 25 percent back in 1945.

In the United States, mass distribution of newspapers developed in the second half of the nineteenth century, with the introduction of industrialized printing techniques and the mass reading audiences made possible by large urban areas. The so-called *penny press* began in the 1880s, when newspaper publishers priced their papers below the actual cost of printing them (papers in New York typically went for 5 cents apiece earlier).[1] The cheaper, mass-produced newspaper made for a mass readership, as newspapers became businesses oriented to selling advertising for their main income. Papers began to focus more on selling their readership to advertisers than selling news and information to their readers. Consequently, owners and managers of papers became primarily concerned with attracting as many readers as possible. This model based on attracting as large a public audience as possible carried over into the businesses of radio and eventually television broadcasting as well. The content of these media, therefore, had to appeal to vast numbers without offending large segments of the public.

The third major source of ethical problems in the mass media results from *the power to shape public discourse.* In the early days of the study of mass communication people assumed that messages in the mass media were very powerful. The *bullet* or *hypodermic needle* view of the effects of mass media reflected this belief. Because something was published or broadcast in the media, people feared it would be believed for just that reason. Scholars studying the effects of mass propaganda in World War I were especially worried about this power. Later studies tempered this fear, and some researchers became convinced the mass media lacked such power altogether. These studies emphasized the moderating influence of the *two-step flow* or *multi-step flow* of messages from the mass media, as they were interpreted by individuals in local communities who were seen as opinion leaders.

More recent theories about the effects of the mass media present a more complex view. While it may be difficult to prove any significant effects from single messages in the media, this view holds the media do shape and determine the topics the public at large thinks about. Consequently, there is the theory of *agenda-setting*, which maintains the mass media may not determine what we think about a particular issue, but they do determine what issues we do think about. This theory highlights the gatekeeping and framing functions managers of the media exercise in deciding what events and topics will be brought to the attention of the public. In addition, in his cultivation theory of the mass media, George Gerbner holds that the main effects of the mass media relates to how much an individual is exposed to media, especially television. According to this theory, people who are heavy users of a medium such as television tend to see the world as more threatening than is warranted. Light users of the media, on the other hand, have a more realistic view about the number of murders and police shootings that are going on in their town or neighborhood.

According to agenda-setting theory and cultivation theory the mass media shape as well as restrict the general impressions people have about the world. There are clear ethical implications of such influence. How do editors and news managers determine what kinds of stories will be covered? How do producers decide what kinds of shows will be broadcast with implications about lifestyles, standard occupations, and the like? Who or what groups have access to the mass media? Are there groups who are shut out or have difficulty getting their message placed in the media? Are important points of view shut out from public view because those views conflict with economic and other interests of those controlling the mass media?

We will now turn to some more specific ethical issues confronting professionals in the mass media.

Ethical Issues in Mass Communication

Professionals in the communication industries belong to one or several associations to further their common interests. Most of these associations have adopted codes of ethics as guidelines for the professional practice of their members. A review of many of these codes of ethics provides us with a common set of ethical concerns. Typical of these codes of ethics are the following:

> The SPJ (Society of Professional Journalists, or Sigma Delta Chi) Code of Ethics
>
> Code of Ethics for Professional Communicators, International Association of Business Communicators (IABC)
>
> PRSA (Public Relations Society of America) Code of Professional Standards
>
> Advertising Ethics and Principles, American Advertising Federation (AAF)
>
> Declaration of Principles on the Conduct of Journalists, International Federation of Journalists
>
> American Society of Media Photographers Code of Ethics
>
> National Press Photographers Association Code of Ethics
>
> American Society of Newspaper Editors Code of Ethics
>
> Code of Ethics: Radio–Television News Directors Association
>
> Public Radio News Directors Inc. (PRNDI) Statement of Ethics
>
> CMA's Code of Ethical Behavior, College Media Advisors, Inc.

In addition, each newspaper, news organization, broadcasting network, as well as national associations in countries outside the United States, usually have their own code of ethics or ethical guidelines for their own professionals. Two of the most influential private organizations in the area of ethical standards in the United States are probably the Poynter Institute and the *New York Times*. The Poynter Institute is especially well known for its Institute for Global Ethics and *Ethics Newslines*. The *New York Times* has compiled an exhaustive fifty-two-page code of conduct for its news and editorial departments, which goes into great detail regarding ethical expectations for its journalists.

A review of these codes of ethics indicates some concerns common to most of these professional groups. The code of the SPJ provides a good summary. It is divided into four sections: Seek Truth; Minimize Harm; Act Independently; Be Accountable. The first section focuses on accuracy, testing that accuracy with corroborating sources, avoiding distortion and stereotyping. The second set of guidelines involves exercising sensitivity, avoiding pandering to *lurid curiosity*, exercising caution about naming names of, for example, sex crime victims, juvenile suspects, and respecting privacy, especially for those not in the public eye. The third set of guidelines, under the heading *Act Independently*, covers issues of potential conflicts of interest. The *Times* lengthy set of guidelines devotes over half of its pages to the need for reporters and editors to avoid any possible perception of special favors or conflicts of interest. Accountability has to do with being transparent about editorial decisions and coverage, admitting mistakes, and inviting input from the public regarding such practices. In addition many of the codes deal with professional obligations of practitioners to clients, business colleagues, and the organizations for which they work. These sections have much in common with general business ethics (the ethics of doing business) and are not as germane to communication issues *per se*.

In an effort to provide an overview of the kinds of ethical issues in media communications, we have grouped many of these issues in the following sections. The first section reviews many of the ways that mass media frame our view of the world through their function as gatekeepers for what is considered news and what isn't. We believe the goals of seeking truth and minimizing harm needs to recognize the power of the mass media to set the public agenda and direct attention to some aspects of our world and not others. This section also touches on the conflict between privacy rights of individuals and public interests. The second heading, *Stereotypes in the Media*, focuses on issues of fairness and providing context in shaping public perceptions of groups and cultures. Entertainment media, as well as journalism, is especially significant in this area. The emphasis here has to be with minimizing harm and avoiding prejudice. The third section brings us to the significant matter of truth and accuracy. The content of the media includes images, photographs, and video as well as verbal content, and the visual images may distort or detract from the overall accuracy of a message.

The Gatekeeping Function: Framing Our View of the World

On the top of the front page of every issue of the *New York Times* there is a box containing the motto: "All the news that's fit to print." But, how does one determine which news is "fit to print?"

Earlier, we referred to the famous movie, *Jaws*, and the effort by the town leaders to keep reports about people being attacked by a shark out of the news. They feared the stories would hurt the town's image as a destination for tourists. Although this case is both extreme and fictional, one can imagine situations in which the local TV station or newspaper feels some responsibility to the local economy and image. This sense of local loyalty could lead to a temptation to downplay stories about local crime or similar risks. In this sort of case, the issues of loyalties and values presented in the Potter Box (see p. 218) come into play in a rather obvious way.

Far more is going on in the world than can be reported in the newspaper or news broadcast in any given day. Decisions, often on the spur of the moment, about what to print or air have to be made. The so-called *bottom-line* considerations can privilege sensationalism and what will attract attention (hence the old cliché, "If it bleeds, it leads"). Catastrophic events which are by their very nature unusual often receive dominant news coverage, causing people to worry about unlikely events while overlooking the dangers of more probable ones. And, the unusual and dangerous can be justified as newsworthy, certainly, because members of the public need to be warned about such potential dangers. We hardly need to be warned when everything is going fine. The utilitarian yardstick—what is in the best interest of the largest number—is invoked in these instances. The ethical principle is thus the greater good is served by making people aware of dangerous circumstances. One must then apply the test of definition, asking whether the facts of the case, objectively considered, do establish this sort of public danger, or is the item sensationalized in the hope of garnering attention and advertising revenue. These cases highlight the power of the media to cultivate a particular image of the world and its dangers.

Similar ethical questions involve whether the newspaper or television news broadcast should show actual close-up pictures (or videotape) of dead children and grieving parents at the scene of tragic accident, such as a drowning at a backyard pool. The argument can be made that such graphic pictures might help prevent such tragedies, since adults may become more aware of the need to supervise kids around pools. In the same way, some news outlets maintain that graphic pictures of auto accident victims increase public awareness of the dangers. Again, we are weighing competing values: in one case, the claimed need for the public to be made aware, graphically, of the dangers, versus the feelings and rights of individuals.

At the time of the 9/11 attack, editors and producers struggled with the question of whether or not to show images of people jumping from the upper floors of the burning buildings. Most decided these pictures were too graphic and disturbing for viewing. In this decision, they seemed to be following the SPJ standard which requires that journalists to take account of "those affected by tragedy or grief."[2] The balancing of newsworthiness while illustrating gruesomely the horrors of that day against the sensibilities of victims, their families, and potential revulsion among viewers represents a similar kind of ethical dilemma arising from gatekeeping.

In the days of the Civil Rights struggle in—but not limited to—the southern United States, news concerning people of color and their interests often did not make it into broadcasts or newspapers as *newsworthy*. Certain groups in society, especially minorities or economically disadvantaged, find their issues are hardly covered in the media. For a long time, HIV infection did not seem to get much coverage in the press because it was not seen as a significant threat to people in the mainstream. Sometimes, publication or broadcast decisions are based on the supposed impact on Americans or Europeans. There was far more coverage of the Tsunami disaster in the Indian Ocean in the December of 2004 than the coverage of the civil war in the Democratic Republic of the Congo, which had killed between three and four million people.

We are not saying that there were not valid reasons for the decisions made in the extensive coverage of the tsunami disaster in Asia. At least one newspaper editor apologized for his decision to give about seven-eighths of his paper's front page on the day following the reports of the Tsunami to the local football team's success. Only one column down the side of the page reported on the disaster in the Indian Ocean. The editor came to feel his decision to approve giving such priority to a sports event on page one over the human tragedy in Asia was mistaken. The question is whether stories involving similar or even greater loss of life, as in the Congo or elsewhere, deserved essentially no coverage at all. These are not easy decisions, but such issues seldom present themselves in simple or clear forms.

Decisions about what stories to broadcast or print can raise issues hinging on privacy as well. A news story might identify individuals, placing them in a bad light or even some danger: a decision involving the rights of the public versus the rights of the individual thereby surfaces. The negative consequence of such intense coverage, or media frenzy, is illustrated in cases such as that of Richard Jewell. He was the security guard at the Olympics in Atlanta following the Olympic Park bombing in 1996. Early news reporting focused on him as the likely bomber, based on what turned out to be erroneous information. In a similar case, reports in the media in 1999 implied that a scientist at the Los Alamos National Laboratory, a man named Wen Ho Lee, had passed nuclear secrets to China. The publicity led to his firing and damaged reputation. Eventually, the case against him had to be dropped, but much harm had already been done. Cases involving sexual assault or involving minors can confront editors with questions of whether or not to provide names. The rape-shield laws in many states prevent rape victims' names being reported, as a general rule. But, the situation is not always clear-cut. In the case involving the professional basketball player, Kobe Bryant, mentioned earlier, a defense attorney unexpectedly announced the name of the alleged victim in open court, making it part of public record. Later, the mother of Bryant's accuser also identified herself at a victims' rights rally.

The highly publicized charges involving Michael Jackson and alleged child molestation charges at his *Neverland Ranch* raised similar dilemmas when the identity of one of the alleged victims became known. Some editors and producers felt it was then OK to go with the names of the alleged victims, while others did not.

Ellen Alderman and Caroline Kennedy in their best-selling book, *The Right to Privacy*, explore questions of the public's rights versus an individual's rights.[3] Their book provides many examples of harms people can suffer from various kinds of reports in the media, not limited to the cases of identifying an alleged victim or perpetrator in a criminal case such as rape. For example, news reports could reveal that someone was adopted, perhaps something they themselves did not know, causing some shock and anguish, for them and for the adoptive parents. A photograph or broadcast could imply or seem to reveal the private lifestyle of people known in the community, such as showing them in bars, nightclubs, gay clubs, or the like. The *appropriation* of someone's image or likeness (using their picture without their knowledge or consent) can cause them embarrassment or mental suffering as well. Revealing in the news that someone has cancer or HIV/AIDS or a sexually transmitted disease can cause similar harms to the individuals.

As a legal right, a right to privacy is implied in the *U.S. Constitution*, if not explicitly stated except in the protection against unreasonable searches and seizures. Alderman and Kennedy point out that although courts have come to recognize such a right, the injunction against infringing on one's privacy applies only to government. Whether individuals are harmed by private disclosures, such as in the media, is a matter of tort law or of ethics. Torts are harms suffered by an individual, which can become the basis of a civil suit involving a plaintiff suing another person or institution to recover damages. As civil cases, they are outside criminal proceedings. The threat of civil suits can restrain media sources from broadcasting individuals' names or private affairs. Codes of ethics for many of the communication professions in fact aim at helping their members avoid such suits. Apart from such dangers, media professionals rely on their own ethics in deciding questions pitting an individual's right to privacy against the public right to know.

A different kind of issue arises when a particular story might involve a major advertiser or a firm owned or controlled by the parent company of the media outlet, raising issues of economic self-interest versus the public good. If the story could be detrimental to a major advertiser, is it suppressed or buried? The question here focuses on the loyalties owed to competing groups, such as economic supporters and the public at large.

The gatekeeping function of news media, broadcast, or print, therefore potentially raises ethical issues. In addition, the way the stories and people in the news are depicted can present us with serious ethical concerns as well. The next section concerns the ethical effects of stereotyping.

Stereotypes in the Media

The frame in which the stories are reported can create impressions or images with ethical consequences. News sources, especially in the United States, gave far more coverage to the *ethnic cleansing* in the Balkans than to the genocide in Rwanda, occurring at about the same time in the 1990s. The conflict in the Balkans, in Europe, was typically characterized as *ethnic*, involving *ethnic cleansing*. The events in Africa were framed as *tribal* conflicts. Why are some conflicts between communities *ethnic* and others *tribal*? The frame *tribal* suggests a primitive setting and culture, and further suggests that the conflicts are somehow normal and to be expected. Imagine if the media referred to the clashes in the Balkans or between Palestinians and Israelis as *tribal*. Many people would find the characterization jarring: Serbians and Croatians—Europeans—are not tribes, they would object. Such frames can be powerful, coloring our expectations about different groups of people. Habitual characterizations can also deaden sympathies we might have for the plight or suffering of others as well.

The cases comparing coverage of conflicts in the Balkans and in Africa sensitize us to the danger of presenting people in stereotypical ways in the media. These issues arise not just in news reporting, but also in entertainment media. People watching films from the early days of movies are often shocked by the blatant racism in some early pictures. Unfortunately some of these earlier portrayals reappear in more recent films and video. The reason may not be hard to seek. Producers and writers know they can use stock characterizations, essentially stereotypes, as a way to define a character or his or her action quickly and easily. The issue revolves around when stock characterization becomes hurtful stereotype. Of course, one can always argue that entertainment is not all that powerful in its effects—if you are bothered by a portrayal, simply turn it off or turn to another station. One writer on media ethics has likened this evocation of the on–off switch to the injunction, "If you're bothered by air pollution, just stop breathing."[4]

When the fourth movie in the popular *Star Wars* series was first screened, the character called Jar-Jar Binks seemed offensive to many people. His manner of talking and shuffling seemed too reminiscent of the racist depiction of African Americans in some of the early films of the last century. There was also objection, although not as much as in the case of Jar-Jar Binks, to the portrayal of the character who was a slave dealer in the same movie. This character seemed to come across with an accent, appearance, and mannerisms that harked back to stereotypical portrayals of Jewish merchants in earlier films and plays. The entertainment industry has also been roundly criticized for portraying gangsters in organized crime, or the *mafia*, as Italian. An animated movie aimed at a young audience, *Shark Tale*, featured a *codfather*, Don Lino, clearly presented as Italian in line with the stereotype.[5] Other standard stereotypes demeaning to different ethnic groups include the Mexican bandit, the Latin American drug kingpin, and the Arab terrorist, among others. More subtle yet still questionable stereotypical depictions also occur, as when the elderly are portrayed as confused and weak or gay men as unusually creative or artistic. The SPJ Code of Ethics is explicit in its injunction to "avoid stereotyping by race, gender, age, religion, ethnicity, geography, sexual orientation, disability, physical appearance or social status."[6]

Questions of communication ethics arise when someone intentionally communicates a message that has effects on other people. If the effects can be judged as harmful, some reasonable justification must be advanced for the communication to be evaluated as ethical. For example, if, according to agenda-setting and cultivation theories, a steady diet of certain kinds of stereotypes and characters in entertainment media can shape public perceptions of whole classes of people, then we have a question of communication ethics, given the potential harm to those depicted negatively. Issues concerning censorship or even matters of good (or bad) taste are not immediately our concern here. The realm of ethics is separable from the realms of legality or taste—although obviously some messages can be, all at the same time, unethical and in violation of communication law and in bad taste.

Stereotypes can creep into news journalism as well as entertainment. The effects can be even more harmful in the news, since the depictions carry the credibility of *news* and are not easily dismissed as fiction or *mere* entertainment. And, again, the effects can be subtle. For example, often television directors rely on *eyewash*, which is stock footage of video the station has on hand. The *eyewash* can be running in the background as an announcer introduces a news topic. A danger of this stock footage is that the people or neighborhood or events shown may in fact have nothing to do with the actual story. In general, the use of such *eyewash* is not necessarily unethical. The practice becomes questionable, however, when certain ethnic groups or neighborhoods are nearly always associated with negative stories, such as those about crime or poverty or poor schools.

Stereotypical thinking can affect decisions about the emphasis or the type of coverage certain stories receive. Does crime in certain neighborhoods get more coverage than in other parts of the city? A murder in a mostly white suburb might seem more newsworthy in the judgment of a news producer than the same crime in an inner-city, mostly African American neighborhood, perpetuating the notion that such crimes there are endemic and therefore not *real news*.

The way certain sensational news stories seem regularly to catch national public attention may reflect stereotypical thinking. A few years ago, national media, especially cable television news stations, ran nearly continuous coverage of what became known as the *Elizabeth Smart case.* Elizabeth Smart was a teenage girl abducted directly from her bedroom; she remained missing for over a year, and was finally discovered being held by a possibly deranged man and his wife. During this time hundreds of children were abducted from their homes, sometimes in similar circumstances, but these cases did not get the same national coverage. What were the features of the Smart case that made it so much more worthy of national attention? One hypothesis is that she and her family were white and fairly well off economically, and so warranted much more attention. The case of the murder of JonBenet Ramsey, which dominated cable networks a few years ago, similarly involved a wealthy, white family, living in what was thought a safe neighborhood. Does the socioeconomic class as well as the ethnicity of the people involved in such cases lead to varying levels of news attention? Are there certain stereotypes at work in determination of newsworthiness in these cases? Communicators need to explicitly work out the values and loyalties implied by these kinds of situations.

The ethical issue lies in whether these sensationalized cases play to certain public stereotypes, suggesting some kinds of people are more important than others. Does the desire for large viewing audiences lead to reinforcing stereotypes in ways harmful to minorities or other identifiable groups? The standard approach to ethical decision making in mass communication is utilitarianism, consideration of the greatest good for the greatest number, as we said. The question is whether the greatest good for the public at large is served by so much attention to these specific cases. One could argue these cases highlight dangers to the public. By focusing so much attention on these stories, the news sources and TV channels are performing a public service, according to this view. On the other hand, one can argue such claims seem questionable, since these issues have received significant attention in the media for many years, and yet it is not clear the coverage has led to a decline of such cases.

Accuracy and Truth in the Media

People turn to the news media for the accurate reporting of facts. Rightfully so, as this is the basic function of the press—to provide the public with the facts so that, in a democracy, the public can decide what is right and what ought to be done. This is also the reason for enshrining freedom of the press in the American Bill of Rights. We also expect the news media to be truthful. One author writing about media communication ethics maintains, "In theory, it would appear that absolute truth is an ideal for which all media practitioners should strive."[7] Truth and accuracy, however, may not always be the same thing. One can be accurate in reporting the facts one chooses to communicate, but leave out other facts that would create a more truthful impression of some event. Goebbels, Hitler's minister for propaganda during World War II, was reported to have maintained that the reports of the propaganda ministry should always be accurate in what they report. Deception can be the result of emphasizing certain facts while downplaying others, or of the way the facts are framed. The selective presentation of facts can be as misleading as lying itself.

The requirement of accuracy also carries with it an obligation to take special care in *ensuring* accuracy of what is reported. The ethical requirement on news outlets and journalists is not just accuracy, but the performance of due diligence to corroborate the accuracy of the facts being presented. This due diligence represents values of and loyalties to one's profession, colleagues, and organization.

These considerations move us from simple or easy ethical determinations to ones less clear. In the first place, it is obvious that those reporting the news ought not to fabricate their information. Because this injunction seems so fundamental, we are astounded when well-known or prize-winning journalists do make up some of their *facts* out of whole cloth. One such writer for the *Boston Globe*, a very well respected newspaper in the Unites States, admitted to making up characters and quotations she used in her columns. Her reason for such fabricating of facts was, she maintained, to "create the desired impact and slam home a salient point."[8] A writer for the *New Republic* admitted not only to deceiving the public but also making up fake interview, press releases, and phony web sites to deceive the fact-checkers at his own publication.[9] The pressures of getting ahead as a reporter or writer or meeting deadlines or perceived expectations of editors do lead to such outright untruths. But, these cases seem so straightforward that they do not raise much question when judging their ethicality.

Cases that are more problematic than these fall somewhere between complete fabrication and the whole truth. Are there times when the news media should withhold all the facts in a case and thereby create, at least to a certain extent, a false impression? Many would argue that in times of war or national crisis, such suppression of all information is warranted (for the greater good of the greatest number). Military secrets, therefore, ought not to be divulged. A few years ago, a commentator got into some trouble for revealing the name of a CIA operative, since identities of such people need to be kept secret for their protection as well for the security needs of the country. The sometime flamboyant television reporter, Geraldo Rivera, was recalled from a war zone in Afghanistan in 2002 when he seemed to reveal the location of a U.S. military operation in a broadcast. Obviously, there are times when representatives of the news media should delete certain facts from their reports. Reporters, editors, and producers exercise their own judgment, typically, when deciding such cases. They are not always clear-cut. When the editors of the *New York Times* and the *Washington Post* decided to publish the so-called *Pentagon Papers* in 1969, during the Viet Nam War, the government at the time claimed the papers had overstepped this boundary. In the event, the Supreme Court of the United States found otherwise.

When the reports are mostly accurate but changed or manipulated to achieve a desired effect, a reporter might claim the changes heightened the good effects the story might achieve. This justification was offered by the reporter fired from the *Boston Globe* just referred to above. This can occur in major works that purport to be factual reporting as well. The famous case of the winner of the Nobel Peace Prize and Latin American activist, Rigoberto Menchu, is such an example. After the publication of her work, *I, Rigoberto*, it came to light that some of her eyewitness accounts, particularly of events such as the executions of members of her own family before her eyes, were actually composites of several events, many of which she had not herself observed. The truth of the oppressiveness of the government described in this case may still be maintained, but the case is weakened by the disclosure of misleading claims of direct observation.

Today, digital photography allows for many kinds of photo enhancements or alterations. These enhancements and alterations are often undetectable in the final photograph or image. It is now possible to replace or add people to news photographs or videos; to visually highlight some areas of the picture while eliminating or editing out others. Two or more pictures can be combined to create a new composite that looks entirely real and believable. Photojournalists who now have all the wonders of digital manipulation in their studios are tempted to *tweak* a photo to create a more dramatic image. In the 1990s movie, *Wag the Dog*, an unscrupulous television producer superimposes video of a girl fleeing across a bridge clutching a small dog on video of a Balkan town in flames. This fictional account has a real-life counterpart in a photograph that ran in Serbian (Yugoslavian) papers in 1987, showing a mother working in a farm with her children around her, all identified as Serbs living in the embattled region of Kosovo. The mother had a rifle slung over her shoulder for protection against Albanian nationalists who allegedly were terrorizing the Serbian population, according to the caption. The picture inflamed public opinion among Serbs against the Albanians in Kosovo. Later it was revealed that the photo was staged, with the photographer himself supplying the rifle for the picture.

The *Code of Ethics* of the American Society of Media Photographers addresses the issue in a general way under the section *Responsibility of the Photojournalists* in its injunction to "never alter the content or meaning of a news photograph, and prohibit subsequent alteration."[10] The next point of the code calls for disclosure of any alterations made in photos used for editorial or illustrative purposes. Interestingly, a writer for the U.S. Army has suggested guidelines the Defense Department is considering regarding what is acceptable and unacceptable in the use of digital enhancements of news photos.[11] Such alterations as color balancing, contrast adjustment, cropping or enlarging that does not distort the meaning are generally considered acceptable. Guidelines would also allow masking or blurring for purposes of protecting privacy or for intelligence or security, as long as such masking would be obvious. Practices ruled unacceptable include those manipulations that actually change the physical relationship among the elements in the photograph, add elements or take out existing elements in the picture, or merge two or more separate photos into a new composite.

Despite these precautions, unaltered pictures can of course be used in ways that slant a story in a particular way. The Elian Gonzalez case which occurred a few years ago illustrates this possibility. The young Cuban boy, Elian, survived the sinking of a small boat carrying Cubans fleeing the island for Florida. His mother did not survive, and so the boy was placed with relatives living in Little Havana in Miami. The U.S. government eventually felt compelled to take Elian from the family to allow the courts to determine custody of the boy (his father wanted to take him back to Cuba to live with him). People who remember the case are most likely to remember especially the striking photo of a helmeted and goggled SWAT team member, holding his rifle in one hand and reaching for the terrified boy in the other. The photo was not altered, but the caption placed over it, the prominence on a newspaper page, and whether other photos displayed other aspects of the story on the same page were all factors that led to differing interpretations of the event.[12]

The manipulation of a message through its visual presentation is certainly nothing new and was widespread before the advent of digital enhancement technology. There have always been concerns about filmed documentaries that claim to present only facts and historical events in an objective way. People remember the storm of controversy over Michael Moore's *Fahrenheit 9/11*, as the nature of the film's status as a documentary became a contentious political issue in the presidential campaign of 2004. An example from the early days of film is the infamous *Triumph of the Will* produced by Leni Riefenstahl in 1934. The filmmaker lived to be over 100, into the twenty-first century, but never succeeded in living down her reputation as a propagandist for Adolph Hitler. She always claimed that she did nothing more than simply film events as they unfolded in front of her at the major NAZI party rally in Nuremburg that year. There is a sequence early in the film in which we see Hitler standing in an open car saluting to the people lining the street. The scene is viewed from behind and above. There is clearly no filming equipment in the car with him. This scene is intercut with a close-up looking over his shoulder in the car, which could have been filmed only with a movie camera mounted on the back of the car itself. This and other sequences belie Riefenstahl's contention that nothing was staged. The two shots are not possible without filming the sequence once without mounted cameras and then again with them. Camera angles and editing throughout the film appear to substantiate the notion that the film is as much propaganda as documentary.

We have now considered situations in which there is outright fabrication of the news and in which there is questionable use of manipulation and distorting in the presentation of the facts. As noted at the beginning of this section, there is further an ethical responsibility to ensure the facts one reports or presents are completely accurate. In other words, it is not enough to simply present what one believes to be the facts at some point in time; one must also corroborate the facts from one source with other sources. These cases are usually more in the gray area between complete truth and manipulation and distortion. How much checking and cross-checking is necessary before a television network or a newspaper goes with a story and its underpinning facts? The following case illustrates the ethical questions involved in the requirement of accuracy.

On May 26, 2004, *The New York Times* ran a *note* from the editors essentially critiquing and even apologizing for the paper's coverage of the issue of whether or not Iraq in fact did possess weapons of mass destruction (WMD) prior to the American invasion of that country in 2002.[13] The editors' note admits the *Times*, along with the government and many other members of the news media, was *taken in*. While the editors were proud of most of the reporting appearing in the *Times* over the two years from the invasion to the May of 2004, they go on to admit, "But we have found a number of instances of coverage that was not as rigorous as it should have been. In some cases, information that was controversial then, and seems questionable now, was insufficiently qualified or allowed to stand unchallenged."[14] The paper became too reliant on informers that were not necessarily reliable. In fact, this problem reveals the practice of relying on informants or sources for stories without relying on independent checking of the facts themselves. An article in the online version of *New York Magazine, New York Metro.com*, placed much of the responsibility on one Pulitzer Prize-winning reporter at the *Times*, who had many contacts in government circles as well as with a prominent Iraqi exile at the time. The article claims that relying solely on supposedly well-placed sources, especially allowing herself to be *embedded* with the Defense Department, led to her accepting the line of those who were eager to place in the paper evidence favorable to their view.[15]

In the previous December, the paper had appointed Daniel Okrent as its *public editor*, essentially an ombudsman representing the interests of readers. In his critique of May 30, 2004, he followed up the extraordinary *editors' note* of the prior week (May 26).[16] After mildly chiding the editors for *burying* their apology on page 10 of the paper, Okrent went on to illuminate systemic weaknesses in the news business contributing to the inadequacies in the *Times'* reporting on WMD. First, he points out that editors as well as reporters are responsible for the content of news stories. Editors must take responsibility for ensuring sufficient cross-checking of stories from *anonymous* sources. Second, even for the prestigious *Times*, the desire for *scoops* occasionally trumps careful checking, which would delay publication. Third, many reporters are eager to *write it onto 1*, meaning getting your story placed on the front page with your byline. Such eagerness can lead to overstating the significance of a particular piece of information, the *breathless* claim of earth-shattering revelations. Okrent feels the editorial system at the *Times* needed to be stronger and more rigorous in its demands on reporters and their use of anonymous sources.

Still another ethical problem is represented in the development and increasing use of what are known as *video news releases*, or VNRs. These communications are typically produced by an advertising or public relations firm in such a way as to look like a genuine news story, with *news correspondents* seeming reporting live on a breaking story. For many smaller media outlets, the prepackaged stories are easy to run and come with often high production values. There may not always be the realization that they are packaged press releases and not actually *news* from an objective news-gathering organization.

Shortly after the *Times* episode, CBS News faced similar criticism in another prominent case for its failure to rigorously check the authenticity of a memorandum that raised questions about President Bush's record in the National Guard during the time of the Viet Nam conflict. Dan Rather of CBS issued an apology to the American public for failing to ensure that the memo in question had been thoroughly checked before broadcasting the story.[17] The CBS network commissioned an outside study of the events surrounding the broadcast about the suspect memo. Although the report, coauthored by a former Republican governor of Pennsylvania, did not find any political bias present in the case, it did find that the news department at CBS proceeded with *myopic zeal* to be first with the story. Although the head of the news division repeatedly demanded rechecking sources for the story, according to the report, his directives were not carried out. In the event, four senior executives and producers at CBS were dismissed because of the case.[18]

The *Statement of Principles* of the American Society of Newspaper Editors inveighs, "Every effort must be made to assure that the news content is accurate, free from bias and in context, and that all sides are presented fairly." (Article IV)[19] The question is whether these cases involving the *New York Times* and CBS News represent unethical practices. The standard of publicity, as advanced by Sissela Bok in her book, *Lying,* suggests the answer depends on to what extent reporters, editors, and producers would be comfortable in publicly explaining and justifying their behavior in these cases. Mistakes may always be clearer in hindsight, of course, and examination after the fact may lead to different conclusions than people came to in the heat of day-to-day operations. Outright fabrication, distortion, and bias may be issues easier to analyze than cases of determining when enough checking of the facts is in fact enough.

The fields of advertising and public relations present special issues when considering obligations of truth and accuracy. Obviously, it is not incumbent on advertisers and public relations practitioners to provide the context of competing claims or points of view, as in the case of journalists. Both sets of professionals are enjoined, in their respective codes of ethics, to refrain from misleading or extravagant claims. For example, the AAF guidelines call for the revealing of "significant facts, the omission of which would mislead the public," and the directive, "Advertising claims shall be substantiated by evidence in possession of the advertiser and advertising agency, prior to making such claims."[20] And, public relations professionals are called on to "adhere to the highest standards of accuracy and truth, avoiding extravagant claims or unfair comparisons . . ."[21]

In contrast to the wording of these standards, note our earlier reference in Chapter 1 to the accepted practice of *puffery* in both advertising and public relations (see p. 14). *Puffery* refers to claims that your product or organization is the *best in the Midwest* or *the leader in its field.* The courts, recall, have held that these kinds of grandiose claims are acceptable because people know they really are not intended to be true in a factual or scientific way. Looking at advertisements on TV or radio or in magazines will quickly show that these kinds of *puffery* claims are widespread. In many cases, advertising skirts issues of accuracy, especially in meeting the standards of not omitting significant facts. We have all marveled at the speed reading (or speaking ability) of the announcers who must read the list of potential side effects of drugs or disclaimers for financing arrangements for cars and the like. Still, the courts have found that the tobacco industry in its advertising for years failed to disclose facts about harmful side effects of tobacco and nicotine. More recently, the manufacturers of pain relievers, such as Vioxx and Celebrex, have had to pull advertising for their products that failed to disclose their potential harmful side effects. These cases remind us that ethics as well as codes of ethics are not usually legally binding. Ethics, after all, is what you do when you don't have to.

Applications of Ethical Principles to Mass Media

We argue in the first chapter that reasoning about ethical issues, dilemmas, or problems can proceed through a process of arguing propositions of fact, value, and policy. First, one ought to determine what the facts in the case are. Does the statement of the ethical problem point to all the relevant elements or facts in the situation? Second, one needs to determine what set of criteria for judgment make the most sense for analyzing the problem. What ethical principles should we bring to bear in determining what is right or wrong in a situation? Finally, we need to argue a proposition of policy. What would be the most ethical action to take? What does our ethical reason tell us is the right action to take?

Model for Ethical Decision Making in Mass Communication

Our approach is similar to a framework developed several years ago by a Harvard divinity professor, Dr. Ralph Potter. His model for ethical reasoning, called now the *Potter Box*, is often proposed as a set of guidelines for ethical decisions in mass communication.[22] Ralph Potter completed his doctorate in 1965 with a dissertation analyzing moral reasoning in regard to the issue of nuclear arms. He credited the sociologist, Talcott Parsons, with the basic principle behind his linked, four-step process for analysis.[23] He later applied his approach to questions of war and opposition to war, in response to the protests in the sixties against the Viet Nam conflict. The four steps are as follows (often laid out graphically in four linked boxes):

1. *Definition*: determine the facts in the case; the facts that cause an ethical issue to arise. This determination should be as thorough as possible, relying on multiple sources and corroboration.
2. *Values*: determine the important or controlling values related to the case. In journalism, values include truth, the value of an informed citizenry, objectivity, fairness, and accuracy. But, there may be competing values operating, such as respect for individuals' privacy, friendship with people involved in the story, our own economic well-being, public safety, and so on.
3. *Ethical principles*: the third step calls for the communicator to weigh competing values by referring to one of the ethical systems, such as those represented by Mill and utilitarianism, or Kant's categorical imperative, or Rawls' egalitarian liberalism, or others.
4. *Loyalties*: determine possible competing loyalties that come into play when considering communicating the message or story. In making their decision, communicators consider to whom they are showing loyalty and whether those or other loyalties are appropriate in this case. Potential competing loyalties are those owed to yourself, to your colleagues, to the institution or organization to which you belong, its (or your) financial sources (advertisers, stock holders), the people who are subjects in the case, and to the public at large.

The process of going through these steps intends to ensure a communicator can articulate the values, principles, and loyalties he is upholding in his ultimate decision concerning communicating a particular news item or story. In other words, this model is intended for making decisions about what messages to send through the media (decisions by editors, publishers, producers, or other gatekeepers).

We could apply this model to the decision concerning whether or not to show televised footage or photos of people jumping from the Twin Towers during the 9/11 attack. In some ways, this was more of an issue for photojournalists' ethics, since the televised images were fleeting and not really clear; photographs, however, captured the moment, stopping a body in free fall and removing doubt about what you were seeing.

What were the *facts*? People did choose to jump to their deaths from the top floors of the World Trade Center rather than face being burned to death. Many eyewitnesses confirmed there were large numbers; it was even dangerous for people on the ground. One story reported, after the collapse of the buildings, was that Fr. Mychal Judge, assumed to be the first fire department casualty at the scene, was administering last rites to a fireman who had been hit by a falling body before he was himself killed by falling debris (other eyewitnesses placed his body inside the lobby under debris, so there is some questions about the exact circumstances of his death). The facts are, then, that there were photographs of actual victims falling (or jumping) from the towers.

What *values* come into play in deciding to print the photos? Different news institutions and different photographers held competing views on this matter. Some felt that you should photograph what actually happens and show the world the full horror of the event. The people jumping were a real and integral part of the event; their actions provide the truest sense of the full horror of the attack, they would say. Other journalists and editors felt that the images were too graphic and were harmful to families and loved ones of those who were trapped on the upper floors. The competing values then are truth and commitment to the full story, on one hand, and the right to privacy, respect, and humane consideration for the victims and their families, on the other. The first group might respond that there were no close-up views allowing anyone to identify the faces of the jumpers. The second group responds that is just the problem—anyone who had a father or mother or husband or wife on the top floors that day could assume the picture was of their loved one.

What *ethical principles* can be brought to bear to decide among the competing values? A utilitarian perspective could suggest that the greater good is realized by disclosing the full record of the event of that day. People even in other countries could identify with the human level of the tragedy by seeing the extreme decision forced on those who chose to jump. There would thus be more support for sympathy for the victims and for the United States itself and more revulsion against the attackers. Unqualified care and concern for the other, however, as represented in dialogical ethics and the ethics of care in virtue ethics, argue that humane care for the victims' privacy trumps the utilitarian principle. The events themselves were so horrific, they could further argue, that little utilitarian value is added by overcoming the principle of care and compassion.

Are there significant *loyalties* to individuals or groups that help us choose among competing values and principles? The more sensational images may, in the short run, attract more readership or audience share. The more striking image may help a photographer or a publication achieve a Pulitzer Prize or similar award. Do the photographer and his or her publication have a loyalty to readers and viewers that take precedence? On the other hand, there were many opportunities for both sensational and striking images on that day (and many awards were later granted for some of those images). The loyalties to humaneness may weigh more heavily in resolving the decision.

Most but not all news outlets chose not to run, or to run only a very few, of the startling photographs discussed in this case. You can now go back through the exercise yourself by going back to the facts and looking at them again (Do we know for certain the motives of the people who jumped? How do we know? Is it a fact their actions shaped public response to the tragedy? And so on). What other values and principles can be brought to bear on these decisions?

In the next section, applying dialogical ethics to mass communication, we look at ways that the notion of loyalties can imply a moral commitment to the humane values in the community, whether local or global.

Dialogical Ethics for Mass Communication

Is it reasonable to apply a dialogical framework for analyzing the ethics of mass communication? It may seem the attempt is problematic. When the communicators are not face to face, in an ongoing relationship, is it possible to speak of true dialogue? Because mediated communication does not permit such a one-on-one interchange, some would deny dialogical ethics can be applied to mass communication. Clifford Christians, an ethicist of mass communication, however, suggests the dialogical perspective can provide guidance for ethical decision making concerning issues in the mass media.

We have seen that the cardinal ethical principle for journalists, and others in the mass media, is truth, which usually implies accuracy. Christians, however, has raised the question of the direct and necessary relationship between truth and accuracy. Note that the assumption is that there is a direct correlation between the truth and the accurate representation of the facts. This assumption represents what philosophers call an *objectivist worldview*, implying one can observe and faithfully record and report the actual state of affairs in the world. This assumption further implies the *correspondence* theory of representation—that facts out in the world correspond to our linguistic descriptions of them. This seems obvious and straightforward but may oversimplify what we can actually observe and report in real life. One always notices, or observes certain aspects of a situation and ignores or fails to notice others. People differ therefore in what they observe and what they report concerning the same event. Which observation and which report are the *accurate* ones? Are they both in some way accurate? There is little argument these days that people see what they expect to see and take more notice of certain elements in their environment while ignoring others. As we saw in our previous discussion of the Twin Towers disaster, there were conflicting reports concerning the location of the body of the Fire Department City of New York (FDNY) chaplain—which is accurate? Which is the *truth*?

Reports meant to be descriptive often represent a particular point of view. During American involvement in Viet Nam, for example, the media regularly reported on the actions of the enemy, referred to as the *Viet Cong*. The term *Viet Cong* is a shortened version of the Vietnamese language phrase referring to Vietnamese members of the Communist party. It became a term that one of the early presidents in South Viet Nam used to refer to his political opponents and then to all the armed insurgents fighting against his government. The term was picked up by members of the U.S. press and became the standard term for the forces in South Viet Nam fighting against the government in Saigon. Was the term accurate as a name for an actual existing organization? Probably not, but reporters after a while tended to use it as if it were.

What we mean by the truth, hence, may imply something different from and even richer than an only partially accurate description of the facts. Christians argues further: "With the dominant scheme [the correspondence theory of reality] no longer tenable, truth should become the province of ethicists who can reconstruct it as the news media's contribution to social dialogue."[24] Taking the attitude of one in dialogue with another, the function of the media becomes to provide a full and nuanced interpretation for the consideration of the public audience. When the journalists, for example, presume to be telling people the facts—reporting the *real* state of affairs—they project an attitude reminiscent of the partner in confrontation who tells his or her partner, "I know the ways things are, and here it is." The question is whether or not the mass media hold the potential for creating conditions allowing for a full understanding of the meaning and conditions of what they report. In some cases, journalists could foster or encourage dialogue within local communities trying to come to grips with the human impact of the news and events in a local community. Can that be done on a national or international scale? Perhaps, the question should be should the mass media try to enact the attitude of dialogical communication in their broadcasting and publishing? Such an attitude places the needs and interests of the *Other*, to use Levinas' perspective, in the forefront. Some will quickly point out that mass media are businesses, and hence the dialogical ideal is just that—too idealistic. We believe, however, that thinking through the implications of the attitude of dialogical communication provides a useful approach to ethical issues in mass communication.

CASE STUDY: EMBEDDED IN MIAMI

It is often said, "The first casualty in war is truth," and the war correspondent has left a mixed trail of wartime reporting. Newspaper reporters began to cover warfare during the Crimean War in the 1850s, but really got started in the American Civil War, which rapidly followed the small war in the Crimea. Jack Reed (World War I and the Russian Revolution) and Ernie Pyle raised war reporting to an art form.[25] The visual medium of television changed the nature of such reporting, especially during Viet Nam. The mass media was said by some to be the cause for the disillusionment the American public came to have toward that conflict. During the first Gulf War in the early 1990s, the U.S. government tried to restrict journalists' access to the battlefield, raising cries of censorship and directed news. In the second Gulf War, the invasion of Iraq in 2003, the U.S. and British armed forces introduced the tactic of *embedding* reporters with military units during the invasion and subsequent fighting. For many journalists and professors of mass communication, this embedding raised ethical questions concerning the independence of embedded reporters and the extent of coverage they could provide (would everything be seen only from the military's point of view?).

In the November of 2003, the city of Miami prepared for a major international meeting of the Free Trade Association of the Americas. In view of the violence and rioting that had accompanied such prior meetings in Seattle and in Cancun, Mexico, the city hit on the idea of *embedding* reporters covering the meeting with the Miami police and Florida Highway Patrol. The city government and police, after the event, hailed the practice as a great success, pointing out that most of the coverage was *positive* (positive toward the police).[26] Groups involved in protesting the meetings claimed that their point of view was essentially shut out from media reporting as a result of the embedding of journalists with the police.

Should reporters cover significant events, in which there is likely to be conflict or confrontation, by being embedded with the military or police units involved? Does such embedding compromise the journalists' independence and ethical responsibilities to their publics?

QUESTIONS FOR ANALYSIS OF THE CASE

1. Do journalists, in your opinion, lose their objectivity when they observe a conflict or confrontation embedded in one side in that conflict? Reporters embedded may come to identify with the soldiers and police officers around (and protecting them). Would that tendency affect their objectivity?

2. Discuss the ethics of the decision by the city and police department to control press and television coverage of the trade meeting in this way. In the same way, consider the ethics of the decision of reporters who chose to allow themselves

to be embedded in this way. Was there a difference (making an ethical difference) between a wartime situation in a foreign land (Iraq) and a local, domestic situation?

3. Journalists like Ernie Pyle were essentially embedded with American army units covering the World War II. Does the fact that his coverage was in print, written just after the events covered, and printed later in newspapers, make a difference? That is, does the instantaneous nature of televised coverage of war or police actions create a different ethical climate?

4. Should journalists, print, or television, favor the police or our military in their coverage of events that are, after all, about protecting the public? To what extent do reporters have an obligation to the public or to the national defense that transcends their ordinary journalistic responsibilities? Where do their values and their loyalties lie in deciding their ethical obligations in this kind of situation?

Chapter Summary

We live in an environment awash with messages from all kinds of mass media. The institutions of the broadcast, Internet, and entertainment media have great potential for shaping our world, or certainly our understanding of the world. As we point out in this chapter, institutions with such power also have great potential for harm or benefit. There is therefore an ethical dimension to nearly all aspects to the roles media play in our lives.

This is a huge topic—entire books and college curricula deal with the questions of media ethics. This chapter is intended as just an introduction and an overview of the kinds of ethical issues confronted by students and practitioners in the various forms of the mass media.

A medium (plural, media) is some device or institution that interposes itself between communicators. Presumably the messages are changed, shaped, or framed in this mediating process. Mass communication, the product of the mass media, assumes a huge, even numberless, audience. Often, the messages seem impersonal or depersonalized. It is also often difficult to identify exactly who or what is the source of these messages.

The *media*, taken as a collective, have varied and diverse purposes: to inform, to persuade, to criticize, to entertain, to instruct, to express emotions or opinions (as in a blog), and so on. Often the lines between and among these various purposes are blurred. With the addition of interactive and handheld devices, the physical channel for disseminating mass communication is becoming even more varied.

Ethical issues arising in mass communication often result from decisions about the rights of individuals versus the rights of society. Also, the good of the public is often in conflict with economic interests of the businesses producing mass communication. And, the media have the power to shape or at least choose the topics for public attention and discussion.

An overview of the kinds of ethical decisions faced by those in the media arises from several issues. First, there are the effects of the gatekeeping function, as media choose and shape what is to be considered *news*. The choices made may result from relying on attention-grabbing stories and pictures. The focus is then on the bottom line of selling time or publications rather than on what is in the best interests of the public. These choices can also pit the right of individuals to privacy against the presumed *newsworthiness* of their actions or disasters.

Secondly, media ethics can be involved in problems associated with stereotyping certain groups in the community or the world. We can come to expect a certain kind of news to come from one community versus another. Stereotypes can also provide a fast and easy way for mass communicators to shortcut the nuances in a story. We can rely on the stereotype to create an image or expectation about a certain group. Crime in more affluent neighborhoods, for example, is seen as more newsworthy and hence receives more coverage than it does in presumably run-down neighborhoods.

Mass communication, particularly journalist and news media, are concerned with accuracy and truth. Obviously, fabrication, knowingly passing off fiction as fact, is clearly unethical. But, communicators also may have an ethical responsibility to take special effort to check and ensure the accuracy. Sometimes events or scenes can be manufactured or manipulated, with the supposed good intention of heightening the urgency or importance of a topic; photos, with today's digital capabilities, can be *tweaked* to highlight a feature in a picture. These misleading practices are ethically suspect. Printing or broadcasting an isolated image, that is not consistent with the rest of the scene, also can present a misleading view of events.

We reviewed two models of frames of reference for analyzing ethical questions that arise in mass communication. The *Potter-Box* takes decision makers through a recurring series of questions, requiring them to think carefully about the facts in a given case, what values argue for treating the subject in different ways, subjecting these considerations to criteria of a well-formed ethical perspective. The final stage in the Potter Box requires the communicator to account for the various loyalties he or she has in making his or her decision about what to communicate.

We also discussed the possibilities for using the attitude derived from dialogical communication as a way to think through ethical decisions in mass communication. The public audience may be conceptualized as the *Other* in dialogue, and therefore treated in way that allows them to participate in arriving at a *true* appreciation of the events being reported or interpreted. Many will argue that such an approach is unrealistic, but it does offer an avenue for contemplating ethical issues in the mass media and mass communication.

QUESTIONS AND TOPICS FOR DISCUSSION

1. How many different kinds of mass media have a major impact on your own life? Is it possible to keep track of how many messages you receive in a day, or in a week, from all these sources? What kinds of messages seem especially to raise ethical problems or concerns?

2. *The Media*, as a generic body, come in for a lot of criticism from politicians and pundits in the media. Collect some criticisms as a group or class and discuss which criticisms seem especially well founded. Which are less well founded?

3. Which type or branch of the mass media seems most trustworthy to you? Which seems least trustworthy? Discuss why you come to these conclusions.

4. Are the ethical standards for entertainment media different from those for more journalistic media? Why? What are the differences that call for different ethical analyses of these different kinds of media (if there are any)?

5. Research a story much in the national news media and talk shows at the present time. Does the prominence of this story reveal anything about gatekeeping and stereotyping in the media? What sort of ethical questions are raised about the selection of these stories and their treatment?

6. Do the media do an ethical job of covering local politics in your community? National politics? How do they perform in covering important national issues—regarding war and peace, economic issues, environmental issues, and questions of human rights?

NOTES

1. Philip Patterson and Lee Wilkins, *Media Ethics: Issues and Cases*, 4th ed. (Boston: McGraw-Hill, 2002), pp. 178–180.

2. *SPJ Code of Ethics* (1997), accessed at http://spj.org/ethics.htm.

3. Ellen Alderman and Caroline Kennedy, *The Right to Privacy* (New York: Vintage Books, 1997).

4. Mary Ann Watson, "Ethics in entertainment television—Introduction and critical essay," *Journal of Popular Film and Television*, 31, (2004): 146–149.

5. *The Christian Science Monitor*, "Stereotypes Bite Back," October 4, 2004.

6. *SPJ Code of Ethics*, Society of Professional Journalists, 1997, accessed at http://spj.org/ethics/code.htm.

7. Louis Alvin Day, *Ethics in Media Communications: Cases and Controversies*, 4th ed. (Belmont, CA: Thompson Wadsworth, 2003), p. 81.

8. "Writers Admit Fabrication, Issue Public Apologies," *Ethics Newsline*, Institute for Global Ethics, Camden, Maine, www.globalethics.org/newline (accessed January 6, 2005).

9. "Writers Admit Fabrication," January 6, 2005.

10. Center for the Study of Ethics in Professions, Illinois Institute of Technology web site, http://ethics.iit.edu/codes/coe/ASMP-CoE.html (accessed January 6, 2005).

11. "DoD Memorandum of Digital Manipulation," reported on the web site of the National Union of Journalists, London, http://media.gn.apc.org/manipdod.html (accessed January 4, 2005).

12. See Phillip Patterson and Lee Wilkins, *Media Ethics: Issues and Cases, 4th ed.* (McGraw-Hill, 2002), pp. 213–217.

13. "The Times and Iraq," *The New York Times,* May 26, 2004, p. A10.

14. "The Times and Iraq," p. A10.

15. Franklin Foer, "The Source of the Trouble," *New York* metro.com, at www.newyorkmetro.com/nymetro/news/media/features/9226/index.html (accessed January 29, 2005).

16. Daniel Okrent, "The Public Editor: Weapons of Mass Destruction? Or Mass Distraction?" *The New York Times.* May 30, 2004.

17. Dan Rather, "Statement of Memos," CBS News, September 20, 2004; the statement is available at www.cbsnews.com/stories/2004/09/20/politics/main644546.shtml.

18. "Four to Leave CBS News in Wake of '60 Minutes' Probe," *The Wall Street Journal,* January 11, 2005, p. B1.

19. *Statement of Principles,* American Society of Newspaper Editors, available at the ASNE web site, www.asne.org/index.cfm?ID=888.

20. *Advertising Ethics and Principles,* adopted 1984, American Advertising Federation, www.aaf.org/about/principles.html, (accessed February 13, 2005).

21. *PRSA Code of Professional Standards,* adopted in 1988 by the Public Relations Society of America, http://jcomm.uoregon.edu/about/ethics/prsa.html, (accessed November 27, 2004).

22. Clifford G. Christians, Mark Fackler, Kim B. Rotzoll, and Kathy Brittain McKee, *Media Ethics: Cases and Moral Reasoning,* 6th ed. (New York: Longman, 2001), pp. 3–8; Patterson and Wilkins, *Media Ethics,* pp. 76–80.

23. Nick Backus and Claire Ferrans, "Theory meets practice: Using the Potter Box to teach business communication ethics," *Proceedings of the Association for Business Communication,* 2004, www.pkb.ubc.ca/abc/ojs/index.php, (accessed February 12, 2005).

24. Clifford Christians, Social Dialogue and Media Ethics. *Ethical Perspectives,* 7, 2000: pp. 182–193, www.ethical-perspectives.be/viewpic.php?LAN=E&TABLE=EP&ID=144, (accessed June 10. 2005).

25. See Philip Knightley, *The First Casualty* (New York: Harcourt Brace Jovanovitch, 1975).

26. John Pacenti, "Embedded Obstacles," *American Journalism Review,* 2004, accessed at www.ajr.org/article_principle.asp?id+3537.

CHAPTER

11 Ethics of Political Communication

To many people, *political communication ethics* sounds like an oxymoron.[1] Over the past several years, politicians rank near the bottom of professions in terms of the public view of their ethics and trustworthiness. When we look again at the early classical writings of Plato and Aristotle, we see the connection that they made among politics, ethics, and communication (rhetoric). Plato reflected the modern attitude—that *rhetors* (the equivalent of politicians in classical Athens) practiced a rhetorical sleight of hand in making the worst seem to be the better case. Recall that in the famous Platonic dialogue, *The Gorgias* (Chapter 2), Plato, in the voice of Socrates, made political rhetoric seem to be like cookery or the art of cosmetics in dressing up the distasteful or the unlovely to appear better than they were: an early application of the concept of *spin*.

On the other hand, Aristotle tried to place politics and rhetoric in a more respectable light by aligning these fields with ethics. You may recall that he said that the character (*ethos*) of the speaker could be the most powerful form of support in a speech of persuasion. In Roman times, Cicero maintained that the ethical politician had a moral duty to practice rhetorical (communication) skill to ensure the triumph of good over evil. To the classical Greeks and Romans, engaging in politics was among the highest duties of a citizen. Today, there seems to be more apathy engendered by cynicism concerning politics. Rather than feeling an obligation to engage in politics, some citizens seem to feel such activity morally beneath them. Not only will they refrain from running for public office—that is getting really actively involved—they will even abstain from voting. Such voter apathy is greatest at the local level and in other than presidential elections. Even in national elections only about half or less of the American electorate casts a ballot. There could be many explanations for widespread voter apathy: people are generally content with the way things are, it is inconvenient or difficult to register and to vote, people do not feel well enough informed, and so on. Still, there is a sense that such apathy is due to distaste for politics and the way political campaigns are conducted.

Political communication ethics clearly overlap issues covered in the previous chapter on media ethics. This is so because political communication relies on the mass media more than ever. Political parties formerly played the central role in vetting potential candidates for the public. Now that political parties are less important, people rely more on the mass media to help them screen candidates.[2] The business aspects of mass communication and journalism can lead to reliance on sensationalism while minimizing attention to the details of public policies and their consequences. "The mass media are first of all businesses," communication scholar Robert Denton reminds us.[3] As such they are focused on ratings more than educating the public on political affairs. But at the same time, the press is called on to play a critical role fundamental to the political system. Dean of the Annenberg School of Communication, Kathleen Hall Jamieson, and her colleague Paul Waldman conclude, "Reporters should help the public make sense of competing political arguments by defining terms, filling in needed information, assessing the accuracy of the evidence being offered, and relating the claims and counterclaims to the probable impact of the proposed policies on citizens and the country."[4]

The blurring of lines between news and entertainment in television also creeps into the picture, as a growing percentage of voters reported in 2000 that they acquired information about candidates and politics from comedy shows, such as *Saturday Night Live*, or entertainment channels such as MTV.[5] Certainly, this figure probably increased in 2004 with the popularity of shows such as Jon Stewart's *The Daily Show* and the monologues of the late-night comedy shows. People in the media other than journalists, in other words, fulfill an increasingly significant role in shaping and framing political communication.

The Internet and other forms of web communication have grown dramatically in their uses for political communication. The Pew Research Center reports that "the Internet has broken through as a major source of campaign news in 2004. Overall 41 percent of voters say they got at least some of their news about the 2004 election online."[6] This report points out further that the percentage of Americans who got most of their campaign news in 2004 from the Internet doubled the number in 2000. In 2004, political blogs (personal web logs) came into their own as part of the political communication process, as we will discuss later in this chapter as well as in Chapter 13. Web sites for candidates, political parties, special interest groups, and individuals now play a major role in the political campaigns and political communication as well.[7]

Our overview of the ethical issues of political communication begins with a review of the practices of modern political communication, including those practices which seem ethically questionable. We will then turn to some specific ethical issues arising from the growing importance of political consultants, lobbyists, and the use of the Internet. Because the theories of John Rawls and Jürgen Habermas seem particularly relevant to issues of political communication, they will each provide a lens for viewing and thinking about these issues. Throughout, we will ask you to bear in mind the distinction between the legality of political communication tactics and their ethicality. Campaign finance laws and other regulations provide a legal framework for what can and cannot be done legally in political communication, while our focus is on ethics of communication practices.

The Practices of Political Communication

The ethics of people in politics have been questioned for a very long time. Clearly, the distaste felt by Plato's Socrates for the sophists and the *rhetors*, the politicians, of his day stems from this attitude. In his advice in the famous book, *The Prince*, Machiavelli of Renaissance Florence did not enhance the ethical reputation of political leaders. Machiavellianism has become the term for sharp and manipulative practices by politicians or anyone who dissimulates to achieve political gain or power. He maintains that some *virtues* would undermine the prince's power, while some vices are desirable to keep and even enhance power. The ruler must know how to be deceitful, while appearing to be the opposite. He also instructs that it is better to be feared than loved, although it is best to avoid being hated, if at all possible. While Machiavelli was concerned with helping a ruler maintain power, most of our interest in political communication over the years has been concerned with getting power and, in the United States, with winning elections. For that reason, we will keep our attention on political communication primarily in election campaigns. As many commentators point out, however, American politics is dominated today by *permanent campaigns*, in which office holders are constantly raising money for or preparing for the next election cycle.

The kinds of political communication tactics often labeled unethical include some of the following, although this list is far from exhaustive:

- Mudslinging and irresponsible *attack ads.*
- Messages for which the source is unknown or unaccountable.
- Communication intended to suppress voter turnout.
- Misrepresentation of opponents' messages or positions.
- *Scare Tactics,* messages intended to arouse unnecessary fear or even panic.
- Racist, Sexist, or similar communications demeaning to a designated group.
- *Push* polls, really disguised attacks on opponents.

This list does not address many concerns about the adverse effects of the vast sums of money involved in and required for political campaigning today. First, the general fear is that such vast sums reduce the access to the public arena of worthy but underfunded groups or interests. The second fear is that money leads to undue influence, especially aimed at those elected as a result of huge campaign contributions. Thirdly, the public agenda can be skewed to reflect the interests of those providing major financial support for candidates. The issues important to the biggest contributors become the major issues in the public debate. The high cost of campaigning means that even after election politicians must devote inordinate amounts of time and energy to fund-raising for the next campaign. Money may be the specter haunting the ethics of political communication in contemporary America. It provides a background for many of the ethical concerns in politics today. The influence of big money can undermine rational decision processes. This is a point we will return to in discussing the ethical theories for evaluating the ethics of political communication in the last section of this chapter.

Kathleen Hall Jamieson has devoted several of her important works to illustrating and analyzing the *good and the bad* of American political communication.[8] Her reviews of American political campaigns make it clear that many of these tactics have a long history, going back to the early days of the United States. Unethical campaigning is nothing particularly new. Early politics in America was a rough and tumble affair, after all. The widespread use of mass media and the Internet may serve to exacerbate the abuses, however, and spread their effects more widely.

Impact of Media and Marketing

In one of her most influential works, *Packaging the Presidency*, Jamieson points out that the Presidential campaign of 1952 really ushered in the era of modern, mass-mediated politics. The campaign between the victorious

General Eisenhower and Governor Adlai Stevenson of Illinois saw the first major use of the medium of television for political campaign uses.[9] The introduction of modern advertising and public relations techniques was a cause for concern at the time. In 1968, Joe McGinnis caused a stir with his book *Selling of the President* (the title provided a catch-phrase that has been used over and over by analysts and pundits when discussing political advertising since 1968). People were troubled by the notion that the foremost political leader of the land could be marketed like any other commodity, such as soap and cigarettes. In that day, it seemed beneath the dignity of political leaders to rely on the so-called *Madison Avenue* techniques. Today, political advertising, especially media advertising, is taken for granted as standard practice for anyone seeking high elective office (or lower, local offices as well). This situation highlights the function of political consultants in modern political communication.

Television became the principal medium for political communication beginning in 1952. The Republican Party lined up the major advertising firm BBD&O (Batten, Barton, Durstine and Osborn) to handle most aspects of media campaigning for Eisenhower, while Young & Rubicom were commissioned to do the advertising for the Citizens for Eisenhower Group, an independent support group presaging the widespread use of Political Action Committees (PACs), in later campaigns. Jamieson points out that Eisenhower's complete reliance on the advice of BBD&O foreshadowed the role media and public relations specialists would come to play in American elections.[10] The new importance of television is shown most vividly in the impact of the famous *Checkers Speech*, delivered by Richard Nixon in 1952 to defend himself against charges that he should have been removed from the Republican ticket because of a secret fund he had used during his days in Congress and the Senate. Commentators since have marveled at the way he handled a questioning of his ethics in this case by reframing the issue in terms of calling for financial disclosures by the other major candidates.

The next campaign of 1956, a rematch of the same candidates (except for the vice presidential candidate on the Democratic ticket), saw increased use of the new medium of television. More significant for ethical considerations, this campaign also initiated breaking with past understandings about the ethics of campaigning at the presidential level. The Democrats, for example, raised questions about President Eisenhower's health, since he had experienced heart problems and ileitis (an intestinal condition). In the recent past in presidential politics, health of a candidate had been seen as off limits: the most notable illustration of this reticence may be seen in the Republicans not making an issue of Franklin Roosevelts' physical disabilities. In addition, the issue of Eisenshower's age was also used against him, questioning his fitness for another four-year term. Admittedly William Henry Harrison's age had been made an issue, but that was back in 1840 (to demonstrate his fitness, he delivered a very long inauguration speech in the open air without a coat—he caught pneumonia and died within a month of taking office). In the 1960 campaign, the religion of a candidate, John F. Kennedy's Catholicism, became an issue, although it had also been an issue in 1928, when Al Smith, the Democrat and a Catholic, had lost to Herbert Hoover. In both cases, religion as an issue was kept outside the mainstream of the national campaigns and parties themselves, because to raise it directly would be seen as ethically out of bounds. Nonetheless, direct or indirect attacks on personal character, beliefs, or infirmities were beginning to come out into the open in these campaigns of 1952–1960.

In the two presidential elections in the mid-1960s, issues of character really came to the fore. The 1964 campaign, between Lyndon Johnson, who had succeeded to the presidency on the assassination of Kennedy, and the conservative Republican, Barry Goldwater, featured one of the most famous points in early television campaign advertising. On the night of September 7, 1964, the famous *Daisy* commercial was aired for the first and last time. The ad featured a little girl in a meadow plucking petals from a daisy while counting them off; when she reached ten, a male voice took over and began a countdown, 10–9–8–7, down to zero and nuclear explosion with a telltale mushroom cloud. Although the ad was used only once by the Democrats, it was played over and over on news shows, giving it much more coverage than the one showing would have achieved. There was a storm of protest over the ad, which seemed to suggest that Goldwater was so unbalanced he would get the country involved in a nuclear war, ending civilization. At that time, such an ad was felt by many to be too unethical in making extreme charges against the rationality or character of an opponent. Such views would seem outdated by the end of the century.

The 1968 campaign came during the height of the Viet Nam conflict, following Johnson's withdrawal from his reelection bid in March of 1968. The nation was shocked by the Tet offensive by the Vietnamese in February, which indicated the war was far from over, and then by the assassinations of Dr. Martin Luther King, Jr., and Robert F. Kennedy, immediately after he had won the important California primary in June. The Democratic Convention in Chicago was marred that summer by riots in the streets outside the convention hall. The Republicans responded in the later campaign by running an ad of a grinning Hubert Humphrey, the Democratic candidate, with jump cuts to bloodshed and rioting in the streets to the tune of "There'll Be a Hot Time in the Old Town Tonight." The implication, of course, was that Humphrey approved of and even laughed at the beatings and violence in the streets. Such blatant misrepresentation would certainly have seemed unethical in 1952, but was becoming more expected in the 1960s into the 1970s.

The so-called *dirty tricks* became more the norm in the 1972 election, contested by the incumbent Richard Nixon and the antiwar Democratic candidate, George McGovern. The Committee to Re-Elect the President, known as CREEP, regularly used tactics such as planting messages, fliers, and ads, which seemed to be from Democratic sources, undermining the Democratic candidates. For example, during the Florida primaries, Donald Segretti of the CREEP had mailings sent out on *Citizens for Muskie* stationery (Edmund Muskie was one of the Democrats running for the nomination). These mailings claimed, falsely, that Hubert Humphrey had a drunken driving arrest and that another Democratic candidate, Henry Jackson, was a homosexual.[11] Without a doubt the most notable ethical lapse occurred when a group of operatives for the president's staff broke into Democratic campaign headquarters in the Watergate complex in Washington to steal their campaign plans and secrets. They thus gave to English an enduring suffix, *-gate*, that could be affixed to any word to make it into the name for a scandal. The backlash from Watergate, however, led to Nixon's forced resignation and a chastened presidential campaign in 1976, when the Washington outsider, Jimmy Carter, defeated Nixon's Vice President and successor, Gerald Ford.

By the time of the 1980 presidential campaign, Carter's prestige was suffering due to the dragging on of the Iran hostage crisis. Followers of a powerful Muslim cleric, the Ayatollah Khomeini, had seized the American Embassy in Tehran and held the American diplomatic staff hostage, eventually for over a year. The Republican nominee was a famous actor from the movies and more especially television, Ronald Reagan.

Impact of PACs

During this 1980 campaign, people who followed politics became very familiar with a new acronym, PAC, for Political Action Committee. The PACs are independent groups or committees, which benefited from a Supreme Court decision in 1976. Spending by the candidates and their official committees and those of the political parties themselves were capped by federal regulations in 1974. The independent committees faced fewer such restrictions as a result of the 1976 decision. The number of PACs subsequently increased from 608 in 1974 to more than 4,000 by 1995. An authority on campaign finance and professor of political science at the University of Virginia, Larry Sabato, concludes that the 1970s marked the beginning of the modern *PAC era*.[12]

In 1980, PAC spending overwhelmingly favored Reagan by a margin of $12 million to $50,000.[13] Of course, Carter enjoyed all the benefits of being the incumbent with almost limitless access to national news media as president. The independent PACs took their toll, however. As Kathleen Hall Jamieson points out, they were able to make outrageous claims that the regular candidate could never get away with. For example, one group in the South claimed that Carter advocated homosexuality and abortion and the undermining of traditional family values. In short, Jamieson concludes, "PAC ads can act as loose cannons careening across the political deck and in the process impede the public's ability to rationally assess political claims."[14] By the elections of 2000 and 2004, these tactics would be further augmented by Internet sites, often sponsored by what are called *527 Groups*, which are again independent advocacy groups that can skirt accountability for what they say in ways that the official candidates and their parties cannot.

The ethical problems associated with PACs can be illustrated by the case of William Horton, as used by PACs supporting the election of George H. W. Bush over Michael Dukakis in 1988. Two ads were the main engines for the development of this story. The first developed by the National Security Political Action Committee was broadcast in September 1988. The ad attempted to draw a tight connection between Dukakis, then governor of Massachusetts, and a convicted murderer named William Horton, an African American man let out on a program allowing weekend furloughs, who had escaped and gone to Maryland, where he raped a woman and attacked her fiancé. Of course, the ad does not inform viewers that Dukakis' Republican predecessor as governor had initiated the furlough program nor that approximately the same number of furloughed convicts escaped under both administrations. Horton's first name in the ad became *Willie* instead of his actual name, possibly to evoke racial stereotypes (the couple attacked in Maryland were both white).

This PAC ad was followed by a second ad produced by the Bush campaign which began to appear in early October. The new ad, in stark black and white, featured a line of convicts circling through a revolving door or prison gate, apparently entering a prison but then coming right back out. The ad referred to the Massachusetts program (similar to those in many other states) and the 268 convicts who had jumped the furlough and escaped during Dukakis' term as governor. The ad implied that some of these escapees had been convicted of first-degree murder and would not be eligible for parole and yet that many had committed crimes such as rape and murder. It did not take much for many people to read the name of *Willie* Horton into this new ad. In fact, of the 268 escapees out of 11,497 furloughed, only four had been convicted of first-degree murder; only one of these four (Horton) had gone on to commit rape and kidnapping.[15] Still, the obvious inference was that hundreds had done so, instead of one. By the middle of October, other PAC ads began to appear showing or interviewing the alleged Maryland victims of Horton, seeming to blame Dukakis for the attacks on the couple. The couple began to hold their own press conferences, and the Bush campaign in speeches and press releases kept up the drumbeat of the *Willie* Horton case, implying that Dukakis was allowing a nationwide crime wave because of his supposed *get-out-of-jail-free-card* program in Massachusetts.[16] Horton's name and image were shown only in the PAC ads and not in those sponsored directly by the Bush campaign itself, which allowed the campaign committee a certain level of deniability in regard to charges of stereotyping or misleading people on that specific case itself; and this case took on a life of its own in the press and in the minds of voters (as revealed in focus groups three years after the campaign).[17]

In addition to the PACs the so-called *527 groups* became especially prominent in the new century. By the 2004 presidential campaign, these 527 groups were having a major impact on election campaigns. A 527 group is so named because of the section number in the tax code of the Internal Revenue Service which permits such organizations. The Bipartisan Campaign Reform Act of 2002 (the BCRA) was intended to curtail the amount of *soft money* flowing to political campaign organizations or candidates. But, the 2002 legislation left untouched these groups set up under the tax code, which allowed unlimited contributions as long as certain reporting requirements were met and regulations followed. These regulations seemed to allow advocating political positions while not directly electioneering for a particular federal candidate. A point of controversy arose regarding these groups in 2004 because several of them did appear to be directly advocating the election or defeat of specific candidates, especially the presidential candidates. Court cases going forward after 2004 as well as proposals for new legislative regulations may restrict the role of these groups in subsequent elections. The impact of these new groups is difficult to sort out because of interlocking connections among PACs, political parties, and 527 groups. For example, PACs can contribute to 527s and vice versa. There are also 501(c) groups, set up under tax code section 501, which can engage in political activities on certain social or educational issues.

Probably the most famous 527 group in 2004 was the "Swift Boat Veterans and POWs for Truth," which claimed that the Viet Nam War record of Democratic candidate John Kerry had been exaggerated, and further claimed that his medals for heroism were not warranted. Many of their messages were disseminated from their web site (www.swiftvets.com/index.php) and online Internet sources but were picked up and given wider distribution by the national press.[18] Although the Swift Boats group may have had the largest impact, the 527 group, Americans Coming Together (ACT), which produced a web site supporting Democratic issues and candidates, was probably the largest of the 527 groups in 2004.

The various PACs and their 527 and 501 cousins raise many ethical questions, as suggested above. First, the messages of such groups may get inordinate play and attention because of the sheer fund-raising potential they represent. Candidates will undoubtedly want to cater to their particular issues and opinions. This tendency could freeze other points of view out of the political marketplace. On the other hand, web logs (blogs) and Internet messaging can be relatively inexpensive. If the national media should pick up and replay the message from an Internet source, even more return for the dollar is gained. It is possible that there are some tendencies countering the extreme costliness of modern politicking given the appearance of these *new media* sources.

Secondly, the lack of accountability of PACs and 527s means that it is hard, especially for ordinary citizens, to check on their facts or interpretations of facts. This lack of accountability can allow for stereotyping, innuendo, and appeals to prejudice, in an effort to short-circuit rational political discourse. We have seen how the various PACs and other organizations reinforce and pick up images and messages from each other. These reinforcing messages create a web of political rhetoric hard for most people to disentangle. The result is thus that assigning ethical responsibility for these practices is problematic. One may not be able to determine the ethical agent responsible in each case. Is the candidate responsible for the ethics of all her supporters, including hundreds of independent or seemingly independent organizations and committees? Is it possible to hold each such group responsible for their ethics of their messages? The proliferation of the various forms of media will probably make these questions more difficult to resolve.

The increasingly central role of media marketing and the rapid growth of the PACs and their growing reliance on Internet communication are the sources for major concerns about communication ethics. In the next two sections, we turn our attention on two other practices and professions involved in the political communication process: political consultants and lobbyists. These professionals deal directly in decisions regarding marketing, fund-raising, and using media outlets and organizations described in this overview of political communication practices.

The Role of Political Consultants

As the role of political parties in choosing and endorsing candidates has declined, the role of political consultants has been on the rise. Candidates now go directly to the voters, largely through the mass media. Of course, there have been consultants and advisers to political candidates for a very long time. Back in the days of the Roman Republic, candidates for office went about public places with a *nomenklatura* at their sides. The title translated from Latin means, literally, *caller of names*. As a potential supporter approached the candidate, the *nomenklatura* would call (actually whisper) the person's name in the ear of the candidate so that he might greet the citizen by name. These assistants probably gave political advice to the candidate as well. Machiavelli, already mentioned, was a political consultant of sorts to the leaders of Florence. In American history, there have been many examples of political advisers, such as William Herndon, Lincoln's good friend, who helped him get elected president in 1860. The political boss, Mark Hanna, was famous in the latter part of the nineteenth century as a power broker who assisted several Republican presidents. Franklin Roosevelt had his *brain trust*, and John Kennedy obviously relied on his brother, Robert Kennedy, as well as advisers such as Ted Sorenson and John Kenneth Galbraith. And, those who watch

Christmas movies as a seasonal ritual are well familiar with the role of William Frawley, who gives political advice to the judge in *Miracle of Forty-Second Street* during the *trial* of Kris Kringle, who claimed to be Santa Claus.

The modern incarnation of the political consultant, however, is associated with the growing importance of mass media and marketing techniques. Joe Napolitan is often considered the modern-day founder of the field. He played an important role in putting together the campaign of John F. Kennedy for president in 1960; he later became a campaign consultant to both President Johnson and to Senator Humphrey in his run for the presidency in 1968. In that same year, 1968, Napolitan joined with a French political consultant to found the International Association of Political Consultants. The American Association of Political Consultants was founded two years later in the United States. Since that time Mary Maitlan and James Carville created a special niche for themselves as celebrity political consultants. Maitlan works exclusively for conservative Republican candidates, while Carville is strongly in the camp of liberal Democrats; nonetheless, they are married to each other and apparently happily so. Dick Morris and George Stephanopoulos have also become famous as political consultants in the 1990s. Morris' famous novel loosely based on the first Clinton campaign for the White House became a successful motion picture, *Primary Colors*; and Stephanopoulos became a regular television commentator.

Public relations firms have appeared with a special emphasis on political campaign communication. Michael Goldman, who heads his own firm specializing in political consultancy, has assisted several national candidates, such as Bill Bradley, Michael Dukakis, as well as Bill Clinton. He says that the job of a political consultant represents an "eclectic mixture of communication, public policy, politics, and education."[19] Political consultants help candidates develop their stands on public issues, formulate campaign and advertising strategies, and assist with speech writing and advertising copy. Consultants work closely with people who conduct opinion polls, since polling has become a central feature of modern political campaigns. They are involved in selecting and buying media time to ensure maximum positive exposure for their candidates. Political consultants have been blamed for *dumbing down* politics with a growing emphasis on simplified sound-bites and attack ads.

In many cases, these consultants as well as other campaign aides have acquired the moniker of *spin doctors*, whose function is to put a *positive spin* on a statement or event that might otherwise be seen as negative. Back in 1984, an editorial writer for the *New York Times*, Jack Rosenthal, predicted the scene in the pressroom after the second debate between Ronald Reagan and Mondale during that year's presidential election campaign:

> A dozen men in good suits and women in silk dresses will circulate smoothly among the reporters, spouting confident opinions. They won't be just press agents trying to impart a favorable spin to a routine release. They'll be the Spin

Doctors, senior advisers to the candidates, and they'll be playing for very high stakes. How well they do their work could be as important as how well the candidates do theirs.[20]

One explanation for the growing prominence of spin and spin-doctors has been the constant coverage of political news during major campaigns by twenty-four-hour cable news networks, such as CNN, Fox, and MSNBC, as well as talk and news radio. The campaign teams want to be sure that their take on the events is *out there* before the instant analysis of media pundits has solidified around a consensus possibly damaging to their candidate.[21]

Political consultants have considered their ethical responsibilities, as seen in the code of ethics formulated by the American Association of Political Consultants.[22] There are nine brief points to the code. The first and ninth are general statements about not degrading the profession of political consulting or supporting individuals or organizations that violate the code. The second and third points concern relationships with clients and colleagues, such as not revealing confidential information. The eighth point deals with correct invoicing for services rendered. That leaves the four points, four through seven, to deal with what we would consider political communication *per se*. The fourth point, condemns appeals based on racism, sexism, religious intolerance or other forms of prejudice; it also calls on consultants to work for equal voting rights for all citizens. The fifth instructs consultants to avoid making false or misleading attacks on opponents or their family members. The sixth states that consultants should document the accuracy of all criticisms of or attacks on an opponent. The seventh and final item dealing specifically with communication requires the consultant to be honest in relationships with news media.

What is the impact of this code of ethics on the activities of political consultants? In the winter of 2002 the American University Center for Congressional and Presidential Studies commissioned a poll of 204 consultants about their role in political campaigns.[23] On the questions of whether there should be a code of ethics, only 11 percent responded in the negative. Asked whether they were aware of the AAPC code of ethics, 73 percent said they were. Only 10 percent believed the code has much effect on consultants' behavior, however. Almost two-thirds (65 percent) felt that the professional organization should be able to censure members who violate the code, although it was unclear what the impact of such a censure would be. Furthermore, over two-thirds of the consultants felt that unethical practices do occur in their profession, although the largest percentage, 44 percent, felt they occur *sometimes*, rather than very often or fairly often. Asked to indicate the most serious ethical problem area in the 2002 elections, nearly half the consultants (47 percent) named *negative campaigning*. The next most serious problem, conflict of interest, received only 14 percent of the responses. A majority also felt that negative campaigning is likely to increase in the future. Concerning the expected increase in negative campaigning, a survey of voters from the 2004 presidential campaign found a dramatic increase in the view that the campaign was excessively negative: 72 percent responded this way in 2004 compared to only 34 percent in 2000.[24] In this survey, consultants and pollsters tended to receive higher grades from the voters than did the press or talk-show hosts (although it is not clear how the general public could have a clear idea about the activities of consultants or pollsters).

Despite consultants' concerns about ethical communication in the American University poll, it became clear that consultants do not agree that many questionable practices are out and out unethical. Making factually untrue statements (lying) is considered unethical by an overwhelming 98 percent, but the practice receiving the second highest ratings as unethical, the use of push polls, was considered clearly unethical by only 48 percent. Practices seen as *questionable*, while not *clearly unethical*, included using statements taken out of context, focusing on personal characteristics of the opponent to the exclusion of issues, and using negative tactics to suppress voter turnout.

The results of these surveys suggest that while there is concern for the ethics of political consultants, there is not much agreement on just what constitutes unethical political communication or campaign practices. A majority of consultants agree only on the notion that outright lying is clearly unethical. The murkiness of campaign communication ethics is seen in the responses by voters and consultants on negative ads or attack ads. There seems to be no clear understanding of what it means to cross the line from ethical to unethical in this area. The consultants appear to suggest that attacks on character, rather than on issues or policies, might cross the line, but when many campaigns turn on the so-called *character issues* the point at which that line is crossed is uncertain.

The Role of Lobbyists

We now turn to a second type of professional communicator concerned with the political process, the lobbyist. While election campaigns are typically periodic events, lobbying is a continuous activity intended to influence legislation or government regulations at the local, state, and national level. Our attempt to distinguish between political campaign consultant and lobbyist in this way, however, may not be as neat as it may sound. We have probably entered the phase of the continuous campaign. Members of Congress, for example, believe fund-raising and campaigning, rather than ending with each election, must be maintained in preparation for the next one. So, both consulting and lobbying are often continuous practices. The lobbyist does not focus on an election campaign, however, but on directly influencing government officials who are in office.

The term seems to go back to the 1830s in the United States when people trying to influence legislation milled about in the lobbies of Congress or state legislatures, waiting to buttonhole members as they went to and from their chambers. Although anyone who tries to affect a legislator's vote on a matter can be said to be *lobbying* that legislator, the individual citizen is not usually considered to be a *lobbyist* in the professional or occupational sense. What is generally meant by a lobbyist is a person who represents an organized special interest and is typically reimbursed or compensated for expenses arising from these activities. The first effort on the national level to define and set rules for lobbyists was the Regulation of Lobbying Act of 1946. The legislation was replaced by the Lobbying Disclosure Act of 1995, amended in 1998. That law defines a lobbyist as follows:

> Any individual who (1) is either employed or retained by a client for financial or other compensation (2) for services that include more than one lobbying contact; and (3) whose "lobbying activities" constitute 20 percent or more of his or her services on behalf of that client during any six-month period.[25]

The key points in this definition are the person is a member of or hired by a specific organization, acts as a lobbyist on more than a single occasion and, in fact, devotes a significant amount of his or her time to lobbying activity. Groups that employ lobbyists include associations such as the Sierra Club, the National Rifle Association, Mothers Against Drunk Driving (MADD), labor unions, and industry groups, such as the National Association of Manufacturers. Other kinds of lobbying groups include professional associations, such as groups representing the telecommunications industry, public utilities, educational associations, such as the American Association of University Professors, and so on. Federal, state, and many local governments require lobbyists to officially register themselves and their organizations in their jurisdiction.

Ethical issues concerning the communication activities of lobbyists revolve around matters of privileged access and undue influence. A typical problem can be illustrated by a case arising in the authors' own state. Legislators in this state serve in a part-time capacity, practicing a regular full-time occupation when the legislature is not in session; often that occupation is the practice of law. When the legislature was deliberating the extension of legalized gambling in the state, it was discovered that two of the leading legislators were also retained in their legal practice by associations representing the gaming industry. Were the legislators or the gaming associations in violation of ethical principles in this instance? Does the special interest group have undue access and influence on the legislators compared to the access and influence of regular constituents, who are simply private members of the public? These questions relate to the concern that special interest groups distort political communication. In some cases, lobbyists actually develop and draft legislation to be introduced by Representatives or legislators—lobbyists thus serve in an unelected capacity in the legislative process. The public interest, it is feared, becomes subordinate to special interests.

In many instances, state and national ethics commissions oversee the activities of lobbyists. Violations of ethical standards in these cases can result in fine or prosecution. In most jurisdictions, there are strict regulations on reporting income and expenses of registered lobbyists and lobbying organizations to ferret out potential conflicts of interest or undue influence.

In addition to legal regulation, the national association of lobbyists, the American League of Lobbyists (the ALL), maintains its own code of ethics for members, approved by its Board in 2000.[26] In the Preamble to the code, the ALL describes lobbying as "an integral part of our nation's democratic process," and "a constitutionally guaranteed right." The first article is labeled "Honesty and Integrity," and calls on members to always be truthful and to "seek to provide factually correct, current and accurate information." The lobbyist is also expected to correct any errors in the information provided, as they are discovered, or to update information that goes out of date. Most of the other articles are concerned with the lobbyists' professional responsibilities and obligations to his or her clients. These articles stress confidentiality, disclosure of other lobbying efforts that might be related to a specific client's interests, conflicts of interest, due diligence, being knowledgeable concerning applicable laws, and so forth. Article 8 deals with a general responsibility to educate the public about the value of lobbying, but this statement is rather vague.

The code of ethics, when it was introduced, was greeted with some skepticism. James Bennet, a staff writer for the *New York Times* wrote in a review in the *Washington Monthly* regarding a new book on Lobbying:

> Oh—about that new ethics code for lobbyists. The American League of Lobbyists tightened its old rules, but in ways that unintentionally highlighted how dodgy the system is. The new rules insisted, for example, that a lobbyist, on learning that something he had told a government official was false, should immediately correct his earlier statements; that a lobbyist should have a *basic understanding* of the *legislative and governmental process*; that a lobbyist should actually perform the work his clients are paying for.[27]

The code is not enforceable, but is intended as guidelines. The ALL hopes that the existence of such a code will help improve the image of lobbyists with the public in general as well as serve as helpful guidelines for professional lobbyists. At the unveiling of the code in 2000, representatives of the organization expressed their hope that journalists familiar with the code would *hammer* those who would violate its principles.[28]

Jonathon Rauch, who has written about the function of lobbyists in the American political process, believes that lobbying has become an indispensable part of that process, even though it tends to distort the debate on public policy.[29] There are very few if any people in America who are not represented in one way or another by a lobbyist in their state or national capital, through some occupational or other interest group. It would be diffi-cult if not impossible to return to a time (if it ever existed) in which this were not the case. The danger, however, is that hundreds of special interest groups fragment the issues of public policy, so that hardly anyone is repre-senting the public at large. Policy is determined by which interest group has the most access, the most resources, or the most skillful spokespersons, not by the force of the better argument. This is a point we feel is especially important in regard to the communication ethics of this situation, and a point we will take up in our discussion of ethical systems for analyzing political communication later in this chapter.

Lobbying communication has received scant attention in academic literature. One group that has focused on this topic, however, is the Wood-stock Theological Center at Georgetown University. This group has conducted conferences and published reports on the ethics of lobbying communication. One such report echoes some of the concerns expressed by Jonathon Rauch, noting that lobbyists play a significant role in political decision making, but that role is often controversial. The report continues as follows:

> Lobbyists play an important but often controversial role in the American polit-ical system. They represent a variety of interest groups attempting to influence government policy. Sometimes these interests are, or seem to be, in conflict with the common good of society at large. Often their methods come under question. The power and influence of lobbyists is a reason often given for bad public policy and cynicism toward politics.[30]

The role of lobbyists is controversial, not because the practice of lobbying is itself unethical, but because of abuses that transgress ethical lobbying prac-tices. The Center holds to the hope that these abuses can be addressed through an application of theological ethical principles, particularly the application of *practical wisdom*, the *phronesis* we have encountered as part of virtue ethics (Chapter 2).

We have been considering so far the ethics of the lobbyist. The essence of lobbying communication lies in the relationship developed between the lobbyist and the Congressional member or legislator. Our discipline of com-munication reminds us that communication in a relationship is reciprocal and always two-way. The partner in this two-way relationship is of course the member of Congress or a legislature. Ethical expectations apply to that person as well as to the lobbyist. To that end, there are myriad sets of rules and regulations regarding ethical conduct by legislators concerning their interaction with lobbyists. The relevant Congressional rules deal with such matters as the following: (1) restrictions on a member's employment by a lobbying firm or organization after completing a term in office; (2) limitations or prohibitions on gifts received; (3) similar restrictions on meals, entertainment, or travel provided by lobbyists; (4) restrictions on honoraria or other fees, such as fees for delivering a speech before an organization. Communication between the lawmaker and the lobbyist must be framed in terms of these limitations.

Each state as well as many municipalities have instituted similar kinds of rules, creating the context for communication between the state and local legislator and lobbyists. A review of all these sets of rules and laws—literally hundreds of pages—would be exhausting as well as exhaustive. Most of these regulations are similar to those laid down for the U.S. Congress. Clearly, there is a great deal of concern about the ethics of the lobbying and its communication practices.

In our discussion of the practices of political communication, we have come across many reasons for people to be skeptical or even cynical about the ethics of the entire process. We now turn to a framework for thinking about the ethics of the practices we have been describing. In presenting this framework, we mean to provide an overview of how various ethical systems could be applied to political communication ethics.

Framework for Ethical Political Communication

As indicated at the beginning of this chapter, we find the political ethical systems of Rawls, as well as contractualism in general, and the concepts of the *ideal speech situation* and *distorted communication* of Habermas particularly applicable for analyzing issues of the ethics of political communication. In addition, the Woodstock Center has suggested the relevance of Aristotle's virtue ethics, developed specifically to apply in political situations. Finally, Mill and Bentham developed utilitarian ethics as a response to the need for political reform and policy making; can many of the political practices described in this chapter be justified from a utilitarian perspective?

Rawls' Perspective

In Chapter 4 of this text, we present the basic tenets of the egalitarian ethics of John Rawls. In that section we contend Rawls' theory is most applicable to situations involving public communication, such as political communication, organizational communication, mass communication, and the like. His project is to construct principles for a just society, stressing equal rights and a just distribution of goods and opportunities. For these reasons, Rawls' approach sheds light on procedures for determining the range and possible limits (if any) on freedom of speech and the press in society, on speech that not only tolerates but respects differences in beliefs, and on the nature of and fair practices in political communication.

Politics deals with the distribution of the goods of society among competing interests, which are represented by various spokespersons. In order to build a *just society*, Rawls recognizes that one must find a way to accommodate the legitimate and rational concerns of these competing groups even when their principles and conception of the good are incompatible. Rawls laid out the initial presentation of his position in his major work, *Justice as Fairness*, as noted in Chapter 4. In the later book, *Political Liberalism*, he attempts to show how a reasonable and just society can be instituted in the complex, modern state (Note that Rawls is not using *liberalism* here in the partisan sense associated with American politics in present times).[31] Complex, modern societies include citizens who hold different, reasonably justified belief systems. Often deeply religious in nature, these belief systems may never be reconciled completely, one to the others. Nonetheless, Rawls believes that an *overlapping consensus* is possible among these varied systems (as long as the systems are themselves rationally defensible and held by reasonable people of good will). In a later book, *The Law of Peoples*, Rawls hopes to extend this way of thinking to a global consensus.[32] From this perspective, political communication which respects the principles implied by these conceptions of *overlapping consensus* and justice as fairness may be said to be ethical.

Rawls' notions of fully rational people debating the foundations of society in the *original position* behind the *veil of ignorance* imply that all such affected groups accede to the reasonableness of the process. Scanlon similarly argues that ethical communication requires that no one could reasonably object to the process. They may not agree with the outcome, to the ultimate distribution of the benefits or goods of the society, but they cannot object to the procedures if Rawls' or Scanlons' guidelines have been followed.

Do the political practices described in this chapter meet the expectations of Rawls or Scanlon for a just and fair political society? That can be determined on a case-by-case consideration. Techniques intended to short-circuit the rational process, by the use of half-truths, distorted messages, taking words out of context, obviously do not meet these standards. The more difficult decisions, however, have to do with those modern mediated practices involving modern mass marketing techniques, political consultants as *hired guns*, and the infusion of PAC money and resources. Clearly, no one in the real political world acts as if in the *original position*, or as if they are behind a *veil of ignorance*. We have seen how mediated messages can frame and imply a conclusion by the skillful juxtaposition of images and text, as in the *Willie Horton* ads from 1988. Can average citizens be expected to have the factual and knowledge base available to determine whether or not they could reasonably object to such messages? Probably not. We have also seen that it is nearly impossible to untangle the relationships among various messages and their sources in the modern media context. In short, many of the modern political communication techniques discussed in this chapter are at least ethically murky from the perspective presented by John Rawls. Specific cases could be evaluated (in terms of communication ethics) by judging the extent to which they reasonably advocate a position or interest while respecting the overlapping consensus necessary for a stable, just political society.

Habermas and the Ideal Speech Situation

The ethical system of Jürgen Habermas, discussed in Chapter 3, is intended to be compatible with universalistic systems based on the Enlightenment ideal of rational discourse. Recall that Habermas holds one ought to test the validity of norms of communication ethics in discussion with other people, instead of relying on the logic of a single person. He claims that valid ethical norms (rules) are those which all in open communication can agree to: the rules are based on a consensus of all affected. His primary concern, as in the case of Rawls, lies in developing a just political society.

How do people arrive at this consensus? Habermas proposes special conditions for the discussion, conditions that he calls *communicative action,* or the *ideal speech situation.* Most of the time in the *real world,* he recognizes, arguments are presented with *strategic* intent rather than *communicative* intent. He is using the word *strategic* here in a special sense to mean communicating in such a way so as to manipulate the response of the other person by the use of verbal stratagems rather than good reasons. Most of the political communication discussed in this chapter can certainly be described as strategic. *Strategic* communication (given this definition) results in what Habermas calls *distorted communication,* distorted because it misleads another or intentionally relies on partial or slanted information. The ideal for ethical political communication, however, is cooperative argumentation, in which all involved use arguments to test their validity with other people (the emphasis is on arriving at the most valid form of an ethical rule rather than winning a case).

Recall that Habermas set forth four criteria for achieving undistorted communication, requiring the following: (1) nobody's relevant contribution may be excluded; (2) all have an equal opportunity to make contributions; (3) participants must mean what they say; and (4) communication must not be in any way coerced (even to the extent of saying something in order to curry favor with someone more powerful). These principles envision an ideal (and idealistic) situation in which people are concerned with nothing but the force of the better argument and reasoning. Such an ideal political discussion requires full and free access of all to the public platform. No one can be cut off or denied this opportunity, regardless of wealth, status, or position. All speakers must proceed in the spirit of cooperation rather than competition. And, everyone must have the opportunity to agree or disagree.

Clearly, the modern role of PACs and similar groups is to give greater voice to the better-funded interests. The costs of mass media marketing is so great today that many smaller or less wealthy causes must be denied access to what we could meaningfully construe to be the public platform. Note the code of ethics of the political consultants' association agrees with some of these principles. Communication intended to suppress voter turnout and participation is deemed unethical by that code. Even so, the sheer costs involved in modern political communication cannot help but exclude and suppress certain interests regardless of actions by other communicators to deny them access. The costs of media production, time, consultants, and organization result in what appears to be an unavoidably distorted political communication situation. It would appear that for the foreseeable future, fully ethical political communication, if defined in terms of undistorted public communication, is an ideal rather than an attainable reality. To bring about a more nearly ethical situation, from this point of view, would require policy makers as well as citizens working toward a situation in which all reasonable voices could be heard in the political arena.

Virtue Ethics and Political Communication

We saw in Chapter 2 that Plato attacked the persuasive practices of politicians of his day because they were overly concerned with winning rather than with the good of the people *per se*. Aristotle attempts to rehabilitate political persuasion by linking political rhetoric with ethics. The proper function of political communication, according to Aristotle, is not logical exposition and proof as in mathematics and science. Logic and science aim at general truths for all circumstances. In the political arena, however, we do not deal with general truths, but with specific events and circumstances. In real life, those who debate public policy do not have the advantages of the scientist in a laboratory. There is usually an urgent need to act without waiting for all the information to come in.

Political communication requires arguments that will be persuasive to an audience under real-life conditions, in which *practical reason* must guide decisions rather than *scientific reason*. The *best possible proof* is not final or universal proof, as one might find in ideal circumstances, but the most effective proof available in ongoing public life.

Aristotle maintains that the *ethos*, the character of the speaker, can be the most powerful means of support in a political communication. Aristotle could advise us today that, in the absence of the ideal speech situation or the original position and veil of ignorance, we must rely on political leaders and communicators of good character, employing *phronesis*, that is, sound practical judgment. This perspective places more responsibility on the receivers of political communication to demand more of those who would be the sources of such communication. One may again protest that the public today cannot be expected to have the facts and the context to analyze the worth of political advertising and campaign spots. Developing codes of ethics for political consultants and lobbyists may show a step in the direction of highlighting sound ethical judgment among these practitioners. In the absence of genuine accountability, especially in view of the proliferation of Internet and web-based communication outlets, even these efforts may be insufficient. As we have said already, even tracking down the source of a particular political message may be nearly impossible.

It may not be possible to ensure political communication is ethical, but we can strive to educate ourselves and the public in general to have some basis for ethical self-defense in the political arena.

Utilitarian Ethics and Political Communication

Finally, the standard approach to correcting abuses in the realm of political communication has relied on the notion that good speech in the public marketplace of ideas can counter bad speech. This precept is the basis for John Stuart Mill's defense of freedom of speech and the press. This defense of free and robust political debate is based on Mill's earlier advocacy of utilitarian ethics. The utilitarian ethic avoids requiring all political advocates to take principled positions envisaged by Rawls and Habermas. Instead of requiring that those in the political arena hold to the standards of undistorted or nonstrategic communication, utilitarians contend that allowing free and full access to all will result in the greater good for the greatest number.

Still, the marketplace idea of political communication seems to rely on full and untrammeled access of all to the political platform, which today means the mediated platform. We have seen that, to a certain extent, web sites and blogs can provide for relatively inexpensive access to some part of the public audience. At the present time, however, it does not appear that web sites and blogs can have the impact of mass media in affecting huge electorates, especially large constituencies in state or national elections. Seen from this angle, utilitarianism can appear to be nearly as idealistic as the situations proposed by Rawls or Habermas.

A second view of utilitarianism, at least, allows us to question the ethics of individual political messages or practices in terms of the touchstone of the greatest good for the greatest number. Do lobbyists for special interests, for example, further greater public interests as well as those of their clients? To make that utilitarian standard work, is it necessary to ensure that all interests have the same lobbying access as all others? Again, we seem to be driven to a position possible in the ideal but not the real. At least the utilitarian yardstick for public policy does provide a rational basis for beginning the analysis of the ethical worth of such practices.

CASE STUDY: PUBLIC AND PRIVATE INFORMATION

George is one of the founders of a fairly new public relations and marketing consulting firm. The firm has begun to branch out into political campaign consulting and has landed its first major client, a candidate for a seat in the House of Representatives from a local district in the general election. The candidate for the other party is a fairly conservative businessman and former clergyman. Some of the main issues in the campaign, as they seem to be developing, deal with legalization of marijuana for medical use. This has been a continuing issue in the state since the legislature had approved such use, but the law had been overturned in higher court proceedings. Other major issues include reform of health care insurance and federal cutbacks for public health services in general.

A reporter friend contacts George to let him know that one of his sources has discovered that the opponent quietly attends AA (Alcoholics Anonymous) meetings at his church on a regular basis. The group and the church hold information about meetings and attendees as confidential and private. It also appears from other sources that the opponent has been treated for depression, although several years earlier. The reporter believes he is still on medication, however. A week later, the reporter calls to say that he has heard rumors that an adult son of the opposing candidate, by a previous marriage, may be living with another male in a large city in a southern state. He has asked sources to investigate any links between this son and the gay community in the city.

George shares this information with his colleagues working on the Congressional campaign. They are very excited and say these revelations could really help in attacking the credibility and fitness of the opponent. George is not so sure that all or any of these reports are appropriate or ethical.

What advice would you give George about developing messages based on any or all of these pieces of information? Should the firm be concerned about whether other independent groups, such as bloggers or 527 groups, pick up and run with any of these reported findings about the other candidate?

QUESTIONS FOR ANALYSIS OF THE CASE

1. The charge of alcoholism could weaken the opponent's support from his conservative and religious base. By participating in AA, the candidate has, in a somewhat public fashion, admitted to his problem—does that make this information fair game for campaign use?

2. The candidate represented by George has a daughter who does not hide the fact that she is herself gay. If the opponent's campaign begins to make an issue of that

fact, is George's group justified in developing ads using the new information provided by the reporter friend?

3. If the reporter goes ahead and reports his findings in his newspaper, does that change the ethical equation? If the information is made public through a different, independent medium, is it all fair game for attacks on the opposing candidate?

Chapter Summary

Many people are turned off by politics and politicians. People often report a low regard for the ethics of people involved in politics, including candidates, legislators, political consultants, advertisers, and lobbyists. The growing importance of the mass media in political campaigning and advertising raises further concerns about the communication ethics of those in politics. The growing use of negative campaigning and attack ads, the reliance on sound bites and racehorse coverage of campaigns seem to contribute to the growing disgust and disdain for political communication.

The rise of Internet campaigning and blogging, along with the appearance of supposedly independent PACs and similar groups, seems to have decreased accountability for political messages. Although politics in America has historically been a robust and even rough-and-tumble affair, the role of television and other electronic mass media raises new ethical issues. A review of campaign strategy and tactics since 1952 indicates more frequent uses of attacks on the health, private lives, and integrity of candidates. Although Congress has tried to restrict abuses, as in the Bipartisan Campaign Reform Act of 2002, other groups have proliferated through the new media rendering the reform efforts somewhat ineffective.

Political consultants have developed a professional association with a professional code of ethics. The difficulty with this movement has been that there is little agreement, even among consultants themselves, about the definitions of what constitutes unethical campaign techniques. Outright lying is generally condemned, but there is much less agreement concerning other questionable rhetorical strategies.

Professional lobbyists have also become a political fact of life in American public policy making. Although lobbyists have been around a long time, at least since the 1830s in the United States, their role and influence seems to have greatly augmented in recent years. There is a concern that powerful private interests, represented though lobbyists, can override the public good in governmental decision making. As with the consultants, there is a professional association with a code of ethics, but it may lack any real enforcement mechanism. There are legal restraints on the conduct of lobbyists and on those who are the targets of such organized communication—the legislators or regulators themselves.

We looked at several perspectives for analyzing the ethics of political communication. The contractualism or egalitarianism of Rawls seems especially well suited for political communication. Rawls looks for ethical ways of developing an *overlapping consensus* among competing political interests. Rawls as well as the system associated with Scanlon requires a procedural method for assessing the ethical adequacy of ways at arriving at public, political consensus.

Critical theorists, such as Jürgen Habermas, also provide a perspective concerned specifically with political communication. Habermas lays down a procedural basis for ethical political discussion, as does Rawls. His procedure requires that all who could be affected have equal access to the public discussion and equal ability and resources for participating meaningfully in that discussion. The purpose of practices referred to as *spin*, and the role of consultants, lobbyists, and PACs are to try to prevent such equality of access and participation.

Virtue ethics imply that in the real world of modern politics, where such equal access is unlikely, we must rely on character and integrity of politicians, consultants, lobbyists, and the voters as well. Utilitarianism holds out the practical implications of the free play of the marketplace of ideas. The more voices that are allowed to compete in the public arena, the more likely it is that ethical and sound policies will result. Still, the utilitarian standard requires some insurance of equal access for all affected parties and interests.

QUESTIONS AND TOPICS FOR DISCUSSION

1. Is the Utilitarian yardstick the most applicable for dealing with the issues in political communication? Discuss the extent to which the political system should work like a market, with the better ideas being those surviving the endless competition.

2. Consider ethical philosophies and perspectives not considered in the final section of the chapter. How could one apply principles of dialogical communication and ethics to systems of political communication? How could one mount a political campaign based on dialogical principles?

3. Discuss a postmodernist and a feminist critique of the role of political campaign consultants, lobbyists, and PACs. Would a postmodern analysis question the very purpose of elections? Do the people actually choose their leaders and policies in a meaningful and significant way?

4. Analyze major political advertisements in a recent major election campaign (see www.factcheck.org, for example, to research the ads). What appeals seem to you to be ethical, and which ones do not?

5. Research the activities of Internet groups such as 527 groups in a recent major election (such as Swift Boat Veterans for Truth, or Moveon.org). Discuss the ethical implications of their communication.

6. Research the lobbying efforts of associations affecting your university or business—such as AAUP, American Association of Colleges and University—or associations such as MADD, the Sierra Club, or the AARP. Discuss the ethical principles illustrated in their communication.

NOTES

1. Robert E. Denton, Jr., ed., *Political Communication Ethics: An Oxymoron?* (Westport, CN: Praeger, 2000).

2. Robert E. Denton, Jr., "How Television Undermines American Democarcy," in *Political Communication Ethics* (see note 1), p. 96.

3. Denton, "How Television Undermines Democracy," p. 99.

4. Kathleen Hall Jamieson and Paul Waldman, *The Press Effect: Politicians, Journalists, and the Stories that Shape the Political World* (Oxford: Oxford University Press, 2003), p. 194.

5. The Pew Research Center for the People and the Press, "The Tough Job of Communicating with Voters," released February 5, 2000, accessed at http://people-press.org/reports/display.php3?ReportID+46.

6. The Pew Research Center for the People and the Press, "Voters Liked Campaign 2004, But Too Much Mud-Slinging," released November 11, 2004, accessed at http://people-press.org/reports/display/php3? Report ID+233.

7. Kathleen Hall Jamieson, How the 2004 Election Changed Political Communication, http://people-press.org/reports/display.php3?ReportID+46 (accessed November 9, 2004).

8. Kathleen Hall Jamieson, *Packaging the Presidency: A History and Criticism of Presidential Campaign Advertising,* 3rd. ed. (Oxford: Oxford University Press, 1996); Kathleen Hall Jamieson and Paul Waldman, *The Press Effect: Politicians, Journalists, and the Stories that Shape the Political World* (Oxford: Oxford University Press, 2003); Kathleen Hall Jamieson, *Dirty Politics: Deception, Distraction, and Democracy* (New York: Oxford University Press, 1992).

9. Jamieson, *Packaging the Presidency,* pp. 42–43.

10. Jamieson, *Packaging the President,* p. 42.

11. Jamieson, *Packaging the President,* p. 279.

12. Larry Sabato, Public Policy Inquiry; Campaign Finance: Who's Giving to Whom, PACs and Parties, 2005, accessed at www.campaignfinancesite.org/book-sabato.html, reprinted from Sabato, *Money, Elections, and Democracy: Reforming Congressional Campaign Finance,* ed. M.L. Nugent and J.R. Johannes (Boulder:Westview Press, 1990), pp. 187–204.

13. Jamieson, *Packaging the President,* p. 417.

14. Jamieson, *Packaging the President,* pp. 426–427.

15. Jamieson, *Dirty Politics,* pp. 17–19.

16. Jamieson, *Dirty Politics,* pp. 21–22; Jamieson, *Packaging the Presidency,* pp. 471–473; Jamieson and Waldman, *The Press Effect,* pp. 2–4.

17. Jamieson and Waldman, *The Press Effect,* pp. 2–4.

18. The Center for Public Integrity, "527s in 2004 Shatter Previous Records for Political Fundraising," www.publicintegrity.org/527, (accessed March 8, 2005).

19. The career site, Salary.com, Dream Job: Political Consultant, www.salary.com/careers/layouthtmls/crel_display_Cat10_Ser174_Par274.html (accessed February 27, 2005).

20. *New York Times,* October 21, 1984.

21. NPR, Present at the Creation: Spin, www.npr.org/programs/morning/features/patc/spin/#editorial, (accessed February 27, 2005).

22. See Code of Ethics, American Association of Political Consultants, 2004; accessed at www.theaapc.org/content/aboutus/.

23. Harris Interactive, *Political Campaign Consultants: Their Role in Political Campaigns, Views on Ethical Practices, and the Perceived Impact of the BCRA on Political Campaigns*, 2003, prepared for the Center for Congressional and Presidential Studies at American University.

24. The Pew Research Center for the People and the Press, Voters Liked Campaign 2004, But Too Much 'Mud-Slinging, at http://people-press.org/reports/display.php3?Report ID+233 (accessed January 6, 2005).

25. United States Congress, *Lobbying Disclosure Act of 1995, as amended 1998* (PL 105–166).

26. American League of Lobbyists, *Code of Ethics*, February 28, 2000, www.alldc.org/ethicscode.htm (accessed January 6, 2005).

27. James Bennett, Cynicism without Solutions, *The Washington Monthly*, 2000, www.washingtonmonthly.com/books/2000/0004.bennet.html, (accessed February 28, 2005).

28. Bennett, *The Washington Monthly*.

29. Jonathon Rauch, *Government's End: Why Washington Stopped Working*, Vol. 2 (Washington, DC: Public Affairs, 1999).

30. Thomas J. Reese, S.J, in Ethics and Public Policy: A New Beginning, [*Woodstock Report*, March 1998, No. 53] Woodstock Theological Center, accessed at www.georgetown.edu/centers/woodstock/report/r-fea53.htm.

31. John Rawls, *Political Liberalism* (New York: Columbia University Press, 1996).

32. John Rawls, *The Law of Peoples* (Cambridge, MA: Harvard University Press, 1999).

12 Ethics in Organizational Communication

CHAPTER OUTLINE

Organizational communication is a growing subfield within the broader discipline of communication studies. Ethical dimensions of organizational communication are therefore also a growing area of concern in the discipline. In the *Real World* there is little doubt that there is also increasing awareness of the dangers of a lack of corporate or organizational ethics. The most famous scandal of recent times, in this regard, was surely the Enron debacle, which, along with similar high-profile corporate scandals, brought about special national legislation in the form of the Sarbanes-Oxley Act of 2002. Communication issues lay at the crux of these cases. These scandals touched on such issues as organizational responsibility for messages sent or suppressed as well as personal responsibility for *whistle-blowing* when organizational wrongdoing became evident to some.

Enron Corporation is an energy trading company that developed in 1985 from a merger of two companies, Houston Natural Gas and InterNorth, a Houston pipeline company. From 1996 through 2000, Enron was named *America's Most Innovative Company* because of its cultivation of a unique niche as a developer of markets in energy futures and other financial commodities related to energy and communication markets. It turned out that the corporation may have been most innovative when it came to fudging accounts and hiding losses to portray a false image of a highly profitable firm. Investigations launched in early 2002 led eventually to indictments of top Enron executives on charges of various forms of fraud and conspiracy. At the heart of the scandals were communications intended to mislead and deceive stockholders, the stock markets, regulators, and the public in general concerning the financial worth of the corporation. The scandal also entangled the accounting and consulting firm of Arthur Andersen, since they had served as auditors for and signed off on Enron's accounting reports and practices. This connection led to revelations of other scandals involving companies such as WorldCom, Global Crossing, and ImClone (this latter connection even led to the legal troubles of media celebrity on *good living*, Martha Stewart).

The effects of Enron and related series of scandals rippled through financial markets, as the value of Enron stock fell from $85 a share to only 30 cents a share in the year 2001. Pensions and stock portfolios of individuals and institutions were severely damaged as a result. Congress felt compelled to take action to ensure firmer oversight of accounting and auditing practices in corporations, and thus was born the *Sarbanes-Oxley* legislation with its stringent rules for corporate accounting. Chief executives and financial officers found themselves under closer scrutiny than ever before. Such cases show that breaches of ethical conduct can also lead to serious legal consequences, although we have tried to draw a conceptual distinction between ethicality and legality throughout this book. It is clear, however, that one powerful motivation for ethical behavior and self-monitoring can be the threat of legal sanctions.

In this chapter we lay out what we believe to be some of the most salient issues of communication ethics in modern, complex organizations. We will begin with a brief overview of organizational communication as a field of study. This overview previews the fundamental areas of ethical concern in considering the range of organizational communication and a general framework for analyzing such communication. We then turn to three views for analyzing ethical issues in organizational communication:

- the impact of organizations on the community or society;
- the impact of organizations on its members, people in the organization;
- the impact of members on the organization itself.

The chapter concludes with the consideration of vantage points for dealing with ethical issues in organizational communication.

Overview of Concerns in Organizational Communication

Organizational communication obviously is concerned with communication of and within an organization, so we must begin with an idea about what we mean by the term *organization*. Following a discussion of the ethical ramifications of this definition, we turn to a quick summary of the developments in the perspectives employed by scholars of organizational communication.

We begin with the often-stated axiom that communicating is fundamental to organizing, since the idea of organizing requires coordination among a group of people.[1] What we mean by an *organization* is hence a recurrent pattern of interactions among people engaged in a common enterprise. The members of an organization can come and go, but the entity we think of as the organization continues with its same identity regardless of changing membership. It can maintain itself over years, even over centuries. This stability of organizations leads us to think of them as moral agents, almost the same as individual people, with goals, purposes, and individual foibles. As one of the authors has noted, "Organizations persist over time, but what really persists are the cooperative efforts of people, who maintain an ongoing pattern of relationships that can be labeled as 'the organization.'"[2]

This conception of organizations as individuals is important to our discussion in this chapter. If they are considered individual agents, organizations can be held accountable for the ethics of their internal and external communication. We therefore tend to look at the ethics of the organization itself as well as the ethics of the individual members acting within the organization. The question then arises concerning where ethical responsibility should lie in various cases—with the organization or with the individuals within the organization? Are leaders, managers, owners, or spokespersons responsible, individually, for the ethics of the organization's communication? In the United States, the Supreme Court held back in 1886 that incorporated organizations could be considered *persons* under the due process clause of the 14th Amendment to the U.S. Constitution. In a series of court decisions in the 1970s and 1980s the rights of free speech accorded to individual citizens were accorded to corporations, reinforcing the idea that they were the same as persons. On the other hand, the Enron prosecutions held individual executives responsible for wrongdoing, while the corporation itself was made to pay various fines. Organizations are thus in some sense moral agents, but people within the organizations can be held accountable as well. In answer to our first question—what is an organization?—we must give a dual response. In one sense, the organization is the set of people, as moral individuals, acting in concert with the interests of the functions of the organization. In another sense, the organization is an individual entity, responsible itself for its actions and its communication.

As a field of study and teaching, organizational communication had its beginnings in the 1950s as teachers of speech communication were asked to develop training in public speaking and group discussion for people in businesses. Courses in business speech, begun as early as the 1930s, then began to proliferate in college curricula. These kinds of courses were combined with material from organizational behavior and management studies, as full-blown courses in organizational communication appeared. Reflecting its beginnings, organizational communication usually employed a functionalist approach. Such an approach focuses on improving the functioning of the organization and its members. The aim of functionalism is to make the organization work most effectively and efficiently. When the two values of effectiveness and efficiency take center stage, ethical considerations tend to recede into the background. And, recall our earlier implications drawn from Plato about ethical communication in the introduction to this book: commitment to the truth, on one hand, and success, on the other, are often in conflict. When pragmatic or *bottom-line* considerations are the first priority, ethics recedes as a priority.

In addition, a functionalist approach tends to consider short-run consequences over long-term effects. The short-run view can obscure the ethical consequences in the long run. Arthur Andersen as well as the other members of public accounting's *Big Five*, provide training in business ethics and did so prior to the revelation of the scandals at Enron, WorldCom, and others. The Enron Corporation itself had a code of ethics and actually required new employees to sign a code of conduct statement on being hired. The problem was not that ethics was excluded from their training process or even their corporate pronouncements, but rather where ethics stood in relationship to other priorities. We are reminded of some of the responses referred to earlier in Chapter 1: Although students say ethics is important in the abstract, they also maintain there are times when one must say, "Now we are talking real life." Functionalism itself need not result in such an attitude, but we need to be aware that it can happen.

In the 1980s, scholars of organizational communication turned more and more to an interpretive view of organizations and their communication. This view built on the concept of organizational or corporate culture. The newer emphasis on corporate cultures grew out of a set of management-oriented works of that time, such as Peters and Waterman's *In Search of Excellence*, Deal and Kennedy's *Corporate Cultures*, and Ouichi's *Theory Z*. These books asserted that an organization's *corporate culture* underlay its effectiveness. Excellent firms had strong cultures; less effective outfits had weak cultures, according to these works. One of the major elements, the basic constituent of corporate culture, was said to be a set of organizational values. In the management vocabulary, these were said to be the firm's core values. Scholars took up the concept of organizational culture in their studies of organizational communication, tending more toward an interpretive approach rather than a functionalist orientation. Looking through the prism of corporate culture, they aimed at developing an understanding of lived experience within complex organizations. The cultural approach emphasized the sets of values that characterized organizations and provided the milieu for members' experiences. And, a concern for values translated more readily into ethical considerations. Do the core values of an organization, in actual practice, really support and reinforce ethical communication? Does the corporate value system, the corporate culture, create a climate conducive to raising and acting on ethical concerns? The approach based on corporate cultures thus can lead to a greater emphasis on ethical issues of organizational communication. As a result, one can speak of a Strong Ethical Cultural Organization (SECO) as the ideal for corporate ethical decision making and communicating.

Critical theory provides a third perspective for thinking about organizational communication, one that inherently highlights ethical concerns. In organizational studies, critical theory specifies an approach based on the neo-Marxist studies originally associated with what is termed the *Frankfurt School*. The points of view represented by this philosophical school are described earlier in Chapter 3 of this text. We have referred to Jürgen Habermas throughout this work as the most influential current representative of this perspective. Critical theorists emphasize values of human emancipation from institutionalized domination of various forms. Their *critique* of society and its institutions aims at producing freer and more authentic lives for people in general. Their emphasis, however, is seen by many scholars, especially in the United States, as too ideological or too political, and not sufficiently objective or empirical in methodological orientation. Nonetheless critical theorists are probably most likely to employ an ethical touchstone in studies of organizational communication.[3] Still, we believe it is safe to say that functionalism, at least implicitly, dominates the research and writing about organizational communication today. Even studies which focus on organizational cultures tend to do so for the purpose of enhancing the effectiveness of the organization and its internal communication.

Ethical Issues in Organizational Communication

We discuss the major issues of organizational communication in terms of three sets of responsibilities or obligations. These responsibilities correspond with three major constituents in the processes of organizational communication: the society or community in which the organization operates; the members, the people who constitute the organization; and the organization itself. Interactions among these three basic constituents provide a nexus for the typical kinds of ethical decision points in organizational communication.

The organization itself has an impact on the other two constituents and each of them, in turn, has impacts on the organizations. The first two sets of ethical issues, therefore, are based on the organization's impact on society or its community and on the organization's members.

Impact on Community and Society

This first area of concern deals with the responsibility and accountability of the organization to its immediate community, society, and the public at large, also known as *Corporate Social Responsibility*, or CSR. Measures, or ethical auditing techniques, have been developed to report an organization's level of meeting such a responsibility: *Corporate Social Performance* (CSP) is a rating of how well an organization is in fact responsive to the true needs of its community. The development of *nonfinancial reporting standards* represents a related auditing technique for measuring the CSP of an organization. The organization's CSP can be evaluated in terms of what is sometimes called a *triple bottom line*, referring to the bottom lines in regard to financial, environmental, and social outcomes. Such terminology is intended to remind people that there is more than one kind of *bottom-line* to consider. Ronald Sims, a professor of business ethics, explains why we should be concerned with an organization's effectiveness in meeting its social responsibility: "Because corporations control vast resources, because they are powerful, and because their wealth and power come from their operations within society, they have an obligation to serve society's needs."[4]

Responsibility to Stakeholders and Community.   When we discuss ethical obligations of organizations, we need to be clear about the individuals, groups, and institutions who may claim some rights in this discussion. These individuals and groups are often referred to as *stakeholders*. Andrews and Herschel in their text on organizational communication point out:

> Many would argue that, indeed, organizations *are* responsible to society—not just to stockholders and their employees but also to customers, the general public, and the environment. However, the scope of that responsibility remains an area of controversy.[5]

The controversy relates to the issue of determining who the stakeholders are in considering the effects of an organization's effects and communication. Ethicist Robert Phillips maintains that the claim that organizations depend on various internal and external constituencies is uncontroversial, but, he goes on, "Refer to these constituencies as stakeholders, however, and the disagreements appear ceaseless."[6]

Simply put, *stakeholders* are any persons or groups who have a *stake* in the operations or effects of an organization. There can be *internal* and *external* stakeholders. The internal groups seem fairly obvious: the management, employees, and shareholders or owners. Determining who the external stakeholder groups are is more problematic; for example, not everyone would agree that shareholders, including anyone who might hold stock in a company through a mutual fund, are internal but rather external stakeholders. Let's take the case of a university—who are the members (internal stakeholders) and who are outside the boundaries of the organization but still stakeholders in some way? Relevant groups for a university would be faculty, staff, administration, students (full time and part time), and, probably, governing boards in cases where there are boards of directors or trustees. Now, let us think what other groups may have a stake in the operations of the university: alumni, parents and family members of current students, financial institutions (providing loans for students or school operations), potential or prospective students, donor organizations such as foundations or corporations, accrediting bodies of various sorts, potential employers of graduates, graduate and professional schools who might receive graduates, neighbors and local community around the university's campus, governmental and regulatory bodies in the community, state and federal government agencies, professional and fraternal associations, text book publishers, providers of technological services, public utilities, news media, other colleges and universities, and on and on. You can probably think of additional entities that could be added to this list.

The question is, does the university have an ethical obligation to all these groups? Is there a difference in degree, so that the moral responsibility is greater toward some groups than it is towards others? One might claim, for example, that students represent the stakeholder group having the highest priority for a university, but others could advance other priorities as well. Now, imagine that we are thinking about a for-profit business. One could again go through a long list of people and groups who could be considered stakeholders, including even competitors. Some relevant stakeholders in this case include customers or clients, suppliers and vendors, regulatory agencies, governmental agencies, trade associations, environmental groups, and so on. Sims suggests the following list of typical stakeholder groups:[7]

- Shareholders
- Employees
- Customers
- Creditors
- Suppliers
- Unions
- Competitors
- Governments
- Local communities
- The general public.

Many would contend that the most important group to whom moral obligations are owed are the shareholders. The primary moral obligation of a business, according to this predominant view, is to increase the wealth of the stockholders by growing the value of company's stock. Every other ethical consideration takes a back seat to this obligation, they would claim. One problem with taking share value as a moral responsibility is that it leads to thinking that whatever boosts the company's stock price becomes moral and the ethical thing to do. Such thinking reinforces cutting corners or engaging in shady practices, such as those practiced at Enron, WorldCom, and others. One of the ironies of the obligation to boost shareholders' return on profits was to provide incentives to Chief Executive Officers (CEOs), and top executives in the form of stock options for compensation.[8] This incentive further reinforced a tendency toward short-run expedients to inflate stock prices.

Not all business corporations agree with this setting of priorities, however. Johnson & Johnson, long known as an organization in tune with its corporate responsibility, gives top priority in the company *Credo* to "the doctors, nurses and patients, to mothers and fathers and all others who use our products and services."[9] Other stakeholder groups given specific attention in the *Credo* include customers, suppliers and distributors, employees, *communities in which we live and work* and the *world community*, and stockholders. One section explicitly addresses the responsibility to community and society in terms of civic duties and environmental protection:

> We must be good citizens—support good works and charities and bear our fair share of taxes. We must encourage civic improvements and better health and education. We must maintain in good order the property we are privileged to use, protecting the environment and natural resources.[10]

In addition to the distinction between internal and external stakeholders, some theorists suggest the categories of *primary* and *secondary* stakeholders. In thinking about the two cases of a nonprofit university and a for-profit business organization, these categories may help us determine ways to order an organization's ethical priorities. Primary stakeholders are those who play a role directly affecting the functioning of the organization. Stockholders, employees, customers, for example, are primary groups. In regard to the university as an example of a nonprofit organization, we may think of students and faculty as representing primary stakeholders, while local employees and professional associations might represent secondary ones. Secondary groups include interested parties with more of an indirect interest in and effect on the organization. These groups might include news media, competitors, professional associations, lobbyist or pressure groups, such as environmental activist groups. One could make the argument that moral obligations to primary groups are of higher concern than obligations to secondary groups. As Sims notes, however, "The level of accountability to a secondary stakeholder tends to be lower, but these groups may wield considerable power and quite often represent legitimate public concerns."[11] Different issues may make salient the concerns of different stakeholder groups, in other words. If our university were trying to get zoning variances for major construction projects on campus, for example, the local community and governmental agencies suddenly take on primary importance.

If the university has a record of open and ethical communication with the local community, the case for construction may be made more easily. Thus, for the nonprofit organization, again we return to an earlier point that good ethics may be good business. There is some evidence for that in the for-profit world as well. One study of selected companies designated corporations that had shown attention to ethical concerns found this group experienced an average growth rate of 11.3 percent compared to the overall average of Dow Jones industries of 6.2 percent. Another study of the five hundred largest companies in the United States similarly found companies which made a public commitment to ethical behavior tended to show better financial performance compared that those who made no such public commitment.[12] These correlations do not demonstrate causation, of course, but are suggestive. And, we should note that investment groups that track *socially responsible* stocks, such as the TIAA-CREF funds, do not show a better performance record for those designated *socially responsible*. Still, practicing good corporate citizenship through ethical public communication can help an organization avoid legal costs (since practicing good ethics usually avoids illegalities as well) and costly public relations embarrassments.

Risk Communication: Public Health and Safety. Organizations have a special responsibility to communicate with the public about dangers their operations or products may pose to people and the environment. The 1980s saw special concern about environmental hazards posed by toxic chemicals, such as dioxin. Cases such as the Love Canal incident—in which the State of New York and then the Carter Administration in 1978 declared a community around a former waste disposal site a state and federal emergency—led to regulatory reporting requirements about chemical hazards and pollution. The major piece of U.S. legislation requiring risk communication is *Title III of the Superfund Amendments and Reauthorization Act of 1986*, PL 99–499 of the U.S. Code. Part of this act mandates creation of local emergency committees, which are to prepare right-to-know procedures for the local community. Companies and other institutions, including universities, must report the release of chemicals into the air, water, land, or waste treatment facility. Reporting about risks thus became legal as well as an ethical obligation. Similar kinds of public risks of operations came to the fore as well. One of the authors of this text worked with two public utilities concerned about how to formulate communications concerning potential dangers of high-energy electrical distribution lines. More recently, cell phone manufacturers have had to deal with fears that cell phone use might cause brain tumors (no conclusive evidence supporting these last two fears has come to light).

Even more recently, public concern has focused on health risks of various products. The long-running effort of big tobacco companies to deny evidence of a link between their products and cancer is of course very well known. The health dangers of faulty silicon-gel breast implants led to a very public fall from grace for Dow Corning:

> In the annals of business ethics, the fall from grace of Dow Corning Corporation was particularly precipitous. Here was one of America's 100 most profitable industrial companies. Its high-level Business Conduct Committee, which dated back to the 1970s, was considered an industry model: It conducted annually some 25 face-to-face audits worldwide with employee groups. More than ninety percent of Dow Corning employees considered the company *highly ethical*, according to a 1988 company survey, an exceptionally high rating.[13]

This case illustrates that even a well-run corporation with a culture seen as effectively concerned with corporate ethics and responsibility could go astray. It appears that in 1991 the board of directors of Dow Corning learned of the dangers of the silicon-gel implants but decided to suppress the information and keep manufacturing and distributing them.

More recently, manufacturers of prescription medicines have had to deal with similar charges. It appears that the makers of a major prescription drug used to reduce pain from arthritis, Vioxx, suppressed scientific evidence that the drug increased a patient's risk for heart problems, such as heart attack and stroke. Naturally, it is the apparent intentional effort to prevent these messages that raises ethical concerns. Other painkillers used for similar treatments, such as Celebrex and naproxen-based drugs, also turned out to have similar potential risky side effects. A problem that has become all too familiar is shown in a recent newspaper headline: "Flawed device: Guidant knew but didn't tell."[14] The problem in this case was that the manufacturer of a type of implanted defribrillator (a device used to shock the heart back into normal rhythm after the occurrence of a dangerous irregularity) apparently kept from doctors and the public that the instrument had malfunctioned, shorted out, at least twenty-five times before it caused the death of a young man in Utah. Of course, there are many other examples of organizations holding back information about risky products, such as cars and tires, out of concern for maintaining the profitability of those products.

Ethical issues raised in risk communication flow not only from suppressing information about dangerous products but from providing information in an effective way preventing undue fear or other harms. For example, the dangers of the defibrillator mentioned above may be remote, presenting a risk in very few cases. The organization therefore seems to have a responsibility to explain the risk in such a way that patients who really need the device will not reject it, subjecting themselves to even greater health risks. Of course, this caveat in no way absolves the manufacturer of the breach in not reporting anything about the danger at all in the first place. Rather, this consideration means that an organization responsible for some sort of public risk has a responsibility to communicate the true nature of the risk in an effective and responsible manner. This obligation may also extend to responding to irresponsible rumors nowadays so easily spread on the Internet. For example, there have been rumors on the Internet for several years about antiperspirants allegedly causing either breast cancer or Alzheimer's disease. More threatening to individuals' health are cases in which an effective remedy is avoided because of such rumors—in such cases it appears that the ethical obligation is to try to refute the rumor. (For some reason, medical advice from strangers on the Internet seems more credible to many people than medical advice from their physicians.)

Risk communication can suddenly turn into full-blown crisis communication. The difference is that organizational *crisis communication* is required after the *risk* has become a disaster—the chemical has leaked massively, the plant has exploded, the radiation has been released into the atmosphere. In crisis communication, the organization through its spokespersons has to control the message in a way that prevents further harm to the public while containing damage to the organization and its reputation. Probably a good example of unethical crisis communication would be the former Soviet government's attempt to hide or cover up information about the nuclear accident at Chernobyl, in what is now Ukraine. Until some of the Scandinavian countries began to detect unusually huge amounts of radiation in their atmospheres and offshore waters, the Soviet government released no information at all about the catastrophe.

The case often cited as illustrating the most effective, as well as ethical, way of dealing with a crisis is Johnson & Johnson's handling of the Tylenol tampering case over twenty years ago. In 1982, seven people in the Chicago area died from cyanide poisoning after taking Tylenol Extra-Strength capsules. It turns out that someone had injected capsules at some point after they had left the manufacturer. Johnson & Johnson immediately admitted the danger, pulled all the medicine from store shelves, and ceased their manufacture until the mystery could be cleared up. Immediate, open, and forthright communication, in the long run, saved the day for the company and for the product. Suppression and denial of evidence of danger have not proven nearly as effective, as shown by several cases reported here. Of course, one could argue that Johnson & Johnson in this case had the advantage that the danger was not inherent in their product or process of manufacture, but had been introduced externally. One could not argue that in the cases of defective tires, automobiles, cigarettes, or prescription drugs.

Johnson & Johnson itself suffered some loss of credibility as a result of a problem in 1998. This case dealt with a diabetes diagnostic tester manufactured by a subsidiary company, called *LifeScan*. It appears that this company failed to inform the Food and Drug Administration (FDA) when it discovered that its device occasionally showed an error message instead of the danger sign of a high glucose warning when the glucose level was very high. Johnson & Johnson ended up paying a fine and pleading guilty to three misdemeanor charges that it had given misinformation (through its subsidiary) to the FDA about the false readings.[15] In this case, Johnson & Johnson has tried to restore its credibility by developing a case study for training top executives based on the LifeScan incident; the training also encourages concerns and dissenting voices so that employees feel free to bring possible problems to the attention of supervisors.

Business and Financial Reporting.   At the beginning of the twenty-first century, corporate communication about financial accounting and dealings took center stage. The many cases already mentioned, beginning with the Enron scandal, explain the emphasis. This and the related scandals specifically focus on misleading communication about the financial dealings and business arrangements of companies. The legislation known as *Sarbanes-Oxley* (HR 3763), passed in 2002 directly in response to the Enron and related scandals, institutes several tough reporting requirements regarding corporation's financial statements and claims. For example, the CEO and CFO (Chief Financial Officer) must sign off on financial statements and reports, placing themselves at risk for personal liability. A new industry has sprung up developing training and special auditing to help companies meet the new requirements of the act, which has come to be known by the acronym SOX. The American Institute of Certified Public Accountants maintains extensive web-based services for professional accountants to assist in implementing the new standards.[16]

One result of the new law is the increased use of a new executive title for large companies, *Chief Ethics Officer*. Federal sentencing guidelines for violators allow for lesser sentences for executives found guilty in these kinds of cases if they can show that their corporation had made a good faith effort to instill ethical practices. The existence of a code of ethics and the office of Chief Ethics Officer or Corporate Ethics Officer are acceptable as evidence that such a good faith effort had been made. The second result has been much wider implementation of written codes of ethics. The requirement that all new hires, especially at the executive rank, sign off on ethics codes has become widespread. Firms specializing in ethics training and consulting for writing ethics codes are also proliferating. *Business Week* reports that some companies now require that documented research into ethical ramifications of business decisions be a regular part of practicing *due diligence*.[17] Of course, we have seen that Arthur Andersen and Enron, as well as Dow Corning, had presumably strong codes of ethics and ethics training. Unless the climate and corporate culture actually reinforce ethical conduct when major, real-life decisions are being considered, the training and codes are inadequate.

This discussion returns us to one issue recurring throughout this text dealing with the relationship between *the ethical* and *the legal*. We have claimed that ethics is revealed when you do something even though you are not legally required to do it—that ethics goes beyond the law. These provisions from *Sarbanes-Oxley* and the Federal sentencing guidelines show that when private ethics are inadequate, the law can step in and create stringent requirements. Since ethical conduct is usually more demanding than legal requirements, being ethical can have the practical benefit of avoiding running afoul of the law. If there were a need to show the practical benefits of communicating ethically, these cases provide good evidence.

In complex organizations, responsibility appears diffuse and people may not always be able to determine who is responsible for what. In these circumstances, *bottom-line* considerations might become the single point of focus so that ethical considerations do not make it to the radar. One can argue, however, that corporate ethical conduct is more profitable, in the long run, than unethical behavior. One can observe that many organizations, such as those mentioned above, have suffered financially from fines, lost sales, and other penalties. As one business ethicist puts it, "acting ethically and legally means saving billons of dollars each year in theft, lawsuits, and settlements."[18] Ethical business could be good business. Recent events, however, suggest that the short-term view is still predominant.

We now turn to a discussion of the second relationship affecting organizational communication ethics, the relationship between the organization and its members.

Impact on Organizational Members

Organizations have special ethical obligations regarding communication with their members. Such obligations imply requirements to deal openly and truthfully with the people constituting the organization. Again, the *Credo* of the Johnson & Johnson Company covers some of the major concerns:

> We are responsible to our employees, the men and women who work with us throughout the world. Everyone must be considered as an individual. We must respect their dignity and recognize their merit. They must have a sense of security in their jobs. Compensation must be fair and adequate, and working conditions clean, orderly and safe. We must be mindful of ways to help our employees fulfill their family responsibilities. Employees must feel free to make suggestions and complaints. There must be equal opportunity for employment, development and advancement for those qualified.[19]

The *Credo* touches on the worth and dignity of the individual, which certainly has implications for how the company communicates with them. Respect for privacy and for allowing worthwhile private lives is also implied. Employees ought to be able to expect a healthy and safe working environment. And, finally, members ought to have some level of freedom or security to speak out, even to register complaints.

In this section, we will take up each of these kinds of ethical concerns although in slightly altered order, beginning with communication about health and safety in the workplace. We then turn to issues relating to privacy and to organizational control over and access to information, including private or even personal information. Whistle-blowing, a type of exercise of a right to complain, is the next major issue that comes up in regard to the relationship between the individual and the organization. When we later look at the impact of individuals on the organizations, we will see that this topic is relevant again. Quality of life issues and related issues of workplace rights and democracy, topics that seem to be addressed in the *Credo* above are addressed next. Quality of life and dignity of the individual also seem to be issues related to diversity in the organization, and so we will take up that topic as well in this section.

To begin, however, we should point out that organizations have some obvious duties regarding keeping members informed about the health and prospects of the organization as well as the members' tenure and future. We have seen that much of the scandals swirling around Enron, World-Com, and others had to do with misleading employees' about the financial health of the businesses. Many people were hurt, who had their retirement savings committed based on expectations of the financial strength of their employer. A second area of concern deals with relocation of business operations. Over the years, employees have felt betrayed when a corporation has closed down a local plant without due warning to relocate operations offshore. In the latter case, the ethical questions deal with what sort of communication the company should have provided to their stateside members.

The second rather obvious area of ethical responsibility lies in timely and useful provision of feedback and performance evaluations. Both giving and receiving performance evaluations can be stressful. To avoid confrontation, some supervisors tend to give vague or misleading formal evaluations (or in some case no formal evaluations at all). The supervisors hope the employees will somehow be aware of their actual low level of performance—after all, they plead, everyone else knows it. The unsuspecting employee then feels blindsided when selected for *right-sizing* (a euphemism for downsizing or laying people off to save money) because they are below average compared to other workers. The organization thus has an ethical responsibility (and in some cases in civil law, a legal responsibility) to provide timely and accurate feedback on work performance.

Now we will proceed to some more specific cases involving organizations' ethical communication.

Safe and Healthful Work Environment.   When people work in an unsafe or unhealthy environment, we might assume that they have chosen to do so, since they see the benefits of salary and employment outweighing potential risks. The key assumption, however, is that they are in fact aware of the risks they are taking. For many years, miners were unaware of the dangers of the dust they continually inhaled while down in the shafts. The dust caused what came to be known as *black-lung* disease. Workers over the years have been exposed to airborne asbestos, dioxin, and even radiation without being fully informed about the dangers. Of course the long list of occupational dangers goes back to the early days of the Industrial Revolution in northern Britain, as even young children were exposed to all sorts of health and safety risks in the early mills and mines. Back in 1788, the British Parliament took one of the first steps toward recognizing the health dangers of occupations when it passed a law for compensation of chimney sweeps (often young boys) for respiratory diseases.

In the United States, organizations were not specifically required to communicate with employees about workplace hazards until the passage of the Occupational Safety and Health Act of 1970. They were required to compensate workers for accidents and diseases incurred on the job—such worker compensation acts went all the way back to 1911—but the purpose was compensation after the harm had been done. The act also instituted the Occupational Safety and Health Administration, also known as OSHA. The OSHA legislation of 1970 mandated a communication requirement. Manufacturers using chemicals, designated as hazardous under the act, were required to inform employees of their presence and the nature of the danger each chemical represented (2,300 chemicals were initially so designated). The regulations also required manufacturers to set up employee training programs about these dangers, safe-handling techniques, and emergency procedures. The legislation and the OSHA agency have continued to expand the list of hazards about which companies need to communicate with their members.

The OSHA and related state and federal regulations remind us again that laws can supplant or enforce what would otherwise be voluntary ethics when there is a perception that organizations have not acted properly. We saw that happen with *Sarbanes-Oxley* in regard to financial reporting; we see it with OSHA regarding workplace safety. In many cases ethical communication, which would call for organizations to inform their own members about the risks they face, might have prevented legal sanctions coming into force.

A second type of hazard in an organization arises from crime and workplace violence. About two million Americans a year experience some sort of workplace violence or threatened violence, according to Justice Department reports. In the United States, murder is the number one cause of death for women while at work, and it is the number-two cause for men at work.[20] This increase in violence at work is a fairly recent phenomenon, since it has tripled over the last twenty years or so. One report suggests the following concern about this growing perception of crime at work:

> A *Gallup Poll* published in September, 2000, found that American workers are increasingly feeling pressure from rapidly changing technology, mounting job stress and fear of random workplace assaults, and that they blame their bosses for giving them little or no guidance on how to deal with it.[21]

Note the key point that the *bosses*, that is, the leaders in the organization, are blamed for a lack of effective communication about these dangers.

The potential remedy is complicated by the concern for the protection of privacy. Let's say that an employee with a history or even criminal record of violent crime applies for a job with a particular employer. First, there are limits on the extent to which the interviewer can pry into the aspects of a criminal record that are not considered *bona fide* work related (it would be permissible to determine whether a convicted embezzler is applying for a bank teller or similar position, for example). Secondly, there may be restrictions on the extent to which the organization can report to other members about the violent or criminal past of an individual employee without violating the rights of that individual. This presents organizational leaders with both a legal and an ethical dilemma—what are the ethical implications of communicating a feeling that a particular member may be a danger to others? On the one hand, you may harm the individual, and, on the other, you may fail to provide others with information they may need to protect themselves. As so often is the case, the ethical (and in this case, legal) course of action may come down to a tough decision. By informing fellow members about the alleged violent (or in some cases, mental) record of another member, you risk being sued by the member for invasion of privacy and slander. The fellow members could turn around and hold you liable for not informing about the other member's record should there be a harmful incident. One may decide that the ethical course of action may be the one that exposes one or the organization to some form of legal liability.

Issues of Privacy and Surveillance.   The considerations just discussed about informing members about another's potential for violence leads into a discussion of the ethical issues surrounding gathering information about organizational members. The major issue involves surveillance. How much of your right to privacy do you surrender when you go to work? The case study at the end of Chapter 4 in this book presented the case of a corporation which planted miniaturized video cameras in locker rooms to tape private conversations and phone calls of employees. Management believed, in this case, what they were doing was for the greater good, although their actions did involve some invasion of the employees' privacy. The digitalization and miniaturization of surveillance devices make the dangers of secret surveillance more salient than ever for many organizational members. One obvious concern lies in placing such devices in dressing rooms or locker rooms in which people could be filmed undressing or changing clothes.

Monitoring of organizational members can take many forms in addition to taping and video surveillance. Today organizations make an effort to monitor computer use by employees, especially web browsing and emailing. Software programs called *keystroke loggers* allow an organization to read every draft and message composed on a company computer, keystroke by keystroke. Some software allows for a company to select certain key words or names, such as a competitor's or a supervisor's, that would cause a message using the key words or names to be sent to a supervisor or other officer for secret review. The keystrokes are saved permanently on the network server or on the stand-along hard drive, so that erasing offending messages would have no effect. One of the developers of such a program has been quoted saying that while there are no legal qualms about using such software, "there may be an ethical one."[22]

Congress did pass the Electronic Communication Privacy Act in 1986 (the ECPA), which would seem to offer some expectation of privacy on the part of employees, even regarding their emails. The ECPA, however, was aimed primarily at phone communications, their recording and wiretapping. It is less clear that it applies to computer communications. Court cases recently have held that communications that are accessed from a *storage device*, such the network system's storage, does not constitute illegal interception of electronic communication and is therefore permitted by the ECPA.[23] The upshot is that organizational members cannot expect that their electronic messages, such as email, and stored voice mail messages, are private. One of the most publicized of recent cases involved the firing of the CEO of Boeing for using email to carry on a romance with another executive at the company.[24] So, in the wake of corporate scandals and *Sarbanes-Oxley*, it is doubtful that even the top executives are now immune to monitoring of their own communication.

In the case of electronic monitoring, the issue of whether to monitor employees' communication, how much, and with what secrecy is clearly an ethical rather than a legal decision. While some companies have admitted the use of software for monitoring members' emails, others have avoided the question or have claimed to have rejected such programs. Delta Airlines, for example, admits to trying out such software on an experimental basis, but then ditched it as not being compatible with their interests or values.[25] Clearly, this is a case in which an organization needs to weigh competing ethical considerations. Such monitoring, for example, could help to realize a valid company policy of preventing sexual or other kinds of harassment, which could be carried on through electronic means. The office romance involving the Boeing executives could conceivably fall into this category. Recreational web browsing, also, could potentially be very costly to the productivity and therefore the bottom line of a company. As in so many cases, weighing the ethical costs and benefits should be systematic and informed, rather than arbitrary. People in leadership positions in the organization need to be able to think through these issues in a consistent and fair fashion.

New state and federal laws have begun to require fingerprinting for background checks for all kinds of hires and even volunteers. For example, the Catholic Archdiocese of Washington, D.C., has fingerprinted new employees for over a decade, and over five years ago began to fingerprint volunteers as well.[26] Again, a new industry has sprouted to provide electronic screening devices for fingerprinting and data gathering for background checks. Two kinds of ethical issues present themselves in this case. First, the organization must think about the best way to communicate the need for background checks, even for volunteers. Second, the organization needs to be alert to expanding such checks beyond what is necessary simply because the technology is available and, in many cases, already paid for.

Other kinds of issues involving privacy and organizational communication arise from modern medical technology. Testing and monitoring for HIV/AIDS has become an issue in this area. Can an organization require testing of employees and then inform other employees about the test results? Some would argue that this situation resembles the question of whether or not to inform organizational members about a member with supposedly criminal or violent tendencies. Other kinds of questions are raised by the privacy of health records of employees. Does an employee have to reveal medical conditions as a prerequisite for hiring or continued employment? The possibility of DNA screening raises similar kinds of ethical questions. Such screening may reveal that someone is at unusually high risk for a type of debilitating or disabling disease. Can a company require such screening and then use the results against the employee in some way? What can the organization communicate to others concerning the results of such screening? It is not clear that the *American with Disabilities Act of 1990* (the ADA) is helpful in dealing with these issues of potential disability or sickness. Where the legal situation is not clear, the ethical system of the organizational involved becomes the more relevant. Should the organization collect and store such data and, if so, what kind of communication about this information is permitted? One of the informal laws of new computerized information systems goes as follows: if it can be collected, it will be; if it can be communicated, it might be.

Rights of Whistle-blowers.   Most of our discussion of the ethical implications of whistle-blowing is in the following section, dealing with an individual's obligations to his or her organization. At this point, however, we feel we should indicate that the organization may have ethical responsibilities to those who would become whistle-blowers.

The question at this point deals with the ethical responsibilities the organization owes to its members, including its whistle-blowers. Janet Wiscomb, writing for the human resources journal, *Workforce*, maintains that corporations should not fear but encourage whistle-blowers. Her thesis is that in the long run the organization will be much better off to create a culture and climate in which people do not fear reprisals for bringing to light serious problems or potentially dangerous conditions.[27] The organization is ethically responsible for helping to develop an organizational culture which protects and even honors those who bring problems to the attention of the organization. Whistle-blowing is nearly always a sign that internal organizational communication is faulty or inadequate.

In some cases, the law prohibits retaliation against whistle-blowers. The *Occupational Safety and Health Act*, for example, specifically provides legal protection for whistle-blowers:

> To help ensure that employees are, in fact, free to participation in safety and health activities, Section 11(c) of the Act prohibits any person from discharging or in any manner discriminating against any employee because the employee has exercised rights under the Act.
>
> These rights include complaining to OSHA and seeking an OSHA inspection, participating in an OSHA inspection, and participating or testifying in any proceeding related to an OSHA inspection.[28]

The legal protections under OSHA are limited to the specific investigations related to the agency, however, and do not afford blanket protection to all kinds of internal whistle-blowing.

As we have seen in several instances, the organization and its leadership must work out its ethical position regarding communication about dangers and risks to the public, possible unlawful activities, or mismanagement. In general, as Wiscombe points out, an ethically responsible organizational culture can prevent the financial and other harms from litigation and negative publicity. An ethically responsible organization, therefore, is one that encourages or certainly permits responsible whistle-blowing without threat of reprisal.

Corporate Democracy and Quality of Life.   Does the organization have an ethical responsibility to foster a climate that reinforces a society's commitment to democratic institutions? This is the question formulated by proponents of *workplace democracy*. This question is also related to issues related to the quality of work life, sometimes institutionalized as QWL (Quality of Work Life) movements and programs. George Cheney, a researcher specializing in organizational communication, has commented, "Surely one of the great ironies of the modern world is that democracy, imperfect as it is in the political realm, seldom extends to the workplace."[29] One's rights under the U.S. Constitution often seem to be waived once inside one's office, workshop, or other place of employment.[30]

In his influential text on organizational theory, Gareth Morgan analyzes different metaphors that have been used over the years for representing organizations. The machine metaphor is fairly obvious, since many people think that an organization is like a machine. One of the more unusual metaphors (although not unusual in terms of the nature of many modern organizations) is the image of the organization as an instrument of domination.[31] The term *toxic organization* captures the idea behind this organizational metaphor. Lack of job security because of the threats of *out-sourcing* and *right-sizing*, and *off-shoring*—all newly created verbs to indicate the pressures on many employees in the modern economy—increased stress on the job.

Let us now return to the first question raised here, does the organization have a responsibility to exercise democracy in its functioning? Early organizational theories would answer, no. Theorists generally describe development of theories of management through several stages, beginning with the so-called *classical theories*, associated with scientific management and bureaucratic organizations. The leadership, or management, clearly had the responsibility to direct the work of other members and especially production workers. The founder of scientific management, Frederick Winslow Taylor, made it clear that workers were not to question orders. It was the job of managers to decide what to do and, of workers, to do it without question. The next stage in management theories, human relations or human resource management, shifted emphasis to engaging members and workers in two-way discussion. Still, the emphasis was on obtaining the workers' assent through understanding, group processes, and participation in some level of decision making.

Models based on systems theories, contingency theories, and organizational culture theories allowed for a wider range of alternative ways of involving members in organizational decision making. In these theories, allowance was made for employee empowerment through quality circles and self-directed work teams. *Teamwork* became a buzzword and an important concept. One newer form of this movement lay in the use of term *job entrepreneurship*, which implies that workers are to strive constantly to find ways to enhance productivity and expand the range of their services. These moves seem to increase individual autonomy and members' participation and thereby workplace democracy.

On the other hand, as many have pointed out, these activities can have the opposite effect. Small groups of peers may become more intrusive and domineering than some bureaucracies. The self-managed groups can be coopted by management, weakening other employees' organizations, such as unions. The lower-level members of the organization come to identify with the interests of upper management, even those interests which run counter to their own needs.[32] In nonprofit organizations run by outside boards, for example, there has been a movement to open board membership to regular organizational members. A university administration may bring faculty and staff members into administrative policy-making bodies, perhaps even at the board level, so that faculty and staff feel committed to decisions since they have participated in their making. The ethical issue here lies in how the organization formulates and openly communicates the purposes of such participatory structures. Participation by members in problem solving and decision making may or may not further the goals of workplace democracy and quality of life. Many participatory systems have been imposed from the top down, which is a sign that intentions may not be fully democratic. Participation may be aimed at decisions regarding *how* to carry out a policy or program, while there was little or no participation in determining *what* the policy or program would be.

These considerations may not answer directly the question of whether there is an ethical requirement on the part of upper management or leadership to allow for democratic participation in decision making and policy making. The ethical issue seems to be whether or not leadership tries to convince the members that they have a significant role—that their participation makes a real difference—when in fact they do not. The question thus is whether the messages are intended to be manipulative or not.

We can approach the issues of corporate democracy from a broader angle. Does the organization, particularly a for-profit organization, have a responsibility regarding the quality of public life and democratic institutions in its social setting or environment? In a way, this question has overtones for the earlier discussion of corporate social responsibility. Perhaps the most prominent case in recent history arose from the opposition to *Apartheid* in the Republic of South Africa prior to the opening of a new democratic system in that country in 1994. Corporations were called on to take a stand: Would their operations there prop up the undemocratic white regime in power prior to 1994 or would their pulling out of the country harm common people because of lost wages and other benefits? BP-Shell and Texaco petroleum companies have faced similar questions regarding their operations in the delta of the Niger River in the Republic of Nigeria. Oil revenues from these and other international firms have provided financial support for corrupt, often military rulers in that country. Again, the ethical question takes the form whether they can do more harm or good by staying in the country or pulling out. A similar case relates to the political regime in Myanmar, or Burma, a country in which foreign investment is the major source of revenue for the regime. In 1996, Reebok, for example, determined not to do business in Burma; other companies such as IKEA, Adidas, and BP Petroleum have also pulled out of the country.[33] How companies communicate their justifications for either action in these cases—pulling out or staying in for *constructive engagement*—becomes an issue of organizational communication ethics.

Organizations in a democratic society need to reflect on their role in communicating that supports or runs counter to the societal values. Of course, *business is business,* and profit for shareholders and productivity are often basic considerations. Recent voices have called for organizations, particularly for-profit organizations, to take account of their impact on members in shaping an atmosphere congruent with democratic functions—their *ethical climate.* Organizations are accountable for how they deliberate about and communicate these issues to their members and to broader societies. *Business as usual* implies the organization can operate in way that does not take account of potential ethical issues. The quality of life for its members and for the broader society is shaped by these considerations.

Diversity in the Organization.   In Chapters 8 and 9 of this book we have discussed different elements of diversity. These different forms of diversity are, of course, present in organizations, especially contemporary complex, global organizations. The questions for this section deal with the ethical responsibility the organization may have toward members in terms of fostering a climate encouraging ethical communication concerning diversity among its membership. Chapter 8 reviewed the ethical implications of communication in various settings with diverse others including people from different cultures. Chapter 9 highlighted in more detail the diversity represented by people with disabilities.

In organizational communication, ethical issues revolving around communication have dealt with matters of discrimination against member of identifiable groups and harassment, particularly sexual or racial harassment. The nexus of many of these ethical issues lies in how people ought to feel while acting as a member of an organization. Communication from the organization or permitted or allowed by the organization helps determine the atmosphere in which people work and participate. When people are made to feel belittled, threatened, humiliated, or harassed, they cannot fully function in their organizational roles or as human beings. Review the list above, and note that any of these dimensions could be the basis for communication that discounts the humanity of another person.

In many cases the discrimination or harassment has been made illegal, although it is not always certain that violators will be prosecuted. Civil rights cases, for example, depend on the priorities of the Justice Department, its budget and funding, and the overall leadership of the Attorney General and the presidential administration. This situation obtains also for investigations and prosecutions under the *American for Disabilities Act* (the ADA), and other antidiscriminatory legislation. In other words, the legality of certain behaviors or policies may be a moot point due to lack of vigorous enforcement. An organization's ethical climate, hence, may be important for ensuring ethical treatment of members rather than the state of legislation. Recently, many for-profit corporations have taken the lead in going beyond the legal requirements in these matters. This can be seen particularly in the case of gender issues and sexual orientation. The Human Rights Campaign,—the largest advocacy group representing gay, lesbian, bisexual, and transgender people in the United States,—has several important corporate sponsors, such as Shell Oil, American Airlines, Volvo, Citigroup, IBM, and so on. The HRC itself reports that corporate America has taken the lead: for example, 49 of the *Fortune 500* top 50 companies have specific nondiscrimination policies covering gay and lesbian employees, and 83 percent of all 500 have such antidiscrimination policies.[34]

Issues of diversity, however, can be more intransigent than these figures may suggest. The so-called *mainstream group*, which changes in definition over time, is often still taken for granted as the default orientation. For many years, of course, white males were the expected norm, and thus African Americans or women stood out as exceptions in organizational settings, especially in leadership or executive roles. Those who study these issues say that the *mainstream* culture or identity is *unmarked*, since it is the one that is to be expected—there is no reason to take any notice of it. Thus, you seldom hear people talk about men doctors or women nurses, because of the sexual stereotyping associated in the past with these occupations. For those who are members of groups in the unmarked category, forms of communication that mark out other groups are hardly noticed at all. There is a certain taken-for-granted nature in verbal and nonverbal messages that single out or draw special attention to the marked groups, whether they are women, Muslims, Gays, or people with disabilities. This can be even as unsubtle or crude as asking someone, "How do *you people* feel about this?"

Many organizations over the years have exacerbated these problems while trying to avoid them. Some diversity training programs have led to suits claiming discrimination against protected groups when the training involved people expressing openly their long-held prejudices. A California-based chain of grocery stores, for example, landed in legal trouble when company-sponsored diversity training involved an exercise in which supervisors were asked to verbalize stereotypes they had heard concerning women or minority group members.[35]

Leadership development and promotions are often a part of a communication climate that subtly undermines a commitment to diversity. Many organizations have tried to employ mentoring programs to socialize new members and to groom others for advancement. One problem over the years with such mentoring programs has been the difficulty at times of matching women and members of minority cultures with leaders in the organization, who have often been mostly white males. A related problem is shown by the coining of the stereotypical term the *Mommy track*, referring to special hours or schedules accommodating parenting.

The story of human and civil rights in the United States has been a story of general progress in terms of expanding rights of and respect for various groups, who have been subjected to discriminatory or harassing communication. On the other hand, the progress has been uneven, often due to reliance on rules and legislation, while the real problem lies in embedded organizational values and culture, which may be subtly resistant to change. In developing an ethical climate, the organization's membership must carefully confront habitual practices that could communicate a lack of full acceptance of the *Other* in all members. Again, this raises the issue of the definition of membership and where other stakeholders fit in the overall scheme of the organizational system. The question again becomes who are members and who are stakeholders who have a right to participate in such an ongoing discussion.

We discuss next the general ethical responsibilities of members and other stakeholders to the organization itself.

Impact on the Organization

The third perspective for looking at ethical issues in organizational communication concerns the final relationship: the impact of others' communication on the organization itself. From this perspective we ask what ethical responsibilities members, stakeholders, and others have toward the organization. Most attention has been directed to the first two sets of issues, derived from the organization's impact on society and on its members. Still, we need to recognize the general assumption that when one joins an organization, one takes on certain ethical obligations. These include loyalty to the group and its members, making a good effort in carrying out one's duties, striving to be competent in the performance of those duties, showing dependability, and, of course, displaying truthfulness and honesty in interactions with others and the organization.

The Case of Whistle-blowing.   Perhaps no situation so clearly involves ethics of organizational communication as much as whistle-blowing. These cases touch on both the responsibilities of the individual member to the organization as well as the organization's responsibility to the individual and to society. We mentioned three whistle-blowers named *Time Magazine's* Persons of the Year in 2002 in Chapter 2: Sherron Watkins of Enron, Cynthia Cooper of WorldCom, and Coleen Rowley of the FBI. *Time* referred to these women as heroes: "They were people who did right just by doing their jobs rightly—which mean ferociously, with eyes open and with the bravery," we all hope to show in similar circumstances.[36] Some whistle-blowers achieve the status of being the subject of a Hollywood film, as was the case with Jeffrey Wigand, who exposed the fact that his tobacco company knowingly controlled nicotine levels in its cigarettes; the film was *The Insider.*

Whistle-blowing refers to the act of communicating bad news about the organization through generally unauthorized channels. External whistle-blowing, considered to be the most risky form, involves going outside the organization to an external agency—the media, government, or sometimes law enforcement—to expose wrongdoing. Internal whistle-blowing, which is how Watkins, Cooper, and Rowley began their efforts, usually means going to the top of the organization chart, often bypassing one's actual superiors. Sherron Watkins, for example, wrote a blistering memo to Ken Lay, then CEO of Enron, laying out the questionable accounting schemes being perpetrated: "I am incredibly nervous," she wrote, "that we will implode in a wave of accounting scandals."[37] What she predicted, of course, did happen. Colleen Rowley, an FBI agent based in Minneapolis, began her whistle-blowing with a detailed letter to the then FBI Director Robert Mueller claiming that bureau higher-ups had squelched a local investigation into alleged 9/11 hijacking conspirator Zacharias Moussaoui, assumed to be the twentieth hijacker, who failed to participate in the attacks on September 11, 2001. Cynthia Cooper went to the board of WorldCom to expose that the company had attempted to cover up about $3.8 billion in losses. These internal cases all became external, however, when the memos or letters were leaked to the media and when Rowley was subpoenaed to testify before a Congressional hearing.

In most cases of whistle-blowing the one blowing the whistle risks a great deal, typically ostracism on the job, often firing, and other forms of retaliation. The whistle-blowers usually are clearly exercising what Michel Foucault called *fearless speech* (see Chapter 2). For example, after leaving Enron, Sherron Watkins had difficulty finding another position. She explained in an interview with the *New York Times* that while she has had some interviews, "When it comes down to the final decision, there's probably one or two people who say" 'Are you crazy? She's a whistle-blower."[38] In another highly publicized case, Roger Boisjoly, an engineer with Morton Thiokol, had advised strongly against the launch of the space shuttle *Challenger* back in 1986. Boisjoly and two other engineers had warned that the temperatures on the day of the proposed launch of the shuttle created an unsafe condition because the rubber O-rings would fail to seal, allowing hot gasses to ignite the external booster rockets. This, of course, is what did happen that awful day when Teacher in Space, Crista McAuliffe and her fellow astronauts lost their lives in the televised, fiery explosion. As a result of his whistle-blowing, Boisjoly felt alienated from coworkers, and forced to take a long sick leave. When he did try to find another job in the industry, like Watkins, he was unsuccessful, seen as a *known whistle-blower*.[39]

A whistle-blower often faces an ethical dilemma, represented by the competing values of loyalty and team spirit, on the one hand, and upholding moral and legal values on the other. Professionals may have a particular obligation to act in a way that protects the public and the clients. An engineer, aware that a bridge or building could catastrophically fail, has a clear obligation to protect lives that would otherwise be lost. A medical nurse or practitioner has a professional duty to protect lives by coming forward when he or she observes risky medical practices. Rowley believed that if FBI senior officers had allowed the Minneapolis investigation to go forward, it may have been possible to prevent the tragedies of 9/11.

On the other hand, people in the organization may feel betrayed by the whistle-blower who appears to break ranks and *wash the dirty linen* out in public. They are not good team players, who did not go through the proper channels, as they had an ethical obligation to do (or so the organization's top brass claims). This latter view holds that whistle-blowers are basically troublemakers. It may seem too easy for us to dismiss this position as too calloused and too facile, calling up stereotypes of *Big Business*, fitting plot lines of various movies. In reality, there may be no typical case, so clearly pitting the underdog, the righteous whistle-blower, against the evil bosses. Nonetheless, a typical response from the organization faced with whistle-blowing is to close ranks and, too often, to try to discredit the whistle-blower.

The mixed reaction given to whistle-blowers is clearly illustrated by the differing responses to W. Mark Felt, the former number-two executive at the FBI during the days of the Watergate investigations in the 1970s, which led to the forced resignation of the then President Richard Nixon. For over thirty years, Felt was the sort of whistle-blower who remains anonymous. Bob Woodward and Carl Bernstein, while they were gathering information for their stories on the Nixon White House and its involvement in the Watergate break-in, gave their anonymous source the code-name of *Deep Throat*. Mr. Felt did not come forward to identify himself until 2005, when he was in his nineties. Some praised him as a hero. One of the top lawyers involved in prosecuting the Watergate case, Richard Ben-Veniste, said that Felt's role showed that "the importance of the whistle-blowers shouldn't be underestimated."[40] Others praised him for taking a great personal risk, when he feared that his superior at the FBI was himself involved in the cover-up. On the other hand, former Nixon speechwriter (and onetime candidate for President) Patrick Buchanan denounced Felt as a traitor.[41]

One of the criticisms leveled at Mark Felt, or *Deep Throat* in the Watergate scandal, was that he had an obligation to report on criminal acts through the Department of Justice or the FBI's chain of command—such reporting was his absolute duty as a law-enforcement officer, they would say. This raises the fundamental question faced by nearly all would-be whistle-blowers: have they truly exhausted internal routes for resolution of the problem? At this point in time, it appears that Mark Felt's response to the charge is that he felt certain his superiors at the FBI were themselves complicit in the ongoing cover-up. In fact, he, like so many internal critics and whistle-blowers, believed they are exhibiting genuine loyalty to his organization by going public to help it correct its faults. You may recall that this was the basis of the defense Socrates mounted when he was on trial for his life for misleading the youth of Athens (he held that Athens should vote him a lifetime benefit for pointing out the faults in the city).

Individual Responsibility and Corporate Environment. Two researchers in organizational communication, Daniel Montgomery and Peter DeCaro, contend that there has been an overemphasis on the individual responsibility for wrongdoing or unethical behavior in organizational communication research.[42] They argue that the focus on the individual and inner, psychological motivations overlooks the systemic effects of the organizational environment and setting. Think of highly publicized cases of wrongdoing, such as the mistreatment of Iraqi prisoners in the prison in Baghdad: individuals took the blame, not the organization or system in which they were operating. Emphasizing individual culpability allows the organization and other members of the organization to continue operations as normal, blaming the problems on a few deviant individuals. So, when we talk about ethical obligations of the individual to the organization, we want to avoid this sort of tendency.

Several recent books on ethics in American life have explored tendencies that appear to suggest a downward spiral in individual integrity, especially in regard to self-sacrifice and discipline in the pursuit of common goals. David Callahan, a cofounder of the public policy group, Demos, pointed to a new individualism bordering on self-centeredness behind increasing slacking, fudging, and cheating on the job.[43] Anita L. Allen, a professor of law and philosophy at the University of Pennsylvania, highlights similar tendencies in her book, *The New Ethics.*[44] Both authors reject the notion that people are different now from they were in the recent past, but attribute declines in ethical behavior in organizations to uncertainty, stress, and the belief that others get ahead by unscrupulous behavior, or, at least, by cutting ethical corners.

One conclusion from these studies is that one must be especially vigilant in scrutinizing one's own ethical standards and actions in the contemporary organizational context. These considerations also highlight the importance of an organization studying the messages it may unintentionally send to members through seeming to reinforce a culture of *get things done at all costs.*

Ethical Vantage Points for Issues in Organizational Communication

Critical theory and postmodernist theorists would question many of the basic premises concerning organizational communication. Modern, corporate organizations exhibit traits of the *modernist,* bureaucratic assumptions. These assumptions include notions that organizations are basically a technology, a set of tools, for accomplishing tasks. An organization is a rational structure, which is in itself neither ethical nor unethical. A neutral posture toward rational organizations, or bureaucracies, one could argue, has been responsible for unfeeling or unhealthy organizational climates. The concept of *managerialism* is one that privileges the ends of managers or top executives over all others—they are the organization, according to this view (we are reminded of *L'Etat c'est moi*, as attributed to France's Louis XIV).

Represented in the clash between organizational functionalism and postmodernism are two competing ideas about what an ethics of organizational communication would look like. On one hand, ethical communication leads to organizational success, however defined; on the other, ethical communication contributes to the humanity of all members, regardless of stated organizational objectives. In this section, we briefly consider alternative approaches derived from different theories about communication ethics. You may want to explore other alternative perspectives as well that could be applied to the kinds of issues raised so far in this chapter. Here we show how three or four perspectives could be brought to bear on these issues.

Dialogical Communication Ethics

Is dialogical communication a possible basis for ethical communication in organizations? In some ways, it appears that organizational communication deals mainly with *business as business*, or the *Real World*, and that idealistic philosophies of the likes of Buber and Levinas may not seem terribly relevant in that world. However, after a well-known Harvard psychologist developed the idea of *multiple intelligences*, practical efforts were made to apply the idea of *emotional intelligence* to organizational and managerial leadership. In their book, *Executive EQ: Emotional Intelligence in Leadership and Organizations*, Robert Cooper and Ayman Sawaf tried to apply some of these ideas to corporate settings.[45] And, *EQ* is of course a take-off on the idea of *IQ* as a standard measure for rational intelligence. They suggest that high EQ is necessary for successful organizational leadership. A mark of high EQ is what they refer to as *authentic presence*, which is close to the idea of the attitude one displays in dialogical communication. Recall that the hallmark of dialogical ethics in communication required authentic presence for the other. Such presence requires openness, acceptance, full regard, and a spirit of nonevaluation of the *Other*.

Cooper and Sawaf argue that there is sufficient evidence in the organizational literature for the value of EQ in effective management. In other words, practices consistent with the approach of dialogical ethics can lay down an effective method for organizational leadership. Feminist theories of organizational communication similarly imply that there is more than unfeeling calculation in effective leadership. Imagine how an *ethics of caring* could be applied in various organizational contexts. If an organization is facing important decisions—such as to relocate or downsize—how would this kind of approach bring out ethical implications of such decisions? Leaders and members could approach difficult decisions in a spirit of cooperative dialogue, informed by authentic caring for each other and their communities. It seems that such an approach could be applied to issues involving corporate social responsibility as well as to issues growing out of organizational responsibilities to its members.

We should bear in mind, of course, that not all complex organizations are for-profit businesses. We can picture cooperative or communal organizations in which a dialogical perspective would need little "bottom-line" justification, which seems needed for corporate firms.

Rawls and Habermas

The theories of John Rawls and Jürgen Habermas also seem especially germane to issues in organizational communication ethics. In a systemic ethical process all stakeholders participate, in a fully understanding way, in decisions that might affect them all. The CSR particularly calls for rules of a social contract. Habermas calls for a realm allowing for undistorted communication, in which all who are affected can meet and converse as equals to work out the most appropriate norms for dealing with a situation. Rawls, like Scanlon, holds that all who would be affected by an organizational structure or set of rules should also agree on the principles that will guide decisions affecting them all.

This sort of discourse ethics calls for a situation in which relevant stakeholders can be communicated with in such a way that their authentic input can be taken into account. An ethical decision by the organization, hence, is one that nearly all those groups affected can assent to (or, in Scanlon's wording, not reasonably object to). Communication that makes management look good, without taking account of the impact on the community or neighborhood, let us say, would be questionable under this situation. This sort of communication ethics, of course, focuses more on process—in how the decision was arrived at or the message formulated—than on ultimate outcomes.

We should bear in mind that the principles of Habermas and Rawls are mainly applicable to a political state or society. There are some basic differences between a state or society, on one hand, and an organization, on the other. First, for an organization, there is more opportunity for entrance and exit, for example. One can choose to join or to leave an organization more easily than joining or leaving (emigrating) from a state or a society. Membership in a state or a society is typically less voluntary than in an organization. Secondly, as business ethicist Robert Phillips points out, the values of one's contributions to an organization are usually more evident than in the case of one's involvement in a state or society.[46] Hence, equality of outcome and of treatment may be less essential in an organization than in a state or society. Rawls' concern about justice applies more fittingly to citizens of a state than to members of an organization, particularly a voluntary organization. Organizational members may ethically receive more rewards than other members, based on what they do for the organization. Also, organizations have specific ends or objectives, while states and societies generally do not. The ethics of organizations can thus be determined, partly, with respect to those ends and their fulfillment of them. Members can act ethically or not in furthering those ends or opt out of the organization altogether if they object to those ends. It is harder to opt out of a political state, in the way that David Thoreau envisioned over a hundred years ago.

Utilitarianism

What would a utilitarian perspective demand in considering communication in organizations? In our courses on communication ethics, we have often found that students seem most comfortable with this perspective. The criterion of what is best for the greatest number seems pragmatic and avoids, or seems to avoid, a lot of hairsplitting. But, the upshot is that often they make an assumption that whatever is best for the organization represents the *greatest number.*

Take the case of the company wanting to relocate one of its many manufacturing plants offshore. Most of the current employees of that particular plant will not be able to go along. The communication issue is as follows: if management informs all employees about the plan to close down the operation in, say, six months, what will the effect be? There could be a precipitate drop in the productivity of that one plant as many employees focus on finding other jobs, or they do only a half-hearted job while still at the plant. Do the interests of all those in the corporation as a whole trump the interests of the local plant workers? Many students respond, yes. The greatest good for the greatest number is achieved by withholding communication from the local workers, according to this position.

Many contemporary utilitarians, such as Peter Singer, would point out that this seemingly obvious solution misses the main thrust of a utilitarian perspective. For a utilitarian, the greatest good must take account of everyone who might in some way be affected. The ethical path is the one that increases the total happiness of everyone, not just the members of the larger corporation. Therefore, one should take account of the likely effects on the broader community, on the economic interests of the region and even the nation at large, and on the country to which the plant is relocating. What if the new location is in a country with lower environmental protection and health and welfare regulations? Will the workers and the citizens of that country be better or worse off as a result of the plant relocation? It is hard to say, but a utilitarian calculus requires taking those considerations into account.

The decision on relocation, in this example, needs a full airing, a utilitarian analysis seems to suggest. In that regard, the approach seems similar to what a Rawlsian or Habermasian analysis might suggest as well. Interestingly, we also seem to come close to the kind of ethical analysis in line with critical theory and postmodernism. Who are the greater number to be benefited (just the organizational members? other stakeholders?)? Should organizational ethics be based on what is best for the *organization*? How can we tell that in the short and long run?

CASE STUDY: GOOD BUSINESS OR BRIBERY?

Janet Smith was a young rising star in overseas investment and development operations for a Miami-based corporation in the communications industry. Janet had graduated near the top of her class from undergraduate school and at the top of her MBA class only five years earlier. She was naturally thrilled to have reached such a position so soon in her career.

The company was beginning a major effort at expanding into overseas markets, especially in what in the business were known as the *transition economies*. A *transition economy* is one, such as in Russia or China as well as in parts of the so-called *developing world*, that is undergoing a change from a more managed economy to one characterized by free-market or capitalist practices. Janet, in her position coordinating her firm's investment activities in Russia and China, became aware of what she believed to be questionable practices. In these countries, where the company was trying to gain a foothold competing with already established transnational firms, it was customary for local officials, who controlled permits and enforcement of regulations, to receive some sorts of *considerations* to facilitate their cooperation. Janet saw financial reports indicating that her company had made arrangements with foreign-based companies and agents to help with such considerations. In addition, these officials and other government representatives expected to receive kickbacks from the awarding of construction contracts as well.

Janet knew from her recent studies that her company fell under the Foreign Corrupt Practices Act, passed in the 1980s, prohibiting bribery to gain foreign business. She might have also been aware, however, that many transnational firms found ways around the act, through the use of indirect partners of the sort she suspected in this case. A report in the *World Bank Transition Newsletter* in 2000, for example, includes the following conclusion: "Yet it is suggestive that FDI [foreign direct investment] originating in the United States—which has been governed by the Foreign Corrupt Practices Act for more than 20 years—does not appear to be characterized by higher standards of corporate ethics than domestic firms or FDI originating in other countries."[47]

When Janet expressed her concerns to her boss in her division, he discounted them. "Don't worry," he said, "all our competitors are doing this, and we have to go along to get along." He continued, "Our responsibility to the division and the company is to 'look the other way' on this one. A lot of money is at stake." When she pressed her ethical concerns, however, with other executives, the consensus was that when she had more experience, she would know that this was how the game was played.

Janet felt her company was violating its basic commitment, contained in its own ethical standards and core values statements, to ethical business practices. She felt her only recourse was to *go public*, but doing so would risk, in fact probably end, her current job and career. What should she do? Does the greatest good in this case require her *looking the other way*?

QUESTIONS FOR ANALYSIS OF THE CASE

1. Is whistle-blowing ethical in this situation? What considerations argue for and against Janet's going public in this instance? What are the facts in the case? What values (personal and corporate) are relevant?

2. Does a utilitarian approach to ethics provide appropriate guidance for Janet in this case? What path allows for the greatest good for the greatest number here? Can one argue that the benefits of the new economy for the people of the countries involved override her ethical qualms?

3. Is Janet trying to apply her own ethical standards in a situation in which the cultures of the other nations call for a different standard? If so, what are the cultural implications of the United States having a law such as the Foreign Corrupt Practices Act? Does such legislation impose American ethical beliefs on other cultures and put American companies at an inappropriate disadvantage?

4. Would considerations from dialogical ethics suggest any helpful route for Janet to follow? How could a dialogical situation be created in this case? Is there any direction to be found by considering the views of Rawls or Habermas?

Chapter Summary

Organizational communication is a growing and important branch in the study of human communication. Our lives are based in and even dominated by all kinds of organizations, making their roles in our lives significant and complex. We note that organizations are often considered to be moral agents, as if they were people or citizens. Hence, we can talk about the ethical responsibilities of organizations in their communication practices. The study of organizational communication has tended to fall under one of three theoretical perspectives: functionalist, interpretivist, and critical.

In considering the ethics of organizational communication, we have looked at three relationships and related ethical impacts:

- The impact of the organization on its community and society;
- The impact of the organization on its members; and
- The impact of members on the organization.

Each type of relationship raises important issues of communication ethics.

Under the impact of the organization on society, issues include questions about the corporate social responsibility of an organization. Special issues include how the organization ethically communicates about risks to public health and safety and responsibilities for financial reporting and business practices.

Under the impact on members, we looked at several ways an organization's communication can significantly affect members. First, we noted that organizations have special obligations to communicate about business plans and financial health that can affect employees' lives, such as plant closings, relocation, default on pension obligations, and the like. Second, they are obligated to be clear about an individual's performance and prospective future. In addition, organizations need to consider how they will communicate with members about health and safety, including risks from workplace violence. New technologies of monitoring (hidden recording devices, electronic eavesdropping, health screening) raise ethical concerns. What is to be done with this type of information? When is it too intrusive? We looked at the act of whistle-blowing from two vantage points—the obligations of organizations to members who might become whistle-blowers and, under the third relationship, the ethics of whistle-blowing itself. We concluded this section by looking at the ethics of providing for workplace democracy and in regard to quality of life as well as ethical communication concerning diversity in the organization.

We then took up a brief discussion of how different ethical theories and perspectives could be brought to bear on the sorts of ethical issues raised in the study of organizational communication. Throughout the book we have held up dialogical ethics as a foundational approach for analyzing communication ethics. The concept of emotional intelligence, or EQ, which stresses the effects of *authentic presence* in leadership or managerial communication may be useful for this analysis, we suggest. We also looked at the relevance of analyses based on the theories of Rawls and Habermas, especially in regard to the idea that all stakeholders be allowed a role in the discussion of organizational problems and decisions. Lastly, we considered the often-used approach of utilitarianism and the test of the greatest good for the greatest number. We raise the question whether utilitarian criteria are not often misused in considering business as well as organizational ethics.

QUESTIONS AND TOPICS FOR DISCUSSION

1. Discuss the various ways that organizations impact our everyday lives. How do we feel we are treated by large, complex organizations with which we deal? Are most large organizations fully ethical in their communication with the public? With their members?

2. What communication problems have we encountered within our own organizations (organizations to which we belong)? How many of these problems exhibit an ethical dimension?

3. Is ethics always applicable in business organizations and settings? Should organizations have their own sets of ethics that recognize that business should be treated differently?

4. Can individuals be held personally accountable for communications from the *organization*? How much collective responsibility do members have for the messages from the organization that are misleading or false?

5. Research several businesses or corporations: how many have written codes of ethics or credos, like Johnson & Johnson? In discussing these written codes, do you see similarities of patterns? What values of communication and ethics of communication are implied by these codes?

NOTES

1. Karl Weick has probably been most influential in supporting this view; see Karl Weick, *The Social Psychology of Organizing*, 2nd ed. (Reading, MA: Addison-Wesley, 1979).

2. William W. Neher, *Organizational Communication: Challenges of Change, Diversity, and Continuity* (Boston: Allyn & Bacon,1997), p. 18.

3. Most notable in developing this line of analysis have been Stanley A. Deetz, *Democracy in an Age of Corporate Colonization* (Albany, NY: State University of New York Press, 1992), and Dennis K. Mumby, *Communication and Power in Organizations: Discourse, Ideology and Domination* (Norwood, NJ: Ablex Publishing Corp., 1994).

4. Ronald R. Sims, *Ethics and Corporate Social Responsibility* (Westport, CN: Praeger, 2003), p. 48.

5. Patricia Hayes Andrews and Richard T. Herschel, *Organizational Communication: Empowerment in a Technological Society* (Boston: Houghton-Mifflin, 1996), p. 318.

6. Robert Phillips, *Stakeholder Theory and Organizational Ethics* (San Francisco: Berrett-Koehler Publishers, 2003), p. 3.

7. Sims, *Ethics and Corporate Social Responsibility*, p. 41.

8. John A. Byrne, Michael Arndt, Wendy Zellner, and Mike McNamee, "Restoring Trust in Corporate America," *Business Week*, June 24, 2002.

9. Johnson & Johnson, "Our *Credo*," at www.acjournal.org/holdings/vol5/iss1/special/seeger.htm (accessed May 26, 2005).

10. Johnson & Johnson, "Our *Credo*."

11. Sims, *Ethics and Corporate Social Responsibility*, p. 74.

12. Sims, *Ethics and Corporate Social Responsibility*, p. 20.

13. Andrew W. Singer, "In Breast Implants Scandal, Where Was Dow Corning's Concern for Women?" *Ethikos and Corporate Conduct Quarterly*, at www.singerpubs.com/ethikos/index.htm (accessed May 27, 2005).

14. *The Indianapolis Star*, May 24, 2005, p. A1.

15. Jeffrey Siglin, "A Company Credo, as Applied or Not," *New York Times*, July 15, 2001.

16. See the site at www.aicpa.org/about/index.htm.

17. Amey Stone, "Putting Teeth in Ethics Codes," *Business Week Online*, February 19, 2004.

18. Sims, *Ethics and Corporate Social Responsibility*, p. 7

19. Johnson & Johnson, "Our *Credo*."

20. Institute for Criminal Justice Education, Inc. (ICJE), www.icje.org/id105.htm, (accessed May 21, 2005).

21. Institute for Criminal Justice Education, Inc. (ICJE), www.icje.org/id105.htm, (accessed May 21, 2005); and see U.S. Department of Justice, Bureau of Crime Statistics, *Workplace Violence, 1992–96*; at www.ojp.usdoj.gov/bjs/abstract/wv96.htm.

22. *The Wall Street Journal*, March 7, 2000, p. A1.

23. Hall, Render, Killian, Heath & Lyman, PSC, attorneys-at-law, company leaflet, "Employment Law Briefing," n.d.

24. *The Wall Street Journal*, May 18, 2005, p. B1.

25. *The Wall Street Journal*, March 7, 2000, p. A16.

26. *The Wall Street Journal*, June 6, 2005, p. B1.

27. Janet Wiscomb, "Don't Fear Whistle-blowers," *Workforce*, 2002, pp. 27–28.

28. www.osha.gov/dep/oia/whistleblower/ (accessed May 30, 2005).

29. George Cheney, "Democracy in the Workplace: Theory and Practice from the Perspective of Communication", *Journal of Applied Communication*, 23 (1995): 168.

30. See Mumby, *Communication and Power in Organizations*, p. 67.

31. Gareth Morgan, *Images of Organization*, 2nd ed.(Thousand Oaks, CA: Sage Publications, 1997).

32. See George Cheney, Lars Thorger Christensen, Theodore E. Zorn, Jr., and Shiv Ganesh, *Organizational Communication in an Age of Globalization* (Long Grove, IL: Waveland Press, 2004), pp. 211–215.

33. *The Wall Street Journal*, June 7, 2005, p. B2.

34. *The Human Rights Campaign* Web Site, at, www.hrc.org/Template.cfm?Section=Press_Room&CONTENTID=27229&TEMPLATE=/ContentManagement/ContentDisplay.cfm (accessed June 7, 2005).

35. *New York Times*, August 1, 1993, p. F3.

36. *Time Magazine*, December 22, 2002.

37. *Time Magazine*, "Person of the Week: 'Enron Whistleblower" Sherron Watkins'," at www.time.com/time/pow/printout/0,8816.194927,00.html (accessed June 9, 2003).

38. *New York Times*, June 6, 2004, at www.nytimes.com/2004 (accessed June 10, 2004).

39. Mike W. Martin, *Meaningful Work: Rethinking Professional Ethics* (Oxford: Oxford University Press, 2000), pp. 139–140.

40. Washingtonpost.com, "Contemporaries Have Mixed Views," June 1, 2005, accessed at www.washingtopost.com/wp-dyn/content/article/2005/31/2005.

41. *New York Times*, June 1, 2005, p. A16.

42. Daniel J. Montgomery and Peter A. DeCaro, "Organizational Communication Ethics: The Radical Perspective of Performance Management", *American Communication Journal*, 5, no. 1 (2001), online at http:// acjournal.org/holdings/vol5/iss1/special/decaro.htm.

43. David Callahan, *The Cheating Culture* (Orlando: Harvest Books, 2004).

44. Anita L. Allen, *The New Ethics* (New York: Miramax Books, 2004).

45. Robert K. Cooper and Ayman Sawaf, *Executive EQ: Emotional Intelligence in Leadership and Organizations* (New York: Berkeley Publishing Group, 1996).

46. Phillips, *Stakeholder Theory*.

47. Joel Hellman, Geraint Jones, and Daniel Kaufman, Are Foreign Investors and Multinationals Engaging in Corrupt Practices in Transition Economies? *World Bank Transition Newsletter*, 11 (2000): 3–4, at www.globalpolicy.org/socecon/tncs/2000/kickback.htm (accessed June 10, 2005).

13 Ethics and Communication Technology

CHAPTER OUTLINE

As we begin the discussion of ethics and communication technology, it might be wise to lay out the scope of what we are discussing. For this chapter, we understand communication technology to mean *computer mediated communication* (or simply CMC), which includes the Internet, email, chat, Instant Messaging, blogs, and web posting. This discussion also covers the use of cell phone features such as picture mail, voice mail, and video mail. *Communication technology* includes any means by which we communicate with one or more people who may not be physically present to us.

It is possible (and even likely) that the reader of this chapter will say, "Ha! They didn't even mention the newest (fill in the blank) technology."

Chances are, this new technology was developed and marketed during the time between this writing and the publication of the book. The evolution of communication technology is occurring that fast.

And that is part of the reason we are writing this chapter.

The Changing Face of Communication and Technology

There are special challenges to studying communication ethics and technology. More than almost any other issue covered so far in this book, technology is changing and evolving daily. Today's *hot* technology to enhance communication will be tomorrow's *yesterday's news*. Do you enjoy email on the computer? Now you can email on a handheld portable device without a desktop or laptop computer in sight. Even that *advanced* technology may be a dinosaur next year, as new devices are introduced. No sooner did we buy that camera phone than the videophone was on the market. In fact, many readers of this book can remember when computers were the size of Volkswagens and mail was carried by the Postal Service instead of through cyberspace. Telephones were hard-wired with rotary dials rather than wireless devices of the size of credit cards. Instant communication was conducted either in person or by telephone and the concept of *Instant Messaging* another person anywhere in the world was the stuff of which futuristic fantasies were made.

Technological advances in communication have made it easier for us to access instantly and simultaneously many people anyplace on the planet. Digital technology has made our communication easier, our voices clearer, and our feedback instantaneous. Great libraries, pictures of historical artifacts, medical research, and, some would say, even the human mind can be accessed and downloaded with a simple command. This is the age of instant communication and access. We have made *Google* a verb as we continue to expand our knowledge and to sate our appetites for more information. We have heard more than once that students have spent so much time *keyboarding* that they actually do not know how to write long-hand anymore. If we do not feel like actually talking to someone, we may *text* them instead.

Communication technology is constantly morphing, constantly revising itself and always aiming to make communication faster, clearer, and accessible to more people. Communication technology makes it easier to communicate by allowing us to employ multiple devices in order to communicate with others. Communication technology allows us to join virtual chat rooms and contribute to the strands of conversation however we wish, or to simply sit and watch as others *talk* to each other on their computer keyboards. It is now possible to transmit our thoughts into the next cubicle or the next continent with the touch of a *send* button, and to wait for the response that often comes within a few minutes. And, if that technology is too slow and cumbersome (and for many, it is), we can *Instant Message* one or dozens of people in virtual *conversations*—changing audiences by simply touching our *reply* button. We can *blog* if we choose, or we can post our thoughts on virtual bulletin boards where anyone who has access can read and respond. Communication technology has indeed changed the ways we talk, write, and interact with one another.

But has technology enhanced our ability to communicate ethically? Not necessarily, and in this chapter we will discuss some of the ethical issues that arise from the rapid and constantly evolving field of communication technology. We do not yearn for the days of the typewriter, mimeograph, or the mainframe computer, and both of us own and enjoy many of the latest communication technology *toys* that both enhance and sometimes confound our communication capabilities. We do, however, believe that as it becomes easier to use technology to communicate, it becomes more difficult to be *present* to the person or people with whom we are communicating.

To illustrate this contention we will look at a few of the more common uses of communication technology, raising communication ethics issues with each. We will more closely examine core ethical issues such as trust and safety as they relate to communication technology. We will revisit some of the ethical principles covered earlier in this book as the base for our position. A case study will be offered for your consideration as we explore ways that communication technology and communication ethics can collide. As always, we will raise questions that we hope will stimulate you to think through these interesting and provocative ethical issues.

The *global village* is now hot-wired, and we can extend our communication almost anywhere. In an instant we can learn how our communication was received. We are *connected* like never before, and the world is our receiver.

The Internet and Web-Based Communication: The World As Audience

It was not all that long ago that when we wished to send a message, we could only send it to one designated place or recipient. One stamp. One envelope. One address. If there were more than one intended recipient we would need to send that number of letters. We hoped the message would arrive in a few days, sometimes a week, and then the wait would begin for the response. We would anxiously wait for the mail carrier each day, and check the mailbox regularly in anticipation. To send that message to a friend in Ghana or Stockholm meant we would wait even longer for the reply—sometimes weeks. Sometimes the wait would be agonizing, as the song performed by The Marvellettes in 1961 illustrates:

> *Please Mr. Postman look and see*
> *If there's a letter in your bag for me.*
> *Why's it taking such a long time*
> *For me to hear from that boy of mine?*

Perhaps if the slow-to-respond boyfriend has simply emailed or Instant Messaged, she would have been spared the anguish of waiting for Mr. Postman. It might not have been good news on her screen, but it would have been quick news.

Today we can send that message to as many people as we wish and even check that the message was received. Ghana or Stockholm, it wouldn't matter—they would get our message at the same time. And if rain, sleet, or snow keeps our mail carrier from her appointed rounds the next morning, so what? Our replies would be in our Inbox when we access our email.

One of the most significant advances in the evolution of communication technology is that the sender can now encode and transmit a message to as many people as she chooses. Once transmitted, however, control over that communication is lost. Once that loss of control occurs, a potential ethical issue arises. Unlike face-to-face communication, we do not always know if the right person has received the message or how the message was interpreted. The more people who have access to the message, the less any one person might control it. With the world as audience, there is little or no confidentiality or safety in sending it. One's friend in Stockholm, for instance, can with a touch of the *forward* button relay that message to her friend in Madrid—and the sender may have intentionally *not* sent the message to Madrid for reasons of his own. There are times in communication when an unlimited audience with unimpeded access to one's communication is not a good thing. Losing control of one's communication causes him to mismanage his ability to be *present* to others, and allows interlopers to assume the role of unintended *Other* (per Levinas) in his communication. The issue of control of communication and its destination and interpretation is a key one, and we will continue the discussion as the chapter unfolds.

Instant Access and Feedback

We are hooked on speed. We have computers in our homes and offices that provide us with centuries of wisdom and intellectual growth at the command of a keyboard. And, more importantly, we want that information NOW. Not in an hour. Now. Our hunger for faster computers and increased bandwidth have caused us to throw away our old 386 processors and buy newer machines with more bells and whistles to move faster and faster down the Information Highway. As we gain information and communicate with ever-increasing speed, however, we run the risk of overlooking some of the ethical issues in our communication. Joel Rudinow and Anthony Graybosch, both Professors of Philosophy, write:

> Due to the inherent nature of the Internet, including its many-to-many mode of communication, its immediacy, and its anonymity, the world's population can potentially have access to any and all forms of information, regardless of where or when it was released, or regardless of its subject.[1]

If we are in such a hurry to access information, or to communicate with others, how can we make ethical judgments about the messages or the people who are responsible for them? Consider the legal as well as ethical issues of downloading songs or first-run movies onto our personal computers. We now have instant access to nearly every song ever recorded, and *pirated* files just wait for our download command preceding the release of many new *blockbuster* films. Is it ethical for us to download that new song we really like without paying for it? The song is right there online, we have the software to download it, and its not like the artist is being hurt by one simple download, is it?

And what about plagiarism? Technology affords us instant access here as well. If your friend on the other coast needs a quick term paper, because someone in his family was ill and he didn't have time to research and write his own, what's wrong with you allowing him to download your paper you wrote last semester in your Economics class? After all, it is your paper and you can do what you want with it, right? Are you really not being ethical by allowing him to claim it as his own? As with any matter of communication ethics, the use of (or refusing to use) technology to give us an unfair advantage is a matter of making what we believe is the right decision.

As students of communication ethics, we must consider the reasons by which we make decisions about these matters in our communication. Simply because we have instant access and feedback available to us, we are not necessarily justified in making use of it.

Possibly communication technology is advancing far more rapidly than reasoned ethical thought can keep up. It is not clear that there is a widely accepted theory of communication ethics applicable to technology, and it is difficult for anyone to establish an ethical theory for communicating in cyberspace. From porn to politics to pop-ups, there seems to be a *Wild West* flavor to the Net in that there is no ethical *sheriff* in town. Unethical communicators ride rampant through the streets of town with no ethical *laws* to govern their communication. Anonymity in communicating through technology empowers the communicator to speak freely, and sometimes without civility. If the communicator is confronted, he or she can merely delete or shut down the communication from the confronter.

In her article, "Norm Origin and Development in Cyberspace: Models of Cybernorm Evolution," April Mara Major writes:

> The element of non-confrontational discussion (meaning that the participants are not face-to-face) coupled with the asynchronistic communication style of these services, allow users a layer of anonymity not found in the non-digital world and leads to more honest and less civil interactions.[2]

It is the condition of online anonymity that often restricts ethical and genuine communication. Like many other forms of communication there are no assurances that any other person is communicating ethically with us. Even in one of the most commonly used modes of communication via technology—email—one has no guarantees that the communication he is reading is genuine.

Email @ Communication Ethics

When we discuss *email ethics*, we are discussing mutually agreed on norms governing the use of the communication media. We attempt to agree on ways to treat one another in our communication. Politeness and civility in our emails are positive communication guidelines, as are the avoidance of profanity or prejudice in our writings. Like the technology itself, studies of email ethics continue to evolve at a rapid rate. Much of what we have read under the label of *ethics*, however, are more guidelines designed to make us better e-citizens as we make use of this communication technology. Insights into communication ethics remain sparse in much of the literature and research.

Most of the people who own or work with computers use email, and we use it for much of our communication in academia, business, and commerce. This electronic communication has made our lives easier and our communication faster. However, as anyone who has used email has discovered, there are inherent problems and dangers involved in this electronic mail system:

- We send or receive by accident messages intended for other recipients.
- We forget that anything we put into an email is fair game for those who would eavesdrop on our private communications.
- Hastily conceived communication written down and sent without deep thought remains in permanent archives somewhere in cyberspace.
- Gossip and rumor don't pass over the backyard fence as they did a generation ago; they become a written and permanent record available for recall anytime in the future.

- Can we ever be certain that our email to a friend while at work is not being archived for review by our boss?
- And since email can be written and sent under false addresses, can we ever be sure the person who appears on the *from* line is really the one who composed and sent the message?

The problem with communicating via email—despite all its speediness and convenience—is that we are never genuinely *present* to the other person, nor are they for us. It is at this critical point that a true examination of communication ethics begins. We will use the theoretical lens of *dialogical ethics* (Chapter 5) to analyze the ethical issues of communication via email. Remember from our earlier discussion of dialogical ethics that the ability and willingness to be fully *present* to the other is crucial for an evaluation of the ethics of our communication.

In conversing through email, or any other electronic form of communication, we are at best a *virtual presence* to the other. In dialogical ethics, true *presence* happens when two people are mutually sharing ideas, hearing and observing the other, and feeding back their responses. We, the authors of this text, have not only researched but also share a common journey through the terrain of communication ethics. We discuss this journey almost every day. As we discuss the development and progress of this book, we are able to see each other's face as we react to ideas, concepts, changes, and shared frustrations and joys over the course of our work. As such, we are *present* to the other for ideas, consolation, support, and encouragement. During those times when we have been forced to email each other about the text, we experienced each other's thoughts and ideas, but the *presence* was missing.

We can be *present* to those we email, at least after a fashion, but that *presence* is more remote and virtual. We can see each other's words, and even make guesses as to feelings or mood when we wrote it. Have you ever had someone say to you that you *sounded* mad in your email? Have you ever considered the communication *disconnect* in such feedback? It happens because we must interpret the virtual *presence* of the other person, rather than observe and react to it as we would if the communication happened in person. "Face and discourse are tied," wrote Emmanuel Levinas. "The face speaks, it is in this that it renders possible and begins all discourse . . . it is discourse, and, more exactly, response or responsibility which is this authentic relationship."[3]

It is in this responsible discourse that the foundations of dialogical communication ethics are found. Not so in electronic communication. When you send a person a message via email, or text messaging, or video messaging, he may not be responsible to you at all. He can choose not to open your email until next week if he desires. Or, he can ignore it altogether. He can even choose to forward it to another friend with the message, "Can you believe what she wrote?" You won't know what he does with your communication because he is *present* to you only to the extent he chooses.

The debate about ethical communication via email continues, and discussion about how we should conduct ourselves when writing electronic communication constantly evolves. We will continue to make use of email because it is so convenient and fast. But we would be making a mistake to think that our email communication is secure or private. It has gone so far as to have some email providers encrypt every email that is sent and decrypt received messages. But the old adage that says "Build a better mousetrap and someone will create an even better mouse" rings true. The cycle of creating impenetrable email protocols while someone else is figuring how to break them appears to be an ongoing struggle. It's not just our emails that are vulnerable to invasion and lack of security. Our cell phone text messages are just as nonsecure.

Let us close this section by emphasizing that we are discussing more than what has been called *netiquette* here. Showing true respect and acceptance for the other person in dialogue is an ethical imperative for one who practices dialogical communication. Respectful and honest communication in email is more than *nice*, it represents ethical communication.

Text Messaging

When you want to use your phone to communicate but don't want to or can't talk on the phone because of the situation, you are likely to use text messaging. Functioning like minicomputers, most cell phones will allow people to *talk* silently with one another by typing, rather than speaking, into their cell phone. It is a hybrid of email and Instant Messenger for the cell phone. Messages arrive silently, and can be sent in silence as well, without people around knowing we are communicating with someone. It is a great way to communicate when we don't want to interrupt people around us, plus it saves us from being charged for a voice call on the phone.

On the other hand, unique among communication technological devices, text messaging is sometimes indicted as the method of choice for one of the most cardinal violations of communication ethics: cheating. In an online article entitled "Text-a-Friend: The High-Tech Approach to Cheating," we discover the following information:

> On December 10, 182 students in South Korea were indicted for using text-messaging to cheat on national college entrance exams, and in January 2003, six students at the University of Maryland admitted to doing the same thing. Because it is a relatively new phenomenon, text-messaging cheating goes unnoticed by unsuspecting teachers, making it especially appealing to students.[4]

As with email and every other form of electronic communication, the technology itself is ethically neutral—it is simply technology. Communicating ethically is determined by the ways we opt to use the technology. And, like many other forms of communication technology, our communication is neither private nor secure. If we can write a text message, someone can *hack* it and monitor the entire communication process. With any development in technology, the intended communication can be used either ethically or unethically. One can freely express a political viewpoint to a friend or colleague through a text message to her phone. But lest he thinks his expressed opinion is private and confidential, consider a recent development in China:

> The Chinese government has approved a company's bid to sell technology that allows text messages sent by mobile phones to be monitored, raising fears that authorities are stepping up efforts to further clamp down on free expression, say Reporters Without Borders . . . Text messaging is hugely popular in China, where the mobile phone market is the largest in the world. Last year, Chinese people sent more than 220 billion text messages – more than half of all text messages sent around the world, reports the BBC.[5]

If communication takes place in an environment in which participants cannot be sure of trust, confidentiality, mutual presence, and support for the well-being of each other, there can be no way of judging the ethics of that communication. If trust is not established, how can one make the claim that we are communicating ethically? Of course, this is true of any form of communication, mediated or not, but it seems to be more of an issue given the nature of CMC, such as email or texting.

Personal Web Logs (Blogs)

A very popular and informative mode of communication technology today is blogs. Recall our earlier discussion (Chapter 12) of political blogs. Communication technology has provided the capability to publicly *post* one's opinions and ideas and to read strands of others' postings as well. We can create *blogs*—web logs—that serve as public diaries to *stream* or broadcast our thoughts and ideas, and receive thoughts and ideas from others. From the comforts of our own homes, we can read firsthand accounts of a young person describing the fears and anxieties of living in Iraq or Afghanistan. We can read and participate in electronic *bulletin boards*, which feature strands of opinions and ideas about any subject imaginable. Communication technology has opened the world to us. We can with the stroke of a key on our keyboard *communicate* in myriad formats on countless topics with countless numbers of people.

But can we consider the communication we are receiving trustworthy? Do we really *know* that the person writing a chilling account of surviving a killer tsunami is really who she says she is? Technology has indeed made it possible to communicate instantly with limitless numbers of people, but how much trust should we place on the truthfulness of our fellow communicators? The imposition of the new technologies has made it more difficult to check our sources. We can assume, at least to an extent, that there are editors and editorial boards ensuring some checking of facts for print and broadcast media. We have no such assurances for a privately produced blogs and bulletin boards.

Jacques Ellul, a French lay theologian noted for his views of the potential and dangers of technology, includes this fascinating story in 1967 in his book, *The Technological Society*:

> In 1960 the weekly *l'Express* of Paris published a series of extracts from texts by American and Russian scientists concerning society in the year 2000 . . . Now we have works from Nobel Prize winners, members of the Academy of Sciences of Moscow, and other scientific notables whose qualifications are beyond dispute . . . By the year 2000, voyages to the moon will be commonplace; so will inhabited artificial satellites. All food will be completely synthetic . . . Disease, as well as famine, will have been eliminated . . . the problems of energy production will have been completely resolved. Serious scientists, it must be repeated, are the source of these predictions . . . Knowledge will be accumulated in 'electronic banks' . . . there will no longer be any need of reading or learning mountains of useless information; everything will be received and registered according to the needs of the moment. There will be no need of attention or effort. What I needed will pass directly from the machine to the brain without going through consciousness.[6]

The greatest minds of 1967 didn't get it at all correct, which is usually the case with prognostication. However, Ellul's final few lines warrant consideration for communication ethicists. As we become *wowed* by the advancements in technology, and enamored by the gadgets and toys we are able to use, we run the risk of becoming *numb* to the ethical considerations that accompany communication through technology. It was Ellul's considered opinion that mass communication was void of ethics and equally as dangerous.

Marshall McLuhan, author of groundbreaking books dealing with culture and technology in the 1960s, follows a similar theme as Ellul when he writes, " . . . the age of anxiety and of electric media is also the age of the unconscious and of apathy."[7]

In order to bring the ethical issues into consciousness, while at the same time allowing ourselves to be *wowed* by the latest communication technology, we will explore some of the major ethical issues in communication technology. Specifically, we will examine the issues of trust and safety as we surf the next section.

Major Ethical Issues in Communication Technology

There are several major ethical issues worthy of consideration. One of those issues is the potential use of communication technology for deception. As we have discussed (and will see in our case study) it is just as easy to deceive someone as it is to be genuine when using technology. Another issue we will discuss is impersonality, a result of communicating distantly and electronically. We are saying that the use of mediated communication technologies exacerbate these tendencies, making them increasingly salient for CMC.

Any discussion of communication technology must take into account a presence, or lack of a presence, of the Other (as discussed in Chapter 5.) As we have emphasized so far, technology gives us the opportunity and means to communicate with people we have never seen in places we have never been. And, as our range of communication steadily increases, the opportunity for face-to-face contact can become proportionately more remote. We may use email and chat rooms and Instant Messenger to converse with countless numbers of people, but the contact with the Other tends to be impersonal and remote. The danger is that individualized or personalized communication has been reduced to an ethically neutral distance to the point where we cannot know, let alone accept, the *Otherness* of the people with whom we are communicating.

Control of the Communication Occasion

Technology can allow a person to *spoof* any other person's email address, so that while it appears that a message is from you, and is in fact from your email address with your name on it, it may in fact come from a third party intent on mischief or deception. In chat rooms or in Instant Messenger, I can portray myself as anybody I think you want me to be. I can change my gender, age, race, or location, if I choose. I will likely use an *alias* and unless you know me personally when we talk online, I can reveal myself to be entirely different from whom I really am. For all its benefits of speed, accessibility, convenience, and broad reach, technology also tempts us to maintain distant and indirect relationships with those with whom we communicate. The Other cannot see or experience our reactions; we can only type out what we are feeling. We can type LOL, or insert a smiley face, or a gloomy face to indicate sadness. We are insulated from vulnerability and surprise, and while we may share time with people online, we do not share space.

Trust and Safety: What can We Reasonably Expect?

It can be misleading when people talk about how technology *frees* them to communicate more immediately and broadly. With the hit of a *reply* button, and a few lines of text, we have responded to someone's communication. Many of us know people who were brought together because they met in a chat room or on another online venue and who then created happy relationships. We email, chat, text each other, IM regularly, and otherwise avail ourselves every day of the technology that allows us to stay in touch. But, while almost everyone we know uses communication technology, we are not necessarily engaged in dialogical communication when online. "Technology that allows action at a distance," writes Amit Pinchevski in the *Southern Communication Journal*, "presents a problem for ethics insofar as it may compromise the immediacy of human interaction and the ways it is articulated—contact, effect, proximity, and response-ability accompanying an encounter with an Other."[8]

To be fair, many users of chat rooms, for example, strongly feel that they have become a part of a genuine community online. People spending hours every day in such communities establish societal rules, provide for self-regulation, care for each other, support one another, and act as socio-emotional support groups for one another. Many people, often teenagers, now eschew phone conversation and use the cell phone to text one another. They describe a sense of privacy and intimacy when only they and the person on the other phone know what has been *said* in text. But is this sense of community and relationship indicative of a community supportive of ethical communication? It is an issue well worth discussing as such communication technology becomes more sophisticated and available worldwide.

Is there any Safe Communication Online?

We can safely say that if we can not verify that what we read online, or in our email inbox, or in chat rooms really comes from the person we think it's coming from, how can we trust the content of the communication? Recalling the section on Emmanuel Levinas in Chapter 5, if the Other presents no *Face*, how can we be fully present in our communication with him or her? In fact, if we are communicating with *virtual Others*, how can we judge his or her response to us if we are communicating from a distance? As we learned about interpersonal communication in Chapter 7, ethical dialogical communication depends on mutual control of the interaction and each person's presence to the other. When a person is with you, communication is immediate and subject to surprise. In dialogue, you see him as he is. He can surprise you with a smile, or a tear, or a folding of his arms as you speak. When you both speak face to face, there is no *delete* button, nor can he pretend you are not there. Control is mutual. Both of you engage and are engaged. There is no mediation of the communication. In Levinas' terms, the *Face* is met and honored. The ethics of managing *presence* are engaged.

In email, or in chat, or in text messaging the locus of control changes and the ethical issues change as well. One can screen the messages you send him electronically. He can delete them, and you would not even be aware of it. He can forward your email to a dozen people and you would not be completely unaware. He can block you, delete you, ignore you, and pretend he never noticed you. And all the while, you can be doing the same with him, and three others with whom you are communicating at the same time. Unlike face-to-face dialogue, it is the *Interface*—not the Face—that is met when communicating through technology. The ethics of managing *distance* and not *presence* are engaged.

Although technology continues to evolve rapidly, technology itself will probably remain ethically neutral. Despite Ellul's predictions forty years ago, communication technology has not yet been hardwired into human conscience (at least, not that we are aware of—the idea of implanting smart chips into individual bodies has been considered). Technology itself is mathematically programmed, wired, and housed in cases, machines, and devices. One school of thought maintains we are the agents of action, and not until a human decision is made does the technology engage to carry out that action. Like firearms or automobiles, communication technology requires human interface. It is still human beings who choose to communicate ethically or unethically with others, while the technology merely carries the message. On the other hand, there are adherents to the theory of technological determinism (such as McLuhan, mentioned earlier, to a certain extent). The very possibilities opened up by a new technology can shape some of those decisions—or at least make us aware of decisions we did not know we could make (such as deceiving you about one's email source online).

Should We Expect Privacy with Technology?   The question of trust and safety of our communication through technology will continue to be an issue for ethicists. One *can* communicate ethically in email, in chat, in text, or in any kind of Internet medium. He can be honest at all times, read carefully everything you write, and try to be respectful of you when you *meet* online. And, he may trust that you are treating him the same way. But does this mean that this still-emerging universe of communication technology ensures ethical communication? No. The one impediment we cannot escape is that online communication is currently more remote and more subject to breaches of privacy than many forms of face-to-face communication.

Those who feel *liberated* at being able to express their thoughts, beliefs, fantasies, deepest values, and dreams to a trusted online companion would be wise to remember that what they write to one person becomes potentially available to millions. This is why some email providers offer *encrypting* and *decoding* technology to subscribers. The providers themselves know that nothing on the Internet is safe or confidential. Online, we are less in control of the communication process than in our ordinary interactions. And with every new person with whom we communicate, we open the door to new viruses, spoofing, spamming, or other deceptions. When that kind of environment is present, trust and integrity are difficult to establish.

The computer industry itself makes some attempt to bring a sense of ethics to the use of technology. Of course, few programmers or administrators of online domains are unethical or dishonest. Some have attempted to codify a system of ethics for users of computers. The Computer Ethics Institute, a Project of the Brookings Institution, established such a code of ethics that apply to communication technology. Being called the *Ten Commandments of Computer Ethics*, the code reads:

1. Thou shalt not use a computer to harm other people.
2. Thou shalt not interfere with other people's computer work.
3. Thou shalt not snoop around in other people's computer files.
4. Thou shalt not use a computer to steal.
5. Thou shalt not use a computer to bear false witness.
6. Thou shalt not copy or use proprietary software for which you have not paid.
7. Thou shalt not use other people's computer resources without authorization or proper compensation.
8. Thou shalt not appropriate other people's intellectual output.
9. Thou shalt think about the social consequences of the program you are writing or the system you are designing.
10. Thou shalt always use a computer in ways that insure consideration and respect for your fellow humans. [9]

Amidst the *thou shalt's* and *thou shalt not's* is a reference to consequentialism and an unmistakable appeal to the *greater good* (utilitarianism.) Yet a closer look at the *commandments* reveals more of a codification of use of technology rather than directives about communication with others. The focus, while admirable, is on technology, and not on how a person ought to communicate with another person. To examine the latter, it is necessary to once again explore the ethical issues of communication technology.

Ethical Framework and Communication Technology

Communication technology is itself *ethics neutral*. As we have discussed in this chapter, however, when we communicate via an electronic medium we understand that we do so with no assurance that all is as it seems. These media seem especially prone to temptations to mislead or deceive communicators.

As we discussed in dialogical ethics, without the *Face* (as used by Levinas) before us we have a difficult time connecting ethically with the person on the other end of our email. We can never be certain that the person with whom we are communicating in IM is really our *Thou* (Buber), or an imposter who has taken on the identity of that person. As Viktor Mayer-Schonberger writes in his contribution to *CyberEthics*:

> Who are we in cyberspace? In a classic *New Yorker* cartoon, a dog sits grinning at a computer terminal and the caption reads, 'In cyberspace, no one knows you're a dog.' The joke captures what is uniquely liberating about going online, the opportunity to be someone else, or to be multiple someone else's[10]

What may be perceived as *uniquely liberating* to some may be viewed as ethical *masking* to others. While it may be great sport for the dog in the cartoon to pretend to be someone else when talking to you online, it makes it more difficult for you to ever trust that you are engaged in ethical communication. And so we conclude communication by technology is lacking one key criterion that determines the ethics of interpersonal communication: there is no face-to-face dimension. Minus that key element, we understand that any communication online cannot be verified as interpersonally ethical.

So what conclusions can we take from a discussion of whether one can ethically communicate using technology? If it is so easy to misrepresent oneself in online conversation, or in email or chat or on a web site, why are we even having this conversation about ethics? If you can't trust anyone you *meet* online to have your best interest at heart, how can you possibly evaluate my participation in the medium as ethical?

As we think about the ever-changing, always fluid nature of communicating through technology, we discover that it is possible to communicate ethically online or in chat or IM or anywhere else in cyberspace. The trick is in claiming ethical control of one's own communication, even while accepting that others may not be so ethical in their communication with you or with anyone else.

In this claiming of personal ethical communication in the use of technology, we can view this issue through the ethical lens we discussed in Chapter 4. Specifically, we call the reader back to Scanlon and his reasonable obligation to others. Simply, what do we owe each other in our communication via technology? If we know of the possibility that others may be misrepresenting themselves online, or if we agree that we have no control over what happens to communication once it is transmitted, how then can we ourselves maintain our ethics?

The same questions can be raised in all forms of communication discussed in this book—from dialogical communication to political communication—and certainly to communication via electronic media. And the answer is the same for all: we cannot guarantee that the other person or agent engaged in communication with us is being ethical. We can trust that he or she is, but we cannot guarantee it. We can trust that our best friend sitting across the table from us is being open and honest with us. We can assume that, because we know that person and because we can see his or her face, he or she is communicating ethically with us. But of course we cannot guarantee it. Many of us have been lied to while the other person looked directly into our eyes. Determining whether communication is or is not ethical depends not on what the other person does or says, but on how we choose to communicate with the other. That is what Scanlon would claim we owe the other in our communication: our best ethical effort in communication.

The authors claim that the only way to assure ethical communication through technology—the only way to fulfill what we owe each other—is to decide that we will be ethical at all times in our communication online. We can hope that others will communicate ethically with us, but we can guarantee that we will engage others ethically even though they can't see us. The question then becomes: can we *personally* communicate ethically in our use of technology? Not because there are *Ten Commandments* telling us to do so but because we choose to engage ethically.

There are three criteria we would recommend as a *litmus test* for ethical communication in the use of technology of all kinds. All three are formed by the determination that we will be truthful in our communication everywhere on the Net or in email or in text messages. The three criteria are:

1. I personally choose to be authentic in my communication, even while realizing the possibility that others are not.
2. I will be consistent in my communication with others, recognizing that my consistency is in the long run how I will be perceived ethically.
3. I will be nonjudgmental in all my communication via technology, because I have no guarantees that I am judging a truth or a fabrication.

We will continue to enjoy the tremendous and rapid changes in communication technology. As long as we are able to remain consistent and truthful in our engagement with others online, it matters less that we have no control of the ethics of someone else's communication. The main thing to bear in mind is that we control the truth from our side of communication. Others, however, may not and that is where people can get hurt. The following case illustrates just how easily a trusting and innocent online communication by one person can turn dangerous and even deadly because of the inherent dangers of trusting completely the ethics of another person's online communication.

CASE STUDY: LET'S MEET AT THE MALL AFTER SCHOOL

Melanie was thrilled. Nothing like this had ever happened to her before and it was exciting and scary at the same time. The gangly and socially awkward fourteen-year-old would describe herself as *OK looking*, but she hated her braces, hated her zits, and even hated the sound of her own voice. Boys were starting to become interesting to her but no boy at school ever gave her a second look. Her parents' reassurances that she would one day grow into a beautiful woman used to make her feel better but now she tended to disregard those words of encouragement because they came from—after all—her parents. Melanie knew that she wasn't the only girl feeling this way, either. She routinely *talked* with girl friends on Instant Messenger or in a private chat room almost every day, sometimes even after her parents asked her to shut down her computer for the night.

One evening her friend Kristen mentioned that she had met this *awesome* guy named Travis in a chat room for teens. She explained that Travis was an *older guy* of nearly seventeen and all the girls thought he *sounded hot*. Kristen informed Melanie that she could introduce her to Travis and that maybe the three of them could *hang out together* online. Melanie saw no harm in that idea and agreed to her friend's plan.

The next evening the online connection was made and Melanie, Kristen, and Travis began regular communication in a private chat room for just the three of them. Travis was very friendly to the girls, and they all began to trust the wisdom of this older boy. It wasn't long before the talk turned to the teens' dissatisfaction with their parents and all their rules. Curfews and the need to *check in* whenever they went out, as well as *old school* thinking by their parents were topics of regular conversation. Travis explained that he had moved out of the house two months ago and now lived with his older brother in an apartment. He could come and go as he pleased, didn't have to call anyone when he was out, and could even drink if he wanted to.

One night, Travis contacted Melanie through Instant Messenger and suggested that it might be time to meet in person. He told her that he was attracted to her and that they should meet somewhere to "see what might happen," and Melanie was thrilled.

"Let's meet at the mall after school tomorrow," Travis offered. "But you probably shouldn't tell Kristen. She might get jealous that I like you more than I do her, and there's no need to hurt her." Melanie could catch a ride with Kristen and her mom, saying that her own mother was going to meet her there an hour later. Once they were alone, she and Travis could go check out his apartment, talk a while, and get to know each other better. He could drive her home before dinner and drop her off a block from her house so no one would see her or know of her deception. Melanie could tell her parents that she was going to study with a friend after school and would be home by dinner. Melanie was excited and a little confused by this escalation of the friendship but she really did think it was time to meet Travis. She already *knew* him from IM and chat, so what was the harm? The plan was set for the next afternoon.

Melanie waited in the prearranged spot in the food court for her friend to arrive. Over an hour passed, and no Travis. By now, both of Melanie's parents might be home, and how could she ever explain this situation to them? Melanie called Kristen from the mall and told her that her mother had been delayed and could not make it to the mall for another hour. Would Kristen mind asking her mom to come pick her up and take her home? Seeing a child stranded, Kristen's mom without hesitation came and got her daughter's friend. On the ride home, Melanie worked out what she thought would be a reasonable excuse for being a little late.

Melanie's parents were indeed both at home but didn't suspect a thing. Melanie would sure yell at Travis tonight for all the hassle he put her through this afternoon. No sooner had she closed the door and put her backpack down when the doorbell rang. Standing on her front porch was a man of about forty-five whom she had never seen before. She was shocked when he showed her a shield and said, "Hello Melanie. I am Detective Foster with the police department. You know me as 'Travis' but that's not my real name. Your parents are home now, and I would like to have a talk with the three of you."

For the next half hour the detective explained to Melanie's shocked and silent parents how he was able to be introduced to, gain the trust of, and eventually arrange an unsupervised meeting with their young daughter. He produced transcripts of all the online communication between the two of them as well as those Melanie had with Kristen. In fact, all of Melanie's email and online communication with and regarding Travis had been monitored and printed for her parents to see.

Detective Foster set up such an elaborate scheme, he claimed, because the department was targeting online predators of young women. He told Melanie that three times he had bumped into her while she waited at the food court. She hadn't noticed any of it. He explained that it was he who was reading the paper not ten feet away from her as she waited for Kristen's mom to pick her up. He had even discreetly slipped his business card into her purse (which she reached in and found). He knew what she looked like and where she lived because she had revealed all that information to him online. He knew what classes she took and when she got out of school. He knew her parents' work schedules and when Melanie was usually alone at home.

Melanie wasn't in trouble—at least not with the police. She had behaved as many young teens behave. She tended to trust what she read online, and *Travis* was able to smoothly break down any cautions she might normally have meeting someone in person. The detective hoped that this *sting* would make Melanie and her parents aware that the Internet was no place to trust what you saw. If a forty-five-year-old detective could be convincing as a seventeen-year-old boy, the possibilities for a predator to become whomever he wanted to become were just as good.

Detective Foster thanked them for their time and got up to go, saying he planned to visit Kristen and her parents on his way home for the night.

QUESTIONS FOR ANALYSIS OF THE CASE

1. The detective used deceptive communication through technology in order to make a point that people may be in danger of deceptive communication through technology. In your opinion, did the detective communicate ethically?

2. Was Melanie's decision to lie to Kristen and her mother about her meeting with Travis—a decision made so as to not *hurt* Kristen—ethical?

3. How do you think the conversation went in Melanie's house after the detective left?

Chapter Summary

Communicating ethically requires a commitment to the other, following the precepts of dialogical communication. It is a commitment of genuineness and honesty in the way we communicate. The odds are much more favorable (although not guaranteed) that we can judge communication as ethical or not by always monitoring how we behave in a relationship. If we can respond to what we *read* from the other (Buber, Levinas), then we have the opportunity to adjust the way we communicate to the other. But in a milieu where the *Other* may be invisible—almost ghostlike—it becomes harder to trust that ethical communication is taking place.

As we have discussed, there are no guarantees that another person is communicating ethically with us even if he or she is seated across a table from us. All we can do is provide our honest and ethical communication every time we log online or tap a text message or post a web page.

The Internet is an ever-evolving and fluid phenomenon. Technology has made it easier than ever before to communicate quickly with endless numbers of people. It allows us access to communicate with others in a magnitude not even imagined a few years ago. It also can bring us viruses and invade our privacy. It can allow someone to steal our identity or ascribe to us words we never uttered.

Communication technology is largely ethics neutral. The Internet is neither ethical nor unethical—any more than is a telephone or a television. We recognize that the very availability of such technology can suggest unethical uses that would not have occurred were that technology not available. The standard of ethical communication using technology, however, is whether we ourselves choose to be ethical in all of our communication. Every keystroke. Each text message. Every chat encounter. Every posting of an email. In an environment where we can never be certain that all is as it appears to be, perhaps we owe each other that much.

QUESTIONS AND TOPICS FOR DISCUSSION

1. Do you agree that we cannot expect communication from others on the Internet or in email or in texting always to be ethical? Do you feel there is more of a temptation to mislead or deceive others online?

2. If we believe that all may not be as it seems online, should we make the effort of being ethically consistent in our communication—should we not assume others are playing games with us and so we can play also?

3. Choose another system of communication ethics discussed in this book that deals with the issue of communicating ethically using technology? How would Kantian ethics or utilitarianism deal with these issues?

NOTES

1. Joel Rudinow and Anthony Graybosch, *Ethics and Values in the Information Age* (Thompson Wadsworth: Belmont, CA, 2002), p. 39.

2. Terry Halbert and Elaine Ingulli, *CyberEthics*, 2nd ed. (Thompson Southwestern, 2005), pp. 132–133.

3. Emmanuel Levinas, *Ethics and Infinity: Conversations With Phillipe Nemo*, trans. Richard A. Cohen (Pittsburgh: Duquesne University Press, 1985), pp. 87–88.

4. Silver Chips Online, available at http://silverchips.mbhs.edu (accessed March 7, 2005).

5. Available at the IFEX (International Freedom of Expression eXchange) web site, www.ifex.org (accessed March 7, 2005).

6. Jacques Ellul, *The Technological Society*, trans. John Wilkinson (New York: Alfred A. Knopf, 1967), p. 432.

7. Marshall McLuhan, *Understanding Media: The Extensions of Man* (New York: McGraw-Hill, 1964), p. 56.

8. Amit Pinchevski, "Ethics on the Line," *Southern Communication Journal*, 68, no. 2 (Winter 2003), p. 152.

9. Computer Ethics Institute, A Project of the Brookings Institution, available at www.brook.edu/its/cei/cei_hp.hrm (accessed March 2, 2005).

10. See Terry Halbert and Elaine Ingulli, *CyberEthics*, 2nd ed. (Thompson Southwestern, 2005), p. 248.

14 Capstone

CHAPTER OUTLINE

When we took on the challenge of writing a book on Communication Ethics we knew it would be a special opportunity. Like many of you who have opened this book, we have been both excited and confounded by the myriad issues involved in any study of communication ethics. The process of researching and organizing this book has been much like the process of felling and removing a tree from your backyard. Much of the process can be easily seen and *chopped up* into manageable sections. But when one gets to the roots—underneath the surface—things are more complex. As we tugged on one root we discovered a tangle of other roots just below the surface. The roots in communication ethics are almost always entwined with roots in philosophy, religion, politics, and so on. Along the way, we got both encouragement ("Haven't you finished that book *yet?*") and challenges ("Can you really teach ethics to students?") from friends and colleagues. While we think we have answered the first question, the second remains in play for us.

Teaching and Learning Ethics: Can It Be Done?

Both authors regularly teach a course in communication ethics at our university and consult the texts that deal specifically with ethics and communication and discuss what we think a young adult should learn during the semester. We carefully teach and explain theory and employ case studies and applications in our teaching. We try to bring *real-world* examples to class and hope for passionate and focused discussion. Some of our students quickly grasp the theories and can readily discuss the similarities and differences among them. It's when we ask them to apply these theories to the *real world* examples that the clarity and focus begin to fade.

It is not that students cannot apply theory to practice—they most certainly can. A quality education has taught them how to do that. We must add a very important fact in our teaching and learning of communication ethics: our students' understanding of the *real world* may not be their professors' understanding of it. Our experiences, worldviews, values, and goals might be quite different, and so our ethical perspectives might differ as well.

Many of our students are not far removed from the protective family umbrella that sheltered them from some harsh experience of the *real world*. Religious values, sociopolitical opinions, and ethical principles about how we treat each other were more acquired from others than achieved through hard, personal introspection. The university provides students with another umbrella. We encourage and expect inquiry and critical thinking, but offer students a *bubble* beneath which they can safely explore their own thoughts, ideas, and ethics without fear of losing a job or income.

As you begin to face the prospect of life after graduation and as the umbrella that will shelter you from the uncertainties of your *real world* will have to be one of your own making, your understanding of communicating ethically with others will grow and evolve. As you partner with another, perhaps start a family, get jobs, become fully participatory citizens, pay taxes, and face your own aging, your sense of ethics will continue to change. But for now, you want to get started. You wish to secure a good beginning to your career. As you move from college to whatever your *real world* will look like, your communication ethics will be in transition as well.

You will no doubt feel like you have to play The *Game*. Your ethics, like the roots from the tree we are digging up, will get tangled in others' ethics in nearly every situation in which you find yourself. Let's briefly revisit our discussion of The *Game* (see Chapter 5) with your emerging ethical beliefs in mind.

The *Game* Revisited

Recall from Chapter 5 the discussion of The *Game*. We revisit this issue now because it often comes up when students are asked to apply ethical standards to cases or issues. As long as the characters and situations are hypothetical, it is easy to apply one or more ethical platforms to a case. Much like selecting food from a cafeteria, it is fairly easy to select the theory or concept that *fits* the case before us. And, if someone suggests a better approach, we easily drop our initial idea for someone else's superior one. After all, it's only *theoretical application* and we do it all the time in academia.

But when we ourselves become the characters in a real-life case study the stakes are suddenly raised. If a future job or raise or promotion is on the table, theory often gives way to self-interest and self-advancement. As more than one student has told us, you have to *play the game* in order to be competitive in today's world. A small lie here. A half-truth there. Choosing to not reveal all the facts we know in order to succeed—that's how The *Game* is played. Say whatever we need to say in order to optimize the possibilities for success. Besides, if we don't play the game, the other person will and the other guy gets hired or promoted.

Students are telling us the rules of The *Game* demand that you take care of *Number One* first and worry about ethics later. We faculty are tempted to mourn our failure to teach the relevance of communication ethics to students until closer scrutiny reminds us that we ourselves play The *Game*. In fact, nearly everyone approaches ethical communication in such fashion at one time or another. And if we have the umbrella of tenure or are otherwise secure in our careers, is it not then and only then safer to communicate more truthfully and openly?

We might be wise to concede that The *Game* will be played as long as emerging professionals face the tremendous burden of succeeding quickly and getting ahead on a fast track. If we as professionals interested in and committed to communicating ethically acknowledge that The *Game* is a strong force in our lives, we may be able to move past the *relativistic ethics* dilemma with which our students may struggle. Teaching communication ethics may not be a terminal experience for our students. Instead, what we may be doing is equipping them with a *starter kit* that will be constantly modified as The *Game* is played throughout their lives.

We do not claim that The *Game* is ethical or right. Anytime a lie or deceit or deliberate misdirection in communication takes place, questions about our ethics must be brought to bear. We do, however, acknowledge that The *Game* is played almost every day, and as such needs to be considered realistically in any discussion of communication ethics.

Weaning oneself from needing to play The *Game*, and becoming a person who communicates consistently from an ethical foundation, is a continually evolving process. As we examine ethical questions and situations throughout our lives, our goal is to try to establish an ethical equilibrium. That is to say, we hope our behavior and our ethics are in sync more and more as we move through life. We seek to become ethically balanced.

Ethical Equilibrium in Communication

As we have discussed throughout this book, the way we treat others in our communication depends on having fertile ground from which our ethics can grow and be modified as we ourselves grow and our values are modified. As we learn and teach communication ethics, we might do well to think again about the roots of that tree we are digging up. The teaching of theory and the introduction of major schools of thought is the material we can see and *chop up* together. When we ask students to apply a system of ethics to their everyday communication with others, they often get tangled in the roots.

To get through that tangle, we need a balanced approach. There is no right or wrong time to begin discussing ethics about how we ought to communicate. As we learn about ethics we will likely begin to make decisions as to whether a particular theory discussed in this book fits our understanding of life. The classroom and an instructor and students unafraid of raising the tough questions are that fertile ground from which a balanced approach to communication ethics will grow. As our time as students ends and we prepare to enter a competitive job market where ethical issues are raised in everyday communication, we should remember to pack our *starter kit* when we leave school and be prepared to add to it as we grow and learn more about ourselves.

In a professional communication class, students had an assignment to present an extemporaneous speech on some aspect of professional communication. Mike drew the topic, "Spin makes the professional world go 'round,' regardless of ethics or morals." Mike announced before he started that he would not comment on the *ethics or morals* part of the topic. When asked after his speech why he opted to omit the ethics part of the assertion, Mike responded, "Who am I to try to tell anyone about ethics or whether communication is right or wrong? It's important, but I am not qualified to discuss the ethics of how people ought to communicate with each other." We include this anecdote because Mike is not a twenty-something just starting to think about his career. He is in his forties, a parent of three children, and employed as a scientist. Even a professional in mid-life is not always prepared to explain his or her ethical stance. While the class agreed ethics should be talked about and questions of right and wrong in communication are important, they claimed they themselves were not qualified to evaluate or judge the communication of others. It turns out that Mike and the others had some very definite judgments to make about the ethics of the executives involved in the Enron scandal and others. But when asked to discuss the ethics of *spin*, they were reluctant to claim an ethical vantage point and seemed to retreat into individual relativism—whatever is good for you is good for you and what is good for me is good for me. (We doubt Mike takes that point of view when discussing morals with his three children.)

We think the key to learning and teaching ethical communication is to be aware of systems of ethics that may apply to whatever situation we may find ourselves in. Almost everyone plays *The Game* at times in his or her life. Some people never stop playing and spend their lives lying or deceiving others in order to *get theirs*. Still, this fact does not mean people must retreat into relativism out of fear that others might judge their actions if they presume to analyze the ethics of others. Maturity may be achieved when we adopt a purposeful, intentional, and balanced system for communicating with others. Eventually our communication and our ethics should become more in sync and that's ethical equilibrium.

Challenges and Issues for Further Studies in Communication Ethics

As we continued to tug at the roots beneath the chapters of this communication ethics book, we encountered many other roots entwined with the ones we were exploring. As we untangled those roots we thought we might make each of them another chapter for study. What we discovered was that each of *those* roots were tangled in other roots and that we were not going to be able to cover all the issues we wanted to explore in this book. Communicating ethically encompasses a huge range of issues, some of which we had to leave for another project. They are important enough to mention, however, and to at least peek at the communication issues we see in each one. In this section, we intend to simply raise a few of the issues we see under each topic. We will not try to answer them here, however. We'll leave that exploration for you to pursue.

We will briefly spotlight the following topics in which communication ethics issues are raised every day.

- Health Communication
- Religious Communication
- Environmental Communication
- Education Communication.

Health Communication

In almost every periodical or in nearly weekly news features we hear about ethical issues in health and medicine. For instance, let's look at the question of confidentiality in health communication. Does a physician have an ethical right to communicate material in our health records to insurance companies? If a teenager, during the course of a routine school examination, is discovered to have a sexually transmitted disease, is the attending physician ethically bound to disclose that to the teen's parent or guardian? If an elderly patient being treated for last-stage cancer is discovered to have a kidney disease that will need extensive attention, does the oncologist have an ethical responsibility to communicate the additional *bad news*, or is it best to say nothing and not add to the dying patient's burden?

Is it ethical for drug companies to advertise on television, extolling the virtues while quickly running through the potential side effects of the drug? And where does the advertising budget for these slick commercials come from? Should they spend money on commercials rather than on research?

The issue of stem-cell research was a *hot* issue at the time of this writing. The ethics issues have spilled over from the health field into politics, religion, and technology. Opinions are sharply divided as to the ethics of the harvesting and development of stem cells. What are the communication ethics that are raised in this important issue?

And when we get past stem-cell ethics, what do we say about cloning? Are there issues a student of communication ethics might raise to the arguments of proponents and opponents of cloning? As the courts and governments weigh in on these legal issues, who speaks to the ethical concerns? And what does the ethicist say? As we tug on the root of communication ethics in cloning, we become entangled in issues of ethics in politics, medicine, and religion.

Religious Communication

The complexity of a communication ethics study of religious communication can be illustrated by some of the decisions the authors went through in writing this book. As we considered the inclusion of a chapter on the ethics of religious communication, we received an interesting mix of feedback from others. Some people encouraged us to explore the issues involved in ethical communication in religion, while others urged us to avoid the topic. Both sides were expressed passionately, and we knew feelings ran deep about the questions of religion, communication, and ethics. In the end, we opted to not include religious communication—other than the study of divine command theory in Chapter 3—not because we were reluctant to tackle the passionate issues involved, but rather because the ethical issues were far too numerous to be contained in a single chapter. By the time we laid out a chapter that covered what we thought to be the key issues of communication ethics in religion, the length would have been roughly half the size of this entire book. We may revisit this controversial issue in the future should we decide to begin another book devoted to this single and complex topic. For this study, however, we point to just a few of the communication ethics issues where the church and religion are concerned.

Issues and challenges for the student of communication ethics are numerous in the area of religion. For instance, is it ethical for televangelists to offer prayers, or prayer cloths, or even salvation itself in exchange for monetary donations from their viewers? What does the communication ethicist have to say to those critics who claim that salvation should not come with a price tag?

Others claim that for evangelizing to be successful, one must catch people at their most emotionally vulnerable point in life in order to persuade them to confess their sins and join the church. In matters of faith, is it ethical for a church official to emotionally stir the listeners in order to make an altar call?

Other issues arise when religion and medicine clash. The issues are almost always centered on how differing views are communicated. A suburban church has made news for its stance on the issue regarding the deaths of three children of parishioners in the past six or seven years. The issue identified is that of faith healing through prayer and intercession instead of visiting a doctor for medical treatment. As the communication ethics student tugs on that religion root, it becomes tangled with roots in law and medicine as well. The matter is being contested in the courts. What are the ethical issues being communicated by this church regarding the deaths of sick children?

Sometimes people can be persuaded to follow and blindly obey a charismatic leader. Unethical communication can potentially lead to disaster. Consider the cults based on the charismatic leadership and communication styles of individuals like Jim Jones and David Koresh. How do we evaluate the communication ethics of Jones who in 1978 persuaded 913 of his followers of the Peoples Temple to commit mass suicide in Jonestown, Guyana? In 1993, six followers of Koresh's cult known as the Branch Davidians and four agents of the Bureau of Alcohol, Tobacco and Firearms died in a deadly siege and inferno in Waco, Texas. Both Jones and Koresh claimed divine-like status, and their communication was to be considered as inspired by God. Research these tragic chapters in our history and consider the communication ethics involved in each.

Next, try to make sense of the claims made by Christians, Muslims, Jews, Buddhists, and nearly every other religion that they alone communicate the one true faith, the history of persecution and warfare in the name of religion, and other ethical issues too numerous to list, and it's easy to understand the enormity of such a study.

These and so many other ethical questions continue to challenge the field of communication ethics. Should we respond, or is it best to leave matters of ethical communication and religion to the churches?

Environmental Communication

Peter Singer along with other ethicists continues to raise ethical concerns about the relationship between humans, animals, and the environment.[1] These ongoing concerns continue to raise challenges from an ethical communication viewpoint. What are the ethical issues, for instance, being communicated in the question of animal rights? Do animal rights proponents always have the ethical right to put animal rights ahead of or even on par with human rights? Is it ethical to defend the habitat of a tiny fish and halt the construction of a dam or the drilling of oil? Who decides, and how are those decisions communicated? Do we develop Alaskan oil fields to lessen our reliance on foreign oil, even if it means the disruption of migratory patterns of certain animals? Who decides? Are there ethical issues in the decision to destroy a heron rookery in order to build a supermarket that will supply food to the community? How is that ethical decision communicated?

How is the issue of global warming being communicated from an ethics point of view? Here the root we are tugging on becomes tangled in science and politics. We hear that the earth is warming and that the protective ozone layer has holes in it. We hear that ice chunks—some the size of small cities—are falling into the sea and endangering our coastlines. Then, we hear equally qualified experts saying that the dangers are being politicized and overstated. Which is it? Are we ethically bound to communicate truthfully about such crucial issues?

Education Communication

Communicating ethically in the classroom is a subject with which we are all familiar. Professors and students alike have a stake and a responsibility in this area. In Chapter 5 we discussed the ethical contributions of Paulo Freire and his concept of empowerment. Most importantly, we supported the claim that teachers owe it to their students to create and nurture an academic environment in which students are free to grow and learn without fear. The communication environment needs to be one of the free sharing of ideas as well as a place where students and teachers are at the same time teachers and learners.

But there are other communication issues with ethical implications that we did not talk about. For example, is it ethical for professors to discuss the performance of a student in her class with a professor who has that student in another class? It is true that faculty do it a lot, but *should* they? If you have Martina in class, and know that she is on the border between a B and a C, and you hear from your colleague that Martina is barely passing his class and seems to be totally uninterested in class meetings, might that not affect you when it comes to grading? Is it ethical for a professor to reveal to another colleague that he is giving Tony a C so that he can maintain his eligibility for football, even though the other professor is considering failing Tony for not showing up to classes? When a professor tells you that you are getting a student in one of your classes next fall who can't ever seem to pay attention in class, is he being ethical in his communication with you?

There are web sites where students can go and anonymously complain about certain professors. A student can name the professor, the class, tell anecdotes about the professor, and basically write anything he wants—all the while remaining unidentified himself. Do you see any ethical issues there?

I can go online and purchase a term paper on the art of Renoir rather than do the boring research myself. It's not even a paper for my major. Besides, rumor has it that the professor doesn't even read those papers, but has a TA or Grad Assistant read them. They'll never know the difference, and, besides, it's how the *Game* is played, right? Or are there ethical issues on the table here as well?

Professors routinely receive requests from students for a letter of recommendation for graduate school, scholarships or awards, or for employment. Most of the time these letters are easy to craft because the student has done very well, she is one of our favorite majors, and is otherwise held in high esteem. Sometimes, however, the student is well liked but has not performed at a high level academically. What should your professors write in those recommendations? If you are the student who has not performed as well as you had wanted, but need that job or that scholarship, do you want your recommending professor to *frame* his letter in such a way that you appear to have done better than you know you have? What if you are the student who has achieved at a very high level academically? Would you want your recommending professor to *frame* her letters of recommendation so that it appears that everyone she recommends has done very well? If everyone is excellent no one is excellent. How honest do you want your letter of recommendation to be? And for those of us who write such letters, how willing are we to help the student by carefully crafting a letter by not mentioning academic underperformance? Are there questions of right and wrong at play here?

Is it ethical for a department Chair to reveal that your class evaluations last semester were better than Angie's? Or is it ethical for a dean to disclose that Don won't be at the department chairs meeting today because his son was expelled from high school yesterday? We aren't claiming these types of communication take place with regularity on some campuses. We are raising the question of whether they *should* take place at all.

As you can see, tugging at any of these communication *roots* leads to larger entanglements just below the surface. These issues, and many others not even explored in this book, are fertile grounds for the student of communication ethics. The *chopping up* of issues we can see is easy. The digging and tugging at a root that threatens to rip up my yard is a much more difficult matter. It is the discovery and tracking of those roots, however, that will help us understand our own ethical beliefs as we continue to grow and learn.

Topic for Discussion: A Personal Code of Ethics

A purposeful and personal system of ethical communication will one day be your signature, and will possibly come from that *starter kit* you put together in a communication ethics class. One way of starting to develop that personal ethical system is to read through a codified system of ethics that regulates the discipline you are thinking of entering. For example, the National Communication Association (NCA)—the authors' professional affiliation—has its own code of ethics. We include it in this chapter to provide such an example.

Credo for Ethical Communication (Approved by the NCA Legislative Council in 1999)

Questions of right and wrong arise whenever people communicate. Ethical communication is fundamental to responsible thinking, decision making, and the development of relationships and communities within and across contexts, cultures, channels, and media. Moreover, ethical communication enhances human worth and dignity by fostering truthfulness, fairness, responsibility, personal integrity, and respect for self and others. We believe that unethical communication threatens the quality of all communication and consequently the well-being of individuals and the society in which we live. Therefore we, the members of the National Communication Association, endorse and are committed to practicing the following principles of ethical communication:

- We advocate truthfulness, accuracy, honesty, and reason as essential to the integrity of communication.
- We endorse freedom of expression, diversity of perspective, and tolerance of dissent to achieve the informed and responsible decision making fundamental to a civil society.
- We strive to understand and respect other communicators before evaluating and responding to their messages.
- We promote access to communication resources and opportunities as necessary to fulfill human potential and contribute to the well-being of families, communities, and society.
- We promote communication climates of caring and mutual understanding that respect the unique needs and characteristics of individual communicators.
- We condemn communication that degrades individuals and humanity through distortion, intimidation, coercion, and violence, and through the expression of intolerance and hatred.
- We are committed to the courageous expression of personal convictions in pursuit of fairness and justice.

- We advocate sharing information, opinions, and feelings when facing significant choices while also respecting privacy and confidentiality.
- We accept responsibility for the short- and long-term consequences for our own communication and expect the same of others.[2]

Note the first sentence in the NCA *Credo* is: "Questions of right and wrong arise whenever people communicate." Communication ethics are not limited to any one form of communication but rather encompass the entire range of our interactions with and judgments about others. *Wherever people communicate* brings into play all of our interactions with others: those we have in person, online, in the media, in our religious experiences, in health, in the classroom, everywhere. The study of communication ethics is about questions of right and wrong, respect for others, common decency and integrity in our discourse with everyone. The manner in which we communicate with the person we love the most is no different (from a communication ethics perspective) from the way we interact with the server at the restaurant we will visit tomorrow.

This code of ethics is an excellent example of an organization's proclamation of beliefs, tenets, and responsibilities. More importantly, the *Credo of Ethics of the National Communication Association* clearly outlines the ethical principles (truthfulness, honesty, accuracy, and reason) that govern the organization and the individuals who claim affiliation with it. In this Code and others like it one finds both an ethical framework and a set of personal guidelines for shaping one's communication with others.

We direct your attention to Chapters 10 and 11, in which we mention other formal codes of ethics. A simple search engine online will direct you to dozens of codes (for example, onlineethics.org lists several codes in English and Spanish).[3] The Center for the Study of Ethics in the Professions at the Illinois Institute of Technology is a useful source for a variety of codes as well.[4] Professor Chris MacDonald at St. Mary's University (Canada) maintains an excellent site with guidelines for developing a code of ethics.[5] In addition, the Markkula Center for Applied Ethics at Santa Clara University in California provides very useful sources for developing ethical codes.[6]

A Personal Code of Communication Ethics

After all you have read in this book and all the cases you have considered, after all the ethical issues and questions that have been raised in your discussions, can you design your own personal Code of Communication Ethics? It's one thing to evaluate and judge the behavior and values of others, but when push comes to shove and you are challenged to codify what you personally believe, what will you come up with? We offer some suggestions for your consideration.

The first thing we recommend is that you realize that any code you establish at this stage of your life will be provisional. That is to say, as you grow and experience the next stage of your life, your personal code of ethics will be revised to fit your own view of the world, as well as your participation in it. The values and ethics your parents and other influential people hold as valid must be examined through your own critical lens. Your immediate goal is to establish yourself as a marketable, evolving, and valuable human being. With those caveats in mind, here are a few questions to ponder as you assess your ethical view of your world. These questions will guide you in finding the fertile grounds from which will grow a personal *Credo* of your own communication ethics.

1. *What is my worldview?*
   How do you perceive life around you? Are people generally good, or bad? Are people generally honest, or deceitful? Do you think humans really care about one another, or do they just want to survive without being bothered? Are men liars? Do women usually deceive? Are we gullible to believe that people are genuine, or should we be skeptical of what others tell us until we can prove them right or wrong? Is the world a good place or one to be feared?

2. *What is my view of Self?*
   Who am I? Am I a person of worth and value? When I look into my mirror, is it an honest and genuine person staring back at me? Are my values and beliefs my own, or did I just accept everything I have been told along the way without examination? What do I truly think I owe to other people? Do I have an *Other?*

3. *Of all the systems of communication ethics discussed in this book, which one or two of them seem the most comfortable to me?*
   What is it about that system(s) that I most agree with? Are there events in my life when this type of communication actually took place? Is there a system the book covered that I reject? On what ethical grounds do I reject that system?

4. *Is there a system or concept covered in this book that I might want to experiment with?*
   How do these systems pertain to my own personal communication? Can I practice this new system of ethical communication with someone I trust, who will give me honest feedback? Can I stay consistent in my communication long enough to truly test the effectiveness of that system?

The issues affecting the formulation of a personal code can be varied. Your personal code can be influenced by the lie you caught your friend in yesterday or by the fact that your friend and you are always truthful with each other, even if it hurts. As you grow and enter into covenants with other people, your code of ethics will change as well.

Keep in mind as you attempt to establish your own code of ethics that what you include today may no longer be relevant—or may need to be considerably modified—tomorrow. The content of your code of ethics is important but subject to periodic update. Even more important, we suggest, is the process by which you establish and modify that code as the conditions of your life change.

A Final Word

The authors are indebted to those who have gone before us in order to introduce students to the field of communication ethics. Our hardest task was to continue to keep in focus the lens of communication as we examined both new and familiar ethical writings. More than once we got caught up in the brilliance of a major ethicist's work only to be brought back to earth with the question, "That's great, but what does it have to do with communication?"

We believe that we learn and teach communication ethics in balance. We expose students to the traditional as well as postmodern ethical schools of thought, and we entice them to think about cases and situations in which they can apply these ethics. But what we are really doing when we teach about ethics is allowing students to grapple with issues that pertain to their lives. We equip them with ways of thinking about ethics and tools to help them evaluate right and wrong in their lives.

Gordon Marino, a professor of philosophy at St. Olaf College, echoed this way of thinking in a column in *The Chronicle of Higher Education*, titled "Before Teaching Ethics, Stop Kidding Yourself":

> People who presume to teach ethics should help their students be honest with themselves about their own interests. Such candor is, of course, part of the Socratic curriculum of coming to know yourself . . . unless our ethics students learn to examine themselves and what they really value, their command of ethical theories and their ability to think about ethics from diverse perspectives are not likely to bring them any closer to being willing and able to do the right thing.[7]

We have titled the book *Communicating Ethically* because we want to stress that communication ethics is an ongoing process—something being worked out as we go along. There is no point at which one stops and says, "now I have a fully developed set of communication ethics, or ethics of any kind."

A Last Look at Dialogue

We are students and professors of the discipline of Communication. By trade, we are explorers of and commentators on the ways people communicate with other people. Keeping our focus on communication has been our challenge throughout our exploration in the field of ethics. The one theme we found ourselves returning to was that of dialogical ethics. It is a perspective squarely in the communication discipline. We can try to understand the concepts of Virtue Ethics, Universalism, Utilitarianism, Contractualism, among others, and all have much to offer. But, it is dialogical ethics that vibrates like a tuning fork inside us. We *know* this concept. We understand how it works.

Dialogical ethics is very much a communication theory. It is also a postmodern theory, which frees us from being bound to a canon of rules and imperatives. The focus is on the people and not the rules. We can *test* our ethical communication by careful analysis of our dialogue with others. Dialogical ethics lends itself to interactions in our diverse and multicultural society.

We can benchmark our ethical growth by carefully examining how we dialogue with others. Before we presume to apply ethical standards to our planet, perhaps we are better served by applying them to our relationships. It's a start.

NOTES

1. Peter Singer, *Writings on an Ethical Life* (New York: HarperCollins, 2000).
2. www.natcom.org. (accessed June 16, 2005).
3. http://onlineethics.org/codes (accessed June 20, 2005).
4. Gordon Marino, *The Chronicle of Higher Education*, February 20, 2004, p. B5.
5. http://ethics.iit.edu/codes/.
6. www.ethicsweb.ca/codes/.
7. www.scu.edu/ethics/.

GLOSSARY

act utilitarianism the type of utilitarianism that holds that in each separate case, one determines what the greatest good for the greatest number would be; in contrast, under rule utilitarianism, one considers what the greatest good (the highest utility) would be if the rule behind the decision in this particular case were made a general rule for all similar cases.

altruism, ethical the belief that in each case one would do what is in the best interest of other people instead of oneself; the opposite is *ethical egoism*, in which one does what is best for oneself in every case.

applied ethics the application of ethical principles to actual situations, usually in a professional or occupational setting.

care, ethics of the ethical system association with Carol Gilligan, in which one's real-life relationships shape one's determination of what is ethical in given situations; the ethical act is performed out of care for another person, rather than because of rules of ethics.

categorical imperative the principle laid down by Immanuel Kant that in all instances the ethical action is the one based on a *maxim*, or rule, that one would want to have applied universally, in all cases. *Hypothetical* imperatives, on the other hand, are ones in which you take into consideration the situational contingencies of a specific case. If something is categorical, the principle applies in all cases without exception.

code of ethics written lists of principles or rules intended to be binding on practitioners of particular professions or occupations. Medical ethics and legal ethics are outstanding examples of systems grounded by such codes. See *professional ethics*.

consequentialism systems of ethics in which the ethical decision or act is determined by the outcomes or the consequences; *utilitarianism* is most representative of ethical consequentialism.

contractualism the system of ethics that assumes an implied contractual relationship exists between people interacting with each other or in a large system. Each person agrees to give up some benefits or rights in the interests of enjoying the most just society or relationships. Rawls and Scanlon provide examples of contractualist ethical systems.

critical theory a group of social and political philosophers, developed from the so-called *Frankfurt School*, who emphasize a critique of social and economic relationships that highlight domination or hegemony of one group in society over another. Jürgen Habermas is the best-known current member of the group of critical theorists.

cultural relativism the position that ethical decisions or actions can be judged only from within the value and belief systems of specific human cultures.

divine command theory of ethics the theory of ethics which holds that the ethical decision or action is determined by religious commandments, doctrine, or set of beliefs.

egalitarianism the system of ethics which stresses that all should enjoy equal outcomes or consequences. All should be treated equally or at least in a way to which all affected could not object. Rawls' *original position* is intended to arrive at a just society in which these principles would obtain.

egoism the position that holds that one's own self-interest should be the basis for all decision making. *Ethical egoism* maintains that if everyone behaved in their own best interests, the overall result would be the most ethical for all. *Phychological egoism* is the position that, as a matter of fact, all people act solely from their own self-interest.

emotivism   the ethical principle that ethical judgments are based on feelings approving or disapproving people's action. This view holds that there is no objective basis for ethical judgments, but rather expressing an ethical evaluation of some action involves expressing one's emotional reaction to it.

empiricism   the philosophical position that all knowledge is derived or derivable only from experience and from the input of the senses. British Empiricists, such as John Locke, were influential in the development of principles leading to utilitarianism.

evolutionary, or biological ethics   the theory that ethical principles are given by or based on biological principles that had survival benefits for organisms as they evolved over time.

feminism   a movement or philosophical position which emphasizes that socially constructed gender categories and principles have allowed for oppression of women based solely or largely on their gender.

grand narrative   a concept associated with postmodernists, which refers to any or all universal systems of belief, such as those backing science, religion, or other such systems.

maximization principle   also known as the principle of maximization of utility. This is the principle, especially behind utilitarianism, that ethical actions are those which maximize the most good for the most people.

Moral Development, stages of   the stages posited by Lawrence Kohlberg based on his studies of children and adolescents that people progress through lower to higher stages of moral reasoning as they mature.

natural law, or natural law theory   the theory that nature determines behavior, with the implication that what is according to nature is therefore moral or right. St. Thomas Aquinas based his theological ethics on natural law; in contrast, evolutionary or biological ethics is also based on *nature* as well.

nihilism   the principle, especially in political theory or philosophy, that there is no fundamental basis for *right* or *wrong* or for humans' knowing what these terms could mean.

original position   the hypothetical condition developed by John Rawls as the philosophical approach to determining the principles for a just society. Assume that people are back in an *original position* from which they are to agree on the general set of rules and principles that will govern their society.

parrhesia (fearless speech)   the term from classical Greek meaning open or fearless speech. Michel Foucault used the term for those situations in which a person speaks up courageously against injustice at some risk to himself.

people-first language   using language which emphasizes or gives priority to a person's humanity rather than a characteristic incidental to their humanity; thus we say *person with a disability*, rather than a *disabled person*.

phronesis   term used by Aristotle, especially in his works on ethics, to designate the exercise of sound, mature judgment in decision making. Aristotle refers to such judgment as the intellectual virtue directing the application of the ethical virtues.

postmodernism   a movement especially among European intellectuals which maintains that modernism (or modernity) has been or should be replaced by a new set of assumptions which give privilege to no one set of universal truths or principles. They further believe that what is referred to as *modern* led to unjust domination or oppression of most people by an elite (determined by economic class, gender, race, or some other similar kind of characteristic).

Potter Box   the model developed by theologian Ralph Potter to assist people in the mass media in making ethical decisions regarding mass communication.

professional ethics   the ethics of someone acting as a practitioner of a specific profession or occupation. Professional ethics are most often codified in a *credo* or a code of ethics incumbent on those licensed or designated to practice that profession.

relativism   the position that all moral or ethical decisions are dependent on (relative to) a particular set of conditions, such as culture or time. One cannot or should not judge the ethics of people in other cultures or times, according to this view.

rule utilitarianism   the type of utilitarianism in which one considers what the greatest good (the highest utility) would be if the *rule* or principle behind the decision in this particular case were made a general rule for all similar cases. Compare *act utilitarianism*.

situationalism, or situational ethics   the system of ethics which allows for different decisions or actions to be ethical depending upon one's individual situation or circumstances. An action may be ethical at one time for particular people, but not at another time or for different people. This position was developed most systematically by the theologian, Joseph Fletcher, who maintains that love (*agape* or spiritual love) for another person is the single controlling ethical principle.

social contract   the concept in political and social philosophies which assumes that the basis for social and political institutions lies in a hypothetical contract drawn up and agreed to before such institutions came into existence. The idea of the social contract is found in Jean-Jacques Rousseau, Thomas Hobbes, and John Locke, and provides the foundation for contractualist theories of ethics.

subjectivism   the ethical position that ethical decisions or judgments are necessarily subjective rather than objective. This idea is often expressed in the notion the a *should* cannot be an *ought*, meaning that ethical judgments are not based on facts. *Emotivism* is quite similar to this position.

Unconditional Positive Regard   the principle underlying dialogical ethics formulated by Carl Rogers, the psychotherapist.

It requires one to give to any other person full, caring and undivided attention without judgment or evaluation. This ethical position respects the different values and beliefs held by participants in true dialogue.

universalism, or universalistic systems of ethics   those systems which hold that one set of rules or principles should cover all ethical decision making for all times and for all places. Kant's system is most representative of universalistic systems.

utilitarianism   one of the major systems of ethics, which holds that the ethical decision or action is that which produces the most utility, that is, the greatest good for the greatest number. Jeremy Bentham and John Stuart Mill are considered the founders of this ethical school of thought; Peter Singer is probably the best-known contemporary advocate of utilitarian ethics. In determining the greatest number of people, every person is to count and no one is to count for more than any other. Singer and others today would extend the principle to sentient beings of all types, not restricted just to human beings.

veil of ignorance   the principle developed by John Rawls in his concept of the Original Position. Each person is to be unaware concerning the actual station or condition he or she will occupy in real life while he or she are agreeing to the general principles that will govern his or her society. His assumption was that people would therefore want all benefits and rights distributed as equally as possible in the society, since they do not know what position they will occupy in life.

virtue ethics   the system of ethics, most closely associated with Aristotle, which holds that the most ethical decision or action is that which would be performed by a person of the highest character. There are no hard-and-fast rules, but one must exercise mature judgment and reason (*phronesis*) in balancing one virtue against others in specific cases. A major contemporary proponent of virtue ethics is Martha Nussbaum.

BIBLIOGRAPHY

Ackah, C. A. (1988). *Akan Ethics*. Accra, Ghana: Ghana Universities Press.

Agger, Ben (1992). *The Discourse of Domination: From the Frankfurt School to Postmodernism*. Evanston, IL: Northwestern University Press.

Alderman, Ellen and Kennedy, Caroline (1997). *The Right to Privacy*. New York: Vintage Books.

Alexander, Richard D. (1987). *The Biology of Moral Systems*. New York: Aldine de Gruyter.

Allen, Anita L. (2004). *The New Ethics*. New York: Miramax Books.

Alterman, Eric (2004). *When Presidents Lie: A History of Official Deception and Its Consequences*. London: Viking Penguin Press.

Anderson, James A. and Englehardt, Elaine E. (2001). *The Organizational Self and Ethical Conduct*. Ft. Worth: Harcourt College Publishers.

Anderson, Rob and Cissna, Kenneth N. (1997). *The Martin Buber—Carl Rogers Dialogue*. Albany: State University of New York Press.

Applbaum, Arthur Isak (1999). *Ethics for Adversaries: The Morality of Roles in Public and Professional Lives*. Princeton, NJ: Princeton University Press.

Arendt, Hannah (1978). *The Life of the Mind*, Volume One ed. Mary McCarthy San Diego: Harcourt Brace Jovanovich.

Arendt, Hannah (1998). *The Human Condition*, intro. Margaret Canovan. Chicago: University of Chicago Press.

Arendt, Hannah (2003). *Responsibility and Judgment*, ed. Jermome Kohn. New York: Schocken Books.

Aristotle (1962). *Nicomachean Ethics*, trans. Martin Ostwald. Indianapolis: Bobbs-Merril.

Aristotle (1980). *Aristotle on Rhetoric: A Theory of Civic Discourse*, trans. George A. Kennedy. New York: Oxford University Press.

Badiou, Alain (2001). *Ethics: An Essay on the Understanding of Evil*. London: Verso.

Barbour, Ian (1993). *Ethics in an Age of Technology*. San Francisco: HarperSanFrancisco.

Benhabib, Seyla (1992). *Situating the Self: Gender, Community and Postmodernism in Contemporary Ethics*. New York: Routledge.

Bennett, William J. (1995). *The Moral Compass*, New York: Simon and Schuster.

Berlin, Isaiah (1991). *The Crooked Timber of Humanity*, ed. Henry Hardy. New York: Alfred A. Knopf.

Berlin, Isaiah (1997). *The Proper Study of Mankind*, ed. Henry Hardy and Roger Hausheer. New York: Farrar, Strauss and Giroux.

Best, Steven and Kellner, Douglas (1991). *Postmodern Theory: Critical Interrogations*. New York: Guilford Press.

Bok, Sissela (1999). *Lying*, 2nd ed. New York: Vintage Books.

Bonhoeffer, Diertich (1955; orig. 1943). *Ethics*, trans. Eberhard Bethge. New York: Simon and Schuster.

Bracci, Sharon L. and Christians, Clifford G., eds. (2002). *Moral Engagement in Public Life*. New York: Peter Lang Publishing.

Buber, Martin (1970). *I and Thou*, trans. Walter Kauffman. New York: Touchstone Books.

Buber, Martin (1947). *Between Man and Man*, trans. Ronald Gregor Smith. London: Kegan Paul.

Burns, James Macgregor (1978). *Leadership*. New York: Harper & Row Publishers.

Callahan, David (2004). *The Cheating Culture*. Orlando: Harcourt.

Campbell, Jeremy (2001). *The Liar's Tale: A History of Falsehood*. New York: W. W. Norton and Company.

Card, Claudia, ed. (1999). *On Feminist Ethics and Politics*. Lawrence, KS: University Press of Kansas.

Carter, Stephen L. (1996). *Integrity*. New York: HarperCollins.

Casebeer, William D. (2003). *Natural Ethical Facts: Evolution, Connectionism, and Moral Cognition*. Cambridge, MA: Massachusetts Institute of Technology Press.

Casmir, Fred L. (1993). Third-Culture Building: A Paradigm Shift for International and Intercultural Communication. *Communication Yearbook 16.* Newbury Park, NJ: Sage Press.

Casmir, Fred L. (1997). Ethics, Culture, and Communication: An Application of the Third-Culture Building Model to International and Intercultural Communication, in *Ethics in Intercultural and International Communication,* ed. Fred L. Casmir. Mahweh, NJ: Lawrence Erlbaum Association.

Cheney, George (1995). Democracy in the Workplace: Theory and Practice from the Perspective of Communication, *Journal of Applied Communication, 23,* 168.

Cheney, George, Christensen, Lars T., Zorn, Theodore E., Jr., and Ganesh, Shiv (2004). *Organizational Communication in an Age of Globalization: Issues, Reflections, Practices.* Long Grove, IL: Waveland Press.

Christians, Clifford G., Fackler, Mark, Rotzoll, Kim B., and McKee, Kathy B. (2001). *Media Ethics: Cases and Moral Reasoning,* 6th ed. New York: Longman.

Cicero (1939). *De inventione,* trans. H. M. Hubbell (1949). Cambridge: Harvard University Press.

Cicero (1970). *On Oratory and Orators,* ed. and trans. J. S. Watson. Carbondale, IL: Southern Illinois University Press.

Cobb, John B., Jr. (2002). *Postmodernism and Public Policy.* Albany: State University of New York Press.

Cole, Eve Browning and Coultrap-McQuin, Susan, eds. (1992). *Explorations in Feminist Ethics: Theory and Practice.* Bloomington, IN: Indiana University Press.

Collins, Edward (1996). Divine Command, Natural-Law, and Mutual Love Ethics. *Theological Studies, 57,* 633–653.

Comte-Sponville, Andre (2001). *A Small Treatise on the Great Virtues,* trans. Catherine Temerson. New York: Henry Holt and Company.

Cooper, Robert K. and Sawaf, Ayman (1996). *Executive EQ: Emotional Intelligence in Leadership and Organizations.* New York: Berkeley Publishing Group.

Damasio, Antonio (2003). *Looking for Spinoza: Joy, Sorrow, and the Feeling Brain.* Orlando: Harcourt.

Day, Louis A. (2003). *Ethics in Media Communication: Cases and Controversies.* Belmont, CA: Thomson Wadsworth.

Deetz, Stanley A. (1992). *Democracy in an Age of Corporate Colonization.* Albany: State University of New York Press.

Denton, Robert E., ed. (2000). *Political Communication Ethics: An Oxymoron?* Westport, CT: Praeger.

Ellul, Jacques (1965). *Propaganda,* trans. Konrad Kellen and Jean Lerner. New York: Alfred A. Knopf.

Ellul, Jacques (1967). *The Technological Society,* trans. John Wilkinson. New York: Alfred A. Knopf.

Englehardt, Elaine E. (2001). *Ethical Issues in Interpersonal Communication.* Orlando: Harcourt College Publishers.

Foucault, Michel (1973). *The Order of Things: An Archaeology of the Human Sciences.* New York: Vintage Books.

Foucault, Michel (1997). *Ethics: Subjectivity and Truth.* New York: The New Press.

Foucault, Michel (2001). *Fearless Speech,* ed. Joseph Pearson. Los Angeles: Semiotext(e).

Fletcher, Joseph (1961). *Situation Ethics: The New Morality.* Philadelphia: The Westminster Press.

Fletcher, Joseph. (1996) Naturalism, situation ethics, and value theory, in *Normative Ethics & Objective Reason,* ed. George F. MacLean. Washington, D.C., PAIDEA Publishers, online at www.ajgoddard.net/Writers/Joseph_Fletcher/joseph_fletcher.html#Con, July 6, 2004.

Frankena, William K. (1973). *Ethics.* Englewood Cliffs, NJ: Prentice Hall.

Freire, Paulo (1993; Orig. 1970). *Pedagogy of the Oppressed,* trans. Myra Bergman Ramos. New York: Continuum International.

Freire, Paulo (1998). *Pedagogy of Freedom: Ethics, Democracy, and Civic Courage,* trans. Patrick Clark. London: Rowman & Littlefield Publishers.

Friedman, Maurice S. (2002). *Martin Buber: The Life of Dialogue,* 4th ed. London: Routledge.

Garver, Eugene (1994). *Aristotle's Rhetoric: An Art of Character.* Chicago: The University of Chicago Press.

Gilligan, Carol (1981). *In a Different Voice: Psychological Theory and Women's Development.* Cambridge, MA: Harvard University Press.

Greenleaf, Robert K. and Spears, Larry C. (1998). *The Power of Servant Leadership: Essays.* San Francisco: Barrett-Koehler Publishers.

Griffin, David R. (1999). Introduction to the SUNY Series in Constructive Postmodern Thought, in *Postmodernism and Public Policy*, ed. John B. Cobb. Albany, NY: State University of New York Press.

Habermas, Jürgen (1979). *Communication and the Evolution of Society*, trans. Thomas McCarthy. Boston: Beacon Press.

Habermas, Jürgen (1984). *The Theory of Communicative Action, Vol. 1: Reason and the Rationalization of Society*, trans. Thomas McCarthy. Boston: Beacon Press.

Habermas, Jürgen (1987). *The Theory of Communicative Action, Vol. 2: Lifeworld and System: A Critique of Functionalist Reason*, trans. Thomas McCarthy. Boston: Beacon Press.

Habermas, Jürgen (1996). *Between Facts and Norms: Contributions to a Discourse Theory of Law and Democracy*, trans. William Rehg. Cambridge, MA: Massachusetts Institute of Technology Press.

Habermas, Jürgen (1997). *Moral Consciousness and Communicative Action*, trans. Christian Lenhardt and Shierry Weber Nicholsen. Cambridge, MA: Massachusetts Institute of Technology Press.

Habermas, Jürgen (1998). *The Inclusion of the Other: Studies in Political Theory*, eds Ciaran Cronin and Pablo De Greiff. Cambridge, MA: Massachusetts Institute of Technology Press.

Halberstam, Joshua (1994). *Everyday Ethics.* New York: Penguin Books.

Halbert, Terry and Ingulli, Elaine (2005). *CyberEthics*, 2nd ed. Thompson Southwestern Press.

Harre, Richard M. (1997). *Sorting Out Ethics.* Oxford: Oxford University Press.

Held, David (1980). *Introduction to Critical Theory: Horkheimer to Habermas.* Berkeley, CA: University of California Press.

Hursthouse, Rosalinde (1991). Virtue Theory and Abortion. *Philosophy and Public Affairs, 20*:1, 224–225.

Jagger, Alyson M. (1998). Globalizing Feminist Ethics. *Hypatia*, 13, pp. 1–2.

Jameson, Frederic (2002). *A Singular Modernity: Essay on the Ontology of the Present.* London: Verso.

Jamieson, Kathleen H. (1992). *Dirty Politics: Deception, Distraction, and Democracy.* New York: Oxford University Press.

Jamieson, Kathleen H. (2000). *Everything You Think You Know about Politics . . . And Why You're Wrong.* New York: Basic Books.

Jamieson, Kathleen H. and Waldman, Paul (2003). *The Press Effect.* Oxford: Oxford University Press.

Johannesen, Richard L. (2002). *Ethics in Human Communication*, 5th ed. Prospect Heights, IL: Waveland Press.

Johnson, Larry and Phillips, Bob (2003). *Absolute Honesty: Building a Corporate Culture that Values Straight Talk and Rewards Integrity.* New York: American Management Association.

Kant, Immanuel (1996). *Groundwork of the Metaphysics of Morals* (1785), in *Practical Philosophy*, ed. and trans. Mary J. Gregor. Cambridge: Cambridge University Press.

Kant, Immanuel (1996). On a Supposed Right to Lie from Philanthropy (1797), in *Practical Philosophy*, ed. and trans. Mary J. Gregor. Cambridge: Cambridge University Press.

Kant, Immanuel (1997). *Lectures on Ethics*, eds Peter Heath and J. B. Schneewind. Cambridge, UK: Cambridge University Press.

Kidder, Rushworth (2003). *How Good People Make Tough Choices.* New York: Quill, HarperCollins.

Kohlberg, Lawrence (1981). *Essays on Moral Development, Vol. I: The Philosophy of Moral Development.* Cambridge: Harper & Row Publishers.

Kohlberg, Lawrence (1984). *Essays on Moral Development, Vol. II: The Psychology of*

Moral Development. Cambridge: Harper & Row Publishers.

Lakoff, George (2002). *Moral Politics: How Liberals and Conservatives Think*. Chicago: University of Chicago Press.

Levinas, Emmanuel (1969). *Totality and Infinity*, trans. Alphonso Lingis. Pittsburgh: Duquesne University Press.

Levinas, Emmanuel (1985). *Ethics and Infinity*, trans. Richard A. Cohen. Pittsburgh: Duquesne University Press.

Levinas, Emmanuel (1998). *Entre Nous: Thinking-of-the-Other*, trans. M. B. Smith and B. Harshaw. New York: Columbia University Press.

Levinas, Emmanuel (1998). *Of God Who Comes to Mind*, trans. Bettina Bergo. Stanford, CA: Stanford University Press.

Levinas, Emmanuel (2000). *God, Death, and Time*, trans. Bettina Bergo. Stanford, CA: Stanford University Press.

Luper, Steven (2002). *A Guide to Ethics*. Boston: McGraw Hill.

Lyotard, Jean-Francois (1984). *The Postmodern Condition: A Report on Knowledge*, trans. Geoff Bennington and Brian Massumi, Forward by Frederic Jameson. Minneapolis: University of Minnesota Press.

McDowell, Banks (1991). *Ethical Conduct and the Professional's Dilemma*. New York: Quorum Books.

MacIntyre, Alisdair (1984). *After Virtue*, 2nd ed. Notre Dame, IN: University of Notre Dame Press.

MacIntyre, Alisdair (1998). *A Short History of Ethics*, 2nd ed. Notre Dame, IN: University of Notre Dame Press.

Macklin, James A., Jr. (1997). *Community over Chaos: An Ecological Perspective on Communication Ethics*. Tuscaloosa, AL: University of Alabama Press.

McLuhan, Marshall (1964). *Understanding Media: The Extensions of Man*. New York: McGraw-Hill.

McNamee, Sheila and Gergen, Kenneth J. (1999), *Relational Responsibility: Resources for sustainable Dialogue*. Thousand Oaks, CA: Sage Publications.

Madison, Gary B. and Fairbairn, Mary, eds (1999). *The Ethics of Postmodernity: Current Trends in Continental Thought*. Evanston, IL: Northwestern University Press.

Makau, Josina and Arnett, Ronald C., eds (1997). *Communication Ethics in an Age of Diversity*. Urbana, IL: University of Illinois Press.

Manning, Rita C. (1992). *Speaking from the Heart: A Feminist Perspective on Ethics*. Lanham, MD: Rowman & Littlefield Publishers.

Martin, Mike W. (2000). *Meaningful Work: Rethinking Professional Ethics*. New York: Oxford University Press.

Mill, John Stuart (1951). *Utilitarianism, Liberty, and Representative Government*, intro. A. D. Linsay. New York: E. P. Dutton & Co.

Mitchell, Jolyon and Marriage, Sophia, eds (2003). *Mediating Religion: Conversations in Media, Religion and Culture*. London: T & T Clark.

Montgomery, Daniel J. and Peter A. DeCaro (2001). Organizational Communication Ethics: The Radical Perspective of Performance Management, *American Communication Journal*, 5:(1), online at http://acjournal.org/holdings/vol5/iss1/special/decaro.htm.

Mumby, Dennis K. (1994). *Communication and Power in Organizations: Discourse, Ideology and Domination*. Norwood, NY: Ablex Publishing Corp.

Mumby, Dennis K. (2001). Power and Politics in *The New Handbook of Organizational Communication*, eds Frederic M. Jablin and Linda L. Putnam. Thousand Oaks, CA: Sage Publications.

Nagel, Thomas (1999). Justice, Justice Thou Shalt Pursue: The Rigorous Compassion of John Rawls, *The New Republic Online*, accessed at www.thenewrepublic.com/archives/1099/102599.

Nagel, Thomas (1999). One-to-One. *London Review of Books* online, accessed at www.lrb.co.uk/v21/no3/nage01_.html, on October 3, 2002.

Neher, William W. (1996). *Organizational Communication: Challenges of Change, Diversity, and Continuity*. Boston: Allyn & Bacon.

Niebuhr, Reinhold (1960). *Moral Man and Immoral Society: A Study in Ethics and Politics*. Louisville, KY: Westminster John Knox Press.

Nietzsche, Friedrich (1966). *Beyond Good and Evil*, trans. Walter Kauffman. New York: Vintage Books.

Noddings, Nel (1984). *Caring: A Feminine Approach to Ethics and Moral Education*. Berkeley, CA: University of California Press.

Nozick, Robert (1989). *The Examined Life*. New York: Simon & Schuster.

Nussbaum, Martha C. (1998). Non-relative Virtues: An Aristotelian Approach, in *Ethics: The Big Questions*, ed. James P. Sterba. Malden, MA: Blackwell Publishers.

Nussbaum, Martha C. (2001). *Sex and Social Justice*. New York: Oxford University Press.

Nussbaum, Martha C. (2001). *Upheavals of Thought: The Intelligence of Emotions*. Cambridge: Cambridge University Press.

O'Brien Hallstein, D. Lynn (1999). A Postmodern Caring: Feminist Standpoint Theories, Revisioning Caring, and Communication Ethics. *Western Journal of Communication*, 63:1.

Oakley, Justin and Cocking, Dean (2001). *Virtue Ethics and Professional Roles*. Cambridge: Cambridge University Press.

Patterson, Philip and Wilkins, Lee (2005). *Media Ethics: Issues and Cases*, 5th ed. Boston: McGraw Hill.

Pearce, W. Barnett (1994). *Interpersonal Communication: Making Social Worlds*. New York: HarperCollins.

Pearce, W. Barnett and Cronen, Vernon (1982). *Communication, Action, and Meaning: The Creation of Social Realities*. New York: Praeger.

Pearce, W. Barnett and Littlejohn, Stephen W. (1997). *Moral Conflict: When Social Worlds Collide*. Thousand Oaks, CA: Sage Publications.

Phillips, Robert (2003). *Stakeholder Theory and Organizational Ethics*. San Francisco: Berrett-Koehler Publishers, Inc.

Rachels, James (1999). *The Elements of Moral Philosophy*. Boston: McGraw Hill.

Rand, Ayn (1962). *Introducing Objectivism*. Objectivism Home Page, at www.anyrand.org/objectivism/io.html.

Rauch, Jonathon (1999). *Government's End: Why Washington Stopped Working*. New York: PublicAffairs.

Rawls, John (1971). *A Theory of Justice*, Cambridge: Harvard University Press.

Rawls, John (1993). *Political Liberalism*. New York: Columbia University Press.

Rawls, John (1999). *The Law of Peoples*. Cambridge, MA: Harvard University Press.

Rawls, John (2001). *Justice as Fairness: A Restatement*, ed. Erin Kelly. Cambridge, MA: Harvard University Press.

Ricoeur, Paul (1998). *Critique and Conviction*, trans. Kathleen Blamey. New York: Columbia University Press.

Ricoeur, Paul (2000). *The Just*, trans. David Pellauer. Chicago: University of Chicago Press.

Rogers, Carl (1951). *Client-Centered Therapy: Its Current Practice, Implications, and Theory*. Boston: Houghton-Mifflin.

Rogers, Carl (1961). *On Becoming a Person*. Boston: Houghton Mifflin Co., p. 24.

Rooksby, Emma (2002). *E-mail and Ethics: Style and Ethical Relations in Computer-mediated Communication*. London: Routledge.

Rorty, Amelie Oskenberg, ed. (1980). *Essays on Aristotle's Ethics*. Berkeley: University of California Press.

Rossy, Candace De (2003). Professional Ethics Begin on the College Campus. *Chronicle of Higher Education*, September 19, 2003, p. B20.

Rudinow, Joel and Graybosch, Anthony (2002). *Ethics and Values in the Information Age*. Belmont, CA: Thompson Wadsworth.

Sagi, Avi and Statman, Alan (1995). Divine Command Morality and Jewish Tradition. *Journal of Religious Ethics*, 23:1, 39–67.

Said, Edward W. (1993). *Culture and Imperialism*. New York: Vintage Books.

Scanlon, Thomas M. (1998). *What We Own Each Other*. Cambridge, MA: Belknap Press of Harvard University Press.

Seeger, Matthew (1997). *Ethics and Organizational Communication*. Cresskill, NJ: Hampton Press, Inc.

Sims, Ronald R. (2003). *Ethics and Corporate Social Responsibility*. Westport, CT: Praeger.

Singer, Peter, ed. (1994). *Ethics*. Oxford: Oxford University Press.

Singer, Peter (1995). *How Are We to Live? Ethics in an Age of Self-Interest*. Amherst, NY: Prometheus Books.

Singer, Peter (2000). *Writings on an Ethical Life*. New York: HarperCollins Publishers.

Slote, Michael (2000). Virtue Ethics, in *The Blackwell Guide to Ethical Theory*, ed. Hugh LaFollette. Malden, MA: Blackwell Publishers, pp. 325–347.

Sterba, James P., ed. (1998). *Ethics: The Big Questions*. Oxford: Blackwell Publishers.

Stevenson, Nick (1999). *The Transformation of the Media: Globalisation, Morality and Ethics*. London: Longman.

Strike, Kenneth A. and Moss, Pamela A. (2003). *Ethics and College Student Life*. Upper Saddle River, NJ: Prentice Hall.

Sullivan, Evelin (2001). *The Concise Book of Lying*. New York: Farrar, Strauss and Giroux.

Taylor, Richard (2002). *Virtue Ethics: An Introduction*. Amherst, NY: Prometheus Books.

Velasquez, Manuel and Rostankowski, Cynthia, eds (1985). *Ethics: Theory and Practice*. Upper Saddle River, NJ: Prentice Hall.

Wallace, R. Jay (2002). Scanlon's Contactualism, *Ethics, 112*, 429.

Watson, Mary Ann (2004). Ethics in entertainment television—Introduction and critical essay, *Journal of Popular Film and Television, 31*, 146–149.

Wilkens, Steve (1995). *Beyond Bumper Sticker Ethics*. Downers Grove, IL: InterVarsity Press.

Williams, Bernard (2002). *Truth and Truthfulness*. Princeton, NJ: Princeton University Press.

Woodstock Theological Center (2002). *The Ethics of Lobbying*. Washington, DC: Georgetown University Press.

Wyschogrod, Edith and McKenny, Gerald P. (2003). *The Ethical*. Oxford: Blackwell Publishing.

Yankelovich, Daniel (1999). *The Magic of Dialogue: Transforming Conflict into Cooperation*. New York: Touchstone Books.

Yarborough, Jean M. (2000). *American Virtues: Thomas Jefferson on the Character of a Free People*. Lawrence, KS: University Press of Kansas.

INDEX